United Kingdom Balance of Payments

The Pink Book

2009 Edition

Editor: Derek Vere
Office for National Statistics

ISBN 978-0-230-57610-0
ISSN 0950-7558

A National Statistics publication

National Statistics are produced to high professional standards as set out in the Code of Practice for Official Statistics. They are produced free from political influence.

About us

The Office for National Statistics

The Office for National Statistics (ONS) is the executive office of the UK Statistics Authority, a non-ministerial department which reports directly to Parliament. ONS is the UK government's single largest statistical producer. It compiles information about the UK's society and economy which provides evidence for policy and decision-making and in the allocation of resources.

The Director of ONS is also the National Statistician.

Palgrave Macmillan

This publication first published 2009 by Palgrave Macmillan.

Palgrave Macmillan in the UK is an imprint of Macmillan Publishers Limited, registered in England, company number 785998, of Houndmills, Basingstoke, Hampshire RG21 6XS.

Palgrave Macmillan in the US is a division of St Martin's Press LLC, 175 Fifth Avenue, New York, NY 10010.

Palgrave Macmillan is the global academic imprint of the above companies and has companies and representatives throughout the world.

Palgrave® and Macmillan® are registered trademarks in the United States, the United Kingdom, Europe and other countries.

A catalogue record for this book is available from the British Library.

10 9 8 7 6 5 4 3 2 1
18 17 16 15 14 13 12 11 10 09

Contacts

This publication

For information about the content of this publication, contact the Editor
Tel: 020 7014 2002
Email: bop@ons.gsi.gov.uk

Other customer enquiries

ONS Customer Contact Centre
Tel: 0845 601 3034
International: +44 (0)845 601 3034
Minicom: 01633 812399
Email: info@statistics.gsi.gov.uk
Fax: 01633 652747
Post: Room 1015, Government Buildings, Cardiff Road, Newport, South Wales NP10 8XG
www.ons.gov.uk

Media enquiries

Tel: 0845 604 1858
Email: press.office@ons.gsi.gov.uk

Publication orders

To obtain the print version of this publication, contact Palgrave Macmillan
Tel: 01256 302611
www.palgrave.com/ons
Price: £52.00

Copyright and reproduction

© Crown copyright 2009

Published with the permission of the Office of Public Sector Information (OPSI)

You may use this publication (excluding logos) free of charge in any format for research, private study or internal circulation within an organisation providing it is used accurately and not in a misleading context. The material must be acknowledged as Crown copyright and you must give the title of the source publication. Where we have identified any third party copyright material you will need to obtain permission from the copyright holders concerned.

For re-use of this material you must apply for a Click-Use Public Sector Information (PSI) Licence from:

Office of Public Sector Information, Crown Copyright Licensing and Public Sector Information, Kew, Richmond, Surrey TW9 4DU

Tel: 020 8876 3444

www.opsi.gov.uk/click-use/index.htm

Printing

This book is printed on paper suitable for recycling and made from fully managed and sustained forest sources. Logging, pulping and manufacturing processes are expected to conform to the environmental regulations of the country of origin.

Printed and bound in Great Britain by Hobbs the Printer Ltd, Totton, Southampton

Typeset by Curran Publishing Services Ltd, Norwich

LONDON BOROUGH OF LAMBETH	
LM 1190714 2	
HJ	25-Sep-2009
STA382.0942	£52.00
C	

Contents

	Page
Introduction	1

Part 1: Current account

		Page
1	Summary of balance of payments	21
2	Trade in goods	31
3	Trade in services	41
4	Income	57
5	Current transfers	73

Part 2: Capital account, financial account and international investment position

		Page
6	Capital account	81
7	Financial account	85
8	International investment position	103

Part 3: Geographical breakdown

		Page
9	Geographical breakdown of current account	123
10	Geographical breakdown of the UK international investment position	167

Part 4: Supplementary information

	Page
Balance of payments and the relationship to national accounts	176
Methodological notes	179
Further information on UK balance of payments	198
Glossary	199
Index	205

List of contributors

Authors and Production Team:
- Jeremy Brocklehurst
- John Bundey
- Alexandra Burnett
- Melanie Edwards
- Angie Francis
- Peter Gittins
- Charles Jumbo
- Deborah Kennion
- Phil Lewin
- John Lowes
- Kevin Madden
- Marilyn Thomas
- Derek Vere
- Damian Whittard

Design: Rob Tornya

The Pink Book: 2009 edition

Preface

The annual Office for National Statistics (ONS) *Pink Book* contains estimates of the balance of payments of the United Kingdom. The presentation of the accounts is based on the *IMF Balance of Payments Manual 5th edition (BPM5)*.

Pink Book data in computer-readable form

Free access to data is available online at www.ons.gov.uk

Access around 40,000 time series, of primarily macro-economic data, drawn from the main tables in a range of our major economic and labour market publications. Download complete releases, or view and download your own customised selection of individual time series.

Also access cross sectional data and metadata from across the Government Statistical Service (GSS), organised by theme and subject. Download many datasets, in whole or in part, or consult catalogue information for all GSS statistical resources, including censuses, surveys, periodicals and enquiry services. Information is posted as PDF electronic documents, or in XLS and CSV formats, compatible with most spreadsheet packages.

Complete copies of this publication are available to download free of charge on the following web page: www.statistics.gov.uk/products/p1140.asp

Quarterly estimates

Quarterly estimates of the main components of the balance of payments for the last two years are published in a quarterly ONS Statistical Bulletin and in more detail in *United Kingdom Economic Accounts*.

The latest estimates are also given in summary form in the *Monthly Digest of Statistics* and in *Financial Statistics*.

National Statistics data

All data in the *Pink Book* are 'National Statistics', are fully compliant with the Code of Practice for Official Statistics and carry the National Statistics kitemark (except for the G7 and World data in table 9.14 which is provided by the IMF).

Comments and enquiries

ONS is keen to receive comments on this publication and suggestions for improvements, which can be considered for future editions of the *Pink Book*. Comments can be sent in writing to:

> **Derek Vere**
> Pink Book Editor
> Business and Balance of Payments Division
> Office for National Statistics
> GR/34
> 1 Myddelton Street
> London EC1R 1UW
> Tel: 020 7014 2000
> Email: bop@ons.gsi.gov.uk

Enquiries regarding balance of payments estimates should be directed to the following:

Trade in goods:
Peter Gittins 01633 455610
(peter.gittins@ons.gsi.gov.uk)

Trade in services, current transfers and capital account:
Marilyn Thomas 01633 455708
(marilyn.thomas@ons.gsi.gov.uk)

Income, financial account and International Investment Position:
John Bundey 020 7014 2002
(john.bundey@ons.gsi.gov.uk)

Damian Whittard 01633 455497
(damian.whittard@ons.gsi.gov.uk)

An introduction to the United Kingdom balance of payments

Introduction

The balance of payments is one of the UK's key economic statistical series. It measures the economic transactions between UK residents and the rest of the world. It also draws a series of balances between inward and outward transactions, provides a net flow of transactions between UK residents and the rest of the world and reports how that flow is funded. Economic transactions include:

- exports and imports of goods, such as oil, agricultural products, other raw materials, machinery and transport equipment, computers, white goods and clothing

- exports and imports of services such as international transport, travel, financial and business services

- income flows, such as dividends and interest earned by foreigners on investments in the UK and by the UK investing abroad

- financial flows, such as direct investment, investment in shares, debt securities, loans and deposits

- transfers, which are offsetting entries to any one-sided transactions listed above, such as foreign aid and funds brought by migrants to the UK

Closely related to the balance of payments is the international investment position series of statistics. The international investment position measures the levels of financial investment with the rest of the world, inward and outward.

International statistical standards

The Office for National Statistics (ONS) follows the international standards relating to balance of payments and international investment position statistics. There are several reasons for this. First, domestic and foreign analysts will be assured that the UK's official balance of payments and international investment position statistics comply with objective, coherent international standards that reflect current, global analytic needs. Second, the UK is a member of the international community and international users need comparable data for comparison between countries. Third, the UK, as a member of the European Union, as well as organisations such as the IMF and OECD, needs to compile its various economic statistics in conformity with standards set by those organisations. Fourth, the UK can compare and reconcile its data with those of other countries. Statistics need to be as comparable as possible in order to carry out this validation.

To facilitate such consistency and to provide guidelines for its members, the IMF issued the *Balance of Payments Manual. T*he first edition appeared in 1948 and the most recent (fifth) edition in 1993. The conceptual framework of the UK balance of payments corresponds to that underlying the fifth edition of the IMF Manual, referred to as *BPM5. BPM5* was implemented in the UK's balance of payments accounts and international investment position statistics in September 1998.

A process of reviewing the existing international standards started in the mid 1980s with the specific objective of harmonising, to the maximum extent possible, the statistical concepts, definitions, statistical units, classifications and terminology. Release of the revised standards started in 1993 with *BPM5* and the third edition of the *System of National Accounts (SNA93)*. *BPM5* was prepared by the IMF in close co-operation with national compilers and with the Statistical Office of the European Communities, the OECD, the United Nations and the World Bank. Those five organisations jointly published *SNA93*. In 1995, the EU produced its own version of *SNA93*, the *European System of Accounts (ESA95),* upon which the UK's national accounts are based and which is consistent with *BPM5*. Both *SNA93* and *BPM5* were amended in 2000 to give more consistent guidance on the treatment of financial derivatives.

The United Nations Statistics Commission and the IMF Board of Directors have subsequently approved the comprehensive and parallel updating of the National Accounts and Balance of Payments manuals, in order to ensure their consistency and achieve greater harmonisation.

Conceptual framework definitions

Balance of payments

Broadly speaking, the UK balance of payments is a statistical statement designed to provide a systematic record of the UK's economic transactions with the rest of the world. It may be described as a system of consolidated accounts in which the accounting entity is the UK economy and the entries refer to economic transactions between residents of the UK and residents of the rest of the world (non-residents).

The balance of payments accounts are concerned not only with payments made but also any economic transactions during a period that give rise to a payment in an earlier or later period, for example, goods may change ownership in one period, though payment may be made in an earlier period (pre-payment) or in a later period (trade credit). They also include transactions for which there may never be a payment, for example, goods shipped under foreign aid or goods shipped between related enterprises. There is also more than one 'balance': the balance of payments is a system of accounts in which many balances can be derived, such as the balance of goods and services, the balance on current account, and the balance on capital and financial account.

Balance of payments statements cover a wide range of economic transactions which include:

(i) goods, services, income and current transfers; and

(ii) capital transactions, such as capital transfers; and

(iii) financial transactions involving the UK claims on, and liabilities to, non-residents.

Category (i) is shown in the current account, category (ii) in the capital account and category (iii) in the financial account.

International investment position

The UK's international investment position is a closely related set of statistics. It can be viewed as the balance sheet recording the UK's stock (or level) of foreign financial assets and liabilities at a particular date. The net international investment position is the difference between the stock of foreign financial assets and foreign liabilities at a particular date.

Viewed more broadly, the international investment position can be shown as a reconciliation statement of the stock of investment at two different points in time by showing financial transactions and other changes (non-transaction changes) such as price changes, exchange rate variations and other adjustments that occurred during the period. Financial transactions which are included in the reconciliation statement are equivalent to the transactions measured in the financial account of the balance of payments. ONS does not currently publish a full reconciliation of the international investment position showing price, exchange rate and other changes.

Classifications such as assets and liabilities, type of investment (direct, portfolio and other investment and reserve assets), and instrument of investment, are used consistently in both the balance of payments and the international investment position.

Concepts of territory and residence

In compiling the UK balance of payments and international investment position, the UK economy is conceived as comprising the economic entities that have a closer association with the territory of the UK than with any other territory. Each such economic entity is described as a resident of the UK. Any economic entity which is not regarded as a resident of the UK is described as a non-resident. The concept of residency is not based on nationality.

The UK's economic territory is defined to include the territories lying within its political frontiers and territorial seas, and in the international waters over which it has exclusive jurisdiction. It also includes its territorial enclaves abroad holding, for example, embassies, consulates, military bases, scientific stations, information or immigration offices, or aid agencies, whether owned or rented by the UK government with the formal agreement of the countries where they are located.

The UK offshore islands – Jersey, Guernsey and Isle of Man – are classified as non-resident to the UK. Thus transactions between UK residents and the islands are in the balance of payments, but transactions between islanders are not counted in the UK balance of payments. The islands are not part of the EU, so statistics relating to them are not required under *ESA95* and they have to be excluded from the UK's economic territory to ensure full UK consistency with *ESA95*. This treatment is also technically consistent with *BPM5* recommendations which states that 'In a maritime country, economic territory includes islands that belong to the country and are subject to the same fiscal and monetary authorities as the mainland; goods and persons move freely to and from the mainland and islands...'. The offshore islands are subject to their own fiscal authorities and have their own tax systems. Furthermore, there are impediments to taking up residency on the Channel Islands.

For balance of payments purposes, residents of an economy are generally deemed to have a centre of economic interest in the economy and to be resident for at least one year. The residents of the UK comprise:

- Resident general government institutions including the Scottish Parliament, Welsh Assembly, Northern Ireland Assembly and local government authorities and statutory bodies. The UK territorial enclaves (for example, embassies, consulates, military bases) physically located abroad are included in the UK's economic territory and are therefore residents; similar entities of other countries physically located within the UK are outside the UK's economic territory and are therefore non-residents

- Resident financial and trading enterprises which include all enterprises engaged in the production of goods and services on a commercial or equivalent basis within the territory of the UK. Enterprises may be incorporated or unincorporated; privately or government owned and/or controlled; and locally or foreign owned and/or controlled.

The definition of an enterprise in terms of the territory in which it is located often makes it necessary to divide a single legal entity into a head office operating in one economy and a branch operating in another economy. Resident enterprises include UK branches of foreign companies and exclude foreign branches of UK companies

- Resident non-profit bodies, those in which individuals and/or enterprises combine, as owners, to produce goods and services within the territory of the UK for purposes other than to provide a financial return for themselves. Examples are churches, charitable organisations and representative business organisations such as chambers of commerce

- Resident households and individuals which broadly encompass all persons residing in the territory of the UK for one year or more, whose general centre of economic interest is considered to be the UK. The UK's official diplomatic and consular representatives, the UK's armed forces, other UK government personnel stationed abroad and their dependants, UK students studying abroad, and UK patients being treated abroad are also included even though they may all be abroad for one year or more. They are treated as UK residents since their centre of interest is considered to be the UK. Generally, the centre of economic interest of persons visiting the UK for less than one year is considered to be outside the UK and they are therefore regarded as non-residents, but if they stay for one year or more they are considered to be residents for balance of payments purposes. Irrespective of their length of stay, non-residents also include foreign diplomatic, consular, military and other government personnel and their dependants, foreign students studying in the UK, and foreign patients being treated in the UK. If an individual maintains residences in the UK and another economy, they are considered to be UK residents if they typically spend more time in their UK residence than their foreign residence during the year

Double-entry system

Rules for the UK double-entry system

Credit entries, changes in all economic resources provided by the UK to non-residents, including:

Exports of goods and services

Income accruing on the resources to UK from residents

Financial liabilities of the UK to non-residents

Transfers which are offsets to debit entries

Debit entries, changes in all economic resources received by the UK from non-residents, including:

Imports of goods and services

Income accruing on the resources to non-residents from UK

Financial claims of UK on non-residents

Transfers which are offsets to credit entries

Examples of UK double-entry recording	Credits	Debits
1. Sales of goods (value 100) to non-residents for foreign exchange (that is, goods provided and bank payment (a bank deposit) received in an account held abroad)		
Goods	100	
Bank deposits, foreign currency assets		100
2. Purchase of goods (value 120) from a non-resident using trade credit (that is, goods received and a claim on a resident (trade credit liability) provided)		
Goods		120
Trade credit liabilities	120	
3. Food aid (value 5) provided to non-residents (that is, goods provided and transfer imputed)		
Goods	5	
Current transfers		5
4. Repayment of a loan (value 25) by a resident company to a non-resident lender (that is, liability to a non-resident reduced and a reduction in bank deposits held abroad)		
Loan repayment	–25	
Bank deposits, foreign currency assets		–25

Conceptually, an economic transaction has two sides: something of economic value is provided and something of equal value is received. The balance of payments reflects this in a double-entry recording system of credits and debits. When an economic value is provided (for example, UK exports a car) a credit entry is made, and when the corresponding economic value is received (for example, a payment for the car) a debit entry is made. For example, when an exporter sells (provides) goods to a non-resident, the exporter may receive cash (a financial asset) or another type of financial asset (for example, a trade credit claim) in return. The export is represented by a credit entry and the financial asset acquired is represented by an offset debit entry. Similar entries are made when an importer buys a car (debit) and pays for it (credit). So a credit entry represents a change in rest of world ownership of any sort of UK asset (real or financial); a debit entry represents a change in UK ownership of rest of world assets.

An understanding of the double-entry recording system is necessary for a complete understanding of balance of payments statistics.

Under the double-entry system, by definition credit entries must equal debit entries. Credit entries are required for exports of goods and services, income receivable, and changes in financial liabilities. Likewise, debit entries are required for imports of goods and services, income payable, and changes in financial assets. Where something of economic value is provided without something of economic value in exchange (that is, without a quid pro quo) the double-entry system requires an offset to be imputed (a transfer entry) of equivalent value. For example, food exported as aid requires a credit entry for the goods provided and a debit transfer as the aid offset.

Sign convention in the UK balance of payments statistics

The sign convention used in presenting the UK balance of payments statistics is to give a positive sign to an increase in either credit or debit entries and a negative sign to a decrease in credit or debit entries. Balances (calculated as credits less debits) or items which are net credits have no sign, while balances which are net debits have a negative sign.

When considering making international comparisons it should be borne in mind that there is no unique or correct sign convention and other countries/institutions use variations. In particular the convention used by the IMF in their publications gives no sign to credit entries and a minus sign to all debit entries (for example, imports and acquisitions of assets).

Errors and omissions

It follows that, in principle, under a double-entry accounting system, the difference between the sum of credit and debit entries must be zero. In practice, some transactions are not measured accurately (that is, errors) and some are not measured at all (that is, omissions). Data sources used to compile the accounts often measure the credit and debit sides from different data sources and may not always do so consistently. There could be many reasons why these sources may not measure the acquisition side of the transaction and the corresponding payments, either in the same accounting period or at the same value. To restore the equality of credit and debit entries, a net errors and omissions item is included in the balance of payments accounts. The item indicates whether credit or debit transactions would be needed to balance the accounts, but does not show where the discrepancy lies. Usually the financial account is considered to be the most likely source.

Valuation

It is important that the balance of payments and international investment position statistics carry values that have economic meaning to enable useful analysis, and to provide meaningful indicators of cross-border economic activity. It is also important for the double-entry accounting system that a uniform valuation is adopted. This means that the credit and debit entries of each transaction – which in practice may be derived from independent sources – should be valued at the same price. In addition, a uniform valuation is essential to sum different types of transactions on a consistent and comparable basis. The use of a uniform valuation principle aids understanding by users. Moreover, statistics for different countries will not be comparable unless both parties to a transaction adopt the same valuation principle. It is also important to use a principle which is consistent with national accounting principles. For all these reasons, market price is used in UK economic statistics for valuing transactions.

Market price is the amount of money that a willing buyer pays to acquire something from a willing seller, when such an exchange is between independent parties and involves only commercial considerations. In practice, one or more of the conditions needed to establish a market price may be absent and other valuations may be used.

For the most part, the price at which a transaction is recorded in the accounts of the transactors or in the administrative records used as data sources will be the market price or a very close approximation of it. This valuation is known as the transactions price and is the practical valuation basis used in the balance of payments, both because it aids consistent recording of credits and debits and because of its usual proximity to the ideal market valuation. The following paragraph discusses a special case of transactions where market prices may not apply, namely transfer pricing between affiliated enterprises in different countries.

Transfer pricing

Where transactions are between affiliated enterprises in different countries, the prices adopted in their books for recording transactions in goods and services and any associated indebtedness and interest – referred to as transfer prices – may not correspond to prices that would be charged to independent parties. There will be some departure from the market price principle if transfer prices are different from those charged to enterprises outside the group. However there are practical difficulties in identifying and suitably adjusting individual cases. Transfer pricing to avoid tax is illegal in the UK so the distortions in the international accounts caused by transfer pricing are not considered widespread. For both reasons, adjustments to account for transfer pricing are rarely made in practice.

Assets and liabilities

As with all international investment position statistics, foreign financial assets and liabilities should, in principle, be valued at their current market price at the reference date. In practice this is not always possible and valuation guidelines are adopted in order to approximate market valuation, particularly for those financial assets and liabilities that are only rarely transacted. For example, in measuring the value of direct investment in equity capital, much of which is never traded or is traded infrequently, market value is approximated by one of the following methods: a recent transaction price, directors' value, or net asset value. Over time, this is likely to underestimate the true market value of foreign direct investment.

Unit of account and conversion

Transactions and stock positions originally denominated in foreign currencies need to be converted to pounds sterling using market rates of exchange prevailing at the time of the transaction (balance of payments) or at the reference date (international investment position). Transactions should be converted at the mid-point of the buying and selling exchange rates applying at the time of transaction. Stocks should be converted at the mid-point of the buying and selling exchange rates applying at the beginning or end of the period. In practice, the actual rate used varies according to the source of the transaction or stock data.

Time of recording

Transactions

The time of recording of transactions in balance of payments and international investment position statistics is, in principle, the time of change of ownership (either actual or imputed). Under the double-entry system, both sides of a transaction should be recorded in the same period. This is consistent with the principle of accrual accounting, which requires that transactions be recorded when economic value is created, transformed, exchanged, transferred or extinguished.

Change of ownership is considered to occur when legal ownership of goods changes, when services are rendered and when income accrues. In the case of transfers, those which are imposed by one party on another, such as taxes and fines, should ideally be recorded at the moment at which the underlying transactions or other flows occur which give rise to the liability to pay; other transfers should be recorded when the goods or services change ownership.

For financial transactions, the time of change of ownership is taken to be the time when transactions are entered in the books of the transactors. That is taken to be the time when a foreign financial asset or liability is acquired, relinquished by agreement, sold or repaid. The commitment or pledging of an asset does not constitute an economic transaction, and no entry should be shown unless a change of ownership actually occurs in the period covered. Likewise, the entries for loan drawings should be based on actual disbursements and not on commitments or authorisations. Entries for loan repayments should be recorded at the time they are due rather than on the actual payment date.

Both sides of a transaction should be recorded in the same period. In practice the time of recording of transactions in the balance of payments and international investment position statistics will reflect the practices in data sources, and may diverge from the principle of time of change of ownership. For the UK, transactions in goods credits (exported goods) are mainly recorded at the time when goods are shipped as this is assessed to be a generally good practical approximation of the time when ownership changes. Goods debits (imported goods) are recorded when customs records relating to the movement of the goods across the frontier are processed, again in the expectation that this is the best practical approximation to change of ownership that can be generally achieved. For the remainder of the current account, the time of the recording of transactions generally complies with the time of change of ownership. Exceptions occur mainly because the record-keeping practices of some data providers may not be on this basis. Financial account transactions usually are recorded appropriately, that is, when the parties record transactions in their books. However, some transactions may be derived from information supplied by intermediaries that are not party to the transactions and may not be aware of the time of change of ownership. Also, some enterprises may adopt accounting practices that lead to inconsistent time of recording; a simple example is that different enterprises may close off their accounts at different times of day.

Stock

The time of recognising the stock of a foreign financial asset or liability follows naturally from the time of recording of a transaction in that asset or liability. For example, if a transaction is undertaken to acquire a foreign financial asset, there will also be a consequential increase in the stock of foreign financial assets at the end of that period. Of course, if the asset is disposed of before the end of the period, it will not contribute to the stocks statistics to be recorded for the period, but the disposal will have given rise to another transaction to be recorded for the period.

Types of transactions in the balance of payments

An economic transaction occurs when something of economic value is provided by one party to another. Transactions that are considered to have economic value comprise those in goods, services, income and financial assets and liabilities. The transactions recorded in a balance of payments statement stem from dealings between two parties, one being a resident and the other a non-resident. The types of transactions included in the balance of payments are exchanges, one-sided transactions and imputed transactions.

Exchanges

Exchanges are the most important and numerous type of transaction. They include transactions in which one transactor provides something of economic value to another transactor and receives in return something of equal value.

Special cases of imputation/estimation

Migrants' transfers

A special statistical treatment is required when a person migrates, that is when the person's status changes from non-resident to resident (or vice versa). When this change occurs, the property owned by the migrant becomes the property of a resident instead of that of a non-resident (or vice versa). This change of ownership of net worth between economies is included in the balance of payments. For example, any financial assets held abroad by the migrant become claims by the UK on the rest of the world.

Offset entries are made corresponding to the transfer of net worth and, by their nature, these are included as transfers in the capital account. This treatment amounts to envisaging a transfer of property from the person in their capacity as a non-resident to the person in their capacity as a resident (or vice versa). In principle, this transaction embraces all the migrant's property, whether or not it accompanies the migrant.

Reinvested earnings

A number of special cases of imputed transactions feature in balance of payments compilation. One case involves the reinvestment of earnings in resident enterprises by their non-resident direct investors. These *reinvested earnings* are regarded as being paid out as investment income and then reinvested in the enterprises from which they originated. They are therefore recorded both as a component of investment income in the current account and as a component of direct investment in the financial account. It is considered analytically useful to identify these transactions separately in economic statistics because of the substantial contribution they make to the stock of direct investment finance in a country.

Financial services

A further case relates to estimation for the implicit fees associated with financial services. These include spread earnings on foreign exchange, derivatives and securities trading and FISIM, which is the implicit margin resulting from interest rate differentials between borrowing and lending.

Exceptions to change of ownership

In economic statistics, transactions are considered to occur when the goods and financial assets change ownership between transactors, when services are provided by one transactor to another, or when income is earned by one transactor from another. However, there are certain situations in which no change of ownership legally occurs, but where transactions are nonetheless considered to have occurred for balance of payments purposes. The situations include financial leases, goods imported into or exported from the UK for processing and return, and transactions between a head office in one country and a branch in another.

Financial leases

A financial lease is regarded as a method of obtaining all the rights, risks and rewards of ownership of real resources without holding legal ownership. Although legal ownership remains with the lessor during the term of the lease, all the risks and responsibilities apply to the lessee. In these cases, the basic nature of the transaction is given precedence over its legal form, by imputing a change of ownership of the resource to the lessee. As a result of this imputation, a financial liability is recognised and lease payments are classified as partly loan repayments in the financial account and partly interest in the current account, rather than as services in the current account.

Goods for processing

In economic statistics, the value of goods entering or leaving the UK for processing and returning to the country of origin after processing should be recorded on a gross basis, that is, recording the goods both when they enter (as imports) and when they leave (as exports), even though there is no legal change of ownership of those goods. Thus a good entering the UK to be processed and returned to the country of origin is recorded as an import at the appropriate value and subsequently as an export – recorded by the customs system at the original value plus the added value of the processing. A symmetrical treatment should be applied to UK goods exported for processing and return. The basis for this treatment is that such goods lose their identity during processing by being transformed or incorporated into different goods. On the other hand, for goods undergoing repairs only the value of the repair, not the gross value of the goods, is included in the goods credits or debits.

Branches

In economic statistics, it is usually necessary to split the activities of a legal entity and recognise two units, a head office in one country and a branch in another. Flows of goods, services, income and finance between the branch and its head office are therefore treated as transactions, even though they are legally part of the same unit. For example, goods and services sent from the head office to its branch are to be treated as exports of goods and services by the head office.

There are two cases where such splitting becomes necessary. The first occurs when production of goods and services is undertaken by the personnel, plant and equipment of the legal entity in an economic territory outside the economic territory of the head office, provided certain conditions apply. These conditions include: the intention to operate in the separate economy indefinitely or over a long period (12 months is used as a rule of thumb); keeping a set of accounts of the branch's activity (that is, income statement, balance sheet, transactions with the parent entity); eligibility to pay income tax in the host country; having a substantial physical presence; and receiving funds for the branch's work which are paid into its own bank account.

The second case occurs when a person or legal entity resident in one economy owns land and buildings located in another economy. Ownership of immovable assets is always attributed in balance of payments and international investment position statistics to residents of the economy in which the assets are located. Thus land in the domestic territory, which is in fact owned by a non-resident, is treated as being owned by a notional resident entity, which in turn has a foreign direct investment liability to the real owner. It should also be recalled that territorial enclaves (for example, embassies, consulates, military bases) are regarded as part of the economic territory of the economy they represent. When these institutions buy and sell the land in these enclaves they are effectively adding to and subtracting from the economic territory of their government. Such transactions in land owned by foreign embassies are recorded in the capital account as the acquisition/disposal of non-produced, non-financial assets.

Other changes in the international investment position

In addition to the financial transactions included in the balance of payments, the international investment position reconciliation statement includes the other changes which contribute to differences between opening and closing positions for a period.

Other changes in position may occur through price changes, exchange rate changes and other adjustments. Price changes are valuation changes that occur because of changes in the market price of a financial instrument, such as a change in the price of a share or debt security, or through revaluing a company's net worth.

Exchange rate changes are due to fluctuations in the value of the pound, in which the accounts are compiled, relative to the currencies in which foreign assets and liabilities are denominated.

Other adjustments can arise from a number of causes such as write-off of bad debts, classification changes, monetisation/demonetisation of gold, and the allocation/cancellation of Special Drawing Rights. A reclassification would occur where a foreign investor's equity investment in an enterprise increased during the reporting period and the increase was sufficient to change the classification of the investor's total equity holding at the end of the period from portfolio investment to direct investment. Monetisation of gold occurs when the Bank of England monetises commodity stocks of gold and adds these to its monetary gold holdings as part of the UK's official reserve assets. Special Drawing Rights in the IMF are also included in the UK's official reserve assets. Allocations and cancellations of these instruments are included as other adjustments.

Gross and net recording

Entries for current and capital account items are generally treated so that credits for each component are recorded separately from debits. Current and capital account transactions, in this context, are described as being recorded gross.

Gross recording contrasts to the recording of transactions in the financial account, which is mainly on a net basis, although for long-term trade credits and loans, gross drawings and repayments are included in the financial account. The net recording of other financial account items means that, for each item, credit transactions are combined with debit transactions to arrive at a single result – either a net credit or net debit – reflecting the net effect of all increases and decreases in holdings of that type of asset or liability during the recording period. There are several types of netting in the financial account, for example, the netting of purchases and sales within an instrument in an asset position, and netting of assets and liabilities as in the case of direct investment.

Standard balance of payments classification

Balance of payments and international investment position statistics need to be arranged in a coherent structure to facilitate their use and adaptation for purposes such as policy formulation, analytical studies, projections, bilateral comparisons, and regional and global aggregations. *BPM5* contains a standard classification and list of standard components of the balance of payments and international investment position. These standards were developed taking into account the views of national compilers and analysts, and the requirement to harmonise concepts and definitions with related international statistical standards and classifications. The classification also reflects the separation of categories that may exhibit different economic behaviour, may be important in a number of countries, are readily collectable, and are needed for harmonising with other bodies of statistics.

The standard balance of payments classification comprises two main groups of accounts – the **current account** and the **capital and financial account**. Transactions classified to the **current account** include goods and services, income and current transfers. Within the capital and financial account, the capital account includes capital transfers and the net acquisition or disposal of non-produced, non-financial assets. The **financial account** includes transactions in financial assets and liabilities.

Transactions in current account and capital account items are generally shown on a gross basis (gross debits and credits separately). Transactions in financial account items are mainly recorded on a net basis.

Current account

Table A (opposite) shows the standard classification of the current account. Each of the broad categories is described briefly below, while individual component items are described in detail in subsequent chapters.

Goods and services are divided into separate accounts for goods and services. **Goods** comprise most movable goods that change ownership between UK residents and non-residents. **Services** comprise services transactions between UK residents and non-residents, together with some transactions in goods where, by international agreement, it is not practical to separate the goods and services components (for example, goods purchased by travellers are classified to services).

Income refers to income earned by UK residents from non-residents and vice versa. Income covers compensation of employees and investment income. **Compensation of employees** comprises wages, salaries and other benefits earned by individuals from economies other than those in which they are residents, as well as earnings from extraterritorial bodies such as foreign embassies, which often employ staff from the economy in which they are located. **Investment income** comprises income earned from the provision of financial capital and is classified by direct, portfolio and other investment income and income earned on the UK's reserve assets.

Transfers represent offsets to the provision of resources between residents and

Summary of balance of payments in 2008

£ million

	Credits	Debits
1. Current account		
A. Goods and services	421 501	459 899
1. Goods	251 102	343 979
2. Services	170 399	115 920
2.1. Transportation	20 880	20 376
2.2. Travel	19 598	37 256
2.3. Communications	4 639	4 122
2.4. Construction	1 127	904
2.5. Insurance	8 036	1 073
2.6. Financial	52 828	14 209
2.7. Computer and information	7 040	3 055
2.8. Royalties and licence fees	7 361	5 500
2.9. Other business	44 697	24 404
2.10. Personal, cultural and recreational	2 091	959
2.11. Government	2 102	4 062
B. Income	263 703	236 763
1. Compensation of employees	1 032	1 738
2. Investment income	262 671	235 025
2.1 Direct investment	69 169	10 638
2.2 Portfolio investment	68 104	73 309
2.3 Other investment (including earnings on reserve assets)	125 398	151 078
C. Current transfers	15 422	29 032
1. General government	5 512	14 606
2. Other sectors	9 910	14 426
Total current account	**700 626**	**725 694**
2. Capital and financial accounts		
A. Capital account	5 590	2 197
1. Capital transfers	4 589	1 297
2. Acquisition/disposal of non-produced, non-financial assets	1 001	900
B. Financial account	−637 083	−655 204
1. Direct investment	52 461	72 528
Abroad		72 528
1.1. Equity capital		23 405
1.2. Reinvested earnings		36 091
1.3. Other capital[1]		13 032
In United Kingdom	52 461	
1.1. Equity capital	49 218	
1.2. Reinvested earnings	15 923	
1.3. Other capital[2]	−12 680	
2. Portfolio investment	240 586	−128 620
Assets		−128 620
2.1. Equity securities		−60 774
2.2. Debt securities		−67 846
Liabilities	240 586	
2.1. Equity securities	44 045	
2.2. Debt securities	196 541	
3. Financial derivatives (net)		−17 746
4. Other investment	−930 130	−580 028
Assets		−580 028
4.1 Trade credits		−158
4.2 Loans		−122 407
4.3 Currency and deposits		−461 054
4.4 Other assets		3 591
Liabilities	−930 130	
4.1. Trade credits	—	
4.2. Loans	−348 261	
4.3. Currency and deposits	−576 783	
4.4. Other liabilities	−5 086	
5. Reserve assets		−1 338
5.1. Monetary gold		—
5.2. Special drawing rights		−24
5.3. Reserve position in the IMF		802
5.4. Foreign exchange		−1 923
Total capital and financial accounts	**−631 493**	**−653 007**
Total current, capital and financial accounts	**69 133**	**72 687**
Net errors and omissions	3 554	

1 Other capital transaction on direct investment abroad represents claims on affiliated enterprises less liabilities to affiliated enterprises
2 Other capital transactions on direct investment in the United Kingdom represents liabilities to direct investors less claims on direct investors

non-residents with no quid pro quo in economic value (for example, the provision of food aid). **Current transfers** are distinguished from **capital transfers**, which are included in the capital account. Current transfers represent the offset to the provision of resources that are normally consumed within a short period (less than twelve months) after the transfer is made. In the example of food aid, the food is presumed to be consumed within twelve months of it being received. The classification of current transfers is by general government and other sectors.

Capital account

The capital account comprises both capital transfers and the acquisition and disposal of non-produced, non-financial assets (such as copyrights). The latter includes land purchases and sales associated with embassies and other extraterritorial bodies. Capital transfers entries are required where there is no quid pro quo to offset the transfer of ownership of fixed assets, or the transfer of funds linked to fixed assets (for example, aid to finance capital works), or the forgiveness of debt. It also includes the counterpart to the transfer of net wealth by migrants, referred to as migrants' transfers.

Financial account

The financial account comprises transactions associated with changes of ownership of the UK's foreign financial assets and liabilities. The main classifications used in the financial account are discussed in conjunction with the international investment position classification below.

The **international investment position** measures the UK's stock of external financial assets and liabilities, whereas the **balance of payments financial account** measures transactions in these assets and liabilities. Hence the classifications used in the financial account and international investment position need to be essentially the same.

Major classifications of the financial account and international investment position

Items in the financial account and international investment position statement are classified on a number of bases. The main ones are **type of investment, assets and liabilities, instrument of investment, sector,** and **original contractual maturity of financial instruments**.

A comparison of the international investment position statement and the balance of payments financial account shows one minor difference. In the category of direct investment in the financial account, reinvested earnings are shown separately whereas, in the international investment position statement, where no separate market price valuation of reinvested earnings can exist, the reinvested earnings are grouped into a composite category for equity and reinvested earnings.

Type of investment

The type of investment used in the UK's balance of payments and international investment position consists of five broad categories:

(i) **Direct investment** capital refers to capital provided to or received from an enterprise, by an investor in another country (that is, an individual, enterprise or group of related individuals or enterprises) who is in a direct investment relationship with that enterprise. A direct investment relationship exists if the investor has an equity interest in an enterprise, resident in another country, of 10 per cent or more of the ordinary shares or voting stock. The direct investment relationship extends to branches, subsidiaries and to other businesses where the enterprise has significant shareholding.

(ii) **Portfolio investment** refers to transactions in equity and debt securities (apart from those included in direct investment and reserve assets). Debt securities comprise bonds and notes and money market instruments. In comparison with direct investment, it indicates investment where the investor is not assumed to have any appreciable say in the operation of the enterprise (for example, less than 10 per cent of the ordinary share or voting stock).

(iii) **Financial derivatives** cover any financial instrument the price of which is based upon the value of an underlying asset (typically another financial asset). Financial derivatives include options (on currencies, interest rates, commodities, indices), traded financial futures, warrants and currency and interest swaps. Under BPM5, transactions in derivatives are treated as separate transactions, rather than being included as integral parts of underlying transactions to which they may be linked as hedges. From 2005 onwards, financial derivatives comprise all UK banks' net derivative transactions. Prior to 2005, only estimates for the settlement receipts/payments on UK banks' interest rate swaps and forward rate agreements are included in financial derivatives.

(iv) **Other investment** is a residual category that captures transactions not classified to direct investment, portfolio investment, financial derivatives or reserve assets of the compiling economy. Other investment covers trade credits, loans (including financial leases), currency and deposits, and a residual category for any other assets and liabilities.

(v) **Reserve assets** refer to those foreign financial assets that are available to, and controlled by, the monetary authorities such as the Bank of England for financing or regulating payments imbalances. Reserve assets comprise: monetary gold, Special Drawing Rights, reserve position in the IMF, and foreign exchange held by the Bank.

Assets and liabilities

A financial **asset** is generally in the form of a financial claim on the rest of the world that is either represented by a contractual obligation (such as a loan) or is evidenced by a security (such as a share certificate). Two financial assets – monetary gold and Special Drawing Rights in the IMF – are not claims on the rest of the world. They are, however, included in international investment assets because they are readily available for payment of international obligations. A financial **liability** represents a financial claim of the rest of the world on the UK. Assets and liabilities in the international investment position statement are components of the balance sheet of an economy with the rest of the world. In the financial account the asset and liability classifications in essence reflect, respectively, transactions in claims on non-residents (assets) and in claims by non-residents (liabilities).

In the international investment position, the difference between assets and liabilities is the net international investment position, also referred to as the net liability position/net asset position, depending on the balance.

For **direct investment**, in both the financial account and international investment position, the main classification is by direction of investment, that is, direct investment abroad and direct investment in the UK. Direct investment abroad is derived by netting liabilities of the UK direct investors to their direct investment enterprises against claims on their direct investment enterprises abroad. Similarly, direct investment in the UK is derived after netting claims of the UK direct investment enterprises against their liabilities to those direct investors abroad.

Instrument of investment

Several instruments of investment are also identified. Some of these are only applicable to one type of capital, that is, the instrument **reinvested earnings** is only applicable to direct investment, while **monetary gold** and **Special Drawing Rights** are only used for reserve assets.

The major instruments and grouping of instruments identified in balance of payments and international investment statistics include:

- monetary gold
- Special Drawing Rights
- foreign exchange
- reserve position in IMF
- equity
- reinvested earnings
- debt securities
- financial derivatives
- trade credit
- loans
- currency and deposits
- other assets/liabilities

Holdings of financial derivatives data are presented as an annex to the international investment chapter.

Similar instruments may be combined into groups or combined with certain types of investment to make statistical presentations less cluttered.

For example:

- trade credit, loans, deposits, and other forms of finance including all debt securities, but excluding equity capital and reinvested earnings, between non-financial enterprises in a direct investment relationship, are combined and shown only as *other direct capital*. Similar aggregation applies to finance between a financial enterprise and a non-financial enterprise and between financial enterprises only in case of permanent debt

- bonds, bills, notes and money market instruments within portfolio investment are shown separately but under a heading of *debt securities*

- a number of financial assets, held as part of the UK's reserves assets (currency and deposits, bills, bonds, notes and money market instruments), are grouped under the category *foreign exchange* within the reserve assets category

Foreign equity and debt

At a broader level, instruments may be combined to show foreign equity and foreign debt. Foreign equity includes equity capital, reinvested earnings and equity securities. Foreign debt is a residual item containing all other instruments. They may be compiled on a gross basis (for example, foreign debt/assets and liabilities) or on a net basis (for example, net foreign debt).

Sectorisation

Transactor units within an economy may be grouped together into institutional sectors. Units within the same institutional sector may be expected to behave similarly in their financial and other dealings and in response to differing economic and political stimuli. The principle of classification by sector, or sectorisation, in the financial account and international investment position is to identify the sector of the domestic creditor for assets and the sector of the domestic debtor for liabilities.

Four sectors are generally distinguished in the standard components of the ONS balance of payments and international investment statistics: **monetary financial institutions**; **central government**; **public corporations**; and **other.**

Within the current and capital accounts, sectorisation is also applied to current and capital transfers, where a split between **general government** and **other** is used.

Original contractual maturity

The fifth edition of the balance of payments manual looks to distinguish between long-term or short-term investment. Investment longer than one year is deemed to be long-term and investment less than one year is deemed to be short-term.

Other financial classifications

Other classifications in the financial account and international investment position include the domicile of liabilities issued by residents, drawings and repayments for long-term liabilities in the form of both trade credits and loans and the currency of assets and liabilities.

Country classification

The general principles applying to the compilation of a global balance of payments statement for the UK can be applied to the preparation of a statement for the UK's transactions with an individual country or a group of countries.

Reliability of estimates

All the value estimates are calculated as accurately as possible; however they cannot always be regarded as being absolutely precise to the last digit shown. Similarly, the index numbers are not necessarily absolutely precise to the last digit shown. Some figures are provisional and may be revised later; this applies particularly to many of the detailed figures for the latest years.

Revisions since ONS *Pink Book* 2008

The current account balance is revised from 2004 onwards.

Goods – the data are revised from 2004 to reflect revised data from HM Revenue & Customs and other data suppliers.

Services – the data are revised back to 2004. The earliest revisions result from a general reassessment of data following the annual supply and use balancing process. Revisions from 2007 additionally reflect the use of final results from ONS's annual International Trade in Services Survey for 2007.

Income, financial account and IIP – the data are revised from 2004. Revisions from 2006 reflect the use of annual inquiry results from the ONS direct investment surveys. Revisions from 2007 additionally reflect the incorporation of the results of ONS annual surveys of securities dealers, mutual funds, insurance companies, and pension funds.

Current transfers – the data are revised back to 2006. Revisions reflect the latest data from HM Treasury for transfers involving the UK Government and the latest data from ONS annual surveys of UK insurance companies and from ONS annual direct investment surveys, which provide estimates of taxes on investment income.

Capital transfers – the data are revised from 2007. Revisions reflect the latest data from HM Treasury and the final results from the ONS annual International Trade in Services survey for 2007.

Symbols and conventions used in the tables

Rounding

As figures have been rounded to the nearest final digit, there may be slight discrepancies between the sums of the constituent items and the totals as shown.

Symbols

The following symbols are used throughout:

.. = not available

-   = nil or less than a million

References

The internationally agreed framework for the presentation of the Balance of Payments and the National Accounts are described in the following publications:

Balance of Payments Manual (5th edition 1993), International Monetary Fund (ISBN 1-55775-339-3). www.imf.org/external/np/sta/bop/BOPman.pdf

Balance of Payments Textbook (1996), International Monetary Fund (ISBN 1-55775-570-1). www.imf.org/external/np/sta/bop/BOPtex.pdf

Balance of Payments and International Investment Position, Australia: Concepts, Sources and Methods (1998) Australian Bureau of Statistics (ISBN 0-642-25670-5). www.abs.gov.au/Ausstats/abs@.nsf/0/ 09998F91F5A8A7BFCA25697E0018FB0A?Open

European System of Accounts (ESA 1995), Office for Official Publications of the European Communities (ISBN 92-827-7954-8)

System of National Accounts (1993), (ISBN 92-1-161352-3). http://unstats.un.org/unsd/sna1993/introduction.asp

Current account

Part 1

Summary of balance of payments

Chapter 1

Current account

The UK has recorded a current account deficit in every year since 1984. Prior to 1984, the current account recorded a surplus in 1980 to 1983. Since the last surplus was recorded in 1983, there have been four main phases in the development of the current account. In the first phase, from 1984 to 1989, the current account deficit increased steadily to reach a high of £25.5 billion in 1989, equivalent to -4.9 per cent of Gross Domestic Product (GDP). During the second phase, from 1990 until 1997, the current account deficit declined to a low of £1.0 billion in 1997. In the third phase, between 1998 and 2006, the current account deficit widened sharply, peaking at £43.8 billion in 2006. This was the highest recorded in cash terms but only equated to -3.3 per cent of GDP. In the past two years, there has been a reduction in the current account deficit – in 2008 it currently stands at £25.1 billion, equivalent to -1.7 per cent of GDP.

The profile for the current account has historically followed that of trade in goods, its biggest and most cyclical component.

Figure 1.1
Current account balance

£ billion

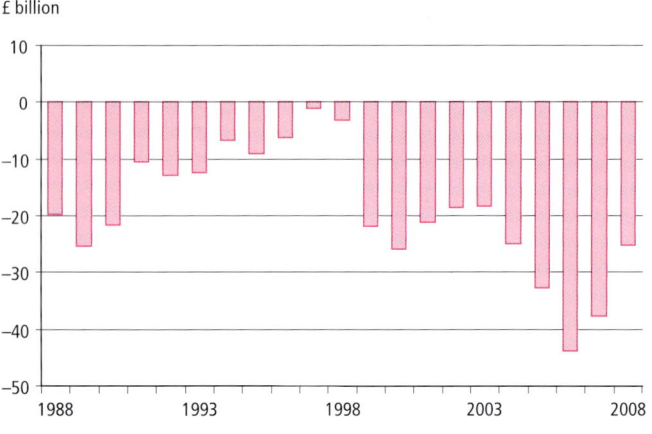

Figure 1.2
Current balance as a percentage of GDP

Per cent

That pattern was broadly followed until it changed in 2001. The pattern re-emerged in 2004 to 2006 with an increasing deficit on trade in goods being mirrored by an increase in the current account deficit. In 2007 and 2008, once more there has been a decoupling of the movements of trade in goods to the movements in the overall current account balance.

The last trade in goods surplus, recorded in 1982, contributed to a current account surplus. Following 1982, the goods balance went into deficit and this increased to a peak of £24.7 billion in 1989, while the current balance deteriorated to a deficit of £25.5 billion. From 1989 until the late 1990s, both the trade in goods and current account deficits broadly fell and then subsequently rose. From 2001 to 2003, while the goods deficit continued to grow, the current account deficit narrowed due to a widening income surplus. From 2004, the deficit on trade in goods increased steadily, matched by a rise in the current account deficit. In 2007 and 2008 however, the increasing deficit on trade in goods was more than offset by increasing surpluses on both trade in services and income. This reduced the current account deficit by £6.1 billion in 2007 and by a further £12.6 billion in 2008.

Trade in goods and services

The trade in goods account recorded net surpluses in the years 1980 to 1982, largely as a result of growth in exports of North Sea oil. Since then however, the trade in goods account has remained in deficit. The deficit grew significantly in the late 1980s to reach a peak of £24.7 billion in 1989, before narrowing in the 1990s to levels of around £10 billion to £14 billion. In 1998 the deficit jumped by over £9 billion, and it has continued to rise since, reaching a cash record of £92.9 billion in 2008.

The trade in services account has shown a surplus for every year since 1966. The surplus on services generally increased

Figure 1.3
Trade in goods and services

Credits less debits

£ billion

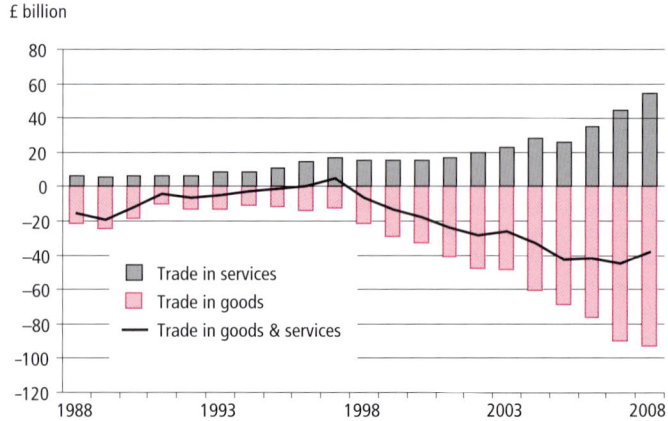

until 1987, during which time it broadly offset the deficit on trade in goods. From 1988 to 1992 the surplus was reasonably steady at around £6 billion annually. The services surplus then increased considerably, reaching £16.8 billion in 1997. It dropped back to £15.0 billion in 1998 but by 2004, had risen to £28.4 billion. It fell back slightly in 2005 then rose to a record £54.5 billion in 2008.

Income

The income account consists of compensation of employees and investment income, the latter dominating the account. Historically the balance on compensation of employees has generally been in deficit. It moved into surplus in the late 1990s but moved back into deficit in 2004, where it has remained.

The investment income balance was in surplus until 1976. From 1977 to 1996 it showed a deficit in nearly every year. Then from 1997 onwards, except for 1999, it has shown a surplus in every year. The surplus on direct investment income has been partly offset by deficits on earnings from portfolio investment equity securities, and other investment - principally UK banks' net interest payments on deposits. From 2002 to 2004 the surplus was around £18 billion in each year. In 2005 the surplus rose to £22.5 billion due to record net earnings of £43.0 billion on direct investment, but then dropped sharply in 2006 to £10.5 billion. Investment income rose in 2007 to £21.5 billion and to a new record level of £27.6 billion in 2008. By sector, net earnings of UK monetary financial institutions (banks and building societies) were £24.2 billion in 2008, compared to £8.9 billion in 2007. This increase was partially offset by a £1.4 billion increase in the net payments by central government in 2008 together with a £7.3 billion fall in net earnings by other sectors.

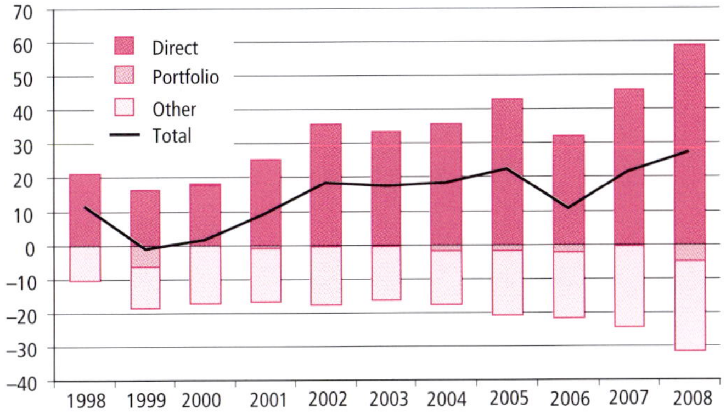

Current transfers

The transfers account has shown a deficit in every year since 1960. The deficit increased steadily to reach £4.8 billion in 1990. In 1991, the deficit reduced to £1.0 billion, reflecting £2.1 billion receipts from other countries towards the UK's cost of the first Gulf conflict. The deficit has since increased, to reach a record £13.6 billion in 2008. Separate data for general government and other sectors are available from 1986 and show that both have been consistently in deficit since 1992. The majority of payments to and receipts from EU institutions are recorded as other sector transactions as they relate to the original payee or ultimate recipient of the payment/receipt. The volatility in this account is driven by fluctuating net contributions to EU Institutions.

Figure 1.5

Current transfers

Credits less debits

£ billion

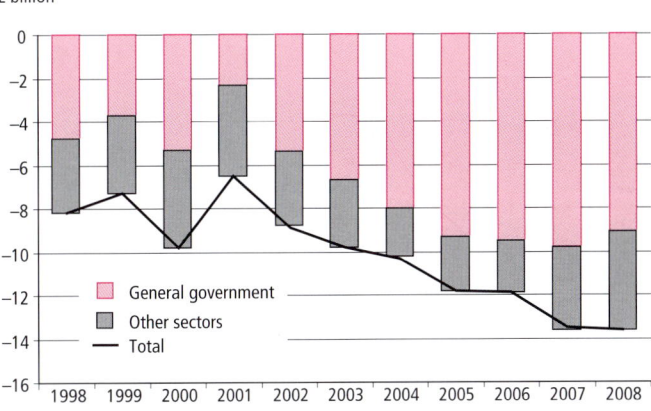

Revisions since *Pink Book 2008*

The current account balance has been revised back to 2004 in this publication, as compared with data published in the *Pink Book 2008*, reflecting the incorporation of GDP balancing adjustments for Trade in Services and annual inquiry results for 2006 and 2007. Details of the sources of these changes are given on pages 17-18 of the Introduction, and the impact of the changes can be seen in Figure 1.6 and in Table 1.1R.

Investment flows, levels and income

One important set of relationships within the balance of payments is the link between the financial account (investment flows), the international investment position (levels or balance sheets), and the income deriving from the balance sheets. This is explained in more detail in the Introduction. Although a reconciliation statement between opening and closing levels and flows is not officially compiled in the UK, Table 1.3 shows the rudiments of this relationship over the years for which consistent detailed data are available. Within the three main

Figure 1.4

Investment income

Credits less debits

£ billion

Figure 1.6

Revisions since *Pink Book 2008*

Credits less debits

£ billion

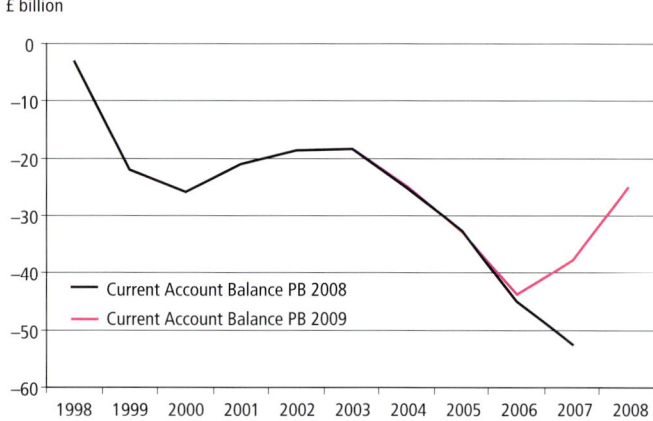

Figure 1.7

International investment position and income

Credits less debits

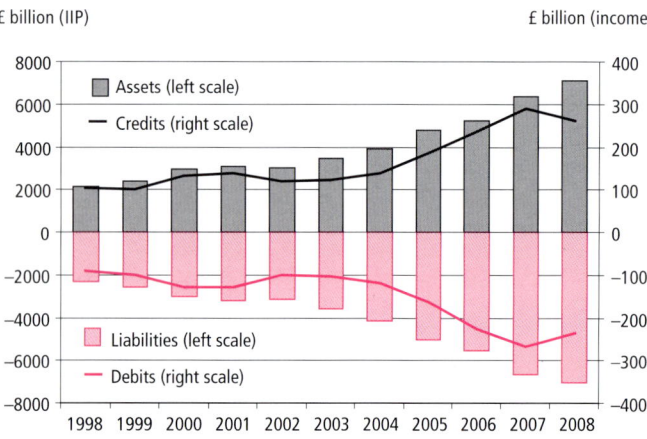

categories of investment (direct, portfolio and other), as well as reserve assets, it can be seen that the difference in the values of the balance sheet at the end of one year and the previous year is approximately equal to the value of the financial transactions in that year. The difference between the two amounts is explained by valuation, exchange rate and other effects such as company write-offs.

The value of both external assets and liabilities in the international investment position has been rising steadily since 1980, reflecting both the increased global investment and the increasing prices of external assets and liabilities. Except for 1990, the UK's external assets exceeded external liabilities in every year until 1995. Between 1995 and 2007, external liabilities exceeded external assets. However, the UK returned to a net asset position in 2008 due mainly to exchange rate effects. The devaluation of sterling against other major currencies increased the value of UK assets and liabilities denominated in foreign currencies. Since a higher proportion of UK assets than of UK liabilities were denominated in foreign currencies, the total value of UK assets held increased by more than did the total value of UK liabilities.

Since 1995, there has been more than a fourfold increase in the levels of both external assets and liabilities. At the end of 2008 each stood at over £7.0 trillion, with a net asset position of £92.9 billion.

Implied 'rates of return'

Another important relationship is that which exists between investment income and the international investment position. This can be considered most easily by looking at the implied 'rates of return' for both assets and liabilities. In total, the implied rate of return on liabilities was higher than on assets from the late 1970s until the mid 1990s. Since 1997, although the return on assets has been higher, both have been at relatively low levels.

The rates of return for direct investment are usually significantly higher than for other forms of investment although the rates have dropped considerably in 2008. Historically, the relatively higher return is probably a consequence, in part, of comparatively lower valuations since direct investment levels are at book value rather than market value used elsewhere, but may also reflect the higher return required to make the longer term investment worthwhile. In recent years however, as the global recession has taken hold, the implied rate of return for direct investment has contracted considerably. Between 2006 and 2008 the implied rate of return for direct investment liabilities declined from 9.6 per cent to 1.6 per cent. This resulted in direct investment liabilities switching from delivering the highest to the lowest rate of return of any investment type.

Within portfolio investment, rates of return on debt securities have been higher than on equity securities. From 1999 to 2003 the difference in the rate of returns generally narrowed before widening in more recent years. In 2008 however, the rate

Figure 1.8

Implied rates of return on assets

Per cent

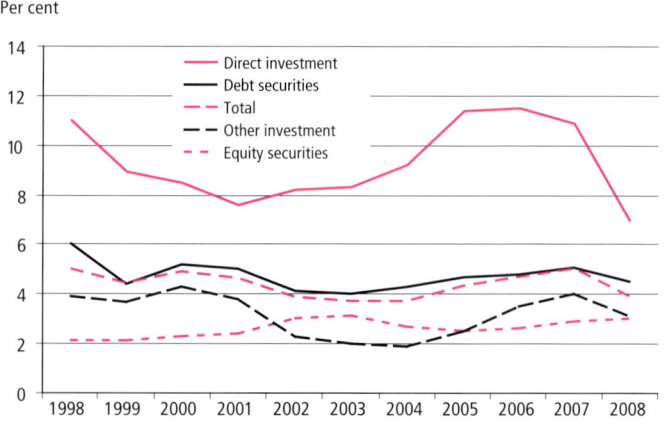

Figure 1.9

Implied rates of return on liabilities

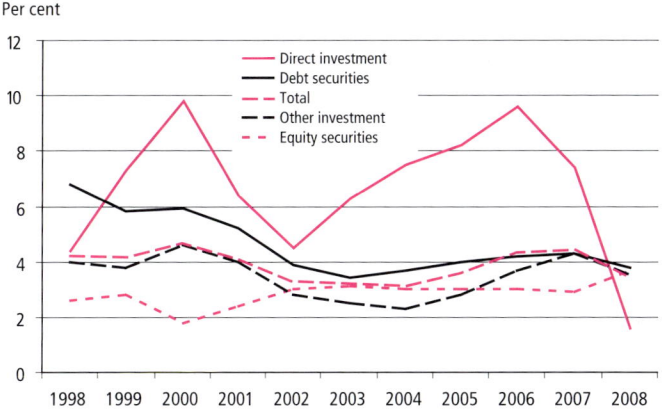

declined once again. This was due to the rate of return on equity continuing to grow, while the rate of return on debt declined as interest rates fell.

Rates of return on other investment were similar to returns on debt in the early 1990s, but between then and 2004 they were generally in decline. From 2005 until 2007 they began to increase again, but fell in 2008. Because other investment constitutes around half of the value of the balance sheets, it is not surprising that the rates of return have reflected the movements in interest rates on loans and deposits such as the base rate and the London Interbank Offered Rate (LIBOR).

1.1 Summary of balance of payments
Balances (credits less debits)

£ million

				Current account								
	Trade in goods	Trade in services	Total goods and services	Compensation of employees	Investment income	Total income	Current transfers	Current balance	Current balance as % of GDP[1]	Capital account	Financial account	Net errors & omissions
	LQCT	KTMS	KTMY	KTMP	HMBM	HMBP	KTNF	HBOG	AA6H	FKMJ	HBNT	HHDH
1946	−101	−274	−375	−20	76	56	166	−153	..	−21	181	−7
1947	−358	−197	−555	−19	140	121	123	−311	..	−21	552	−220
1948	−152	−64	−216	−20	223	203	96	83	0.7	−17	−58	−8
1949	−137	−43	−180	−20	206	186	29	35	0.3	−12	−103	80
1950	−54	−4	−58	−21	378	357	39	338	2.6	−10	−447	119
1951	−692	32	−660	−21	322	301	29	−330	−2.3	−15	426	−81
1952	−272	123	−149	−22	231	209	169	229	1.4	−15	−229	15
1953	−244	123	−121	−25	207	182	143	204	1.2	−13	−177	−14
1954	−210	115	−95	−27	227	200	55	160	0.9	−13	−174	27
1955	−315	42	−273	−27	149	122	43	−108	−0.6	−15	34	89
1956	50	26	76	−30	203	173	2	251	1.2	−13	−250	12
1957	−29	121	92	−32	223	191	−5	278	1.3	−13	−313	48
1958	34	119	153	−34	261	227	4	384	1.7	−10	−411	37
1959	−116	118	2	−37	233	196	–	198	0.8	−5	−68	−125
1960	−404	39	−365	−35	201	166	−6	−205	−0.8	−6	−7	218
1961	−144	51	−93	−35	223	188	−9	86	0.3	−12	23	−97
1962	−104	50	−54	−37	301	264	−14	196	0.7	−12	−195	11
1963	−123	4	−119	−38	364	326	−37	170	0.6	−16	−30	−124
1964	−551	−34	−585	−33	365	332	−74	−327	−1.0	−17	392	−48
1965	−263	−66	−329	−34	405	371	−75	−33	−0.1	−18	49	2
1966	−111	44	−67	−39	358	319	−91	161	0.4	−19	22	−164
1967	−601	157	−444	−39	354	315	−118	−247	−0.6	−25	179	93
1968	−708	341	−367	−48	303	255	−119	−231	−0.5	−26	688	−431
1969	−214	392	178	−47	468	421	−109	490	1.0	−23	−794	327
1970	−18	455	437	−56	527	471	−89	819	1.6	−22	−818	21
1971	205	617	822	−63	454	391	−90	1 123	2.0	−23	−1 330	230
1972	−736	722	−14	−52	350	298	−142	142	0.2	−35	477	−584
1973	−2 573	907	−1 666	−68	970	902	−336	−1 100	−1.5	−39	1 031	108
1974	−5 241	1 292	−3 949	−92	1 010	918	−302	−3 333	−4.0	−34	3 185	182
1975	−3 245	1 708	−1 537	−102	257	155	−313	−1 695	−1.6	−36	1 569	162
1976	−3 930	2 872	−1 058	−140	760	620	−534	−972	−0.8	−12	507	477
1977	−2 271	3 704	1 433	−152	−678	−830	−889	−286	−0.2	11	−3 286	3 561
1978	−1 534	4 215	2 681	−140	−300	−440	−1 420	821	0.5	−79	−2 655	1 913
1979	−3 326	4 573	1 247	−130	−342	−472	−1 777	−1 002	−0.5	−103	864	241
1980	1 329	4 414	5 743	−82	−2 268	−2 350	−1 653	1 740	0.8	−4	−2 157	421
1981	3 238	4 776	8 014	−66	−1 883	−1 949	−1 219	4 846	1.9	−79	−5 312	545
1982	1 879	4 261	6 140	−95	−2 336	−2 431	−1 476	2 233	0.8	6	−1 233	−1 006
1983	−1 618	5 406	3 788	−89	−1 050	−1 139	−1 391	1 258	0.4	75	−3 287	1 954
1984	−5 409	6 101	692	−94	−326	−420	−1 566	−1 294	−0.4	107	−7 130	8 317
1985	−3 416	8 499	5 083	−120	−2 609	−2 729	−2 924	−570	−0.2	185	−1 657	2 042
1986	−9 617	8 182	−1 435	−156	71	−85	−2 094	−3 614	−0.9	135	−122	3 601
1987	−11 698	8 604	−3 094	−174	−730	−904	−3 437	−7 435	−1.7	333	10 606	−3 504
1988	−21 553	6 388	−15 165	−64	−1 188	−1 252	−3 293	−19 710	−4.1	235	16 989	2 486
1989	−24 724	5 866	−18 858	−138	−2 309	−2 447	−4 228	−25 533	−4.9	270	13 614	11 649
1990	−18 707	6 643	−12 064	−110	−4 586	−4 696	−4 802	−21 562	−3.8	497	22 272	−1 207
1991	−10 223	6 312	−3 911	−63	−5 642	−5 705	−999	−10 615	−1.8	290	7 855	2 470
1992	−13 050	6 353	−6 697	−49	−1 037	−1 086	−5 228	−13 011	−2.1	421	16 311	−3 721
1993	−13 066	8 174	−4 892	35	−2 547	−2 512	−5 056	−12 460	−1.9	309	22 278	−10 127
1994	−11 126	8 161	−2 965	−170	1 521	1 351	−5 187	−6 801	−1.0	33	−3 240	10 008
1995	−12 023	11 165	−858	−296	−546	−842	−7 363	−9 063	−1.2	533	−1 717	10 247
1996	−13 722	14 312	590	93	−2 460	−2 367	−4 539	−6 316	−0.8	1 260	−940	5 996
1997	−12 342	16 801	4 459	83	241	324	−5 745	−962	−0.1	958	−7 294	7 298
1998	−21 813	15 003	−6 810	−10	11 813	11 803	−8 172	−3 179	−0.4	489	4 480	−1 790
1999	−29 051	15 562	−13 489	201	−1 244	−1 043	−7 322	−21 854	−2.4	747	29 505	−8 398
2000	−32 976	15 002	−17 974	150	1 812	1 962	−9 775	−25 787	−2.6	1 703	23 133	951
2001	−41 212	17 200	−24 012	66	9 359	9 425	−6 515	−21 102	−2.1	1 318	27 194	−7 410
2002	−47 705	19 632	−28 073	67	18 219	18 286	−8 870	−18 657	−1.7	932	24 204	−6 479
2003	−48 607	22 612	−25 995	59	17 464	17 523	−9 835	−18 307	−1.6	1 466	22 553	−5 712
2004	−60 900	28 414	−32 486	−494	18 339	17 845	−10 276	−24 917	−2.1	2 064	29 358	−6 505
2005	−68 589	25 742	−42 847	−610	22 465	21 855	−11 849	−32 841	−2.6	1 503	29 024	2 314
2006	−76 312	34 782	−41 530	−958	10 531	9 573	−11 885	−43 842	−3.3	975	38 225	4 642
2007	−89 754	44 807	−44 947	−734	21 509	20 775	−13 538	−37 710	−2.7	2 566	31 676	3 468
2008	−92 877	54 479	−38 398	−706	27 646	26 940	−13 610	−25 068	−1.7	3 393	18 121	3 554

1 Using series YBHA: GDP at current market prices.

1.1R Summary of balance of payments
Revisions since ONS Pink Book 2008

£ million

			Current account									
	Trade in goods	Trade in services	**Total goods and services**	Compensation of employees	Investment income	**Total income**	Current transfers	Current balance	Current balance as % of GDP[1]	Capital account	Financial account	Net errors & omissions
	LQCT	KTMS	KTMY	KTMP	HMBM	HMBP	KTNF	HBOG	AA6H	FKMJ	HBNT	HHDH
1946	–	–	–	–	–	–	–	–	..	–	–	–
1947	–	–	–	–	–	–	–	–	..	–	–	–
1948	–	–	–	–	–	–	–	–	–	–	–	–
1949	–	–	–	–	–	–	–	–	–	–	–	–
1950	–	–	–	–	–	–	–	–	–	–	–	–
1951	–	–	–	–	–	–	–	–	–	–	–	–
1952	–	–	–	–	–	–	–	–	–	–	–	–
1953	–	–	–	–	–	–	–	–	–	–	–	–
1954	–	–	–	–	–	–	–	–	–	–	–	–
1955	–	–	–	–	–	–	–	–	–	–	–	–
1956	–	–	–	–	–	–	–	–	–	–	–	–
1957	–	–	–	–	–	–	–	–	–	–	–	–
1958	–	–	–	–	–	–	–	–	–	–	–	–
1959	–	–	–	–	–	–	–	–	–	–	–	–
1960	–	–	–	–	–	–	–	–	–	–	–	–
1961	–	–	–	–	–	–	–	–	–	–	–	–
1962	–	–	–	–	–	–	–	–	–	–	–	–
1963	–	–	–	–	–	–	–	–	–	–	–	–
1964	–	–	–	–	–	–	–	–	–	–	–	–
1965	–	–	–	–	–	–	–	–	–	–	–	–
1966	–	–	–	–	–	–	–	–	–	–	–	–
1967	–	–	–	–	–	–	–	–	–	–	–	–
1968	–	–	–	–	–	–	–	–	–	–	–	–
1969	–	–	–	–	–	–	–	–	–	–	–	–
1970	–	–	–	–	–	–	–	–	–	–	–	–
1971	–	–	–	–	–	–	–	–	–	–	–	–
1972	–	–	–	–	–	–	–	–	–	–	–	–
1973	–	–	–	–	–	–	–	–	–	–	–	–
1974	–	–	–	–	–	–	–	–	–	–	–	–
1975	–	–	–	–	–	–	–	–	–	–	–	–
1976	–	–	–	–	–	–	–	–	–	–	–	–
1977	–	–	–	–	–	–	–	–	–	–	–	–
1978	–	–	–	–	–	–	–	–	–	–	–	–
1979	–	–	–	–	–	–	–	–	–	–	–	–
1980	–	–	–	–	–	–	–	–	–	–	–	–
1981	–	–	–	–	–	–	–	–	–	–	–	–
1982	–	–	–	–	–	–	–	–	–	–	–	–
1983	–	–	–	–	–	–	–	–	–	–	–	–
1984	–	–	–	–	–	–	–	–	–	–	–	–
1985	–	–	–	–	–	–	–	–	–	–	–	–
1986	–	–	–	–	–	–	–	–	–	–	–	–
1987	–	–	–	–	–	–	–	–	–	–	–	–
1988	–	–	–	–	–	–	–	–	–	–	–	–
1989	–	–	–	–	–	–	–	–	–	–	–	–
1990	–	–	–	–	–	–	–	–	–	–	–	–
1991	–	–	–	–	–	–	–	–	–	–	–	–
1992	–	–	–	–	–	–	–	–	–	–	–	–
1993	–	–	–	–	–	–	–	–	–	–	–	–
1994	–	–	–	–	–	–	–	–	–	–	–	–
1995	–	–	–	–	–	–	–	–	–	–	–	–
1996	–	–	–	–	–	–	–	–	–	–	–	–
1997	–	–	–	–	–	–	–	–	–	–	–	–
1998	–	–	–	–	–	–	–	–	–	–	–	–
1999	–	–	–	–	–	–	–	–	–	–	–	–
2000	–	–	–	–	–	–	–	–	–	–	–	–
2001	–	–	–	–	–	–	–	–	–	–	–	–
2002	–	–	–	–	–	–	–	–	–	–	–	–
2003	–	–	–	–	–	–	–	–	–	–	–	–
2004	–	268	268	–	15	15	–	283	–	–	9 794	–10 077
2005	–	–133	–133	–	–17	–17	–	–150	–	–	–1 557	1 707
2006	1	1 674	1 674	–213	–311	–524	39	1 189	0.1	–	–3 650	2 461
2007	–502	3 035	2 533	–69	12 238	12 169	156	14 858	1.1	–75	–8 154	–6 629

1 Using series YBHA: GDP at current market prices.

1.2 Current account

£ million

		1987	1988	1989	1990	1991	1992	1993	1994	1995	1996	1997
Credits												
Exports of goods and services												
Exports of goods	LQAD	79 531	80 711	92 611	102 313	103 939	107 863	122 229	135 143	153 577	167 196	171 923
Exports of services	KTMQ	29 122	29 093	31 542	34 270	34 723	37 617	43 605	48 072	53 570	61 851	65 555
Total exports of goods and services	KTMW	108 653	109 804	124 153	136 583	138 662	145 480	165 834	183 215	207 147	229 047	237 478
Income												
Compensation of employees	KTMN	413	445	476	543	551	551	595	681	887	911	1 007
Investment income	HMBN	46 267	54 540	71 536	76 353	73 652	65 168	70 944	72 585	85 490	89 794	93 360
Total income	HMBQ	46 680	54 985	72 012	76 896	74 203	65 719	71 539	73 266	86 377	90 705	94 367
Current transfers												
General government	FJUM	1 475	1 929	1 507	2 050	4 892	2 180	2 826	2 138	1 730	2 828	2 173
Other sectors	FJUN	4 468	4 584	5 244	6 025	7 611	10 397	9 612	9 521	10 891	13 371	10 735
Total current transfers	KTND	5 943	6 513	6 751	8 075	12 503	12 577	12 438	11 659	12 621	16 199	12 908
Total	HBOE	**161 276**	**171 302**	**202 916**	**221 554**	**225 368**	**223 776**	**249 811**	**268 140**	**306 145**	**335 951**	**344 753**
Debits												
Imports of goods and services												
Imports of goods	LQBL	91 229	102 264	117 335	121 020	114 162	120 913	135 295	146 269	165 600	180 918	184 265
Imports of services	KTMR	20 518	22 705	25 676	27 627	28 411	31 264	35 431	39 911	42 405	47 539	48 754
Total imports of goods and services	KTMX	111 747	124 969	143 011	148 647	142 573	152 177	170 726	186 180	208 005	228 457	233 019
Income												
Compensation of employees	KTMO	587	509	614	653	614	600	560	851	1 183	818	924
Investment income	HMBO	46 997	55 728	73 845	80 939	79 294	66 205	73 491	71 064	86 036	92 254	93 119
Total income	HMBR	47 584	56 237	74 459	81 592	79 908	66 805	74 051	71 915	87 219	93 072	94 043
Current transfers												
General government	FJUO	1 316	2 226	2 055	1 995	3 218	3 506	4 156	4 795	4 811	5 081	5 087
Other sectors	FJUP	8 064	7 580	8 924	10 882	10 284	14 299	13 338	12 051	15 173	15 657	13 566
Total current transfers	KTNE	9 380	9 806	10 979	12 877	13 502	17 805	17 494	16 846	19 984	20 738	18 653
Total	HBOF	**168 711**	**191 012**	**228 449**	**243 116**	**235 983**	**236 787**	**262 271**	**274 941**	**315 208**	**342 267**	**345 715**
Balances												
Trade in goods and services												
Trade in goods	LQCT	−11 698	−21 553	−24 724	−18 707	−10 223	−13 050	−13 066	−11 126	−12 023	−13 722	−12 342
Trade in services	KTMS	8 604	6 388	5 866	6 643	6 312	6 353	8 174	8 161	11 165	14 312	16 801
Total trade in goods and services	KTMY	−3 094	−15 165	−18 858	−12 064	−3 911	−6 697	−4 892	−2 965	−858	590	4 459
Income												
Compensation of employees	KTMP	−174	−64	−138	−110	−63	−49	35	−170	−296	93	83
Investment income	HMBM	−730	−1 188	−2 309	−4 586	−5 642	−1 037	−2 547	1 521	−546	−2 460	241
Total income	HMBP	−904	−1 252	−2 447	−4 696	−5 705	−1 086	−2 512	1 351	−842	−2 367	324
Current transfers												
General government	FJUQ	159	−297	−548	55	1 674	−1 326	−1 330	−2 657	−3 081	−2 253	−2 914
Other sectors	FJUR	−3 596	−2 996	−3 680	−4 857	−2 673	−3 902	−3 726	−2 530	−4 282	−2 286	−2 831
Total current transfers	KTNF	−3 437	−3 293	−4 228	−4 802	−999	−5 228	−5 056	−5 187	−7 363	−4 539	−5 745
Total (Current balance)	HBOG	**−7 435**	**−19 710**	**−25 533**	**−21 562**	**−10 615**	**−13 011**	**−12 460**	**−6 801**	**−9 063**	**−6 316**	**−962**

1.2 Current account
continued

£ million

		1998	1999	2000	2001	2002	2003	2004	2005	2006	2007	2008
Credits												
Exports of goods and services												
Exports of goods	LQAD	164 056	166 166	187 936	189 093	186 524	188 320	190 874	211 608	243 633	220 858	251 102
Exports of services	KTMQ	69 228	76 525	81 883	87 773	94 012	102 357	112 922	119 186	134 246	150 645	170 399
Total exports of goods and services	KTMW	233 284	242 691	269 819	276 866	280 536	290 677	303 796	330 794	377 879	371 503	421 501
Income												
Compensation of employees	KTMN	840	960	1 032	1 087	1 121	1 116	931	974	938	981	1 032
Investment income	HMBN	102 551	100 733	131 902	137 447	120 543	122 069	137 380	185 766	236 684	290 321	262 671
Total income	HMBQ	103 391	101 693	132 934	138 534	121 664	123 185	138 311	186 740	237 622	291 302	263 703
Current transfers												
General government	FJUM	1 767	3 542	2 465	4 991	3 663	3 968	4 177	4 294	4 383	4 315	5 512
Other sectors	FJUN	10 682	8 510	8 018	8 926	8 571	8 079	9 590	13 106	14 090	9 731	9 910
Total current transfers	KTND	12 449	12 052	10 483	13 917	12 234	12 047	13 767	17 400	18 473	14 046	15 422
Total	HBOE	**349 124**	**356 436**	**413 236**	**429 317**	**414 434**	**425 909**	**455 874**	**534 934**	**633 974**	**676 851**	**700 626**
Debits												
Imports of goods and services												
Imports of goods	LQBL	185 869	195 217	220 912	230 305	234 229	236 927	251 774	280 197	319 945	310 612	343 979
Imports of services	KTMR	54 225	60 963	66 881	70 573	74 380	79 745	84 508	93 444	99 464	105 838	115 920
Total imports of goods and services	KTMX	240 094	256 180	287 793	300 878	308 609	316 672	336 282	373 641	419 409	416 450	459 899
Income												
Compensation of employees	KTMO	850	759	882	1 021	1 054	1 057	1 425	1 584	1 896	1 715	1 738
Investment income	HMBO	90 738	101 977	130 090	128 088	102 324	104 605	119 041	163 301	226 153	268 812	235 025
Total income	HMBR	91 588	102 736	130 972	129 109	103 378	105 662	120 466	164 885	228 049	270 527	236 763
Current transfers												
General government	FJUO	6 585	7 271	7 778	7 340	9 085	10 657	12 225	13 637	13 881	14 087	14 606
Other sectors	FJUP	14 036	12 103	12 480	13 092	12 019	11 225	11 818	15 612	16 477	13 497	14 426
Total current transfers	KTNE	20 621	19 374	20 258	20 432	21 104	21 882	24 043	29 249	30 358	27 584	29 032
Total	HBOF	**352 303**	**378 290**	**439 023**	**450 419**	**433 091**	**444 216**	**480 791**	**567 775**	**677 816**	**714 561**	**725 694**
Balances												
Trade in goods and services												
Trade in goods	LQCT	−21 813	−29 051	−32 976	−41 212	−47 705	−48 607	−60 900	−68 589	−76 312	−89 754	−92 877
Trade in services	KTMS	15 003	15 562	15 002	17 200	19 632	22 612	28 414	25 742	34 782	44 807	54 479
Total trade in goods and services	KTMY	−6 810	−13 489	−17 974	−24 012	−28 073	−25 995	−32 486	−42 847	−41 530	−44 947	−38 398
Income												
Compensation of employees	KTMP	−10	201	150	66	67	59	−494	−610	−958	−734	−706
Investment income	HMBM	11 813	−1 244	1 812	9 359	18 219	17 464	18 339	22 465	10 531	21 509	27 646
Total income	HMBP	11 803	−1 043	1 962	9 425	18 286	17 523	17 845	21 855	9 573	20 775	26 940
Current transfers												
General government	FJUQ	−4 818	−3 729	−5 313	−2 349	−5 422	−6 689	−8 048	−9 343	−9 498	−9 772	−9 094
Other sectors	FJUR	−3 354	−3 593	−4 462	−4 166	−3 448	−3 146	−2 228	−2 506	−2 387	−3 766	−4 516
Total current transfers	KTNF	−8 172	−7 322	−9 775	−6 515	−8 870	−9 835	−10 276	−11 849	−11 885	−13 538	−13 610
Total (Current balance)	HBOG	**−3 179**	**−21 854**	**−25 787**	**−21 102**	**−18 657**	**−18 307**	**−24 917**	**−32 841**	**−43 842**	**−37 710**	**−25 068**

1.3 Summary of international investment position, financial account and investment income

£ billion

		1998	1999	2000	2001	2002	2003	2004	2005	2006	2007	2008
Investment abroad												
International investment position												
Direct investment	HBWD	309.8	438.3	618.8	616.9	637.2	691.1	678.1	705.9	741.7	913.9	1 075.2
Portfolio investment	HHZZ	703.8	838.3	906.1	937.4	844.0	935.8	1 092.1	1 360.9	1 531.1	1 693.8	1 762.2
Other investment	HLXV	1 098.4	1 097.3	1 379.7	1 521.9	1 545.2	1 813.7	2 118.0	2 714.8	2 916.6	3 750.2	4 261.4
Reserve assets	LTEB	23.3	22.2	28.8	25.6	25.5	23.8	23.2	24.7	22.9	26.7	36.3
Total	HBQA	**2 135.4**	**2 396.1**	**2 933.4**	**3 101.9**	**3 051.9**	**3 464.5**	**3 911.4**	**4 806.3**	**5 212.3**	**6 384.6**	**7 135.0**
Financial account transactions												
Direct investment	-HJYP	73.8	125.6	155.6	42.8	35.0	40.9	51.5	44.0	45.0	136.1	72.5
Portfolio investment	-HHZC	32.1	21.4	65.6	86.6	1.0	36.3	141.0	151.0	138.8	92.0	-128.6
Financial derivatives (net)	-ZPNN	3.0	-2.7	-1.6	-8.4	-1.0	5.4	7.9	-9.6	-7.4	19.0	-17.7
Other investment	-XBMM	30.0	41.5	241.7	170.7	70.4	260.4	325.2	501.3	395.9	747.3	-580.0
Reserve assets	-LTCV	-0.2	-0.6	3.9	-3.1	-0.5	-1.6	0.2	0.7	-0.4	1.2	-1.3
Total	-HBNR	**138.7**	**185.2**	**465.2**	**288.5**	**105.0**	**341.4**	**525.8**	**687.3**	**571.9**	**995.7**	**-655.2**
Investment income												
Direct investment	HJYW	29.9	33.1	45.0	46.7	51.5	55.1	63.3	79.2	83.6	90.2	69.2
Portfolio investment	HLYX	29.3	25.9	33.0	34.9	32.5	32.5	36.7	45.4	55.1	66.1	68.1
Other investment	AIOP	42.2	40.6	52.9	54.9	35.8	33.6	36.7	60.5	97.3	133.3	124.6
Reserve assets	HHCB	1.1	1.2	1.0	1.0	0.8	0.8	0.7	0.7	0.6	0.6	0.8
Total	HMBN	**102.6**	**100.7**	**131.9**	**137.4**	**120.5**	**122.1**	**137.4**	**185.8**	**236.7**	**290.3**	**262.7**
Investment in the UK												
International investment position												
Direct investment	HBWI	213.6	250.2	310.4	363.5	340.6	355.5	383.3	494.2	578.3	630.2	676.7
Portfolio investment	HLXW	739.9	933.2	1 067.6	1 013.2	925.3	1 082.9	1 227.9	1 461.7	1 702.6	1 917.6	1 943.4
Other investment	HLYD	1 350.3	1 400.9	1 651.6	1 861.9	1 906.0	2 143.2	2 520.8	3 103.0	3 284.0	4 119.4	4 422.1
Total	HBQB	**2 303.8**	**2 584.3**	**3 029.5**	**3 238.5**	**3 171.9**	**3 581.6**	**4 132.1**	**5 058.9**	**5 564.8**	**6 667.2**	**7 042.1**
Financial account transactions												
Direct investment	HJYU	45.1	55.1	80.6	37.3	16.8	16.8	31.2	97.8	84.9	98.2	52.5
Portfolio investment	HHZF	25.0	106.3	172.2	40.8	49.7	105.6	97.3	129.0	153.9	203.3	240.6
Other investment	XBMN	73.1	53.3	235.6	237.6	62.6	241.5	426.6	489.5	371.3	725.9	-930.1
Total	HBNS	**143.2**	**214.7**	**488.3**	**315.7**	**129.2**	**364.0**	**555.2**	**716.3**	**610.1**	**1 027.4**	**-637.1**
Investment income												
Direct investment	HJYX	8.6	17.0	27.4	21.4	16.0	21.9	27.6	36.2	51.6	44.8	10.6
Portfolio investment	HLZC	29.5	32.2	32.4	36.1	33.3	32.9	38.7	47.6	57.6	66.5	73.3
Other investment	HLZN	52.7	52.7	70.2	70.5	53.0	49.8	52.7	79.6	117.0	157.5	151.1
Total	HMBO	**90.7**	**102.0**	**130.1**	**128.1**	**102.3**	**104.6**	**119.0**	**163.3**	**226.2**	**268.8**	**235.0**
Net investment												
International investment position												
Direct investment	HBWQ	96.2	188.1	308.4	253.5	296.6	335.6	294.7	211.7	163.4	283.8	398.6
Portfolio investment	CGNH	-36.0	-94.9	-161.5	-75.7	-81.3	-147.0	-135.8	-100.8	-171.5	-223.8	-181.3
Other investment	CGNG	-251.9	-303.6	-271.9	-339.9	-360.8	-329.5	-402.9	-388.2	-367.3	-369.2	-160.7
Reserve assets	LTEB	23.3	22.2	28.8	25.6	25.5	23.8	23.2	24.7	22.9	26.7	36.3
Net investment position	HBQC	**-168.4**	**-188.2**	**-96.2**	**-136.5**	**-120.0**	**-117.2**	**-220.7**	**-252.6**	**-352.6**	**-282.5**	**92.9**
Financial account transactions												
Direct investment	HJYV	-28.7	-70.5	-75.0	-5.5	-18.3	-24.1	-20.3	53.8	39.9	-38.0	-20.1
Portfolio investment	HHZD	-7.0	84.9	106.6	-45.7	48.7	69.4	-43.7	-21.9	15.1	111.3	369.2
Financial derivatives	ZPNN	-3.0	2.7	1.6	8.4	1.0	-5.4	-7.9	9.6	7.4	-19.0	17.7
Other investment	HHYR	43.1	11.8	-6.1	66.9	-7.7	-18.9	101.4	-11.8	-24.6	-21.4	-350.1
Reserve assets	LTCV	0.2	0.6	-3.9	3.1	0.5	1.6	-0.2	-0.7	0.4	-1.2	1.3
Net transactions	HBNT	**4.5**	**29.5**	**23.1**	**27.2**	**24.2**	**22.6**	**29.4**	**29.0**	**38.2**	**31.7**	**18.1**
Investment income												
Direct investment	HJYE	21.3	16.1	17.6	25.3	35.5	33.2	35.7	43.0	32.0	45.4	58.5
Portfolio investment	HLZX	-0.2	-6.4	0.5	-1.2	-0.8	-0.4	-2.0	-2.2	-2.4	-0.4	-5.2
Other investment	CGNA	-10.5	-12.2	-17.3	-15.7	-17.2	-16.1	-16.0	-19.0	-19.6	-24.1	-26.5
Reserve assets	HHCB	1.1	1.2	1.0	1.0	0.8	0.8	0.7	0.7	0.6	0.6	0.8
Net earnings	HMBM	**11.8**	**-1.2**	**1.8**	**9.4**	**18.2**	**17.5**	**18.3**	**22.5**	**10.5**	**21.5**	**27.6**

Trade in goods

Chapter 2

Summary

The balance on trade in goods has shown a deficit in all but six years since 1900, with the value of imports exceeding the value of exports. The last surplus on trade in goods was recorded for 1982. In the period 1992 to 1997, the deficit settled into the range of £11 billion – £14 billion before widening in every subsequent year.

In 2008, the deficit increased to a record £92.9 billion. This was the result of an increase of 10.7 per cent in the value of imports (from £310.6 billion to a record £344.0 billion). The increase of 13.7 per cent in the value of exports (from £220.9 billion to a record £251.1 billion) only partly offsets this increase in imports, since total imports are significantly larger than total exports.

When looking at trade figures, users should be aware that both exports and imports are affected by VAT MTIC fraud leading to increases in both imports and exports in 2006 and falls in 2007. In addition, following a change in the pattern of MTIC fraud, interpretation of the breakdown between EU and non-EU trade is more difficult. Originally, most carousel chains only involved EU member states. From 2004 onwards, there were also carousel chains that included non-EU countries, for example, Dubai and Switzerland. However, the MTIC trade adjustments are added to the EU import estimates as it is this part of the trading chain that is not recorded. Changes to the pattern of trading associated with MTIC fraud can therefore make it difficult to analyse trade by commodity group and by country as increases or decreases inflate or reduce both imports and exports. In particular, adjustments affect trade in capital goods and intermediate goods – these categories include mobile phones and computer components, which are now covered by the UK's reverse charge derogation. (For more information on MTIC fraud, see the Methodological notes relating to chapter 2.)

The deficit with EU countries narrowed from a record £42.0 billion in 2007 to £39.2 billion in 2008. This was as a result of a 10.4 per cent rise in exports, only partly offset by a smaller 6.2 per cent rise in imports. The deficit with non-EU countries widened from £47.8 billion in 2007 to a new record of £53.6 billion in 2008. This was the result of a 16.2 per cent rise in imports, which was only partly offset by an 18.2 per cent rise in exports (non-EU imports being significantly larger than exports).

Volume changes

Export volumes increased in every year between 1982 and 2001. The growth in exports slowed during the years 1991 to 1993 reflecting a decline in economic activity abroad. There was a period of strong growth between 1994 and 1997 followed by a marked slowdown in 1998. After a slight pick up in growth in 1999 and accelerated growth in 2000, export volume growth slowed again in 2001. In 2002, export volumes fell as world economic activity slowed, and volumes remained fairly flat in 2003. Volumes rose in each year from 2004 to 2006 as world economic activity grew (in addition, there was an increase in trade associated with MTIC fraud – as shown in Table 2.4 – in 2005 and 2006). There was a sharp fall in export volumes in 2007 of 10.0 per cent, linked to a fall in trade associated with MTIC fraud. Excluding estimates for trade associated with VAT MTIC fraud, exports fell by 1.5 per cent. In 2008, the volume of exports fell by 0.2 per cent.

Import volumes have also been generally increasing since 1981. However, a downturn in the UK economy resulted in a fall in the volume of imports in 1991. Since then, imports grew steadily in each year up until 2006. There was a fall of 2.9 per cent in import volumes in 2007 (again linked to the fall back in trade associated with MTIC fraud) but a rise of 3.8 per cent excluding adjustments for trade associated with VAT MTIC fraud. The volume of imports fell by 2.1 per cent in 2008.

In 2008, the volume of exports to EU countries fell by 5.0 per cent but the volume of exports to non-EU countries rose by 7.0

Figure 2.1
Trade in goods

£ billion

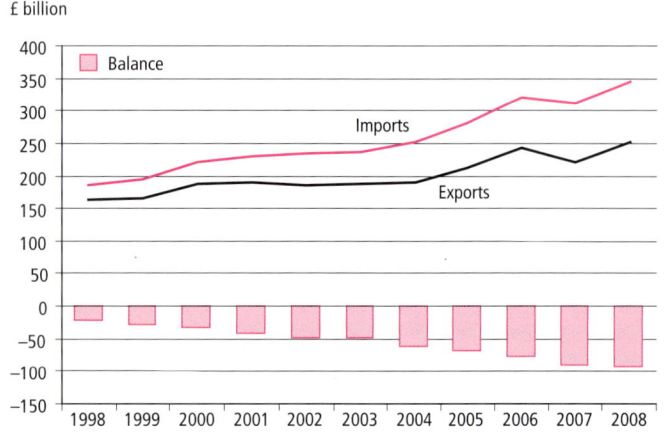

Figure 2.2
Export and import volume indices

Indices 2005 = 100

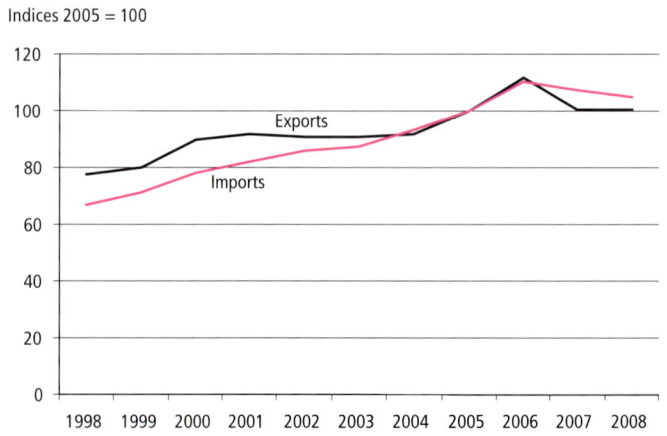

per cent. The volume of imports from EU countries fell by 3.2 per cent and the volume of imports from non-EU countries fell by 0.9 per cent.

Price changes

Both export and import prices rose every year between 1989 and 1995. The largest annual rises, 12.4 per cent for exports and 10.0 per cent for imports, occurred between 1992 and 1993 when sterling depreciated sharply following the UK's withdrawal from the Exchange Rate Mechanism (ERM). Both export and import prices fell significantly from 1997 to 1999. This reflected falls in world commodity prices and the price of crude oil feeding through into the price of manufactured goods. They were fairly flat from then until 2004 but then rose fairly steadily through to 2007.

The price indices for crude oil increased by about 50 per cent in 1999 and by a further 70 per cent in 2000 before falling back in 2001 and 2002, only to rise again in 2003 and 2004, and to an even greater extent, in 2005 and 2006. There was only a small increase in oil prices between 2006 and 2007, but a larger increase (about 45 per cent) in 2008.

Figure 2.3

Export and import price indices

Indices 2005 = 100

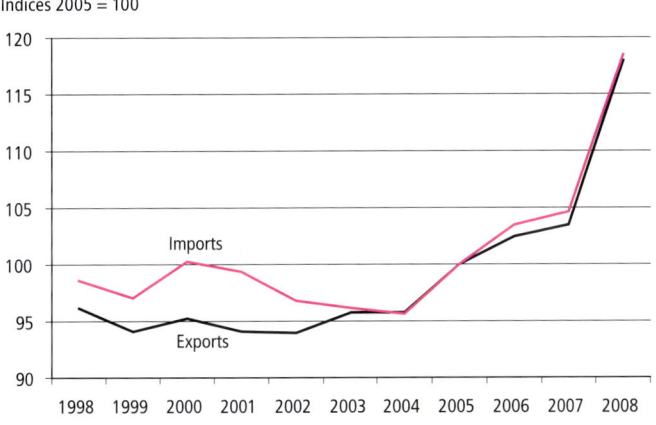

In 2008, the overall export and import price indices rose steeply by 14.1 per cent and 13.2 per cent respectively. Excluding the oil price effect, export prices rose by 10.7 per cent and import prices by 9.9 per cent in 2008. This was, to some extent, as a result of the depreciation of sterling throughout the year.

Trade in oil

While the overall balance on trade in goods has shown a deficit every year since 1982, exports of oil had consistently exceeded imports of oil in each year between 1980 and 2004 before recording a deficit in 2005. In 1985 trade in oil showed a record surplus of £8.0 billion as oil prices reached record levels.

Figure 2.4

Trade in oil

£ billion

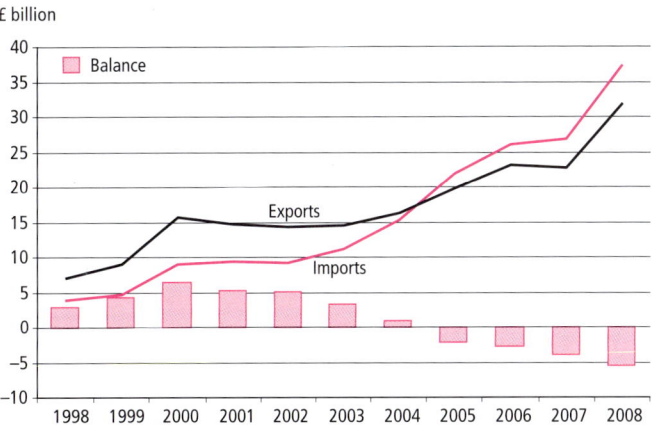

As a result of the Piper Alpha disaster, disruptions to production in the North Sea subsequently diminished the surplus during the period 1988 to 1991. Until 1996 the annual surplus increased steadily as UK production recovered and world crude oil prices increased. Falling oil prices in 1997 and 1998 then led to a reduction in the surplus to £3.0 billion in 1998 before sharp rises in prices saw the surplus increase to £4.4 billion in 1999 and £6.5 billion in 2000 – the highest surplus since 1985. The fall in the price of crude oil reduced the oil trade surplus to £5.3 billion in 2001 and to £5.1 billion in 2002. Crude oil production peaked in 2000 and, with the exception of 2007 when the very large Buzzard field began production, has been in decline since as reserves on the UK Continental Shelf are depleted. As a result, from 2002 onwards the volume of exports of crude oil has dropped and the volume of crude oil imports has generally increased. Coupled with rising prices, this resulted in further falls in the surplus, to £3.4 billion in 2003 and £0.9 billion in 2004 followed by the first deficit since 1979 – of £2.2 billion in 2005. The deficit increased steadily between 2006 and 2008, partly reflecting higher imports of oil other than crude oil. There was a record deficit in 2008 of £5.4 billion, largely caused by a deficit of £3.6 billion in crude oil (the largest deficit since 1976).

Trade in commodities other than oil

Finished manufactures accounted for around half of both total exports and total imports in the last ten years. Their share of total exports rose from 54 per cent in 1994 to a peak of 60 per cent in 1998 before falling back steadily to 53 per cent in 2004. However, they rose to 56 per cent in 2006, before falling back to 50 per cent in 2007 and 47 per cent in 2008. Their share of total imports rose from 55 per cent in 1995 to a peak of 62 per cent in 2002 then fell back to a level of 57 per cent in 2005 before rising to a level of 58 per cent in 2006 then falling to 53 per cent in 2007 and 50 per cent in 2008. The rises in 2006 and subsequent falls largely reflect the effect of trade associated with VAT MTIC fraud.

Within finished manufactures, the balance on trade in capital goods was in surplus every year between 1990 and 1999 but has moved significantly into deficit since then. The balance on trade in ships and aircraft was in surplus up to 1997 but then moved into deficit. The deficit peaked in 2002 and has subsequently narrowed to some extent although it rose in 2006. Trade in motor cars, other consumer goods, and intermediate goods, has been in deficit in each of the last ten years. The deficit on motor cars peaked in 2001 during a period of disruption caused by restructuring in the industry which affected production in the UK. The deficit for consumer goods other than cars has increased steadily over the last ten years.

Within semi-manufactured goods, the UK has been a net exporter of chemicals and a net importer of other semi-manufactured goods in each of the last ten years.

The balance on trade in coal, gas and electricity was in surplus from 1999 to 2003 but moved into deficit in 2004 and, to a greater extent, from 2005 onwards. This has reflected higher imports of gas and electricity through the interconnectors. There was a record deficit of £7.0 billion in 2008, which was more than double the deficit of £3.2 billion in 2007.

In volume terms, exports of capital goods rose by 1.3 per cent in 2008, while exports of intermediate goods fell by 4.1 per cent. Exports of cars rose by 0.9 per cent, but exports of other consumer goods fell by 5.8 per cent. Exports of ships and aircraft rose by 3.6 per cent. Exports of chemicals rose by 2.6 per cent, but exports of other semi-manufactured goods fell by 4.5 per cent. Exports of basic materials rose by 5.5 per cent and of food, beverages and tobacco by 4.8 per cent. Exports of coal, gas and electricity rose by 24.3 per cent, reflecting higher exports of gas and electricity through the interconnectors.

Figure 2.6
Trade in other consumer goods

£ billion

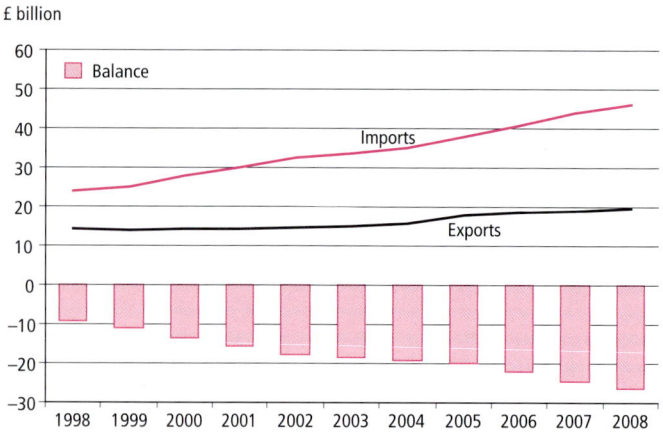

By volume, imports of capital goods fell by 1.1 per cent in 2008, and imports of intermediate goods fell 1.9 per cent. Imports of motor cars fell by 12.4 per cent, particularly reflecting difficult market conditions in the final quarter. Imports of consumer goods other than cars fell by 0.9 per cent. Within semi-manufactured goods, imports of chemicals fell by 3.5 per cent and of other semi-manufactured goods by 1.9 per cent. Imports of coal, gas and electricity rose by 39.5 per cent, reflecting higher imports of gas and electricity through the interconnectors.

Figure 2.5
Trade in motor cars

£ billion

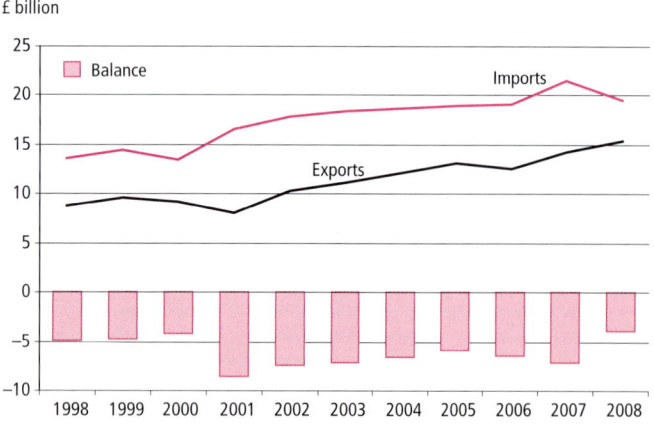

2.1 Trade in goods
Summary table

£ million

		SITC[1]	1998	1999	2000	2001	2002	2003	2004	2005	2006	2007	2008
Exports													
Food, beverages and tobacco	BQMV	0+1	10 216	9 947	9 908	9 630	9 993	10 879	10 577	10 647	10 945	11 769	13 719
Basic materials	ELBK	2+4	2 512	2 284	2 603	2 571	2 855	3 335	3 770	3 981	4 892	5 523	6 625
Oil													
Crude oil	BQNX	333	4 473	6 148	10 522	10 489	9 804	9 241	9 338	10 948	12 784	12 634	16 548
Oil products	BQNY	334+335	2 545	2 975	5 062	4 326	4 517	5 367	6 862	8 846	10 389	10 122	15 296
Total oil	BOKL	33	7 018	9 123	15 584	14 815	14 321	14 608	16 200	19 794	23 173	22 756	31 844
Coal, gas and electricity	BQNF	32+34+35	495	806	1 473	1 571	1 679	1 950	1 685	1 702	2 128	1 944	3 542
Semi-manufactured goods													
Chemicals	BQOB	5	22 102	23 071	24 992	27 514	28 386	31 373	32 009	33 388	37 179	38 891	43 586
Precious stones and silver	BQOD	667+681.1	2 833	3 633	4 744	4 709	4 728	5 138	4 909	5 541	4 976	4 770	6 085
Other	BQOC	Rest of 6	18 410	16 669	17 929	18 072	17 109	17 981	19 549	20 951	22 688	24 608	26 371
Total semi-manufactured goods	BQMX	5+6	43 345	43 373	47 665	50 295	50 223	54 492	56 467	59 880	64 843	68 269	76 042
Finished manufactured goods													
Motor cars	BQOE	781	8 710	9 585	9 178	8 046	10 297	11 183	12 108	13 074	12 557	14 294	15 418
Other consumer goods[2]	BQOF		14 448	13 840	14 280	14 360	14 606	14 997	15 779	17 726	18 657	19 105	19 727
Intermediate goods[2]	BQOG		35 637	36 659	41 130	42 089	40 025	37 370	36 672	38 636	42 221	37 871	40 355
Capital goods[2]	BQOH		33 654	33 324	37 169	37 715	34 944	31 500	29 432	38 131	55 593	29 844	33 052
Ships and aircraft	BQOI	792+793	6 125	5 730	7 261	6 978	6 508	7 143	7 302	6 917	7 338	8 294	9 007
Total finished manufactured goods	BQMQ	7+8	98 574	99 138	109 018	109 188	106 380	102 193	101 293	114 484	136 366	109 408	117 559
Commodities and transactions not classified according to kind	BOKJ	9	1 896	1 495	1 685	1 023	1 073	863	882	1 120	1 286	1 189	1 771
Total	LQAD		**164 056**	**166 166**	**187 936**	**189 093**	**186 524**	**188 320**	**190 874**	**211 608**	**243 633**	**220 858**	**251 102**
Imports													
Food, beverages and tobacco	BQMW	0+1	17 250	17 787	17 660	18 485	19 375	21 187	22 150	23 695	25 013	26 747	31 099
Basic materials	BQNA	2+4	5 631	5 429	6 307	6 442	5 958	6 139	6 338	6 770	7 887	9 561	11 014
Oil													
Crude oil	BQNM	333	1 967	2 106	4 825	4 878	4 752	5 705	8 191	11 212	14 272	13 602	20 166
Oil products	BQOA	334+335	2 009	2 569	4 223	4 647	4 461	5 527	7 116	10 777	11 695	13 185	17 110
Total oil	BQAQ	33	3 976	4 675	9 048	9 525	9 213	11 232	15 307	21 989	25 967	26 787	37 276
Coal, gas and electricity	BQNG	32+34+35	916	753	968	1 270	1 066	1 079	2 240	3 932	4 921	5 141	10 565
Semi-manufactured goods													
Chemicals	BQOJ	5	17 379	18 619	20 633	22 745	23 987	26 139	27 929	29 208	31 727	34 645	37 712
Precious stones and silver	BQOL	667+681.1	4 025	4 788	5 454	5 260	4 247	4 346	4 673	5 238	6 131	5 173	5 635
Other	BQOK		23 670	22 142	23 778	24 905	24 488	25 560	27 626	28 231	31 484	34 619	36 203
Total semi-manufactured goods	BQMR	5+6	45 074	45 549	49 865	52 910	52 722	56 045	60 228	62 677	69 342	74 437	79 550
Finished manufactured goods													
Motor cars	BQOM	781	13 618	14 433	13 403	16 619	17 800	18 374	18 724	18 928	19 105	21 480	19 466
Other consumer goods[2]	BQON		23 792	24 905	28 011	29 953	32 414	33 477	35 093	37 684	40 689	43 798	46 150
Intermediate goods[2]	BQOO		37 091	41 538	48 455	46 085	44 829	40 893	42 126	45 877	53 152	49 785	52 753
Capital goods[2]	BQOP		30 190	32 256	37 944	38 463	39 473	38 251	40 222	49 033	62 530	41 420	43 219
Ships and aircraft	BQOQ	792+793	6 526	6 093	7 405	9 289	9 929	8 646	7 539	7 771	9 269	9 182	10 311
Total finished manufactured goods	BQMY	7+8	111 217	119 225	135 218	140 409	144 445	139 641	143 704	159 293	184 745	165 665	171 899
Commodities and transactions not classified according to kind	BQAO	9	1 805	1 799	1 846	1 264	1 450	1 604	1 807	1 841	2 070	2 274	2 576
Total	LQBL		**185 869**	**195 217**	**220 912**	**230 305**	**234 229**	**236 927**	**251 774**	**280 197**	**319 945**	**310 612**	**343 979**

1 Standard International Trade Classification, Revision 3.

2 Derived from the *Classification by Broad Economic Categories defined in terms of SITC, Revision 3*, published by the United Nations.

2.1 Trade in goods
Summary table
continued

£ million

Balances		SITC[1]	1998	1999	2000	2001	2002	2003	2004	2005	2006	2007	2008
Food, beverages and tobacco	BQOS	0+1	−7 034	−7 840	−7 752	−8 855	−9 382	−10 308	−11 573	−13 048	−14 068	−14 978	−17 380
Basic materials	BQOR	2+4	−3 119	−3 145	−3 704	−3 871	−3 103	−2 804	−2 568	−2 789	−2 995	−4 038	−4 389
Oil													
Crude oil	BQMG	333	2 506	4 042	5 697	5 611	5 052	3 536	1 147	−264	−1 488	−968	−3 618
Oil products	BQMH	334+335	536	406	839	−321	56	−160	−254	−1 931	−1 306	−3 063	−1 814
Total oil	BQNE	33	3 042	4 448	6 536	5 290	5 108	3 376	893	−2 195	−2 794	−4 031	−5 432
Coal, gas and electricity	BQNH	32+34+35	−421	53	505	301	613	871	−555	−2 230	−2 793	−3 197	−7 023
Semi-manufactured goods													
Chemicals	BQMI	5	4 723	4 452	4 359	4 769	4 399	5 234	4 080	4 180	5 452	4 246	5 874
Precious stones and silver	BQMK	667+681.1	−1 192	−1 155	−710	−551	481	792	236	303	−1 155	−403	450
Other	BQMJ	Rest of 6	−5 260	−5 473	−5 849	−6 833	−7 379	−7 579	−8 077	−7 280	−8 796	−10 011	−9 832
Total semi-manufactured goods	BQOT	5+6	−1 729	−2 176	−2 200	−2 615	−2 499	−1 553	−3 761	−2 797	−4 499	−6 168	−3 508
Finished manufactured goods													
Motor cars	BQML	781	−4 908	−4 848	−4 225	−8 573	−7 503	−7 191	−6 616	−5 854	−6 548	−7 186	−4 048
Other consumer goods[2]	BQMM		−9 344	−11 065	−13 731	−15 593	−17 808	−18 480	−19 314	−19 958	−22 032	−24 693	−26 423
Intermediate goods[2]	BQMN		−1 454	−4 879	−7 325	−3 996	−4 804	−3 523	−5 454	−7 241	−10 931	−11 914	−12 398
Capital goods[2]	BQMO		3 464	1 068	−775	−748	−4 529	−6 751	−10 790	−10 902	−6 937	−11 576	−10 167
Ships and aircraft	BQMP	792+793	−401	−363	−144	−2 311	−3 421	−1 503	−237	−854	−1 931	−888	−1 304
Total finished manufactured goods	BQOV	7+8	−12 643	−20 087	−26 200	−31 221	−38 065	−37 448	−42 411	−44 809	−48 379	−56 257	−54 340
Commodities and transactions not classified according to kind	BQOU	9	91	−304	−161	−241	−377	−741	−925	−721	−784	−1 085	−805
Total	LQCT		−21 813	−29 051	−32 976	−41 212	−47 705	−48 607	−60 900	−68 589	−76 312	−89 754	−92 877

1 Standard International Trade Classification, Revision 3.

2 Derived from the *Classification by Broad Economic Categories defined in terms of SITC, Revision 3*, published by the United Nations.

2.2 Trade in goods: volume indices

2005=100

		SITC[1]	1998	1999	2000	2001	2002	2003	2004	2005	2006	2007	2008
Exports													
Food, beverages and tobacco	BQPP	0+1	100	98	98	94	97	102	101	100	101	104	109
Basic materials	BQPQ	2+4	75	71	78	76	84	94	98	100	114	128	135
Oil													
Crude oil	BOGH	333	154	145	149	164	159	138	122	100	96	92	87
Oil products	BOGO	334+335	54	57	82	74	69	78	82	100	106	102	109
Total oil	BONC	33	99	97	113	117	112	107	101	100	101	96	97
Coal, gas and electricity	BOGP	32+34+35	49	73	114	128	141	157	120	100	104	103	128
Semi-manufactured goods													
Chemicals	BQLB	5	63	69	75	84	88	94	97	100	112	116	119
Precious stones and silver	BQLD	667+681.1	35	44	55	60	73	86	90	100	91	96	105
Other	BQLC	Rest of 6	94	89	94	94	90	91	97	100	105	112	107
Total semi-manufactured goods	BQPR	5+6	70	72	79	84	87	92	96	100	107	113	113
Finished manufactured goods													
Motor cars	BQLE	781	66	73	76	66	82	86	94	100	94	106	107
Other consumer goods[2]	BQLF		79	78	80	80	83	84	90	100	102	104	98
Intermediate goods[2]	BQLG		86	92	105	108	100	93	94	100	112	98	94
Capital goods[2]	BQLH		71	74	88	92	85	76	74	100	138	77	78
Ships and aircraft	BQLI	792+793	73	69	88	83	78	105	104	100	104	112	116
Total finished manufactured goods	BQPS	7+8	77	80	91	92	89	86	87	100	117	94	92
Total	BPBP		77.7	80.2	89.9	91.8	90.7	90.5	91.9	100.0	111.5	100.4	100.6
Imports													
Food, beverages and tobacco	BQPT	0+1	74	78	79	82	85	91	97	100	103	106	105
Basic materials	BQPU	2+4	96	94	103	107	100	98	98	100	109	121	120
Oil													
Crude oil	BQPV	333	73	53	70	78	79	87	106	100	107	98	101
Oil products	BQPW	334+335	89	83	80	96	72	82	94	100	93	112	90
Total oil	ELAM	33	79	66	74	86	75	85	100	100	100	105	96
Coal, gas and electricity	BQPX	32+34+35	32	33	42	43	45	39	69	100	107	129	180
Semi-manufactured goods													
Chemicals	BQLQ	5	61	68	74	81	89	94	101	100	107	115	111
Precious stones and silver	BQLS	667+681.1	53	63	68	72	70	78	91	100	114	109	105
Other	BQLR	Rest of 6	88	87	89	93	95	98	102	100	103	108	106
Total semi-manufactured goods	BQPY	5+6	72	76	80	86	90	94	100	100	106	111	108
Finished manufactured goods													
Motor cars	BQLT	781	68	71	68	88	92	95	98	100	102	113	99
Other consumer goods[2]	BQLU		60	63	69	72	81	85	92	100	108	116	115
Intermediate goods[2]	BQLV		73	84	96	93	94	89	95	100	113	106	104
Capital goods[2]	BQLW		49	53	64	66	73	73	79	100	128	89	88
Ships and aircraft	BQLX	792+793	101	93	103	117	127	113	102	100	116	118	119
Total finished manufactured goods	BQPZ	7+8	63	68	77	80	85	85	90	100	115	105	102
Total	BQBJ		66.8	71.2	77.9	82.0	85.8	87.4	93.4	100.0	110.4	107.2	104.9

1 Standard International Trade Classification, Revision 3.

2 Derived from the *Classification by Broad Economic Categories defined in terms of SITC, Revision 3*, published by the United Nations.

2.3 Trade in goods: price indices

2005=100

		SITC[1]	1998	1999	2000	2001	2002	2003	2004	2005	2006	2007	2008
Exports													
Food, beverages and tobacco	BPAI	0+1	94	94	93	96	96	100	99	100	102	106	120
Basic materials	BPAW	2+4	81	77	80	82	82	87	93	100	106	110	128
Oil													
Crude oil	BQAC	333	26	38	64	58	56	60	70	100	119	124	178
Oil products	BQAD	334+335	46	51	60	57	65	70	81	100	112	114	160
Total oil	BQAL	33	32	42	64	58	59	64	74	100	116	119	169
Coal, gas and electricity	BQAF	32+34+35	53	58	68	65	63	67	78	100	117	108	156
Semi-manufactured goods													
Chemicals	BQLJ	5	105	100	99	98	96	100	98	100	101	102	113
Precious stones and silver	BQLL	667+681.1	145	147	155	143	116	107	98	100	100	90	102
Other	BQLK	Rest of 6	94	90	91	91	91	95	97	100	103	104	119
Total semi-manufactured goods	BQAA	5+6	104	99	100	99	96	99	98	100	101	102	114
Finished manufactured goods													
Motor cars	BQPM	781	99	99	92	92	95	99	98	100	102	104	112
Other consumer goods[2]	BQLM		101	98	99	99	98	100	98	100	103	102	112
Intermediate goods[2]	BQLN		104	100	97	97	100	102	100	100	100	106	116
Capital goods[2]	BQLO		120	113	107	104	104	104	100	100	98	94	103
Ships and aircraft	BQLP	792+793	120	118	116	120	120	100	101	100	102	106	113
Total finished manufactured goods	BQAB	7+8	109	104	101	100	101	102	100	100	100	101	110
Total	BQKR		96.1	94.1	95.2	94.1	94.0	95.8	95.8	100.0	102.5	103.4	118.0
Imports													
Food, beverages and tobacco	ELAN	0+1	97	94	93	94	95	98	96	100	103	108	128
Basic materials	ELAO	2+4	88	86	90	89	89	93	96	100	109	118	138
Oil													
Crude oil	ELAS	333	24	36	63	57	54	59	69	100	120	124	180
Oil products	ELAT	334+335	21	29	48	44	57	62	70	100	119	124	178
Total oil	ELBB	33	22	32	55	50	56	60	70	100	119	124	179
Coal, gas and electricity	ELAU	32+34+35	56	45	48	56	47	50	75	100	116	115	183
Semi-manufactured goods													
Chemicals	BQLY	5	96	91	94	94	92	95	94	100	102	103	116
Precious stones and silver	BQMA	667+681.1	144	144	153	140	115	107	98	100	99	88	100
Other	BQLZ	Rest of 6	94	89	93	94	90	91	96	100	109	114	122
Total semi-manufactured goods	ELAQ	5+6	98	94	98	97	93	94	95	100	105	107	118
Finished manufactured goods													
Motor cars	BQMB	781	107	107	104	100	102	102	101	100	99	100	105
Other consumer goods[2]	BQMC		103	102	105	108	104	103	100	100	101	100	107
Intermediate goods[2]	BQMD		112	109	111	109	104	100	98	100	101	104	112
Capital goods[2]	BQME		128	124	122	120	114	108	105	100	99	96	101
Ships and aircraft	BQMF	792+793	84	84	93	102	100	99	95	100	103	102	113
Total finished manufactured goods	ELAR	7+8	112	110	111	110	106	103	100	100	100	100	107
Total	BQKS		98.6	97.0	100.2	99.4	96.8	96.2	95.7	100.0	103.5	104.6	118.4

1 Standard International Trade Classification, Revision 3.

2 Derived from the *Classification by Broad Economic Categories defined in terms of SITC, Revision 3*, published by the United Nations.

2.4 Adjustments to trade in goods on a balance of payments basis

£ million

		1998	1999	2000	2001	2002	2003	2004	2005	2006	2007	2008
Exports												
Overseas trade statistics (f.o.b.)	HGAA	165 859	168 221	189 665	190 806	187 763	189 038	191 018	212 202	245 236	220 539	248 546
Coverage adjustments												
Second-hand ships	HBYK	219	154	105	137	187	141	251	248	248	248	248
Repairs to ships and aircraft	EPAQ	12	12	12	12	12	12	12	12	12	12	12
Goods not changing ownership	HCLJ	−2 565	−2 291	−2 343	−2 761	−2 788	−2 744	−2 012	−2 753	−2 471	−2 319	−313
Goods procured in ports	KTPB	564	645	865	869	881	982	1 129	1 415	1 562	1 579	1 915
Industrial gold	DEJO	46	33	33	44	66	76	37	7	9	38	66
Other	BQPO	55	56	57	57	55	57	61	60	66	61	−76
Total coverage adjustments	EHHH	−1 671	−1 391	−1 271	−1 642	−1 587	−1 476	−522	−1 011	−574	−381	1 852
Other adjustments	EPAR	−131	−664	−460	−71	348	758	378	417	−1 029	700	704
Total	LQAD	**164 056**	**166 166**	**187 936**	**189 093**	**186 524**	**188 320**	**190 874**	**211 608**	**243 633**	**220 858**	**251 102**
Imports												
Overseas trade statistics (c.i.f.)	HGAD	192 025	199 926	224 413	229 510	228 608	236 934	253 151	272 850	303 272	311 941	341 748
Coverage adjustments												
Second-hand ships	HBTY	185	281	112	166	113	248	223	224	224	224	224
Ships delivered abroad	CGER	217	127	540	577	586	572	302	499	304	304	304
Repairs to ships and aircraft	EPBA	35	15	11	9	9	30	54	56	56	56	56
Goods not changing ownership	HBYS	−2 565	−2 291	−2 343	−2 761	−2 788	−2 744	−2 012	−2 753	−2 471	−2 319	−313
Goods procured in ports	KTPC	744	780	1 035	1 218	1 438	1 865	2 240	3 331	2 358	3 490	4 495
Industrial gold	DEJP	135	149	164	145	163	236	230	196	253	273	271
Smuggling - alcohol	QHCP	331	266	279	43	25	29	29	28	28	28	..
Smuggling - tobacco	QHCT	693	990	1 072	1 033	1 063	1 140	1 136	1 144	1 144	1 144	..
Other	EHHI	28	13	21	10	8	8	7	6	8	7	..
Total coverage adjustments	EHHJ	−197	330	891	440	617	1 384	2 209	2 731	1 904	3 207	6 036
Valuation adjustments												
Freight	BPGF	−4 362	−4 660	−5 106	−5 423	−5 450	−5 465	−5 494	−5 534	−5 549	−5 536	−5 455
Insurance	ENAG	−548	−594	−654	−662	−662	−704	−736	−774	−848	−874	−933
Total	HCLT	−4 910	−5 254	−5 760	−6 085	−6 112	−6 169	−6 230	−6 308	−6 397	−6 410	−6 388
Other adjustments												
Impact of MTIC fraud	BQHF	–	1 678	2 794	7 060	11 495	4 486	2 689	11 060	22 378	2 137	2 272
Other adjustments	EPBB	−1 051	−1 462	−1 428	−620	−379	292	−45	−136	−1 212	−263	311
Total other adjustments	CLAK	−1 051	216	1 366	6 440	11 116	4 778	2 644	10 924	21 166	1 874	2 583
Total	LQBL	**185 869**	**195 217**	**220 912**	**230 305**	**234 229**	**236 927**	**251 774**	**280 197**	**319 945**	**310 612**	**343 979**

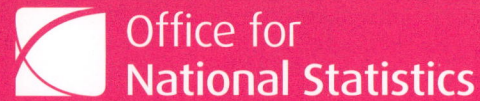

Other titles from the
Office for National Statistics

Reliable, authoritative resources to help **stay ahead** in these **turbulent** and **fast-moving** times

www.palgrave.com/ons/

Trade in services

Chapter 3

Summary

A surplus has been recorded for trade in services in every year since 1966. There was an increase in the surplus from £44.8 billion in 2007 to £54.5 billion in 2008. During the latest year, exports of services increased by 13.1 per cent while imports of services grew by 9.5 per cent (compared to growths of 12.2 per cent and 6.4 per cent respectively in 2007). Of the 11 main product groupings, nine showed surpluses and two (travel and government services) showed deficits. The increase in the surplus was mainly driven by an increase in the financial services surplus, reflecting an increase in exports of FISIM by monetary financial institutions.

Figure 3.1
Trade in services

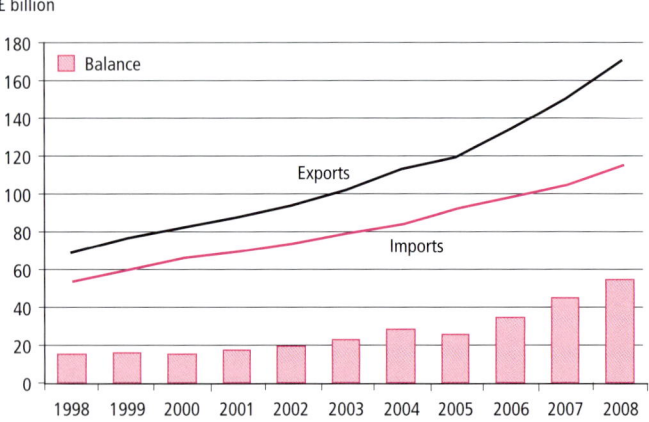

Transportation

Transportation services relate mainly to freight services on exports and imports of goods, and provision of passenger services. They are presented by mode of transport: sea, air and other. In 2008 transportation services accounted for 12 per cent of total exports and 18 per cent of total imports of services.

Sea transportation recorded a surplus of £4.3 billion in 2008 continuing on from surpluses for the previous four years. Prior to this sea transportation recorded deficits. This surplus reflects an increase in exports of freight services provided by UK shipping operators. The move from deficit to surplus can be explained by the increase in the size of the UK fleet following the introduction of tonnage tax in July 2000.

The UK has recorded a deficit on air transport services in every year since the mid 1980s. The deficit increased from £2.8 billion in 2007 to £2.9 billion in 2008.

Figure 3.2
Trade in sea and air transport services
Exports less imports

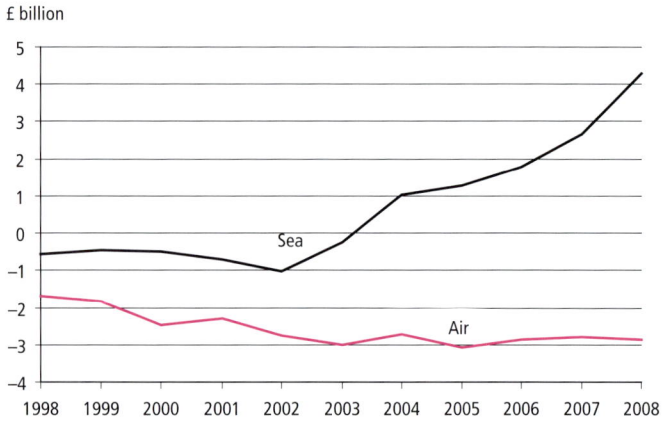

Travel

In 2008, travel expenditure by non-residents visiting the UK accounted for 12 per cent of total exports of services, while expenditure by UK residents traveling abroad accounted for 32 per cent of total imports of services. The travel deficit has grown significantly since the late 1990s. The £17.7 billion deficit in 2008 was the highest on record, up from £16.4 billion in 2007. Exports of travel services to non-resident visitors to the UK increased by 1.6 per cent in 2008 to £19.6 billion, while imports by UK residents traveling abroad grew by 4.4 per cent to £37.3 billion.

Figure 3.3
Trade in travel services

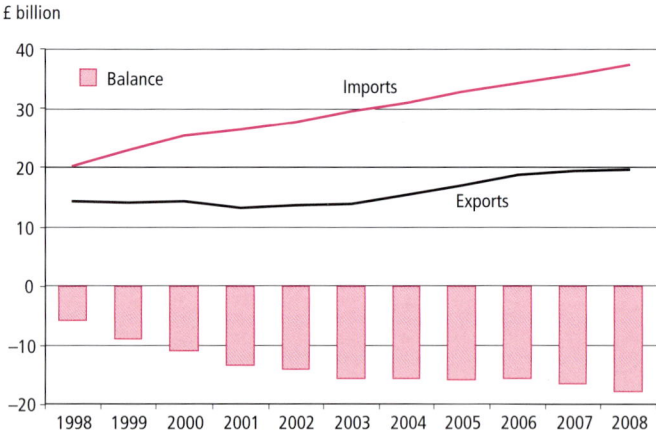

Financial services

Exports and imports of financial services from banks, fund managers and securities dealers for example, have been presented separately since *Pink Book* 2001. As in *Pink Book* 2008, Financial Services contains estimates for financial intermediation services indirectly measured (FISIM). In 2008 financial services accounted for 31 per cent of total exports and for 12 per cent of total imports of services. The overall financial services balance rose from £31.7 billion in 2007 to £38.6 billion in 2008. This rise was mainly due to increases in exports of financial services by UK banks whose income from commissions and fees, spread earnings and FISIM grew by £8.1 billion in the period.

Figure 3.4
Trade in financial services

£ billion

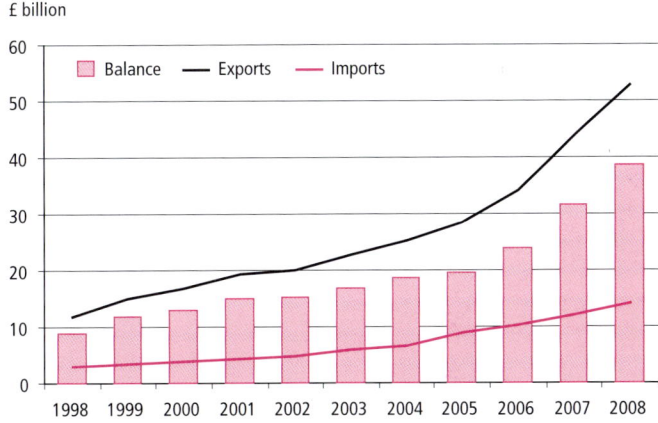

Figure 3.5
Trade in other business services

£ billion

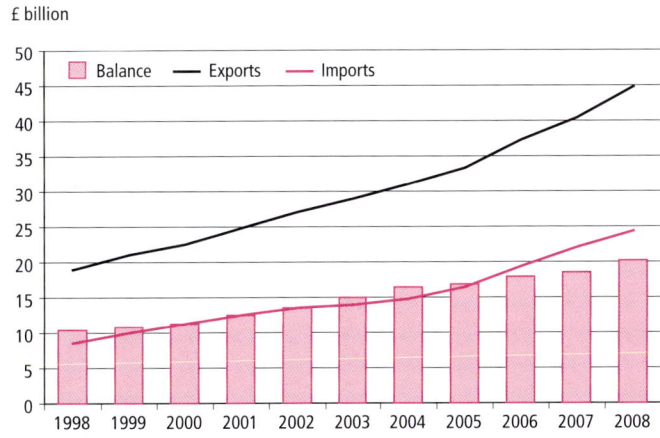

Other business services

Other business services covers a broad range of services including operational leasing, trade related services such as merchanting, and consultancy services such as advertising, engineering and legal services. Data for other business services are only available consistent with BPM5 definitions from 1991. Since 1998 the level of exports of other business services has more than doubled, and the level of imports has almost trebled. In 2008 other business services accounted for 26 per cent of total exports and for 21 per cent of total imports of services. The balance rose by 9.6 per cent in 2008 to £20.3 billion from £18.5 billion in 2007. Exports increased by £4.2 billion to £44.7 billion, while imports rose by £2.4 billion to £24.4 billion.

3.1 Trade in services
Summary table

£ million

		1998	1999	2000	2001	2002	2003	2004	2005	2006	2007	2008
Exports												
Transportation	FJOD	11 522	11 764	12 675	12 768	12 522	13 629	15 997	17 334	16 880	17 722	20 880
Travel	FJPF	14 302	14 060	14 446	13 110	13 595	13 876	15 414	16 871	18 803	19 292	19 598
Communications	FJPH	1 289	1 564	1 864	2 034	2 219	2 479	3 183	3 697	3 945	4 263	4 639
Construction	FJPI	332	275	220	174	195	245	278	600	790	996	1 127
Insurance	FJPJ	2 851	3 280	2 680	3 667	5 601	5 427	4 964	1 552	3 832	5 353	8 036
Financial	FJPK	11 811	15 021	16 837	19 370	19 935	22 778	25 228	28 370	34 199	43 874	52 828
Computer and information	FJPL	1 826	2 433	2 865	3 253	3 954	4 986	6 143	5 956	6 806	7 081	7 040
Royalties and license fees	FJPM	4 270	5 092	5 389	5 673	5 786	6 174	6 434	7 315	7 471	7 555	7 361
Other business	FJPN	19 013	21 017	22 395	24 844	27 026	28 937	31 115	33 263	37 328	40 511	44 697
Personal, cultural and recreational	FJPR	880	962	1 305	1 358	1 601	1 892	2 145	2 243	2 136	1 878	2 091
Government	FJPU	1 132	1 057	1 207	1 522	1 578	1 934	2 021	1 985	2 056	2 120	2 102
Total	**KTMQ**	**69 228**	**76 525**	**81 883**	**87 773**	**94 012**	**102 357**	**112 922**	**119 186**	**134 246**	**150 645**	**170 399**
Imports												
Transportation	FJPV	13 799	14 180	15 972	16 282	16 922	17 416	18 350	19 897	18 875	18 813	20 376
Travel	APQA	20 201	22 930	25 385	26 376	27 697	29 355	30 873	32 781	34 291	35 692	37 256
Communications	FJQZ	1 582	1 805	1 867	1 993	2 040	2 158	2 642	3 201	3 683	3 620	4 122
Construction	FJRA	115	98	55	107	104	120	142	570	625	805	904
Insurance	FJRB	577	575	721	762	758	778	830	891	979	1 022	1 073
Financial	FJRE	2 887	3 252	3 789	4 263	4 776	5 903	6 604	8 910	10 317	12 130	14 209
Computer and information	FJRF	494	691	838	1 175	1 316	1 792	1 857	2 207	2 554	2 664	3 055
Royalties and license fees	FJRG	4 015	4 285	4 379	4 494	4 609	4 810	5 007	5 202	5 166	5 053	5 500
Other business	FJRH	8 557	10 143	11 206	12 424	13 464	13 928	14 738	16 469	19 438	21 990	24 404
Personal, cultural and recreational	FJRL	489	608	779	724	797	855	884	831	856	952	959
Government	FJRO	1 509	2 396	1 890	1 973	1 897	2 630	2 581	2 485	2 680	3 097	4 062
Total	**KTMR**	**54 225**	**60 963**	**66 881**	**70 573**	**74 380**	**79 745**	**84 508**	**93 444**	**99 464**	**105 838**	**115 920**
Balances												
Transportation	FJRP	−2 277	−2 416	−3 297	−3 514	−4 400	−3 787	−2 353	−2 563	−1 995	−1 091	504
Travel	FJSR	−5 899	−8 870	−10 939	−13 266	−14 102	−15 479	−15 459	−15 910	−15 488	−16 400	−17 658
Communications	FJST	−293	−241	−3	41	179	321	541	496	262	643	517
Construction	FJSU	217	177	165	67	91	125	136	30	165	191	223
Insurance	FJSV	2 274	2 705	1 959	2 905	4 843	4 649	4 134	661	2 853	4 331	6 963
Financial	FJTA	8 924	11 769	13 048	15 107	15 159	16 875	18 624	19 460	23 882	31 744	38 619
Computer and information	FJTB	1 332	1 742	2 027	2 078	2 638	3 194	4 286	3 749	4 252	4 417	3 985
Royalties and license fees	FJTC	255	807	1 010	1 179	1 177	1 364	1 427	2 113	2 305	2 502	1 861
Other business	FJTD	10 456	10 874	11 189	12 420	13 562	15 009	16 377	16 794	17 890	18 521	20 293
Personal, cultural and recreational	FJTH	391	354	526	634	804	1 037	1 261	1 412	1 280	926	1 132
Government	FJUL	−377	−1 339	−683	−451	−319	−696	−560	−500	−624	−977	−1 960
Total	**KTMS**	**15 003**	**15 562**	**15 002**	**17 200**	**19 632**	**22 612**	**28 414**	**25 742**	**34 782**	**44 807**	**54 479**

3.2 Transportation

£ million

		1998	1999	2000	2001	2002	2003	2004	2005	2006	2007	2008
Exports												
Sea transport												
Passenger												
Passenger revenue	FJAL	462	463	630	488	569	993	846	608	444	430	469
Time charter receipts	FJAM	–	9	8	–	11	–	36	51	37	73	75
Total passenger	FJOF	462	472	638	488	580	993	882	659	481	503	544
Freight												
Dry cargo												
Freight on UK exports	HECV	322	375	400	406	481	525	444	544	530	552	636
Freight on cross-trades	HDVI	1 602	1 511	1 453	1 609	1 844	2 069	3 180	3 874	2 831	2 744	3 082
Time charter receipts	FJAO	109	90	140	106	118	196	640	912	1 049	1 491	1 939
Wet cargo												
Freight on UK exports	HEIX	60	59	98	82	96	126	173	174	130	142	219
Freight on cross-trades	HECX	442	350	458	497	420	742	1 305	1 194	1 222	1 395	2 530
Time charter receipts	FJAP	70	87	104	336	162	247	472	748	603	554	763
Total Freight	FJOG	2 605	2 472	2 653	3 036	3 121	3 905	6 214	7 446	6 365	6 878	9 169
Disbursements in the UK	FJAR	1 139	1 063	1 042	1 086	1 008	952	801	800	939	896	867
Total sea transport	FJOE	4 206	4 007	4 333	4 610	4 709	5 850	7 897	8 905	7 785	8 277	10 580
Air transport												
Passenger revenue	FJOJ	4 242	4 402	4 690	4 455	4 162	3 856	3 907	4 073	4 266	4 065	4 064
Freight on UK exports and cross trades	FJOK	408	380	428	365	350	368	394	397	391	493	528
Other												
Disbursements in the UK	FJAX	1 565	1 765	1 994	2 167	1 991	2 111	2 302	2 506	2 973	3 310	4 065
Other revenue	HBWB	236	294	303	258	247	240	267	182	183	225	205
Total other	FJOL	1 801	2 059	2 297	2 425	2 238	2 351	2 569	2 688	3 156	3 535	4 270
Total air transport	FJOI	6 451	6 841	7 415	7 245	6 750	6 575	6 870	7 158	7 813	8 093	8 862
Other transport												
Rail												
Passenger	FJOS	108	132	109	113	90	91	112	133	139	172	188
Freight	FJOT	16	17	20	16	12	15	16	17	17	16	16
Total rail	FJOR	124	149	129	129	102	106	128	150	156	188	204
Road												
Passenger	FJOW	–	–	–	–	–	–	–	–	–	–	–
Freight	FJOX	703	730	750	728	905	1 042	1 046	1 065	1 070	1 108	1 178
Total road	FJOV	703	730	750	728	905	1 042	1 046	1 065	1 070	1 108	1 178
Pipeline transport	FJPD	38	37	48	56	56	56	56	56	56	56	56
Total other transport	FJOM	865	916	927	913	1 063	1 204	1 230	1 271	1 282	1 352	1 438
Total	FJOD	**11 522**	**11 764**	**12 675**	**12 768**	**12 522**	**13 629**	**15 997**	**17 334**	**16 880**	**17 722**	**20 880**

3.2 Transportation
continued

£ million

		1998	1999	2000	2001	2002	2003	2004	2005	2006	2007	2008
Imports												
Sea transport												
Passenger												
Passenger expenditure	FJBP	494	429	413	450	486	476	476	463	533	627	437
Time charter payments	FJBQ	22	24	24	19	19	15	25	15	38	48	50
Total passenger	FJPX	516	453	437	469	505	491	501	478	571	675	487
Freight												
Dry cargo												
Freight on UK imports	HCJO	2 063	2 202	2 531	2 552	2 698	3 023	2 693	2 620	2 548	2 524	2 508
Time charter payments	FJBS	217	122	149	316	236	221	667	562	279	58	135
Wet cargo												
Freight on UK imports	HCNJ	282	415	280	305	330	355	417	434	422	407	360
Time charter payments	FJBT	181	89	172	176	140	184	359	636	655	721	1 257
Freight on UK coastal routes	HFAA	135	135	172	202	199	190	177	194	188	187	194
Total Freight	FJPY	2 878	2 963	3 304	3 551	3 603	3 973	4 313	4 446	4 092	3 897	4 454
Other												
Disbursements - dry cargo	FJBU	1 291	953	1 036	1 231	1 528	1 508	1 917	2 505	1 202	843	1 093
Disbursements - wet cargo	FJBW	78	76	55	54	81	118	138	183	164	215	267
Total other	FJPZ	1 369	1 029	1 091	1 285	1 609	1 626	2 055	2 688	1 366	1 058	1 360
Total sea transport	FJPW	4 763	4 445	4 832	5 305	5 717	6 090	6 869	7 612	6 029	5 630	6 301
Air transport												
Passenger expenditure	FJQB	4 197	4 650	5 192	5 255	5 559	5 949	6 231	6 761	7 021	7 076	7 052
Freight	FJQC	583	685	740	822	818	768	681	688	666	650	645
Disbursements abroad	FJCA	3 372	3 336	3 951	3 468	3 132	2 880	2 692	2 798	2 996	3 172	4 040
Total air transport	FJQA	8 152	8 671	9 883	9 545	9 509	9 597	9 604	10 247	10 683	10 898	11 737
Other transport												
Rail												
Passenger	FJQK	121	154	167	168	172	151	167	170	187	193	208
Freight	FJQL	21	26	37	43	44	46	47	44	43	51	44
Total rail	FJQJ	142	180	204	211	216	197	214	214	230	244	252
Road												
Passenger	FJQO	–	–	–	–	–	–	–	–	–	–	–
Freight	FJQP	694	836	1 001	1 169	1 428	1 480	1 611	1 772	1 881	1 989	2 034
Total road	FJQN	694	836	1 001	1 169	1 428	1 480	1 611	1 772	1 881	1 989	2 034
Pipeline transport	FJQV	48	48	52	52	52	52	52	52	52	52	52
Total other transport	FJQE	884	1 064	1 257	1 432	1 696	1 729	1 877	2 038	2 163	2 285	2 338
Total	FJPV	**13 799**	**14 180**	**15 972**	**16 282**	**16 922**	**17 416**	**18 350**	**19 897**	**18 875**	**18 813**	**20 376**

3.2 Transportation
continued

£ million

		1998	1999	2000	2001	2002	2003	2004	2005	2006	2007	2008
Balances												
Sea transport												
Passenger	FJRR	−54	19	201	19	75	502	381	181	−90	−172	57
Freight												
Dry cargo	FJNJ	−247	−348	−687	−747	−491	−454	904	2 148	1 583	2 205	3 014
Wet cargo	FJNM	109	−8	208	434	208	576	1 174	1 046	878	963	1 895
Other	FJVC	−135	−135	−172	−202	−199	−190	−177	−194	−188	−187	−194
Total Freight	FJRS	−273	−491	−651	−515	−482	−68	1 901	3 000	2 273	2 981	4 715
Other												
Dry cargo	FJVF	−1 291	−953	−1 036	−1 231	−1 528	−1 508	−1 917	−2 505	−1 202	−843	−1 093
Wet Cargo	FJVG	−78	−76	−55	−54	−81	−118	−138	−183	−164	−215	−267
Other	FJVI	1 139	1 063	1 042	1 086	1 008	952	801	800	939	896	867
Total other	FJRT	−230	34	−49	−199	−601	−674	−1 254	−1 888	−427	−162	−493
Total sea transport	FJRQ	−557	−438	−499	−695	−1 008	−240	1 028	1 293	1 756	2 647	4 279
of which												
Ships owned or chartered-in by UK residents	FLMZ	1 278	1 680	1 855	1 728	1 697	2 852	3 990	4 204	4 508	5 496	6 911
Ships operated by non-residents	FLNF	−1 835	−2 118	−2 354	−2 423	−2 705	−3 092	−2 962	−2 911	−2 752	−2 849	−2 632
Air transport												
Passenger	FJRV	45	−248	−502	−800	−1 397	−2 093	−2 324	−2 688	−2 755	−3 011	−2 988
Freight	FJRW	−175	−305	−312	−457	−468	−400	−287	−291	−275	−157	−117
Other	FJRX	−1 571	−1 277	−1 654	−1 043	−894	−529	−123	−110	160	363	230
Total air transport	FJRU	−1 701	−1 830	−2 468	−2 300	−2 759	−3 022	−2 734	−3 089	−2 870	−2 805	−2 875
Other transport												
Rail												
Passenger	FJSE	−13	−22	−58	−55	−82	−60	−55	−37	−48	−21	−20
Freight	FJSF	−5	−9	−17	−27	−32	−31	−31	−27	−26	−35	−28
Total rail	FJSD	−18	−31	−75	−82	−114	−91	−86	−64	−74	−56	−48
Road												
Passenger	FJSI	–	–	–	–	–	–	–	–	–	–	–
Freight	FJSJ	9	−106	−251	−441	−523	−438	−565	−707	−811	−881	−856
Total road	FJSH	9	−106	−251	−441	−523	−438	−565	−707	−811	−881	−856
Pipeline transport	FJSP	−10	−11	−4	4	4	4	4	4	4	4	4
Total other transport	FJRY	−19	−148	−330	−519	−633	−525	−647	−767	−881	−933	−900
Total	FJRP	−2 277	−2 416	−3 297	−3 514	−4 400	−3 787	−2 353	−2 563	−1 995	−1 091	504

3.3 Travel

£ million

		1998	1999	2000	2001	2002	2003	2004	2005	2006	2007	2008
Exports												
Business												
Expenditure by seasonal & border workers	FJCQ	132	114	147	163	219	169	203	234	270	263	260
Other	FJNO	3 857	3 998	4 084	3 615	3 618	3 478	3 735	4 110	4 749	4 627	4 574
Total business travel	FJPG	3 989	4 112	4 231	3 778	3 837	3 647	3 938	4 344	5 019	4 890	4 834
Personal												
Health related	FJCX	79	93	66	83	64	144	68	71	78	81	83
Education related	FJDD	2 696	2 534	2 484	2 723	2 592	2 881	3 072	3 357	3 694	3 860	3 957
Other	FJDG	7 538	7 321	7 665	6 526	7 102	7 204	8 336	9 099	10 012	10 461	10 724
Total personal travel	FJTU	10 313	9 948	10 215	9 332	9 758	10 229	11 476	12 527	13 784	14 402	14 764
Total	FJPF	14 302	14 060	14 446	13 110	13 595	13 876	15 414	16 871	18 803	19 292	19 598
Imports												
Business												
Expenditure by seasonal & border workers	FJDO	118	197	192	215	102	225	159	202	214	222	228
Other	FJNP	4 231	4 352	4 811	4 479	4 336	4 135	4 243	4 695	4 962	5 142	5 282
Total business travel	FJQY	4 349	4 549	5 003	4 694	4 438	4 360	4 402	4 897	5 176	5 364	5 510
Personal												
Health related	FJDT	3	10	19	16	12	33	45	60	63	66	69
Education related	FJDV	133	180	99	108	110	102	117	165	172	179	187
Other	APPW	15 716	18 191	20 264	21 558	23 137	24 860	26 309	27 659	28 880	30 083	31 490
Total personal travel	APQW	15 852	18 381	20 382	21 682	23 259	24 995	26 471	27 884	29 115	30 328	31 746
Total	APQA	20 201	22 930	25 385	26 376	27 697	29 355	30 873	32 781	34 291	35 692	37 256
Balances												
Business												
Expenditure by seasonal & border workers	FJCR	14	−83	−45	−52	117	−56	44	32	56	41	32
Other	FJCW	−374	−354	−727	−864	−718	−657	−508	−585	−213	−515	−708
Total business travel	FJSS	−360	−437	−772	−916	−601	−713	−464	−553	−157	−474	−676
Personal												
Health related	FJCY	76	83	47	67	52	111	23	11	15	15	14
Education related	FJDE	2 563	2 354	2 385	2 615	2 482	2 779	2 955	3 192	3 522	3 681	3 770
Other	FJDH	−8 178	−10 870	−12 599	−15 032	−16 035	−17 656	−17 973	−18 560	−18 868	−19 622	−20 766
Total personal travel	FJTW	−5 539	−8 433	−10 167	−12 350	−13 501	−14 766	−14 995	−15 357	−15 331	−15 926	−16 982
Total	FJSR	−5 899	−8 870	−10 939	−13 266	−14 102	−15 479	−15 459	−15 910	−15 488	−16 400	−17 658

3.4 Communications services

£ million

		1998	1999	2000	2001	2002	2003	2004	2005	2006	2007	2008
Exports												
Postal and courier services												
Postal services	FJTN	88	109	118	97	110	112	124	121	127	119	121
Courier services	FJTO	13	52	29	80	67	111	320	390	374	415	495
Total postal and courier services	FJED	101	161	147	177	177	223	444	511	501	534	616
Telecommunications services	FJAS	1 188	1 403	1 717	1 857	2 042	2 256	2 739	3 186	3 444	3 729	4 023
Total	FJPH	**1 289**	**1 564**	**1 864**	**2 034**	**2 219**	**2 479**	**3 183**	**3 697**	**3 945**	**4 263**	**4 639**
Imports												
Postal and courier services												
Postal services	FJTP	218	239	260	200	200	225	181	166	159	156	186
Courier services	FJTQ	39	48	18	55	58	90	294	310	280	408	408
Total postal and courier services	FJEI	257	287	278	255	258	315	475	476	439	564	594
Telecommunications services	FJAT	1 325	1 518	1 589	1 738	1 782	1 843	2 167	2 725	3 244	3 056	3 528
Total	FJQZ	**1 582**	**1 805**	**1 867**	**1 993**	**2 040**	**2 158**	**2 642**	**3 201**	**3 683**	**3 620**	**4 122**
Balances												
Postal and courier services												
Postal services	FJTR	−130	−130	−142	−103	−90	−113	−57	−45	−32	−37	−65
Courier services	FJTS	−26	4	11	25	9	21	26	80	94	7	87
Total postal and courier services	FJEE	−156	−126	−131	−78	−81	−92	−31	35	62	−30	22
Telecommunications services	FJAQ	−137	−115	128	119	260	413	572	461	200	673	495
Total	FJST	**−293**	**−241**	**−3**	**41**	**179**	**321**	**541**	**496**	**262**	**643**	**517**

3.5 Insurance services

£ million

		1998	1999	2000	2001	2002	2003	2004	2005	2006	2007	2008
Exports												
Life insurance and pension funds	FJEU	838	1 557	1 417	2 174	797	8	−713	−1 464	−1 264	−502	216
Freight insurance	FJJL	76	47	41	49	80	129	90	72	43	146	113
Other direct insurance[1]	FJEW	439	653	412	−579	2 164	1 935	3 350	729	1 805	3 674	4 531
Reinsurance	FJEX	331	−49	−296	1 011	1 473	2 241	1 023	970	1 691	489	1 507
Auxiliary insurance services (insurance brokers)	FJEY	1 167	1 072	1 106	1 012	1 087	1 114	1 214	1 245	1 557	1 546	1 669
Total[2]	FJPJ	**2 851**	**3 280**	**2 680**	**3 667**	**5 601**	**5 427**	**4 964**	**1 552**	**3 832**	**5 353**	**8 036**
Imports												
Life insurance and pension funds	FJRC	–	–	–	–	–	–	–	–	–	–	–
Freight insurance	FJRD	577	575	721	762	758	778	830	891	979	1 022	1 073
Other direct insurance	FJFC	–	–	–	–	–	–	–	–	–	–	–
Reinsurance	FJFD	–	–	–	–	–	–	–	–	–	–	–
Auxiliary insurance services	FJFE	–	–	–	–	–	–	–	–	–	–	–
Total	FJRB	**577**	**575**	**721**	**762**	**758**	**778**	**830**	**891**	**979**	**1 022**	**1 073**
Balances												
Life insurance and pension funds	FJSW	838	1 557	1 417	2 174	797	8	−713	−1 464	−1 264	−502	216
Freight insurance	FJSX	−501	−528	−680	−713	−678	−649	−740	−819	−936	−876	−960
Other direct insurance	FJJM	439	653	412	−579	2 164	1 935	3 350	729	1 805	3 674	4 531
Reinsurance	FJJN	331	−49	−296	1 011	1 473	2 241	1 023	970	1 691	489	1 507
Auxiliary insurance services	FJJO	1 167	1 072	1 106	1 012	1 087	1 114	1 214	1 245	1 557	1 546	1 669
Total	FJSV	**2 274**	**2 705**	**1 959**	**2 905**	**4 843**	**4 649**	**4 134**	**661**	**2 853**	**4 331**	**6 963**

1 Other direct insurance by UK insurance companies includes facultative reinsurance on marine, aviation and transport business.
2 Exports of insurance services are net of expenditure abroad by UK insurance companies.

3.6 Financial services

£ million

		1998	1999	2000	2001	2002	2003	2004	2005	2006	2007	2008
Exports												
Monetary financial institutions												
Commissions and fees	APUP	2 108	2 506	3 041	2 986	3 215	2 677	3 458	4 198	5 562	6 676	6 172
Spread earnings	APVA	1 737	1 628	1 809	2 370	2 922	4 536	4 908	5 914	6 974	9 451	11 098
FISIM[1] on loans	TGWM	553	1 202	876	1 585	1 692	2 132	2 004	1 992	2 268	3 476	6 693
of which £	LOFR	*304*	*659*	*480*	*869*	*928*	*1 169*	*998*	*844*	*1 040*	*1 661*	*1 491*
FISIM on deposits	TGWP	697	1 707	1 341	2 141	2 333	3 148	2 939	2 975	3 233	4 978	8 712
of which £	LOFU	*401*	*984*	*772*	*1 233*	*1 344*	*1 813*	*1 573*	*1 370*	*1 549*	*2 480*	*2 408*
Total monetary financial institutions	ZXTE	5 095	7 043	7 067	9 082	10 162	12 493	13 309	15 079	18 037	24 581	32 675
Fund managers	FNMM	849	866	868	853	1 045	1 528	1 925	2 632	3 199	4 856	5 019
Securities dealers												
Commissions and fees	CDFI	2 831	3 996	5 632	5 211	4 290	3 922	4 316	4 628	6 316	8 429	8 362
Spread earnings	QZCM	1 233	1 209	1 033	1 492	1 168	1 316	1 666	1 918	2 544	2 815	1 746
Total securities dealers	ZXTF	4 064	5 205	6 665	6 703	5 458	5 238	5 982	6 546	8 860	11 244	10 108
Baltic Exchange	APRJ	320	320	336	377	357	398	577	777	744	802	999
Other institutions	ZSHJ	1 483	1 587	1 901	2 355	2 913	3 121	3 435	3 336	3 359	2 391	4 027
Total including FISIM	FJPK	**11 811**	**15 021**	**16 837**	**19 370**	**19 935**	**22 778**	**25 228**	**28 370**	**34 199**	**43 874**	**52 828**
Total FISIM[1]	C6FD	1 250	2 909	2 217	3 726	4 025	5 280	4 943	4 967	5 501	8 454	15 405
Total excluding FISIM	C9NI	**10 561**	**12 112**	**14 620**	**15 644**	**15 910**	**17 498**	**20 285**	**23 403**	**28 698**	**35 420**	**37 423**
Imports												
Monetary financial institutions	APVW	549	733	1 003	1 157	1 475	1 701	1 556	1 693	2 002	2 336	3 055
Fund managers	FNMS	171	143	160	229	219	336	420	527	574	727	859
Securities dealers[2]	RWMG	689	829	1 199	1 296	1 009	795	862	1 244	1 643	985	1 119
Baltic Exchange	APSZ	23	27	39	27	35	18	26	42	38	33	51
Other institutions	ZXTG	1 455	1 520	1 388	1 554	2 038	3 053	3 740	5 404	6 060	8 049	9 125
of which FISIM on loans	TGZJ	*449*	*478*	*387*	*373*	*669*	*864*	*1 142*	*1 571*	*1 798*	*2 041*	*2 144*
FISIM on deposits	TGZU	*470*	*466*	*443*	*576*	*554*	*966*	*1 480*	*2 251*	*2 658*	*3 163*	*4 166*
Total including FISIM	FJRE	**2 887**	**3 252**	**3 789**	**4 263**	**4 776**	**5 903**	**6 604**	**8 910**	**10 317**	**12 130**	**14 209**
Total FISIM[1]	C6F7	919	944	830	949	1 223	1 830	2 622	3 822	4 456	5 204	6 310
Total excluding FISIM	C9NJ	**1 968**	**2 308**	**2 959**	**3 314**	**3 553**	**4 073**	**3 982**	**5 088**	**5 861**	**6 926**	**7 899**
Balances												
Monetary financial institutions	ZXLV	4 546	6 310	6 064	7 925	8 687	10 792	11 753	13 386	16 035	22 245	29 620
Fund managers	ZXLW	678	723	708	624	826	1 192	1 505	2 105	2 625	4 129	4 160
Securities dealers	ZXLX	3 375	4 376	5 466	5 407	4 449	4 443	5 120	5 302	7 217	10 259	8 989
Baltic Exchange	ZXLY	297	293	297	350	322	380	551	735	706	769	948
Other institutions	ZXLZ	28	67	513	801	875	68	−305	−2 068	−2 701	−5 658	−5 098
Total including FISIM	FJTA	**8 924**	**11 769**	**13 048**	**15 107**	**15 159**	**16 875**	**18 624**	**19 460**	**23 882**	**31 744**	**38 619**
Total FISIM[1]	IH3K	331	1 965	1 387	2 777	2 802	3 450	2 321	1 145	1 045	3 250	9 095
Total excluding FISIM	IH3L	**8 593**	**9 804**	**11 661**	**12 330**	**12 357**	**13 425**	**16 303**	**18 315**	**22 837**	**28 494**	**29 524**

1 FISIM is an acronym for Financial Intermediation Services Indirectly Measured. It represents the implicit charge for the service provided by monetary financial institutions paid for by the interest differential between borrowing and lending rather than through fees and commissions.
2 For securities dealers, the move to a gross presentation means that imports of non-financial services are moved to the other business services accounts (see table 3.9).

3.7 Computer and information services

£ million

		1998	1999	2000	2001	2002	2003	2004	2005	2006	2007	2008
Exports												
Computer services	FJCN	1 640	2 056	2 478	2 725	3 328	3 705	4 747	4 662	4 999	5 363	5 102
Information services	FJCO	186	377	387	528	626	1 281	1 396	1 294	1 807	1 718	1 938
Total	FJPL	**1 826**	**2 433**	**2 865**	**3 253**	**3 954**	**4 986**	**6 143**	**5 956**	**6 806**	**7 081**	**7 040**
Imports												
Computer services	FJDL	473	593	745	859	1 122	1 478	1 445	1 832	2 260	2 366	2 610
Information services	FJDM	21	98	93	316	194	314	412	375	294	298	445
Total	FJRF	**494**	**691**	**838**	**1 175**	**1 316**	**1 792**	**1 857**	**2 207**	**2 554**	**2 664**	**3 055**
Balances												
Computer Services	FJJP	1 167	1 463	1 733	1 866	2 206	2 227	3 302	2 830	2 739	2 997	2 492
Information services	FJJQ	165	279	294	212	432	967	984	919	1 513	1 420	1 493
Total	FJTB	**1 332**	**1 742**	**2 027**	**2 078**	**2 638**	**3 194**	**4 286**	**3 749**	**4 252**	**4 417**	**3 985**

3.8 Royalties and license fees

£ million

		1998	1999	2000	2001	2002	2003	2004	2005	2006	2007	2008
Exports												
Film and television	FJFO	775	868	934	982	880	911	890	972	1 252	1 295	1 498
Other royalties and license fees	FFVJ	3 495	4 224	4 455	4 691	4 906	5 263	5 544	6 343	6 219	6 260	5 863
Total	FJPM	**4 270**	**5 092**	**5 389**	**5 673**	**5 786**	**6 174**	**6 434**	**7 315**	**7 471**	**7 555**	**7 361**
Imports												
Film and television	FJFQ	882	932	1 020	1 176	1 315	1 449	1 533	1 456	1 385	1 193	1 322
Other royalties and license fees	FFVP	3 133	3 353	3 359	3 318	3 294	3 361	3 474	3 746	3 781	3 860	4 178
Total	FJRG	**4 015**	**4 285**	**4 379**	**4 494**	**4 609**	**4 810**	**5 007**	**5 202**	**5 166**	**5 053**	**5 500**
Balances												
Film and television	FFVV	−107	−64	−86	−194	−435	−538	−643	−484	−133	102	176
Other royalties and license fees	FFWB	362	871	1 096	1 373	1 612	1 902	2 070	2 597	2 438	2 400	1 685
Total	FJTC	**255**	**807**	**1 010**	**1 179**	**1 177**	**1 364**	**1 427**	**2 113**	**2 305**	**2 502**	**1 861**

3.9 Other Business services

£ million

		1998	1999	2000	2001	2002	2003	2004	2005	2006	2007	2008
Exports												
Merchanting and other trade related services												
Merchanting	FJFS	569	868	626	782	699	573	549	942	327	1 140	1 132
Other trade related services	FJFX	732	1 504	1 759	1 881	1 720	1 899	1 698	1 780	1 850	1 760	1 726
Total merchanting and other trade related services	FJPO	1 301	2 372	2 385	2 663	2 419	2 472	2 247	2 722	2 177	2 900	2 858
Operational leasing services	FJPP	40	92	299	248	190	239	342	329	508	394	748
Miscellaneous business, professional and technical services												
Legal, accounting and management consulting												
Law society	FJGE	824	760	1 171	1 339	1 465	1 335	1 470	1 615	2 139	2 611	2 897
Commercial bar association	FJCP	61	62	61	77	85	95	86	116	113	107	76
Other legal services	FJGD	275	349	288	363	481	600	435	553	450	358	487
Accounting	FJBX	477	603	662	642	728	733	892	1 087	1 327	1 343	1 384
Business management and management consulting	FJNV	952	1 101	1 083	1 069	2 545	3 127	3 288	3 998	5 328	6 005	7 045
of which Recruitment and training	TVLQ	..	..	..	..	*354*	*359*	*350*	*342*	*387*	*389*	*491*
Advertising and market research	FJGP	1 174	1 150	1 432	1 622	1 703	2 155	1 965	2 403	2 295	2 373	2 481
Research and development	FJDP	2 300	2 801	2 421	2 933	2 899	3 467	4 467	4 705	4 846	5 204	5 280
Architectural, engineering and other technical services												
Architectural	FJGT	67	82	76	153	71	106	110	95	178	271	346
Engineering	FJGU	2 987	2 676	2 441	3 239	3 049	3 475	3 501	3 291	3 643	3 596	4 294
Surveying	FJGV	41	45	68	66	62	57	137	226	149	107	161
Other Technical	FJGW	1 083	1 027	1 113	1 220	1 931	1 629	1 698	1 616	1 441	1 087	1 502
Agricultural, mining and on-site processing services	FJHC	52	47	54	41	31	202	234	259	322	401	548
Other miscellaneous business services	FJHH	6 398	6 749	7 561	7 688	7 748	7 140	8 101	7 869	9 362	10 130	10 089
of which Other business services exported by UK banks	APVQ	*1 008*	*1 325*	*1 414*	*1 277*	*1 490*	*2 118*	*1 892*	*2 134*	*2 156*	*2 250*	*2 443*
Services between affiliated enterprises, n.i.e.	FJHF	981	1 101	1 280	1 481	1 619	2 105	2 142	2 379	3 050	3 624	4 501
Total miscellaneous business, professional, and technical services	FJPQ	17 672	18 553	19 711	21 933	24 417	26 226	28 526	30 212	34 643	37 217	41 091
Total	FJPN	**19 013**	**21 017**	**22 395**	**24 844**	**27 026**	**28 937**	**31 115**	**33 263**	**37 328**	**40 511**	**44 697**
Imports												
Merchanting and other trade related services												
Merchanting	FJHN	65	38	71	55	148	35	81	80	81	80	80
Other trade related services	FJHR	633	884	965	952	854	752	1 122	608	589	639	633
Total merchanting and other trade related services	FJRI	698	922	1 036	1 007	1 002	787	1 203	688	670	719	713
Operational leasing services	FJRJ	193	226	560	457	450	456	784	687	807	799	898
Miscellaneous business, professional and technical services												
Legal, accounting and management consulting												
Legal[1]	FJHX	249	307	490	380	486	453	416	429	534	533	587
Accounting	FJVJ	108	119	213	228	251	300	324	328	358	314	401
Business management and management consulting	FJNW	371	387	456	569	1 428	1 924	2 328	2 601	2 970	3 481	4 086
of which Recruitment and training	TVLV	..	..	..	..	*237*	*264*	*357*	*121*	*134*	*142*	*150*
Advertising and market research	FJID	581	719	789	841	860	946	842	1 100	1 398	1 802	1 785
Research and development	FJDQ	753	781	723	661	644	1 148	1 806	2 021	2 197	2 264	3 309
Architectural, engineering and other technical services												
Architectural	FJIF	12	12	13	35	25	50	11	4	21	11	20
Engineering	FJIG	1 228	977	724	1 075	868	1 107	1 325	1 067	1 278	1 525	1 451
Surveying	FJIH	26	15	55	31	29	24	48	88	40	28	64
Other Technical	FJII	435	410	429	431	463	368	384	556	433	465	568
Agricultural, mining and on-site processing services	FJIN	27	50	71	142	77	53	63	100	122	172	182
Other miscellaneous business services	FJIP	3 157	4 448	4 839	5 498	5 741	5 181	4 006	5 362	6 853	7 887	8 001
of which Other business sevices imported by UK banks	APWA	*509*	*794*	*520*	*448*	*619*	*760*	*497*	*591*	*528*	*820*	*994*
Other business services imported by Security dealers	RWMH	*986*	*1 511*	*2 294*	*2 027*	*1 358*	*1 149*	*1 462*	*3 036*	*4 234*	*5 496*	*5 050*
Services between affiliated enterprises, n.i.e.	FJHG	719	770	808	1 069	1 140	1 131	1 198	1 438	1 757	1 990	2 339
Total miscellaneous business, professional and technical services	FJRK	7 666	8 995	9 610	10 960	12 012	12 685	12 751	15 094	17 961	20 472	22 793
Total	FJRH	**8 557**	**10 143**	**11 206**	**12 424**	**13 464**	**13 928**	**14 738**	**16 469**	**19 438**	**21 990**	**24 404**

3.9 Other Business services
continued

£ million

		1998	1999	2000	2001	2002	2003	2004	2005	2006	2007	2008
Balances												
Merchanting and other trade related services												
Merchanting	FJFT	504	830	555	727	551	538	468	862	246	1 060	1 052
Other trade related services	FJFY	99	620	794	929	866	1 147	576	1 172	1 261	1 121	1 093
Total merchanting and other trade related services	FJTE	603	1 450	1 349	1 656	1 417	1 685	1 044	2 034	1 507	2 181	2 145
Operational leasing services	FJTF	−153	−134	−261	−209	−260	−217	−442	−358	−299	−405	−150
Miscellaneous business, professional and technical services												
Legal, accounting and management consulting												
Legal	FJGG	911	864	1 030	1 399	1 545	1 577	1 575	1 855	2 168	2 543	2 873
Accounting	FJGI	369	484	449	414	477	433	568	759	969	1 029	983
Business management and management consulting	FJGK	581	714	627	500	1 117	1 203	960	1 397	2 358	2 524	2 959
Advertising and market research	FJGQ	593	431	643	781	843	1 209	1 123	1 303	897	571	696
Research and development	FJGS	1 547	2 020	1 698	2 272	2 255	2 319	2 661	2 684	2 649	2 940	1 971
Architectural, engineering and other technical services	FJGY	2 477	2 416	2 477	3 106	3 728	3 718	3 678	3 513	3 639	3 032	4 200
Agricultural, mining and on-site processing services	FJHD	25	−3	−17	−101	−46	149	171	159	200	229	366
Services between affiliated enterprises, n.i.e.	FJHL	262	331	472	412	479	974	944	941	1 293	1 634	2 162
Other	FJHI	3 241	2 301	2 722	2 190	2 007	1 959	4 095	2 507	2 509	2 243	2 088
Total miscellaneous business, professional, and technical services	FJTG	10 006	9 558	10 101	10 973	12 405	13 541	15 775	15 118	16 682	16 745	18 298
Total	FJTD	10 456	10 874	11 189	12 420	13 562	15 009	16 377	16 794	17 890	18 521	20 293

3.10 Personal, cultural and recreational services

£ million

		1998	1999	2000	2001	2002	2003	2004	2005	2006	2007	2008
Exports												
Audiovisual and related services												
Film and television	FKJO	480	531	726	737	856	1 077	1 274	1 357	1 248	989	983
Other	FFWH	167	189	252	172	184	204	286	215	200	162	301
Total audiovisual and related services	FJPS	647	720	978	909	1 040	1 281	1 560	1 572	1 448	1 151	1 284
Other personal, cultural and recreational services	FJPT	233	242	327	449	561	611	585	671	688	727	807
Total	FJPR	**880**	**962**	**1 305**	**1 358**	**1 601**	**1 892**	**2 145**	**2 243**	**2 136**	**1 878**	**2 091**
Imports												
Audiovisual and related services												
Film and television	FKJX	411	496	532	512	615	463	587	584	571	755	757
Other	FFWN	35	40	55	46	39	59	89	44	68	70	67
Total audiovisual and related services	FJRM	446	536	587	558	654	522	676	628	639	825	824
Other personal, cultural and recreational services	FJRN	43	72	192	166	143	333	208	203	217	127	135
Total	FJRL	**489**	**608**	**779**	**724**	**797**	**855**	**884**	**831**	**856**	**952**	**959**
Balances												
Audiovisual and related services	FJTI	201	184	391	351	386	759	884	944	809	326	460
Other personal, cultural and recreational services	FJTJ	190	170	135	283	418	278	377	468	471	600	672
Total	FJTH	**391**	**354**	**526**	**634**	**804**	**1 037**	**1 261**	**1 412**	**1 280**	**926**	**1 132**

3.11 Government services

£ million

		1998	1999	2000	2001	2002	2003	2004	2005	2006	2007	2008
Exports												
Expenditure by foreign embassies and consulates in the UK	FJUK	371	385	385	389	393	397	401	405	409	413	418
Military units and agencies												
Expenditure by US forces in UK	FJKB	293	247	271	262	262	264	264	264	264	264	264
Other military receipts by UK government	HCOJ	40	21	58	48	67	248	312	286	366	309	177
Total military units and agencies	FJIX	333	268	329	310	329	512	576	550	630	573	441
Other												
EU institutions	FKIE	216	213	226	525	487	494	543	565	586	607	662
Other receipts	HCQO	212	191	267	298	369	531	501	465	431	527	581
Total other	FJJA	428	404	493	823	856	1 025	1 044	1 030	1 017	1 134	1 243
Total	FJPU	**1 132**	**1 057**	**1 207**	**1 522**	**1 578**	**1 934**	**2 021**	**1 985**	**2 056**	**2 120**	**2 102**
Imports												
Expenditure abroad by UK embassies and consulates	FJUJ	177	219	106	142	215	190	177	167	187	110	82
Expenditure abroad by UK military units and agencies	FJJD	1 116	1 972	1 584	1 629	1 494	2 144	1 892	1 817	2 124	2 499	3 284
Civil non-EU services	FJJF	216	205	200	202	188	296	512	501	369	488	696
Total	FJRO	**1 509**	**2 396**	**1 890**	**1 973**	**1 897**	**2 630**	**2 581**	**2 485**	**2 680**	**3 097**	**4 062**
Balances												
Embassies and consulates	FJIW	194	166	279	247	178	207	224	238	222	303	336
Military units and agencies	FJIY	–783	–1 704	–1 255	–1 319	–1 165	–1 632	–1 316	–1 267	–1 494	–1 926	–2 843
Other	FJJB	212	199	293	621	668	729	532	529	648	646	547
Total	FJUL	**–377**	**–1 339**	**–683**	**–451**	**–319**	**–696**	**–560**	**–500**	**–624**	**–977**	**–1 960**

Income

Chapter 4

Summary

The balance on income has been in surplus for all years since 2000. The income surplus grew strongly between 2000 and 2002 to reach £18 billion and then remained at around this size until 2005, when it increased to £21.9 billion. The surplus then dropped to £9.6 billion in 2006 before increasing over the next two years to reach a record £26.9 billion in 2008. The movements in the income surplus from 2000 have largely been due to movements in the net earnings on direct investment.

In the decade to 2001, earnings on both investment abroad and investment in the UK nearly doubled. In 2002 however, both fell sharply: credits down 12 per cent and debits down 20 per cent. This was largely due to cuts in official interest rates, both abroad and in the UK, post September 11 (2001) and throughout 2002, and subsequent falls in interest receipts and payments on loans and deposits. From 2003 to 2007 income increased significantly and by 2007 both investment income credits and debits were more than double the earnings seen in 2002. This reflected stronger profits on foreign direct investment and a higher rate of return on both portfolio and other investment, together with significant levels of investment over the period. In 2008 income credits and debits both fell, mostly due to lower earnings on direct investment.

Figure 4.1

Income

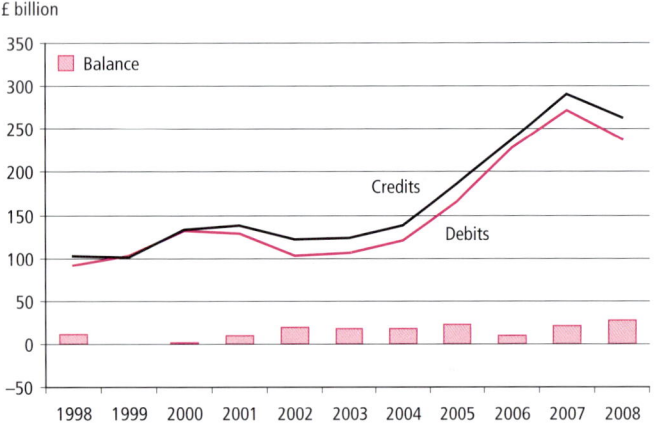

Earnings on direct investment abroad were the largest component of investment income credits between 2002 and 2005, accounting for over 40 per cent of total earnings, compared to only 29 per cent in 1995. The boom in UK merger and acquisition activity in the late 1990s and 2000 and subsequent growth in earnings from abroad has been the main driver of this change. Since 2006 other investment income, which is mostly earnings from loans and deposits, has been the largest component of investment income credits, accounting for 47 per cent of total earnings in 2008. Earnings on portfolio investment abroad have been broadly rising in line with total investment income, accounting for 26 per cent of total earnings from abroad in 2008.

Growth in foreign earnings on investment in the UK from 2003 to 2007 was predominantly in other investment, and the fall in 2008 was mainly due to a sharp drop in foreign earnings on direct investment. Other investment is consistently the largest component of foreign earnings on investment and accounts for more than half of all investment income paid from 2006.

By component, direct investment has recorded a surplus in every year since 1986. Within portfolio investment, a net surplus on interest receipts and payments on debt securities has largely been outweighed by net dividend payments on equity securities. Other investment has recorded a net deficit in every year since 1987.

Figure 4.2

Investment income

Credits less debits

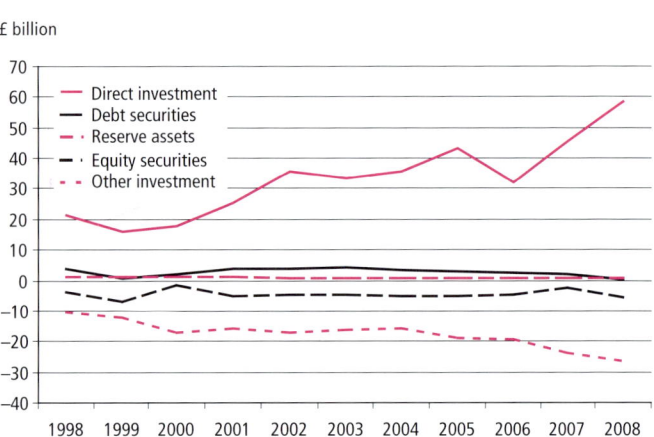

By sector, net earnings of UK monetary financial institutions (banks and building societies) were £24.2 billion in 2008, compared to £8.9 billion in 2007. This rise was mainly driven by a rise in the balance on direct investment, due to foreign investors in the UK monetary financial sector reporting losses of £28.3 billion, compared to UK investors abroad reporting profits of near zero. Over the same period, insurance companies' net earnings on direct investment switched from net earnings of £2.5 billion to net payments of £2.6 billion.

The balance on compensation of employees has shown a deficit since 2004, and has stood at £0.7 billion in the last two years.

Direct investment

Direct investment income credits have exceeded debits in every year since 1986, and the surplus increased to a record £58.5 billion in 2008, £13.1 billion higher than the surplus in 2007. Earnings on direct investment abroad decreased by 23 per cent in 2008, to £69.2 billion, due to foreign earnings by banks falling to virtually zero and those by insurance companies going negative, together with falls in the earnings of private non-financial corporations, other financial intermediaries and public corporations. Foreign earnings on direct investment in the UK fell by 76 per cent to £10.6 billion, from £44.8 billion in 2007. This decrease resulted from increased losses reported by foreign-owned monetary financial institutions, together with lower earnings reported by private non-financial corporations and other financial intermediaries. Foreign earnings on direct investment in the UK tend to be more erratic than earnings on direct investment abroad, partly because of their concentration in the financial sector. Foreign-owned banks and other financial corporations often locate in the UK to be close to the financial markets in London and their profits have previously reflected the difficult trading conditions, that is, in 1998, to a lesser extent 2002, and more recently in 2007 and 2008.

heavily in 2008, resulting in a fall in dividend receipts. Their dividend receipts were £4.5 billion in 2007 compared with £1.5 billion in 2002, and were £3.5 billion in 2008. UK monetary financial institutions' interest receipts on foreign debt securities rose to a record £34.5 billion in 2007, up 26 per cent on 2006 due to increased investment in those instruments and higher interest rates, and then fell slightly in 2008 to £34.2 billion. Earnings on bonds and notes by UK insurance companies, pension funds and other financial intermediaries (securities dealers, unit and investment trusts) were at record highs in 2008, due to increased investment. On the debits side, foreign earnings from UK equity have more than doubled since 1998, rising from £9.9 billion to £25.6 billion in 2008. Strong foreign investment into UK debt securities has led to a sharp rise in interest paid, reaching a record £47.7 billion in 2008.

Figure 4.3
Direct investment income
£ billion

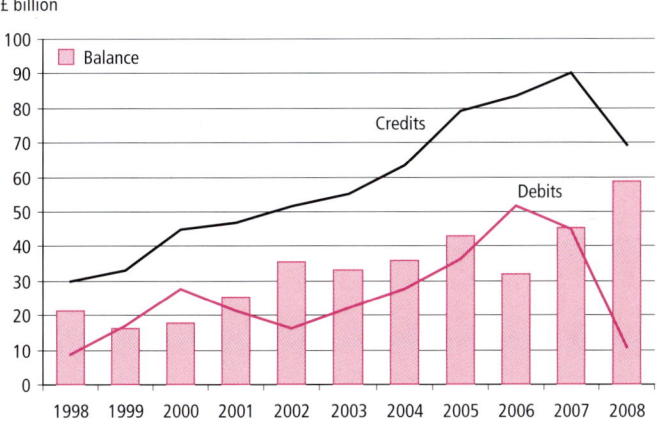

Figure 4.4
Portfolio investment income
£ billion

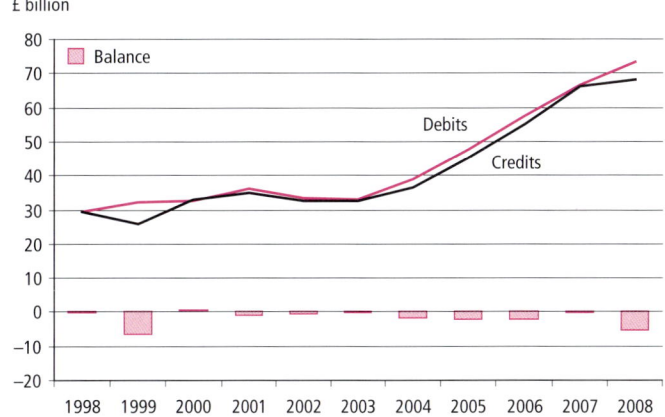

Portfolio investment

The UK has generally recorded a deficit on portfolio investment, with a net surplus on debt securities being more than offset by a net deficit on equity securities. By instrument, in all years since 1987 the UK has paid out more dividends on UK equity securities owned by non-residents than have been received on foreign equity securities owned by UK residents. In contrast, the UK has recorded a surplus on debt securities in each of the last 12 years, with a surplus on earnings from bonds and notes only partly offset by a deficit on money market instruments. UK monetary financial institutions doubled their net earnings on portfolio investment between 2001 and 2007, moving from a surplus of £9.7 billion in 2001 to a record surplus of £19.5 billion in 2007, before falling back to a surplus of £16.1 billion in 2008. UK monetary financial institutions traditionally tended to hold debt securities rather than equity securities, but from 2003 to 2007 they steadily increased their levels of investment in foreign equity securities, which resulted in a similar rise in dividend receipts; however, they disinvested

Other investment

Movements in the other investment balance are mainly driven by interest rate changes, which impact on interest paid and received on loans and deposits. As the UK has an excess of other investment liabilities over assets, there is generally a deficit on other investment income, with rising interest rates leading to a rising deficit and falling interest rates to a falling deficit. Rising global interest rates from 2005 through to 2007 led to the other investment deficit increasing from £19.0 billion to £24.1 billion over that period. In 2008, the deficit rose to £26.5 billion: the deficit for monetary financial institutions fell slightly but the deficit for other non-governmental sectors increased, due to a greater fall in credits than in debits. Earnings on deposits and loans abroad by UK banks accounted for over 80 per cent of total other investment credits in 2008. The vast majority of these earnings are made from foreign currency, reflecting the international nature of banking in the UK (as many of the banks trading with the rest of the world are actually branches or subsidiaries of foreign banks).

Figure 4.5

Other investment income

£ billion

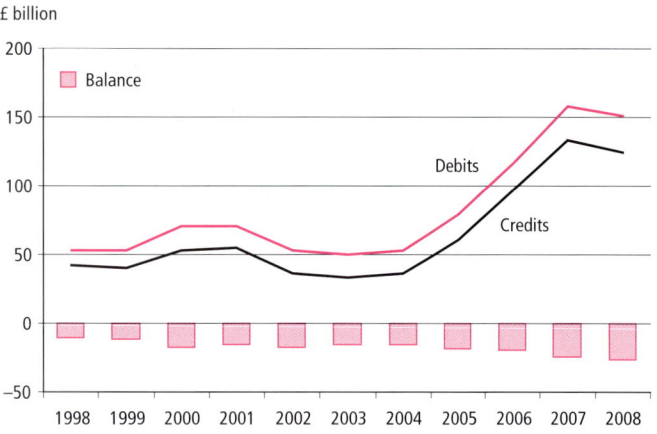

Figure 4.6

Investment income of banks

Credits less debits

£ billion

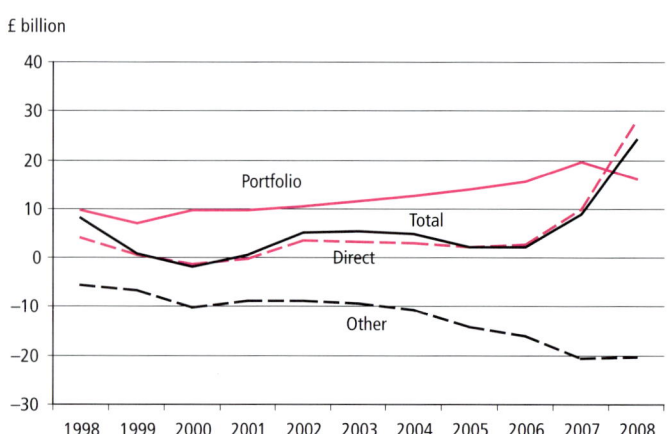

Sectoral breakdown of investment income

UK monetary financial institutions remain the single biggest investing sector, earning 53 per cent of total UK investment income credits and paying out 49 per cent of debits in 2008. Monetary financial institutions have earned an investment income surplus in every year since 2001, reaching a record £24.2 billion in the latest period. When considering the sector's overall contribution to the UK's balance of payments, it is important to also include monetary financial institutions' financial service fees and commissions, spread earnings and FISIM (Financial Intermediation Services Indirectly Measured) earned from foreign clients – a net £29.6 billion in 2008. Central government recorded a net annual deficit of around £3 billion to £5 billion from 1992 to 2005. More recently, this deficit has risen to £9.8 billion and continues to be mainly attributable to debits on gilts. Other sectors, predominantly private non-financial corporations and non-monetary financial institutions, have historically recorded net surpluses. In 2005, these other sectors recorded a record surplus of £24.3 billion, though this dropped back to a surplus of £12.9 billion in 2008. This was largely due to strong net earnings on direct investment by UK private non-financial corporations, which peaked in 2005.

4.1 Income
Summary table

£ million

		1998	1999	2000	2001	2002	2003	2004	2005	2006	2007	2008
Credits												
Compensation of employees	KTMN	840	960	1 032	1 087	1 121	1 116	931	974	938	981	1 032
Investment income												
Earnings on direct investment abroad	HJYW	29 919	33 144	45 042	46 741	51 473	55 093	63 292	79 192	83 573	90 250	69 169
Earnings on portfolio investment abroad												
Earnings on equity securities	HCPL	6 061	7 773	9 872	9 861	10 530	10 385	11 186	13 254	16 964	20 616	20 079
Earnings on debt securities	HLYW	23 237	18 095	23 101	25 021	21 954	22 165	25 522	32 125	38 158	45 502	48 025
Total portfolio investment	HLYX	29 298	25 868	32 973	34 882	32 484	32 550	36 708	45 379	55 122	66 118	68 104
Earnings on other investment abroad	AIOP	42 202	40 560	52 902	54 863	35 766	33 635	36 675	60 536	97 344	133 343	124 621
Earnings on reserve assets	HHCB	1 132	1 161	985	961	820	791	705	659	645	610	777
Total investment income	HMBN	102 551	100 733	131 902	137 447	120 543	122 069	137 380	185 766	236 684	290 321	262 671
Total	HMBQ	**103 391**	**101 693**	**132 934**	**138 534**	**121 664**	**123 185**	**138 311**	**186 740**	**237 622**	**291 302**	**263 703**
Debits												
Compensation of employees	KTMO	850	759	882	1 021	1 054	1 057	1 425	1 584	1 896	1 715	1 738
Investment income												
Foreign earnings on direct investment in the UK	HJYX	8 585	17 003	27 435	21 437	16 016	21 919	27 620	36 154	51 620	44 826	10 638
Foreign earnings on portfolio investment in the UK												
Earnings on equity securities	ZMRB	9 930	14 687	11 354	14 865	15 351	15 011	16 396	18 440	21 698	22 966	25 576
Earnings on debt securities	HLZB	19 526	17 538	21 086	21 239	17 956	17 892	22 308	29 151	35 865	43 545	47 733
Total portfolio investment	HLZC	29 456	32 225	32 440	36 104	33 307	32 903	38 704	47 591	57 563	66 511	73 309
Earnings on other investment in the UK	HLZN	52 697	52 749	70 215	70 547	53 001	49 783	52 717	79 556	116 970	157 475	151 078
Total investment income	HMBO	90 738	101 977	130 090	128 088	102 324	104 605	119 041	163 301	226 153	268 812	235 025
Total	HMBR	**91 588**	**102 736**	**130 972**	**129 109**	**103 378**	**105 662**	**120 466**	**164 885**	**228 049**	**270 527**	**236 763**
Balances (Net earnings)												
Compensation of employees	KTMP	−10	201	150	66	67	59	−494	−610	−958	−734	−706
Investment income												
Direct investment	HJYE	21 334	16 141	17 607	25 304	35 457	33 174	35 672	43 038	31 953	45 424	58 531
Portfolio investment												
Earnings on equity securities	HLZO	−3 869	−6 914	−1 482	−5 004	−4 821	−4 626	−5 210	−5 186	−4 734	−2 350	−5 497
Earnings on debt securities	HLZP	3 711	557	2 015	3 782	3 998	4 273	3 214	2 974	2 293	1 957	292
Total portfolio investment	HLZX	−158	−6 357	533	−1 222	−823	−353	−1 996	−2 212	−2 441	−393	−5 205
Other investment	CGNA	−10 495	−12 189	−17 313	−15 684	−17 235	−16 148	−16 042	−19 020	−19 626	−24 132	−26 457
Reserve assets	HHCB	1 132	1 161	985	961	820	791	705	659	645	610	777
Total investment income	HMBM	11 813	−1 244	1 812	9 359	18 219	17 464	18 339	22 465	10 531	21 509	27 646
Total	HMBP	**11 803**	**−1 043**	**1 962**	**9 425**	**18 286**	**17 523**	**17 845**	**21 855**	**9 573**	**20 775**	**26 940**

4.2 Investment income
Sector analysis

£ million

		1998	1999	2000	2001	2002	2003	2004	2005	2006	2007	2008
Credits (Earnings of UK residents on investment abroad)												
Monetary financial institutions												
Banks	CGNB	55 666	51 681	68 723	71 021	53 145	52 216	56 335	79 798	113 787	150 520	139 722
Building societies	GJXE	134	176	292	333	337	276	281	325	426	555	731
Total monetary financial institutions	CGND	55 800	51 857	69 015	71 354	53 482	52 492	56 616	80 123	114 213	151 075	140 453
Central government	CGNY	1 267	1 165	989	965	823	795	707	669	654	620	786
Public corporations	CGNP	410	329	364	438	371	389	900	1 440	712	872	414
Other sectors	CGNW	45 074	47 382	61 534	64 690	65 867	68 393	79 157	103 534	121 105	137 754	121 018
Total	HMBN	**102 551**	**100 733**	**131 902**	**137 447**	**120 543**	**122 069**	**137 380**	**185 766**	**236 684**	**290 321**	**262 671**
Debits (Foreign earnings on investment in UK)												
Monetary financial institutions (banks and building societies)	CGPN	47 592	51 061	70 800	70 621	48 335	47 090	51 600	78 020	112 092	142 181	116 303
Central government	CGNZ	5 826	5 027	4 564	4 233	3 868	4 141	4 803	6 028	7 029	9 043	10 607
Local authorities	CGOB	16	12	7	4	2	–	–	–	–	–	–
Public corporations	CGOD	20	–	–	–	–	–	16	18	18	18	17
Other sectors	CGSE	37 284	45 877	54 719	53 230	50 119	53 374	62 622	79 235	107 014	117 570	108 098
Total	HMBO	**90 738**	**101 977**	**130 090**	**128 088**	**102 324**	**104 605**	**119 041**	**163 301**	**226 153**	**268 812**	**235 025**
Balances (Net earnings)												
Monetary financial institutions (banks and building societies)	CGSO	8 208	796	–1 785	733	5 147	5 402	5 016	2 103	2 121	8 894	24 150
Central government	CGOE	–4 559	–3 862	–3 575	–3 268	–3 045	–3 346	–4 096	–5 359	–6 375	–8 423	–9 821
Local authorities	-CGOB	–16	–12	–7	–4	–2	–	–	–	–	–	–
Public corporations	CGOF	390	329	364	438	371	389	884	1 422	694	854	397
Other sectors	CGTX	7 790	1 505	6 815	11 460	15 748	15 019	16 535	24 299	14 091	20 184	12 920
Total	HMBM	**11 813**	**–1 244**	**1 812**	**9 359**	**18 219**	**17 464**	**18 339**	**22 465**	**10 531**	**21 509**	**27 646**

4.3 Earnings on direct investment

£ million

		1998	1999	2000	2001	2002	2003	2004	2005	2006	2007	2008
Credits (Earnings of UK residents on direct investment abroad)												
Earnings on equity												
Dividends and distributed branch profits												
Dividends	CNZN	12 246	8 795	14 679	14 412	15 255	29 482	26 620	29 623	30 673	29 104	34 762
Distributed branch profits	HDNG	1 158	1 278	2 231	2 552	2 381	2 723	3 573	6 264	5 452	3 786	−946
Total dividends and distributed branch profits	HMAE	13 404	10 073	16 910	16 964	17 636	32 205	30 193	35 887	36 125	32 890	33 816
Reinvested earnings	-HDNY	14 071	21 392	25 178	27 220	32 209	21 456	31 076	43 555	47 878	58 879	36 091
Earnings on property investment	HHBW	89	264	358	433	380	399	439	453	488	528	606
Total earnings on equity	HMAK	27 564	31 729	42 446	44 617	50 225	54 060	61 708	79 895	84 491	92 297	70 513
Earnings on other capital [1]	HDNQ	2 355	1 415	2 596	2 124	1 248	1 033	1 584	−703	−918	−2 047	−1 344
Total	HJYW	29 919	33 144	45 042	46 741	51 473	55 093	63 292	79 192	83 573	90 250	69 169
Debits (Foreign earnings on direct investment in the UK)												
Earnings on equity												
Dividends and distributed branch profits												
Dividends	BCEA	6 945	8 198	9 472	14 418	7 638	8 170	10 461	14 918	15 292	17 489	16 395
Distributed branch profits	CYFD	−2 534	323	2 713	2 251	−1 079	56	1 995	2 659	6 338	−5 581	−29 528
Total dividends and distributed branch profits	HMAH	4 411	8 521	12 185	16 669	6 559	8 226	12 456	17 577	21 630	11 908	−13 133
Reinvested earnings	CYFV	1 522	4 607	10 788	−992	3 647	7 429	8 558	10 501	22 195	24 288	15 923
Earnings on property investment	HESG	259	1 167	1 258	1 398	1 507	1 614	1 663	1 796	1 901	2 228	2 545
Total earnings on equity	HMAG	6 192	14 295	24 231	17 075	11 713	17 269	22 677	29 874	45 726	38 424	5 335
Earnings on other capital [1]	CYFN	2 393	2 708	3 204	4 362	4 303	4 650	4 943	6 280	5 894	6 402	5 303
Total	HJYX	8 585	17 003	27 435	21 437	16 016	21 919	27 620	36 154	51 620	44 826	10 638
Balances (Net earnings)												
Earnings on equity												
Dividends and distributed branch profits												
Dividends	LTMA	5 301	597	5 207	−6	7 617	21 312	16 159	14 705	15 381	11 615	18 367
Distributed branch profits	LTMB	3 692	955	−482	301	3 460	2 667	1 578	3 605	−886	9 367	28 582
Total dividends and distributed branch profits	HHZA	8 993	1 552	4 725	295	11 077	23 979	17 737	18 310	14 495	20 982	46 949
Reinvested earnings	LTMC	12 549	16 785	14 390	28 212	28 562	14 027	22 518	33 054	25 683	34 591	20 168
Earnings on property investment	LTMD	−170	−903	−900	−965	−1 127	−1 215	−1 224	−1 343	−1 413	−1 700	−1 939
Total earnings on equity	HHYY	21 372	17 434	18 215	27 542	38 512	36 791	39 031	50 021	38 765	53 873	65 178
Earnings on other capital [1]	HMAM	−38	−1 293	−608	−2 238	−3 055	−3 617	−3 359	−6 983	−6 812	−8 449	−6 647
Total	HJYE	21 334	16 141	17 607	25 304	35 457	33 174	35 672	43 038	31 953	45 424	58 531

1 Earnings on other capital consists of interest accrued to/from direct investors from/to associated enterprises abroad.

4.4 Earnings on direct investment
Sector analysis

£ million

		1998	1999	2000	2001	2002	2003	2004	2005	2006	2007	2008
Credits (Earnings of UK residents on investment abroad)												
Monetary financial institutions (banks)	HCVU	1 682	2 613	3 639	4 596	4 464	5 700	5 806	8 036	8 920	8 010	21
Insurance companies	CNZD	793	1 488	930	790	628	2 326	3 556	4 385	4 338	5 010	−449
Other financial intermediaries	HCWW	2 209	2 990	3 017	2 924	3 232	4 293	5 097	6 883	7 375	8 080	5 722
Private non-financial corporations	HCUS	25 136	25 944	37 335	38 269	42 949	42 499	48 448	59 465	62 405	68 189	63 435
Public corporations	HDMG	14	17	17	40	54	87	153	153	219	609	52
Household sector [1]	HHLI	85	92	104	122	146	188	232	270	316	352	388
Total	HJYW	29 919	33 144	45 042	46 741	51 473	55 093	63 292	79 192	83 573	90 250	69 169
Debits (Foreign earnings on direct investment in UK)												
Monetary financial institutions (banks)	GPAZ	−2 433	2 109	4 979	4 795	1 008	2 537	2 858	5 722	6 292	−2 031	−28 253
Insurance companies	HDPK	1 333	4	612	−955	179	898	1 844	2 241	3 544	2 525	2 169
Other financial intermediaries												
Securities dealers	HDQX	−643	1 124	1 495	1 272	1 337	449	1 600	1 489	1 224	3 772	−512
Other	HFBT	415	361	780	593	829	1 754	1 083	2 533	4 594	4 501	6 664
Total other financial intermediaries	HFCY	−228	1 485	2 275	1 865	2 166	2 203	2 683	4 022	5 818	8 273	6 152
Private non-financial corporations	BCEB	9 913	13 405	19 569	15 732	12 663	16 281	20 235	24 169	35 966	36 059	30 570
Total	HJYX	8 585	17 003	27 435	21 437	16 016	21 919	27 620	36 154	51 620	44 826	10 638
Balances (Net earnings)												
Monetary financial institutions (banks)	LTME	4 115	504	−1 340	−199	3 456	3 163	2 948	2 314	2 628	10 041	28 274
Insurance companies	LTMF	−540	1 484	318	1 745	449	1 428	1 712	2 144	794	2 485	−2 618
Other financial intermediaries	LTMG	2 437	1 505	742	1 059	1 066	2 090	2 414	2 861	1 557	−193	−430
Private non-financial corporations	LTMH	15 223	12 539	17 766	22 537	30 286	26 218	28 213	35 296	26 439	32 130	32 865
Public corporations	HDMG	14	17	17	40	54	87	153	153	219	609	52
Households	HHLI	85	92	104	122	146	188	232	270	316	352	388
Total	HJYE	21 334	16 141	17 607	25 304	35 457	33 174	35 672	43 038	31 953	45 424	58 531

1 The household sector includes non-profit institutions serving households.

4.5 Earnings on portfolio investment

£ million

		1998	1999	2000	2001	2002	2003	2004	2005	2006	2007	2008
Credits (Earnings of UK residents on portfolio investment abroad)												
Earnings on equity securities (shares) by:												
Monetary financial Institutions (banks)	HHRX	521	609	865	1 261	1 473	2 299	2 676	3 410	4 132	4 478	3 475
Central Government	LOEN	–	–	–	–	–	–	–	8	7	8	8
Insurance companies and pension funds												
Insurance companies	CGOM	1 715	1 939	2 237	2 289	2 455	2 075	2 194	2 430	2 997	3 365	4 409
Pension funds[1]	HPDL	2 023	2 132	1 861	1 543	1 598	1 456	1 790	2 428	2 827	2 923	3 139
Total insurance companies and pension funds	CGOX	3 738	4 071	4 098	3 832	4 053	3 531	3 984	4 858	5 824	6 288	7 548
Other financial intermediaries	CGOY	1 610	2 914	4 677	4 465	4 690	4 275	4 202	4 501	6 274	8 990	7 931
Private non-financial corporations	EGMS	9	10	41	124	127	110	126	135	166	189	241
Household sector[2]	HEOG	183	169	191	179	187	170	198	342	561	663	876
Total earnings on equity securities	HCPL	6 061	7 773	9 872	9 861	10 530	10 385	11 186	13 254	16 964	20 616	20 079
Earnings on debt securities												
Earnings on bonds and notes by:												
Monetary financial institutions												
Banks	HHRY	13 369	11 153	15 538	16 066	15 259	15 036	17 161	20 952	24 921	31 909	31 620
Building societies	GJXE	134	176	292	333	337	276	281	325	426	555	731
Total monetary financial institutions	HPCQ	13 503	11 329	15 830	16 399	15 596	15 312	17 442	21 277	25 347	32 464	32 351
Central Government	HF6Q	–	–	–	–	–	–	–	–	–	81	4
Insurance companies and pension funds												
Insurance companies	CGON	1 122	1 075	1 121	1 370	1 718	1 998	1 767	2 161	2 397	2 405	3 428
Pension funds[1]	HPDM	415	509	517	565	621	703	903	931	1 086	1 731	2 253
Total insurance companies and pension funds	CGOZ	1 537	1 584	1 638	1 935	2 339	2 701	2 670	3 092	3 483	4 136	5 681
Other financial intermediaries	CGPA	3 759	2 807	2 762	3 468	2 071	2 206	2 808	4 799	5 754	5 142	7 002
Private non-financial corporations	EGNF	61	54	43	108	111	117	210	206	167	120	171
Household sector[2]	HEOH	312	266	286	260	240	255	238	269	278	285	308
Total earnings on bonds and notes	HCPK	19 172	16 040	20 559	22 170	20 357	20 591	23 368	29 643	35 029	42 228	45 517
Earnings on money market instruments by:												
Monetary financial institutions (banks)	HBMX	3 933	1 908	2 292	2 569	1 233	984	1 451	1 665	1 937	2 001	1 873
Central government	LSPA	–	–	–	18	26	19	9	2	–	–	–
Other financial intermediaries	NHQV	49	73	131	118	130	205	249	319	464	563	296
Private non-financial corporations	HGBX	83	74	119	146	208	366	445	496	728	710	339
Total earnings on money market instruments	HCHG	4 065	2 055	2 542	2 851	1 597	1 574	2 154	2 482	3 129	3 274	2 508
Total earnings on debt securities	HLYW	23 237	18 095	23 101	25 021	21 954	22 165	25 522	32 125	38 158	45 502	48 025
Total	HLYX	**29 298**	**25 868**	**32 973**	**34 882**	**32 484**	**32 550**	**36 708**	**45 379**	**55 122**	**66 118**	**68 104**

1 The pension funds data only covers self-administered funds, see glossary.
2 The household sector includes non-profit institutions serving households.

4.5 Earnings on portfolio investment
continued

£ million

		1998	1999	2000	2001	2002	2003	2004	2005	2006	2007	2008
Debits (Foreign earnings on portfolio investment in the UK)												
Earnings on equity securities (shares) issued by:												
Monetary financial institutions (banks and building societies)	HBQJ	305	319	132	147	119	123	133	151	176	271	360
Other sectors[1]	HBQK	9 625	14 368	11 222	14 718	15 232	14 888	16 263	18 289	21 522	22 695	25 216
Total foreign earnings on UK equity securities	ZMRB	9 930	14 687	11 354	14 865	15 351	15 011	16 396	18 440	21 698	22 966	25 576
Earnings on debt securities												
Earnings on bonds and notes												
Issues by central government												
UK foreign currency bonds and notes	ZMRA	339	311	339	265	128	20	37	38	37	36	18
Earnings on British government stocks by:												
Foreign central banks (exchange reserves)	HESK	1 392	1 244	1 309	1 168	1 119	1 053	1 110	1 190	1 309	1 624	1 846
Other foreign residents	HCEV	4 014	3 418	2 899	2 710	2 530	2 990	3 489	4 614	5 478	7 102	8 318
Total foreign earnings on British government stocks	HENI	5 406	4 662	4 208	3 878	3 649	4 043	4 599	5 804	6 787	8 726	10 164
Total issues by central government	HBQU	5 745	4 973	4 547	4 143	3 777	4 063	4 636	5 842	6 824	8 762	10 182
Local authorities' bonds	HHGH	–	–	–	–	–	–	–	–	–	–	–
Public corporations' bonds	HESY	–	–	–	–	–	–	–	–	–	–	–
Issues by monetary financial institutions (banks and building societies)												
Bonds	HGUV	1 540	1 621	1 977	1 897	1 945	2 102	2 696	3 271	3 882	4 645	4 901
European medium term notes and other medium-term paper:												
Issued by UK banks	HCEY	1 071	1 035	1 138	1 350	1 418	1 788	2 587	3 417	4 409	5 845	7 006
Issued by UK building societies	HCFB	80	54	109	100	86	53	71	103	113	145	85
Total medium-term paper	HGMM	1 151	1 089	1 247	1 450	1 504	1 841	2 658	3 520	4 522	5 990	7 091
Total issues by monetary financial institutions	HBOT	2 691	2 710	3 224	3 347	3 449	3 943	5 354	6 791	8 404	10 635	11 992
Issues by other sectors[1]	HGUW	4 796	5 046	6 153	5 909	6 054	6 539	8 393	10 184	12 087	14 464	15 260
Total foreign earnings on UK bonds and notes	HLZA	13 232	12 729	13 924	13 399	13 280	14 545	18 383	22 817	27 315	33 861	37 434
Earnings on money market instruments												
Earnings on treasury bills (issued by central government)												
Sterling treasury bills	XAMR	49	38	3	13	20	24	120	144	153	281	425
Euro treasury bills	HHNV	18	3	–	–	–	–	–	–	–	–	–
Total earnings on treasury bills	HHZU	67	41	3	13	20	24	120	144	153	281	425
Earnings on certificates of deposit (Issued by monetary financial institutions)												
Issued by UK banks	HCEB	4 371	3 075	4 910	6 049	3 473	2 324	2 437	3 855	5 238	6 292	7 000
Issued by UK building societies	HGUY	19	21	35	20	17	40	70	60	66	120	134
Total earnings on certificates of deposit	HCEE	4 390	3 096	4 945	6 069	3 490	2 364	2 507	3 915	5 304	6 412	7 134
Earnings on commercial paper												
Issued by monetary financial institutions												
Issued by UK banks	HCEC	928	586	803	813	572	570	755	1 246	1 684	1 766	1 978
Issued by UK building societies	HHBC	51	100	161	110	36	42	86	197	370	393	108
Total earnings on mfi issued commercial paper	HCEF	979	686	964	923	608	612	841	1 443	2 054	2 159	2 086
Issued by other sectors[1]	HHZT	858	986	1 250	835	558	347	457	832	1 039	832	654
Total earnings on commercial paper	HHBO	1 837	1 672	2 214	1 758	1 166	959	1 298	2 275	3 093	2 991	2 740
Total foreign earnings on UK Money Market Instruments	HLYZ	6 294	4 809	7 162	7 840	4 676	3 347	3 925	6 334	8 550	9 684	10 299
Total foreign earnings on UK debt securities	HLZB	19 526	17 538	21 086	21 239	17 956	17 892	22 308	29 151	35 865	43 545	47 733
Total	HLZC	**29 456**	**32 225**	**32 440**	**36 104**	**33 307**	**32 903**	**38 704**	**47 591**	**57 563**	**66 511**	**73 309**

1 These series relate to non-governmental sectors other than monetary financial institutions.

4.5 Earnings on portfolio investment
continued

£ million

		1998	1999	2000	2001	2002	2003	2004	2005	2006	2007	2008
Balances (net earnings)												
Earnings on equity securities (shares)	HLZO	−3 869	−6 914	−1 482	−5 004	−4 821	−4 626	−5 210	−5 186	−4 734	−2 350	−5 497
Earnings on debt securities												
Earnings on bonds and notes	HLZQ	5 940	3 311	6 635	8 771	7 077	6 046	4 985	6 826	7 714	8 367	8 083
Earnings on money market instruments	HLZR	−2 229	−2 754	−4 620	−4 989	−3 079	−1 773	−1 771	−3 852	−5 421	−6 410	−7 791
Total earnings on debt securities	HLZP	3 711	557	2 015	3 782	3 998	4 273	3 214	2 974	2 293	1 957	292
Total	HLZX	**−158**	**−6 357**	**533**	**−1 222**	**−823**	**−353**	**−1 996**	**−2 212**	**−2 441**	**−393**	**−5 205**

1 These series relate to non-governmental sectors other than monetary financial institutions.

4.6 Earnings on portfolio investment
Sector analysis

£ million

		1998	1999	2000	2001	2002	2003	2004	2005	2006	2007	2008
Credits (Earnings of UK residents on portfolio investment abroad)												
Earnings from portfolio investment abroad by UK: Monetary financial institutions												
Banks	AINB	17 823	13 670	18 695	19 896	17 965	18 319	21 288	26 027	30 990	38 388	36 968
Building societies	GJXE	134	176	292	333	337	276	281	325	426	555	731
Total monetary financial institutions	AIND	17 957	13 846	18 987	20 229	18 302	18 595	21 569	26 352	31 416	38 943	37 699
Central government	LOEO	–	–	–	18	26	19	9	10	7	89	12
Insurance companies and pension funds	AINE	5 275	5 655	5 736	5 767	6 392	6 232	6 654	7 950	9 307	10 424	13 229
Other financial intermediaries	AINF	5 418	5 794	7 570	8 051	6 891	6 686	7 259	9 619	12 492	14 695	15 229
Private non-financial corporations	AINI	153	138	203	378	446	593	781	837	1 061	1 019	751
Household sector[1]	AINK	495	435	477	439	427	425	436	611	839	948	1 184
Total	HLYX	29 298	25 868	32 973	34 882	32 484	32 550	36 708	45 379	55 122	66 118	68 104
Debits (Foreign earnings on portfolio investment in the UK)												
Foreign earnings from portfolio investment in UK: Monetary financial institutions (banks and building societies)	HBXI	8 365	6 811	9 265	10 486	7 666	7 042	8 835	12 300	15 938	19 477	21 572
Central government	HBXM	5 812	5 014	4 550	4 156	3 797	4 087	4 756	5 986	6 977	9 043	10 607
Local authorities	HHGH	–	–	–	–	–	–	–	–	–	–	–
Public corporations	HESY	–	–	–	–	–	–	–	–	–	–	–
Other sectors	HBXR	15 279	20 400	18 625	21 462	21 844	21 774	25 113	29 305	34 648	37 991	41 130
Total	HLZC	29 456	32 225	32 440	36 104	33 307	32 903	38 704	47 591	57 563	66 511	73 309
Balances (Net earnings)												
Monetary financial institutions	LTMI	9 592	7 035	9 722	9 743	10 636	11 553	12 734	14 052	15 478	19 466	16 127
Central government	ZPOF	–5 812	–5 014	–4 550	–4 138	–3 771	–4 068	–4 747	–5 976	–6 970	–8 954	–10 595
Local authorities	-HHGH	–	–	–	–	–	–	–	–	–	–	–
Public corporations	-HESY	–	–	–	–	–	–	–	–	–	–	–
Other sectors	LTMJ	–3 938	–8 378	–4 639	–6 827	–7 688	–7 838	–9 983	–10 288	–10 949	–10 905	–10 737
Total	HLZX	–158	–6 357	533	–1 222	–823	–353	–1 996	–2 212	–2 441	–393	–5 205

1 The household sector includes non-profit institutions serving households.

4.7 Earnings on other investment

£ million

		1998	1999	2000	2001	2002	2003	2004	2005	2006	2007	2008
Credits (Earnings of UK residents on other investment abroad)												
Earnings on trade credit												
Central government	XBGJ	–	–	–	–	–	–	–	–	–	–	–
Other sectors[1]	HGQD	177	–	–	–	–	–	–	–	–	–	–
Total earnings on trade credit	AIOM	177	–	–	–	–	–	–	–	–	–	–
Earnings on loans												
Long-term												
Bank loans under ECGD guarantee	AINM	664	594	508	378	235	205	198	235	258	283	268
Inter-government loans by the UK	XBGI	9	4	4	4	3	4	2	2	2	2	1
Loans by Commonwealth Development Corporation (public corporations)	HGEN	123	115	101	74	74	74	74	74	74	74	74
Loans by the Export credit Guarantee Department	CY95	273	197	246	324	243	228	673	1 213	419	189	288
Loans by specialist leasing companies[1]	HBXC	–	–	–	–	–	–	–	–	–	–	–
Total long-term loans	AIOO	1 069	910	859	780	555	511	947	1 524	753	548	631
Short-term loans	VTUN	54	37	36	36	36	36	36	36	36	36	36
Total earnings on loans	CGKJ	1 123	947	895	816	591	547	983	1 560	789	584	667
Earnings on deposits												
By UK monetary financial institutions (banks)												
Sterling deposits	IFD7	6 538	6 183	7 159	6 380	4 833	5 034	7 162	8 260	10 714	21 576	22 932
Foreign currency deposits	IFD8	28 956	28 621	38 722	39 771	25 648	22 958	21 881	37 240	62 905	82 263	79 533
Total deposits by UK banks	IFD9	35 494	34 804	45 881	46 151	30 481	27 992	29 043	45 500	73 619	103 839	102 465
Deposits by securities dealers	HGTD	789	854	1 376	2 908	1 733	1 762	1 904	3 338	5 186	6 071	4 884
Deposits by other UK residents[1]	CGJK	4 141	3 567	4 202	4 499	2 636	3 029	4 416	9 805	17 402	22 494	16 294
Total earnings on deposits abroad	CGJQ	40 424	39 225	51 459	53 558	34 850	32 783	35 363	58 643	96 207	132 404	123 643
Earnings on other assets (Non-governmental sectors other than monetary financial institutions)												
Trusts and annuities	HHLF	352	388	548	489	325	305	329	333	348	355	311
Foreign currency exchanges	HHKX	–	–	–	–	–	–	–	–	–	–	–
Miscellaneous central government receipts	HPPK	126	–	–	–	–	–	–	–	–	–	–
Total earnings on other assets	CGKM	478	388	548	489	325	305	329	333	348	355	311
Total	AIOP	42 202	40 560	52 902	54 863	35 766	33 635	36 675	60 536	97 344	133 343	124 621

1 These series relate to non-governmental sectors other than monetary financial institutions.

4.7 Earnings on other investment
continued

£ million

		1998	1999	2000	2001	2002	2003	2004	2005	2006	2007	2008
Debits (Foreign earnings on other investment in the UK)												
Earnings on trade credit												
Public corporations	XBGW	–	–	–	–	–	–	–	–	–	–	–
Other sectors [1]	HHLW	140	–	–	–	–	–	–	–	–	–	–
Total earnings on trade credit	CGMA	140	–	–	–	–	–	–	–	–	–	–
Earnings on loans												
Loans to:												
Central government	CGLF	14	13	14	77	71	54	47	42	52	–	–
Local authorities	CGLG	16	12	7	4	2	–	–	–	–	–	–
Public corporations	CGLH	20	–	–	–	–	–	16	18	18	18	17
Securities dealers	CGLI	5 770	5 433	8 530	10 525	8 522	7 653	7 557	11 413	15 461	18 243	16 576
Other [1]	CGMD	3 874	4 017	4 074	3 477	3 549	3 322	4 089	6 983	10 534	13 704	10 692
Total earnings on loans	CGNO	9 694	9 475	12 625	14 083	12 144	11 029	11 709	18 456	26 065	31 965	27 285
Earnings on deposits (Monetary financial institutions)												
Deposits with UK banks[2]												
Sterling deposits	IFE2	8 445	8 550	10 209	10 333	8 439	8 711	11 407	12 991	15 548	28 676	32 750
Foreign currency deposits	IK6A	32 949	33 367	46 037	44 778	31 038	28 621	28 282	46 733	74 001	95 641	89 753
Total deposits with UK banks	IK6B	41 394	41 917	56 246	55 111	39 477	37 332	39 689	59 724	89 549	124 317	122 503
Deposits with UK building societies	HHLS	266	224	310	229	184	179	218	274	313	418	481
Total earnings on deposits	HMAS	41 660	42 141	56 556	55 340	39 661	37 511	39 907	59 998	89 862	124 735	122 984
Earnings on other liabilities (Non-governmental sectors other than monetary financial institutions)												
Imputed income to foreign households from UK insurance companies technical reserves	HBWS	1 203	1 133	1 034	1 124	1 196	1 243	1 101	1 102	1 043	775	809
Other liabilities	CGME	–	–	–	–	–	–	–	–	–	–	–
Total earnings on other liabilities	CGMH	1 203	1 133	1 034	1 124	1 196	1 243	1 101	1 102	1 043	775	809
Total	HLZN	52 697	52 749	70 215	70 547	53 001	49 783	52 717	79 556	116 970	157 475	151 078
Balances (Net earnings)												
Trade credit	LTMK	37	–	–	–	–	–	–	–	–	–	–
Loans	LTML	–8 571	–8 528	–11 730	–13 267	–11 553	–10 482	–10 726	–16 896	–25 276	–31 381	–26 618
Currency and deposits	LTMM	–1 236	–2 916	–5 097	–1 782	–4 811	–4 728	–4 544	–1 355	6 345	7 669	659
Other investment	LTMN	–725	–745	–486	–635	–871	–938	–772	–769	–695	–420	–498
Total	CGNA	–10 495	–12 189	–17 313	–15 684	–17 235	–16 148	–16 042	–19 020	–19 626	–24 132	–26 457

1 These series relate to non-governmental sectors other than monetary financial institutions.
2 UK banks' payments on non-resident deposits includes payments on loans received and repurchase agreements.

4.8 Earnings on other investment
Sector analysis

£ million

		1998	1999	2000	2001	2002	2003	2004	2005	2006	2007	2008
Credits												
(Earnings of UK residents on other investment abroad)												
Earnings from other investment by UK:												
Monetary financial institutions (banks)	CGMM	36 161	35 398	46 389	46 529	30 716	28 197	29 241	45 735	73 877	104 122	102 733
Central government	CGMN	135	4	4	4	3	4	2	2	2	2	1
Public corporations	ZPOP	396	312	347	398	317	302	747	1 287	493	263	362
Other sectors	CGMR	5 510	4 846	6 162	7 932	4 730	5 132	6 685	13 512	22 972	28 956	21 525
Total	AIOP	**42 202**	**40 560**	**52 902**	**54 863**	**35 766**	**33 635**	**36 675**	**60 536**	**97 344**	**133 343**	**124 621**
Debits												
(Foreign earnings on other investment in the UK)												
Foreign earnings from other investment in UK:												
Monetary financial institutions												
Banks	HCEQ	40 697	40 210	54 905	52 970	37 144	34 184	36 750	56 749	86 316	119 242	113 791
Building societies	HHLS	266	224	310	229	184	179	218	274	313	418	481
Total monetary financial institutions	HMAS	41 660	42 141	56 556	55 340	39 661	37 511	39 907	59 998	89 862	124 735	122 984
Central government	CGLF	14	13	14	77	71	54	47	42	52	–	–
Local authorities	CGLG	16	12	7	4	2	–	–	–	–	–	–
Public corporations	CGMV	20	–	–	–	–	–	16	18	18	18	17
Other sectors	CGMZ	10 987	10 583	13 638	15 126	13 267	12 218	12 747	19 498	27 038	32 722	28 077
Total	HLZN	**52 697**	**52 749**	**70 215**	**70 547**	**53 001**	**49 783**	**52 717**	**79 556**	**116 970**	**157 475**	**151 078**
Balances												
(Net earnings)												
Monetary financial institutions	LTMO	–5 499	–6 743	–10 167	–8 811	–8 945	–9 314	–10 666	–14 263	–15 985	–20 613	–20 251
Central government	LTMP	121	–9	–10	–73	–68	–50	–45	–40	–50	2	1
Local authorities	-CGLG	–16	–12	–7	–4	–2	–	–	–	–	–	–
Public corporations	LTMQ	376	312	347	398	317	302	731	1 269	475	245	345
Other sectors	LTMR	–5 477	–5 737	–7 476	–7 194	–8 537	–7 086	–6 062	–5 986	–4 066	–3 766	–6 552
Total	CGNA	**–10 495**	**–12 189**	**–17 313**	**–15 684**	**–17 235**	**–16 148**	**–16 042**	**–19 020**	**–19 626**	**–24 132**	**–26 457**

Current transfers

Chapter 5

Summary

The deficit for current transfers more than doubled between 1990 and 2000, growing from £4.8 billion in 1990 to £9.8 billion in 2000. After decreasing to £6.5 billion in 2001, the deficit increased again in each of the seven subsequent years, to £13.6 billion at the end of 2008 – the highest cash figure on record.

The deficit on general government transfers narrowed, from a deficit of £9.8 billion in 2007 to a deficit of £9.1 billion in 2008. Over the same period the deficit for other sectors increased from £3.8 billion in 2007 to £4.5 billion in 2008.

Figure 5.1
Current transfers

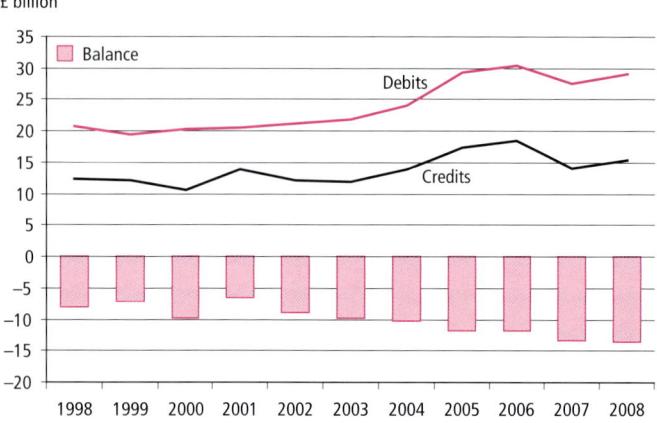

General government transfers

General government transfers include: taxes and social contributions received from non-resident workers and businesses; current transfers with international organisations (for example, EU Institutions); bilateral aid; social security payments abroad; military grants; and miscellaneous transfers. On the credits side, the total increased by £1.2 billion to £5.5 billion for 2008. Debits increased by £0.5 billion between 2007 and 2008 to £14.6 billion.

Figure 5.2
Transfers by general government

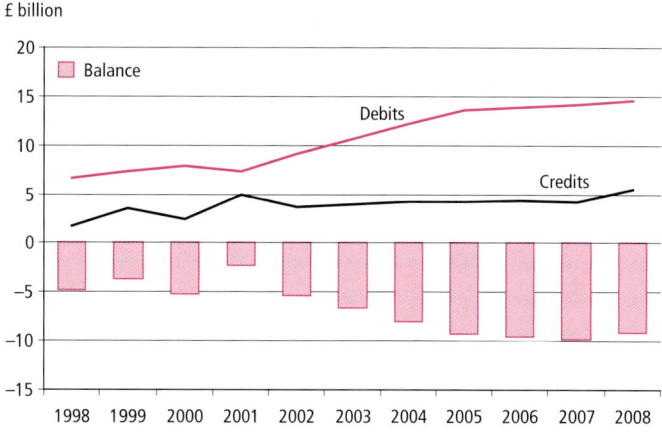

Other sector transfers

Non-government transfers include those EU transfers where the UK Government simply acts as the agent for the final beneficiary (for example, social fund and agricultural guidance fund receipts) or original payer (for example, VAT based contributions). Other sectors transfers also include: taxes on income and wealth paid by UK workers and outward direct investors to foreign governments; insurance premiums and claims; and other transfers (workers remittances, and other private transfers such as gifts). Other sectors credits rose by £0.2 billion between 2007 and 2008, while other sectors debits increased by £0.9 billion over the same period.

Figure 5.3
Transfers by other sectors

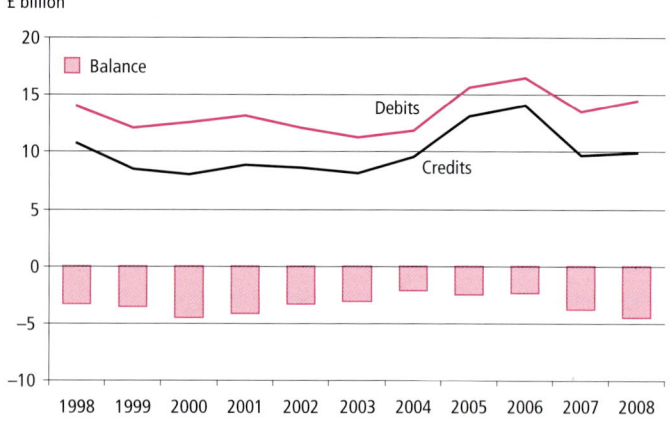

EU institutions

Transfers with EU institutions constitute the largest single component within current transfers. They showed a deficit in every year from 1986 to 2008; the lowest deficit recorded over the last ten years is £2.3 billion (in 2001) and the highest deficit £5.7 billion (in 2007). The deficit decreased by £0.9 billion between 2007 and 2008.

Figure 5.4
Transfers with other EU institutions

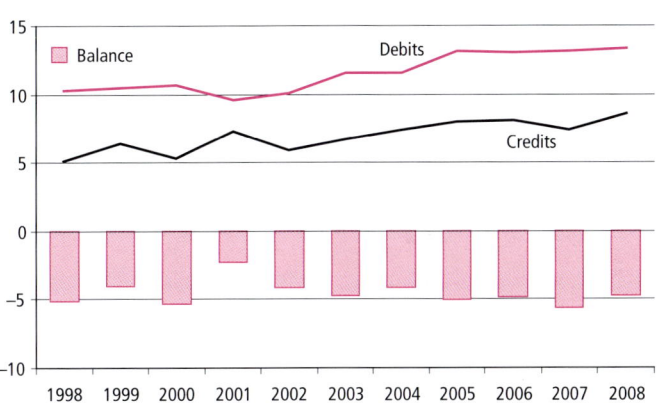

5.1 Current transfers

£ million

		1998	1999	2000	2001	2002	2003	2004	2005	2006	2007	2008
Credits												
General government												
Current taxes on income, wealth etc.	FJKI	354	337	357	398	527	375	482	546	681	608	585
Other taxes on production	FJKH	–	–	–	–	–	–	–	–	–	–	–
Other subsidies on production	FJBC	–	–	–	–	–	–	–	–	–	–	–
Social contributions	FJBH	29	29	24	25	24	23	22	22	28	31	40
Social benefits	FJBL	–	–	–	–	–	–	–	–	–	–	–
EU Institutions:												
(a) Abatement	FKKL	1 377	3 171	2 084	4 560	3 099	3 560	3 592	3 655	3 570	3 523	4 862
(b) Other EU receipts	FKIJ	7	5	–	8	13	10	81	71	104	153	25
Miscellaneous receipts	FKIK	–	–	–	–	–	–	–	–	–	–	–
Total general government	FJUM	1 767	3 542	2 465	4 991	3 663	3 968	4 177	4 294	4 383	4 315	5 512
Other sectors												
Current taxes on income, wealth etc.	FJBJ	–	–	–	–	–	–	–	–	–	–	–
Other taxes on production	FJGC	–	–	–	–	–	–	–	–	–	–	–
Other subsidies on production	FJBA	–	–	–	–	–	–	–	–	–	–	–
Social contributions	FJAB	70	60	31	34	53	21	14	–8	28	–5	28
EU Institutions:												
(a) Agricultural Guarantee Fund	EBGL	2 935	2 781	2 571	2 336	2 381	2 691	3 315	3 408	3 219	2 952	3 108
(b) Social Fund[1]	H5U2	783	434	659	370	412	427	364	842	1 225	751	583
(c) ECSC Grant	FJKP	1	–	–	1	–	–	2	–	–	–	–
Net non-life insurance premiums[2]	NQQP	4 253	2 495	2 086	3 471	3 008	2 208	3 181	6 133	6 831	3 320	3 590
Non-life insurance claims[3]	FJFA	7	10	18	25	19	19	47	16	39	50	44
Other receipts of households[4]	FKIL	2 633	2 730	2 653	2 689	2 698	2 713	2 667	2 715	2 748	2 663	2 557
Total other sectors	FJUN	10 682	8 510	8 018	8 926	8 571	8 079	9 590	13 106	14 090	9 731	9 910
Total	KTND	**12 449**	**12 052**	**10 483**	**13 917**	**12 234**	**12 047**	**13 767**	**17 400**	**18 473**	**14 046**	**15 422**
Of which: Receipts from EU institutions	FKIM	5 103	6 391	5 314	7 275	5 905	6 688	7 354	7 976	8 118	7 379	8 578

1 Social fund receipts by local government are included up to 2003. From 2004 they are included in general government other EU receipts.
2 Premiums paid to UK insurance companies.
3 Claims paid to UK residents by foreign insurance companies.
4 Includes estimates for workers' remittances and for non-profit institutions serving households.

5.1 Current transfers
continued

£ million

		1998	1999	2000	2001	2002	2003	2004	2005	2006	2007	2008
Debits												
General government												
Current taxes on income, wealth etc.	FJKK	–	–	–	–	–	–	–	–	–	–	–
Other taxes on production	FJKN	–	–	–	–	–	–	–	–	–	–	–
Other subsidies on production	FJCE	–	–	–	–	–	–	–	–	–	–	–
Social contributions	FJCH	–	–	–	–	–	–	–	–	–	–	–
Social security benefits	FJCK	1 162	1 183	1 218	1 292	1 388	1 452	1 596	1 650	1 728	1 834	1 998
Contributions to international organisations												
EU Institutions:												
(a) GNP: 4th Resource	HCSO	3 516	4 403	4 243	3 859	5 259	6 622	7 565	8 597	8 358	7 996	8 628
(b) GNP adjustments	HCSM	404	229	136	–1	76	150	–16	135	163	327	–205
(c) Inter governmental agreements	HCBW	–	–	–	–	–	–	–	–	–	–	–
(d) Other	FKIN	–1	11	6	24	10	18	–3	106	8	6	–
Other organisations:												
(a) Military	HDKF	139	118	157	195	192	152	160	141	159	139	165
(b) Multilateral economic assistance	HCHJ	314	245	503	434	539	367	622	495	945	1 102	1 025
(c) Other	HCKL	200	268	454	403	248	201	394	550	615	505	646
Bilateral aid:												
(a) Non-project grants	FJKT	142	133	175	185	206	268	303	306	300	349	372
(b) Technical cooperation	FJKU	692	651	859	904	1 038	1 320	1 474	1 497	1 467	1 699	1 818
Military grants	HDJO	17	30	27	45	129	107	130	160	138	130	159
Total general government	FJUO	6 585	7 271	7 778	7 340	9 085	10 657	12 225	13 637	13 881	14 087	14 606
Other sectors												
Current taxes on income, wealth etc.	FJCI	454	682	775	523	644	444	535	589	428	533	742
Other taxes on production	FJLB	–	–	–	–	–	–	–	–	–	–	–
Other subsidies on production	FJCC	–	–	–	–	–	–	–	–	–	–	–
Social contributions	FJBG	–	–	–	–	–	–	–	–	–	–	–
Social benefits	FJCM	70	60	31	34	53	21	14	–8	28	–5	28
EU Institutions:												
(a) Customs duties and agricultural levies	QYRD	2 076	2 024	2 086	2 069	1 919	1 937	2 145	2 237	2 329	2 412	2 636
(b) Sugar levies	GTBA	42	46	44	31	25	18	25	24	–	–	–
(c) VAT based contributions	HCML	3 758	3 920	4 104	3 624	2 720	2 775	1 764	1 980	2 165	2 293	2 255
(d) VAT adjustments	FSVL	470	–109	100	–49	88	–35	25	19	2	26	15
(e) ECSC Production levy	GTBB	–	–	–	–	–	–	–	–	–	–	–
Net non-life insurance premiums[1]	FJDB	7	10	18	25	19	19	47	16	39	50	44
Non-life insurance claims[2]	NQQR	4 253	2 495	2 086	3 471	3 008	2 208	3 181	6 133	6 831	3 320	3 590
Other payments by households[3]	FKIQ	2 906	2 975	3 236	3 364	3 543	3 838	4 082	4 622	4 655	4 868	5 116
Total other sectors	FJUP	14 036	12 103	12 480	13 092	12 019	11 225	11 818	15 612	16 477	13 497	14 426
Total	KTNE	**20 621**	**19 374**	**20 258**	**20 432**	**21 104**	**21 882**	**24 043**	**29 249**	**30 358**	**27 584**	**29 032**
Of which: Payments to EU institutions	FKIR	10 265	10 524	10 719	9 557	10 097	11 485	11 505	13 098	13 025	13 060	13 329

1 Premiums paid by UK residents to foreign insurance companies.
2 Claims paid by UK insurance companies to non-residents.
3 Includes estimates for workers' remittances and for non-profit institutions serving households.

5.1 Current transfers
continued

£ million

		1998	1999	2000	2001	2002	2003	2004	2005	2006	2007	2008
Balances												
General government												
Current taxes on income, wealth etc.	FJKJ	354	337	357	398	527	375	482	546	681	608	585
Other taxes on production	FJIZ	–	–	–	–	–	–	–	–	–	–	–
Other subsidies on production	FJBD	–	–	–	–	–	–	–	–	–	–	–
Social contributions	FJBI	29	29	24	25	24	23	22	22	28	31	40
Social benefits	FJBM	–1 162	–1 183	–1 218	–1 292	–1 388	–1 452	–1 596	–1 650	–1 728	–1 834	–1 998
Other current transfers	FJKW	–4 039	–2 912	–4 476	–1 480	–4 585	–5 635	–6 956	–8 261	–8 479	–8 577	–7 721
Total general government	FJUQ	–4 818	–3 729	–5 313	–2 349	–5 422	–6 689	–8 048	–9 343	–9 498	–9 772	–9 094
Other sectors												
Current taxes on income, wealth etc.	FJHU	–454	–682	–775	–523	–644	–444	–535	–589	–428	–533	–742
Other taxes on production	FJHT	–	–	–	–	–	–	–	–	–	–	–
Other subsidies on production	FJHV	–	–	–	–	–	–	–	–	–	–	–
Social contributions	FJHJ	70	60	31	34	53	21	14	–8	28	–5	28
Social benefits	FJJG	713	374	628	336	359	406	350	850	1 197	756	555
Other current transfers[1]	FJLT	–3 683	–3 345	–4 346	–4 013	–3 216	–3 129	–2 057	–2 759	–3 184	–3 984	–4 357
Total other sectors	FJUR	–3 354	–3 593	–4 462	–4 166	–3 448	–3 146	–2 228	–2 506	–2 387	–3 766	–4 516
Total	KTNF	**–8 172**	**–7 322**	**–9 775**	**–6 515**	**–8 870**	**–9 835**	**–10 276**	**–11 849**	**–11 885**	**–13 538**	**–13 610**
Of which: EU institutions	FKIS	–5 162	–4 133	–5 405	–2 282	–4 192	–4 797	–4 151	–5 122	–4 907	–5 681	–4 751

1 Includes an estimate for workers' remittances.

Capital account, financial account and international investment position

Part 2

Capital account

Chapter 6

Summary

The capital account has remained in surplus for over 20 years. A surplus of £3.4 billion was recorded in 2008, constituting the highest recorded cash surplus. The increase of £0.8 billion during the year followed the £1.6 billion increase during the previous year, which was mainly due to a fall in other sectors debt forgiveness debits following large scale debt relief to Nigeria in 2005 and 2006.

Figure 6.1
Capital account

6.1 Capital account

£ million

		1998	1999	2000	2001	2002	2003	2004	2005	2006	2007	2008
Credits												
Capital transfers												
General government												
Debt forgiveness	FJUU	–	–	–	–	–	–	–	–	–	–	–
Other capital transfers	FJLY	–	–	–	–	–	–	–	–	–	–	–
Total general government	FJMD	–	–	–	–	–	–	–	–	–	–	–
Other sectors												
Migrants' transfers	FJMG	967	1 144	1 371	2 267	1 864	1 951	2 298	2 491	2 725	2 953	3 200
Debt forgiveness	FJNC	–	–	–	–	–	–	–	–	–	–	–
Other capital transfers												
EU Institutions:												
Regional development fund	FKIT	357	285	989	543	296	622	1 062	1 402	618	707	972
Agricultural fund for regional development[1]	FJXL	56	47	82	26	–	2	49	80	50	150	417
Other capital transfers	EBGO	43	–	–	322	–	–	–	–	–	–	–
Total EU institutions	FKIV	456	332	1 071	891	296	624	1 111	1 482	668	857	1 389
Total other sectors	FJMU	1 423	1 476	2 442	3 158	2 160	2 575	3 409	3 973	3 393	3 810	4 589
Total capital transfers	FJMX	1 423	1 476	2 442	3 158	2 160	2 575	3 409	3 973	3 393	3 810	4 589
Sales of non-produced, non-financial assets	FJUX	89	152	165	177	172	218	193	337	631	783	1 001
Total	FKMH	**1 512**	**1 628**	**2 607**	**3 335**	**2 332**	**2 793**	**3 602**	**4 310**	**4 024**	**4 593**	**5 590**
Debits												
Capital transfers												
General government												
Debt forgiveness	FJUV	146	22	22	18	15	16	13	16	13	11	73
Other capital transfers (project grants)	FJMB	182	171	225	237	263	345	389	396	388	449	480
Total general government	FJME	328	193	247	255	278	361	402	412	401	460	553
Other sectors												
Migrants' transfers	FJMH	531	499	461	1 300	582	547	515	551	669	697	744
Debt forgiveness												
Monetary financial institutions[2]	FJNF	–	–	–	–	–	–	–	–	–	–	–
Public corporations[3]	HMLY	27	49	55	188	236	130	109	1 249	1 356	76	–
Total debt forgiveness	IZZZ	27	49	55	188	236	130	109	1 249	1 356	76	–
Other capital transfers	FJMS	–	–	–	–	–	–	–	–	–	–	–
Total other sectors	FJMV	558	548	516	1 488	818	677	624	1 800	2 025	773	744
Total capital transfers	FJMY	886	741	763	1 743	1 096	1 038	1 026	2 212	2 426	1 233	1 297
Purchases of non-produced, non-financial assets	FJUY	137	140	141	274	304	289	512	595	623	794	900
Total	FKMI	**1 023**	**881**	**904**	**2 017**	**1 400**	**1 327**	**1 538**	**2 807**	**3 049**	**2 027**	**2 197**
Balances												
Capital transfers												
General government												
Debt forgiveness	FJUW	−146	−22	−22	−18	−15	−16	−13	−16	−13	−11	−73
Other capital transfers	FJMC	−182	−171	−225	−237	−263	−345	−389	−396	−388	−449	−480
Total general government	FJMF	−328	−193	−247	−255	−278	−361	−402	−412	−401	−460	−553
Other sectors												
Migrants' transfers	FJMI	436	645	910	967	1 282	1 404	1 783	1 940	2 056	2 256	2 456
Debt forgiveness	FJNG	−27	−49	−55	−188	−236	−130	−109	−1 249	−1 356	−76	–
Other capital transfers	FJMT	456	332	1 071	891	296	624	1 111	1 482	668	857	1 389
Total other sectors	FJMW	865	928	1 926	1 670	1 342	1 898	2 785	2 173	1 368	3 037	3 845
Total capital transfers	FJMZ	537	735	1 679	1 415	1 064	1 537	2 383	1 761	967	2 577	3 292
Non-produced, non-financial assets	NHSG	−48	12	24	−97	−132	−71	−319	−258	8	−11	101
Total	FKMJ	**489**	**747**	**1 703**	**1 318**	**932**	**1 466**	**2 064**	**1 503**	**975**	**2 566**	**3 393**

1 Up to 2006 this series includes the European Agricultural Guidance Fund.
2 This series also appears in the Financial Account (see Table 7.7).
3 This series also appears in the Financial Account (see Table 7.7) as series HMLW.

Financial account

Chapter 7

Summary

Investment abroad and into the UK both increased dramatically from the mid-1990s, reflecting the increased globalisation of the world economy. Between 2000 and 2007, other investment dominated cross-border investment, primarily banking activity. In 2008 however, other investment, both abroad and in the UK, has recorded net disinvestment as the global financial crisis deepened leading to a reduction in loans internationally and a repatriation of deposits. In recent years, including the latest, the UK has needed to borrow from abroad to finance a continuing current account deficit, which has resulted in inward investment (UK liabilities) exceeding outward investment (UK assets).

In 2005 and 2006, direct investment in the UK exceeded direct investment abroad for the first time since 1990. However in 2007 and 2008, once again direct investment abroad exceeded direct investment in the UK. In 2007 this was driven by strong growth in equity capital and other capital transactions. In 2008, negative growth in UK direct investment abroad was

Figure 7.1
Financial account

£ billion

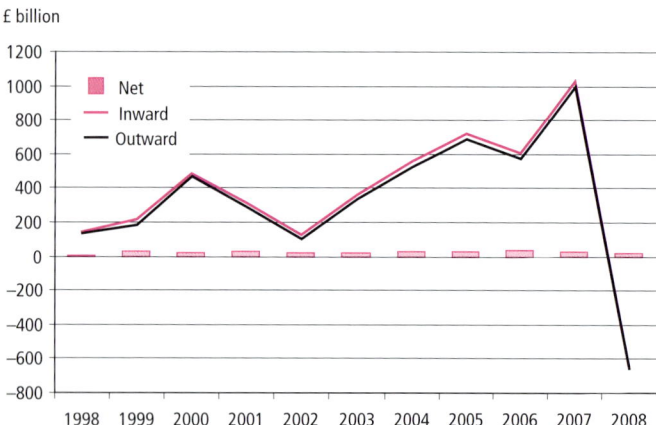

Figure 7.2
UK investment abroad

£ billion

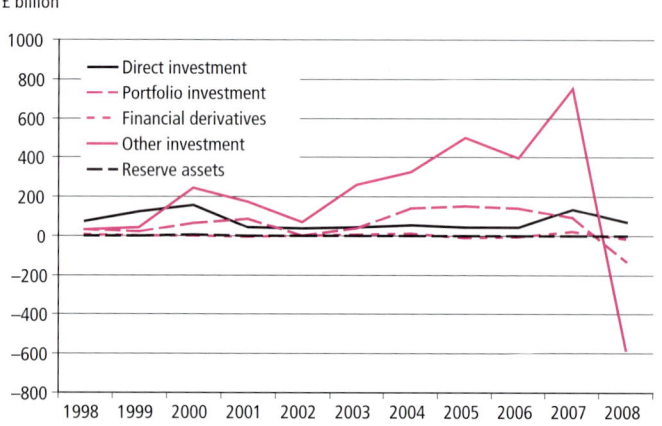

Figure 7.3
Foreign investment in the UK

£ billion

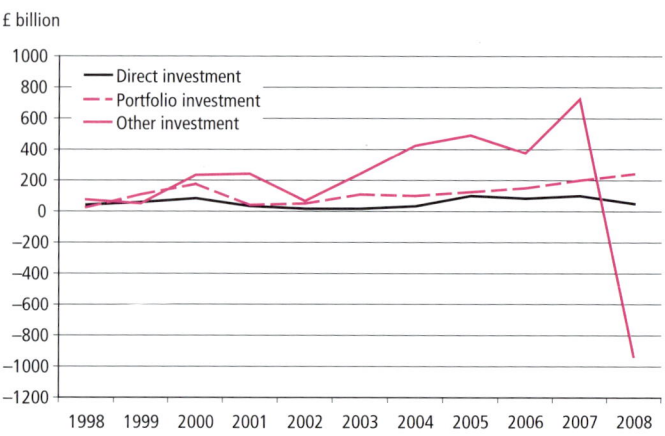

offset by negative growth in direct investment in the UK to maintain the UK's position as a net outward direct investor. Higher negative growth rates in equity capital invested abroad resulted in reinvested earnings being the single largest contributor to outward direct investment in 2008.

Historically, portfolio investment tended to record net investment abroad although the pattern over the past decade has seen more frequent positions of net inward than net outward portfolio investment. The reasons for these recent periods of net inward investment are varied. In 1999 and 2000 high investment in UK equity resulted from substantial UK direct investment acquisitions in foreign telecom and pharmaceutical companies, which were funded by the issue of UK shares to foreign shareholders; this is recorded as portfolio investment in the UK. In 2006 and 2007, due to the UK's relatively high interest rate, the attractiveness of UK debt securities to foreign investors led to net inward portfolio investment in the UK. In 2008, this position was maintained as the acceleration of the global financial crisis drove up demand for less risky long-term debt securities, even though interest rates had dropped considerably in the UK, while UK equity offered greater value for money to international investors as sterling depreciated.

Other investment is the largest and most volatile form of investment. The amounts recorded in the gross flows of loans and deposits are as much a consequence of how the transaction is carried out between resident and non-resident banks, as overall market conditions. However in 2008, the considerable deterioration of other investment, both abroad and in the UK, was a response to the global financial crisis which led to a loss of confidence, deposits being repatriated and credit markets tightened.

The financial account in 2008 recorded a net inflow of £18.1 billion compared with a net inflow of £31.7 billion in 2007. UK investment abroad declined considerably in 2008, actually recording a record net disinvestment abroad of £655.2 billion - this was following record net investment of £995.7 billion in 2007. Investment in the UK also recorded a considerable retraction with record net disinvestment in the UK of £637.1 billion following net investment of £1,027.4 billion in 2007. The net disinvestment abroad in 2008 was driven by other investment and portfolio investment which was only partially offset by direct investment. In the same period, net disinvestment in the UK was due to net disinvestment in other investment, partially offset by direct and portfolio investment.

Direct investment

Outward direct investment peaked at £155.6 billion in 2000, reflecting booming merger and acquisition activity – the largest outward acquisitions were the investment in Mannesmann AG by Vodafone Airtouch for a reported £100 billion and the purchase of Atlantic Richfield Company by BP Amoco Plc for a reported £18 billion. Overall outward direct investment then declined to £35.0 billion in 2002. Since 2004, outward merger and acquisition activity increased, with 441 acquisitions and 104 disposals recorded in 2007; outward direct investment increased to £136.1 billion. In 2008, as a result of the global recession, direct investment abroad decreased to £72.5 billion. This was due to lower investment in equity capital and lower reinvested earnings whilst other capital transactions remained relatively stable. During this period, the number of outward mergers and acquisitions declined to 298 and disposals fell to 71. Significant transactions reported in 2008 included the acquisition of Altadis S.A. by Imperial Tobacco Group Plc for £9.3 billion and Choicepoint Inc by Reed Elsevier Group Plc for £1.8 billion, and the disposal of seven French regional banks by HSBC Holdings Plc for £1.7 billion. These transactions are reflected in the equity capital component of direct investment abroad. However, the major component of outward investment in 2008 was reinvested earnings.

Until 2004, inward direct investment showed a pattern similar to outward investment, with record direct investment in the UK of £80.6 billion in 2000, followed by lower levels of investment due to the slowdown in global merger and acquisition activity. From then on, there was a considerable increase in the amount of inward acquisitions, including the purchase of Abbey National by Banco Santander in 2004, the Shell restructuring in 2005 and the purchase of Alliance Boots Plc by AB Acquisitions Ltd in 2007. The latter being one of a number of inward acquisitions behind the record in inward direct investment in 2007 of £98.2 billion. In 2008 investment in the UK dropped considerably to £52.5 billion due to lower investment in equity capital together with lower reinvested earnings, which were slightly offset by lower net disinvestment in other capital. Some of the most significant acquisitions in 2008 included Reuters Group Plc by The Thomson Corporation for £8.5 billion and Imperial Chemical Industries Plc by Akzo Nobel N.V. for £8.1 billion.

Figure **7.4**

Direct investment

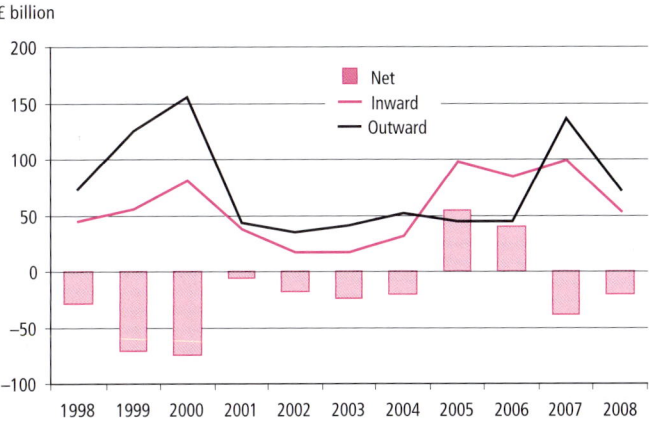

Portfolio investment

Generally investment in foreign debt has exceeded investment in foreign equities. Portfolio investment abroad showed net investment in every year from 1995 to 2007, reaching £92.0 billion in 2007 after peaking at £151.0 billion in 2005. In 2008 however, portfolio investment abroad showed net disinvestment of £128.6 billion. There was net disinvestment of £60.8 billion in equity securities and net disinvestment of £67.8 billion in debt securities. The switch from net investment to net disinvestment for equity securities was mainly due to disinvestment by UK banks and pension funds, while the switch for debt securities was almost entirely due to UK banks. Prior to 2008, net disposals of foreign equity securities occurred in years coinciding with financial shocks: the UK's exit from the Exchange Rate Mechanism in 1992, the South-East Asia crisis in 1997, and the collapse in equity markets in 2002. The net disposal of equity securities in 2008 is the highest on record. Net disinvestment of debt securities has not happened since 1994 and is also the largest on record.

Portfolio investment in the UK has shown net investment in every year for which data are available. In the early 1990s, the majority of inward investment was in bonds and notes. This switched to UK-issued equity in the late 1990s as the counterpart to the outward direct investment occurring then. Since 2002, there has been strong net investment in UK debt securities. The attractiveness of UK debt to foreign investors may have reflected higher interest rates in the UK compared to other major economies, and a switch from dollar to sterling-issued debt due to the fall in the value of the dollar during this period. In 2008 exchange rates with the dollar, euro and yen declined rapidly, as did interest rates in the UK, yet portfolio investment in the UK remained buoyant. In 2008 portfolio investment in the UK was a record £240.6 billion which was driven by investors purchasing long-term debt securities. Investment in debt securities was a record £196.5 billion which was due to the growth of investment in government stocks and in non-government bonds and notes other than those issued by monetary financial institutions. Money market instruments recorded net disinvestment of £16.1 billion in 2008. Equity securities also performed strongly growing by over two-and-a-half times between 2007 and 2008. This was due in part to equity securities in the UK representing improved value for money to the international investor as sterling depreciated against other major currencies.

Figure 7.5
Portfolio investment

£ billion

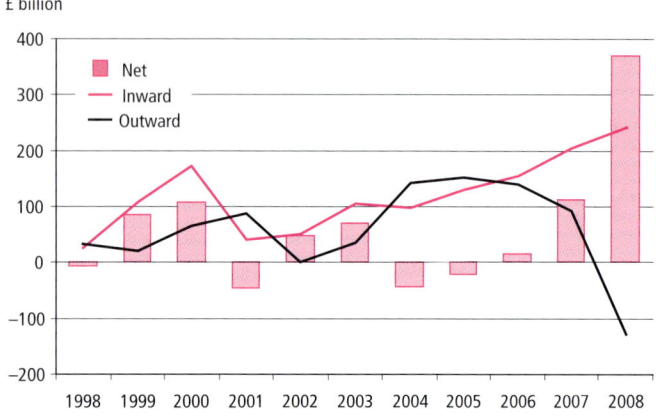

Figure 7.6
Other investment

£ billion

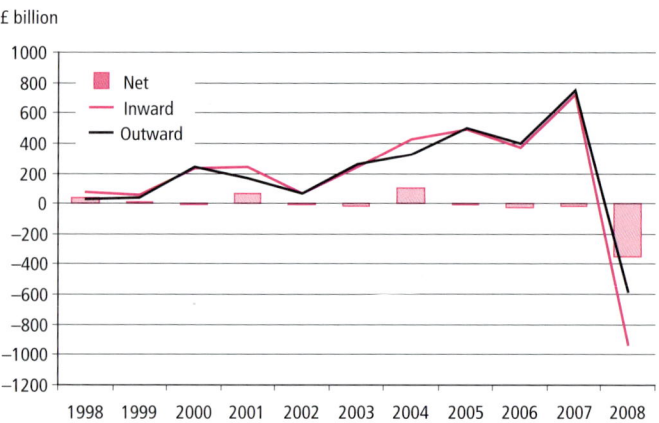

Sectoral breakdown of the financial account

In 2008, UK banks reported net outward investment of £57.3 billion, the third year out of the last four when the UK banks had recorded net outward investment – from 1999 to 2004, UK banks reported six consecutive years of net inward investment. The net outward investment of UK banks in 2008 was mostly due to other investment, mainly net withdrawals of deposits from UK banks, more than offsetting net inward investment in portfolio investment. Central government reported net inward investment of £59.1 billion in 2008, generated mainly from bonds and notes as part of portfolio investment. Other UK sectors showed net inward investment of £15.6 billion due once again to a large increase in transactions in bonds and notes as part of portfolio investment.

Other investment

In recent years, other investment has shown net investment both abroad and in the UK. Loans and deposits by UK banks constitute the major component of other investment. Loans and deposits by UK banks are carried out predominantly in foreign currency, so will be partly influenced by relative exchange rates and interest rates as well as the global financial conditions generally. In 2008, due to the tightening of credit driven by the escalation of the financial crisis, other investment abroad showed record net disinvestment of £580.0 billion, the first net disinvestment since 1991. The switch was driven by banks receiving net repayments on loans abroad together with banks and securities dealers making net withdrawals from deposits abroad.

Other investment in the UK showed record net disinvestment of £930.1 billion in 2008, following net investment of £725.9 billion in 2007. The disinvestment was driven by net repayments by securities dealers of short-term loans and net withdrawals of deposits from banks in the UK.

7.1 Financial account
Summary table

£ million

		1998	1999	2000	2001	2002	2003	2004	2005	2006	2007	2008
UK investment abroad (UK assets = net debits)												
Direct investment abroad												
Equity capital	-HJYM	47 640	101 897	147 679	16 890	26 155	20 639	19 896	15 612	26 819	62 864	23 405
Reinvested earnings	-HDNY	14 071	21 392	25 178	27 220	32 209	21 456	31 076	43 555	47 878	58 879	36 091
Other capital transactions	-HMAB	12 075	2 313	−17 275	−1 283	−23 323	−1 206	538	−15 162	−29 699	14 387	13 032
Total direct investment abroad	-HJYP	73 786	125 602	155 582	42 827	35 041	40 889	51 510	44 005	44 998	136 130	72 528
Portfolio investment abroad												
Equity securities	-HBVI	2 713	14 455	20 521	44 464	−3 189	19 684	56 647	61 323	19 597	28 201	−60 774
Debt securities	-XBMW	29 359	6 934	45 042	42 089	4 199	16 584	84 367	89 632	119 241	63 819	−67 846
Total portfolio investment abroad	-HHZC	32 072	21 389	65 563	86 553	1 010	36 268	141 014	150 955	138 838	92 020	−128 620
Financial derivatives (net)	-ZPNN	3 043	−2 685	−1 553	−8 417	−1 001	5 401	7 875	−9 556	−7 449	19 001	−17 746
Other investment abroad	-XBMM	29 992	41 545	241 666	170 663	70 375	260 401	325 220	501 260	395 898	747 335	−580 028
Reserve assets	-LTCV	−164	−639	3 915	−3 085	−459	−1 559	196	656	−426	1 191	−1 338
Total	-HBNR	**138 729**	**185 212**	**465 173**	**288 541**	**104 966**	**341 400**	**525 815**	**687 320**	**571 859**	**995 677**	**−655 204**
Investment in the UK (UK liabilities = net credits)												
Direct investment in the UK												
Equity capital	HJYR	27 895	46 709	59 811	20 954	11 809	4 464	23 716	82 949	55 393	87 809	49 218
Reinvested earnings	CYFV	1 522	4 607	10 788	−992	3 647	7 429	8 558	10 501	22 195	24 288	15 923
Other capital transactions	HMAD	15 637	3 750	9 967	17 386	1 326	4 883	−1 066	4 395	7 301	−13 947	−12 680
Total direct investment in the UK	HJYU	45 054	55 066	80 566	37 348	16 782	16 776	31 208	97 845	84 889	98 150	52 461
Portfolio investment in the UK												
Equity securities	XBLW	41 935	64 309	121 302	15 730	1 903	20 088	1 957	6 379	−10 564	12 170	44 045
Debt securities	XBLX	−16 897	42 030	50 875	25 099	47 837	85 560	95 387	122 670	164 484	191 103	196 541
Total portfolio investment in the UK	HHZF	25 038	106 339	172 177	40 829	49 740	105 648	97 344	129 049	153 920	203 273	240 586
Other investment in the UK	XBMN	73 117	53 312	235 563	237 558	62 648	241 529	426 621	489 450	371 275	725 930	−930 130
Total	HBNS	**143 209**	**214 717**	**488 306**	**315 735**	**129 170**	**363 953**	**555 173**	**716 344**	**610 084**	**1 027 353**	**−637 083**
Net transactions (net credits less net debits)												
Direct investment												
Equity capital	HBWN	−19 745	−55 188	−87 868	4 064	−14 346	−16 175	3 820	67 337	28 574	24 945	25 813
Reinvested earnings	HBWT	−12 549	−16 785	−14 390	−28 212	−28 562	−14 027	−22 518	−33 054	−25 683	−34 591	−20 168
Other capital transactions	HBWU	3 562	1 437	27 242	18 669	24 649	6 089	−1 604	19 557	37 000	−28 334	−25 712
Total net direct investment	HJYV	−28 732	−70 536	−75 016	−5 479	−18 259	−24 113	−20 302	53 840	39 891	−37 980	−20 067
Portfolio investment												
Equity securities	HBWV	39 222	49 854	100 781	−28 734	5 092	404	−54 690	−54 944	−30 161	−16 031	104 819
Debt securities	HBWX	−46 256	35 096	5 833	−16 990	43 638	68 976	11 020	33 038	45 243	127 284	264 387
Total net portfolio investment	HHZD	−7 034	84 950	106 614	−45 724	48 730	69 380	−43 670	−21 906	15 082	111 253	369 206
Financial derivatives	ZPNN	−3 043	2 685	1 553	8 417	1 001	−5 401	−7 875	9 556	7 449	−19 001	17 746
Other investment	HHYR	43 125	11 767	−6 103	66 895	−7 727	−18 872	101 401	−11 810	−24 623	−21 405	−350 102
Reserve assets	LTCV	164	639	−3 915	3 085	459	1 559	−196	−656	426	−1 191	1 338
Total	HBNT	**4 480**	**29 505**	**23 133**	**27 194**	**24 204**	**22 553**	**29 358**	**29 024**	**38 225**	**31 676**	**18 121**

7.2 Financial account
Sector analysis

£ million

		1998	1999	2000	2001	2002	2003	2004	2005	2006	2007	2008
UK investment abroad (UK assets = net debits)												
By:												
Monetary financial institutions												
Banks	-HFAM	82 060	6 654	224 924	123 916	59 677	181 513	326 315	396 393	427 338	690 726	−521 222
Building societies	HEQN	1 334	949	4 382	1 476	−903	−1 786	868	−2 230	2 649	2 969	−561
Total monetary financial institutions	-HFAQ	83 394	7 603	229 306	125 392	58 774	179 727	327 183	394 163	429 987	693 695	−521 783
Central government	-HFAN	−43	−250	4 228	−2 568	463	−2 217	1 103	1 588	630	4 698	2 005
Public corporations	-HFAO	−7	304	582	62	−164	−571	−370	−1 671	−4 694	−18	−315
Other sectors	-HFAP	55 385	177 555	231 057	165 655	45 893	164 461	197 899	293 240	145 936	297 302	−135 111
Total	-HBNR	**138 729**	**185 212**	**465 173**	**288 541**	**104 966**	**341 400**	**525 815**	**687 320**	**571 859**	**995 677**	**−655 204**
Investment in the UK (UK liabilities = net credits)												
In:												
Monetary financial institutions (banks and building societies)	CGUL	31 159	29 617	242 746	148 717	114 955	204 512	340 046	321 335	428 038	777 460	−579 092
Central government	HFAR	439	−4 434	−243	−97	−4 538	13 657	13 526	29 688	26 219	28 810	61 131
Local authorities	HFAS	−87	−106	−188	22	26	204	651	134	232	−42	361
Public corporations	HFAT	−5	–	–	–	–	–	283	−7	−12	−6	−9
Other sectors	GGCJ	111 703	189 640	245 991	167 093	18 727	145 580	200 667	365 194	155 607	221 131	−119 474
Total	HBNS	**143 209**	**214 717**	**488 306**	**315 735**	**129 170**	**363 953**	**555 173**	**716 344**	**610 084**	**1 027 353**	**−637 083**
Net transactions (net credits *less* net debits)												
In assets and liabilities of:												
Monetary financial institutions (banks and building societies)	GGCK	−52 235	22 014	13 440	23 325	56 181	24 785	12 863	−72 828	−1 949	83 765	−57 309
Central government	HFAV	482	−4 184	−4 471	2 471	−5 001	15 874	12 423	28 100	25 589	24 112	59 126
Local authorities	HFAS	−87	−106	−188	22	26	204	651	134	232	−42	361
Public corporations	HFAW	2	−304	−582	−62	164	571	653	1 664	4 682	12	306
Other sectors	GGCL	56 318	12 085	14 934	1 438	−27 166	−18 881	2 768	71 954	9 671	−76 171	15 637
Total	HBNT	**4 480**	**29 505**	**23 133**	**27 194**	**24 204**	**22 553**	**29 358**	**29 024**	**38 225**	**31 676**	**18 121**

7.3 Direct investment

£ million

		1998	1999	2000	2001	2002	2003	2004	2005	2006	2007	2008
Direct investment abroad												
(UK assets = net debits)												
Equity capital												
Claims on affiliated enterprises												
(net acquisition of ordinary shares)												
Purchases of ordinary shares	-HDOA	60 627	114 693	181 488	40 221	35 374	26 128	27 114	24 939	46 960	74 697	28 267
Sales of ordinary shares	-HDOC	–13 677	–13 620	–34 693	–25 073	–10 440	–8 479	–9 105	–10 691	–21 702	–13 944	–7 355
Total claims on affiliated enterprises	-HJYL	46 950	101 073	146 795	15 148	24 934	17 649	18 009	14 248	25 258	60 753	20 912
Net acquisition of property	-HHVG	690	824	884	1 742	1 221	2 990	1 887	1 364	1 561	2 111	2 493
Total equity capital	-HJYM	47 640	101 897	147 679	16 890	26 155	20 639	19 896	15 612	26 819	62 864	23 405
Reinvested earnings	-HDNY	14 071	21 392	25 178	27 220	32 209	21 456	31 076	43 555	47 878	58 879	36 091
Other capital transactions [1]												
Claims on affiliated enterprises												
Debt securities issued by affiliated enterprises												
Purchases of debt securities	-HDOD	396	636	952	2 263	513	1 598	1 902	2 260	2 060	3 691	3 261
Sales of debt securities	-HDOE	–315	–578	–496	–304	–1 080	–2 312	–608	–1 054	–2 795	–1 708	–1 873
Other claims on affiliated enterprises												
Change in inter-company accounts	-HDOF	20 721	15 806	15 110	5 072	17 140	10 178	18 531	17 765	–229	31 031	75 329
Change in branch indebtedness	-HDOI	1 493	–483	–3 360	5 153	–610	1 783	–472	–4 108	585	3 724	7 701
Total claims on affiliated enterprises	-HJYN	22 295	15 381	12 206	12 184	15 963	11 247	19 353	14 863	–379	36 738	84 418
Liabilities to affiliated enterprises												
Change in inter-company accounts	-HDOG	8 453	14 340	28 278	12 880	38 774	10 568	20 950	29 075	26 371	21 400	70 328
Change in branch indebtedness	-HDOJ	1 767	–1 272	1 203	587	512	1 885	–2 135	950	2 949	951	1 058
Total liabilities to affiliated enterprises	-HJYO	10 220	13 068	29 481	13 467	39 286	12 453	18 815	30 025	29 320	22 351	71 386
Total other capital transactions	-HMAB	12 075	2 313	–17 275	–1 283	–23 323	–1 206	538	–15 162	–29 699	14 387	13 032
Total	-HJYP	73 786	125 602	155 582	42 827	35 041	40 889	51 510	44 005	44 998	136 130	72 528
Direct investment in the UK												
(UK liabilities = net credits)												
Equity capital												
Liabilities to direct investors												
Quoted ordinary shares												
Purchases of quoted ordinary shares	CYFY	24 660	40 393	16 253	3 502	5 951	1 739	19 181	64 495	44 436	20 646	24 852
Sales of quoted ordinary shares	CYFZ	–4 336	–10 526	–2 038	–1 185	–775	–1 200	–	–540	–177	–629	–192
Unquoted ordinary shares												
Purchases of unquoted ordinary shares	CYGA	7 147	20 721	48 154	20 381	11 068	4 238	6 411	21 681	16 160	69 906	24 632
Sales of unquoted ordinary shares	CYGB	–274	–4 692	–4 187	–2 535	–5 183	–708	–2 499	–3 284	–5 493	–4 472	–1 567
Total liabilities to direct investors	HJYQ	27 197	45 896	58 182	20 163	11 061	4 069	23 093	82 352	54 926	85 451	47 725
Net acquisition of property	CGLO	698	813	1 629	791	748	395	623	597	467	2 358	1 493
Total equity capital	HJYR	27 895	46 709	59 811	20 954	11 809	4 464	23 716	82 949	55 393	87 809	49 218
Reinvested earnings	CYFV	1 522	4 607	10 788	–992	3 647	7 429	8 558	10 501	22 195	24 288	15 923
Other capital transactions [1]												
Liabilities to direct investors												
Debt securities issued by affiliated enterprises												
Purchases of debt securities	CYGC	783	558	710	1 318	598	1 844	3 464	2 294	5 135	8 190	4 928
Sales of debt securities	CYGD	–183	–567	–183	–571	–377	–484	–1 153	–269	–745	–3 550	–1 303
Other liabilities to direct investors												
Change in inter-company accounts	CYGH	25 700	17 253	11 338	17 420	10 756	–1 264	–931	14 032	5 351	–364	7 072
Change in branch indebtedness	CYGL	392	–210	869	285	403	1 738	470	351	2 666	–1 103	–1 668
Total liabilities to direct investors	HJYT	26 692	17 034	12 734	18 452	11 380	1 834	1 850	16 408	12 407	3 173	9 029
Claims on direct investors												
Change in inter-company accounts	CYGF	11 199	13 266	2 495	561	9 990	–2 112	2 723	10 850	5 619	17 242	21 440
Change in branch indebtedness	CYGK	–144	18	272	505	64	–937	193	1 163	–513	–122	269
Total claims on direct investors	HJYS	11 055	13 284	2 767	1 066	10 054	–3 049	2 916	12 013	5 106	17 120	21 709
Total other capital transactions	HMAD	15 637	3 750	9 967	17 386	1 326	4 883	–1 066	4 395	7 301	–13 947	–12 680
Total	HJYU	45 054	55 066	80 566	37 348	16 782	16 776	31 208	97 845	84 889	98 150	52 461

1 From Pink Book 2005 the presentation of Other capital transactions no longer mirror each other between UK assets and liabilities: both are now shown from the perspective of the direct investor.

Chapter 7: Financial account

7.3 Direct investment
continued

£ million

		1998	1999	2000	2001	2002	2003	2004	2005	2006	2007	2008
Net transactions (net credits less net debits)												
Equity capital												
Net acquisition of ordinary shares	LTMS	–19 753	–55 177	–88 613	5 015	–13 873	–13 580	5 084	68 104	29 668	24 698	26 813
Net acquisition of property	LTMT	8	–11	745	–951	–473	–2 595	–1 264	–767	–1 094	247	–1 000
Total equity capital	HBWN	–19 745	–55 188	–87 868	4 064	–14 346	–16 175	3 820	67 337	28 574	24 945	25 813
Reinvested earnings	HBWT	–12 549	–16 785	–14 390	–28 212	–28 562	–14 027	–22 518	–33 054	–25 683	–34 591	–20 168
Other capital transactions	HBWU	3 562	1 437	27 242	18 669	24 649	6 089	–1 604	19 557	37 000	–28 334	–25 712
Total	HJYV	**–28 732**	**–70 536**	**–75 016**	**–5 479**	**–18 259**	**–24 113**	**–20 302**	**53 840**	**39 891**	**–37 980**	**–20 067**

7.4 Direct investment
Sector analysis

£ million

		1998	1999	2000	2001	2002	2003	2004	2005	2006	2007	2008
Direct investment abroad (UK assets = net debits)												
By:												
UK Monetary financial institutions (banks)	-HCWJ	971	1 028	3 378	4 283	2 825	1 942	16 231	9 533	11 337	10 218	8 278
Insurance companies	-CNZE	969	–2 135	2 166	–256	1 388	3 038	4 357	1 454	8 587	8 274	–1 443
Other financial intermediaries	-HCXL	11 676	8 469	9 716	4 468	4 071	13 858	–1 374	2 389	2 122	23 077	779
Private non-financial corporations	-HCVH	59 663	117 330	139 101	32 575	25 859	18 598	31 048	28 885	23 162	92 331	62 757
Public corporations	-HDND	20	280	574	201	258	–185	–85	155	–2 003	265	1
Household sector[1]	-AAQN	487	630	647	1 556	640	3 638	1 333	1 589	1 793	1 965	2 156
Total	-HJYP	**73 786**	**125 602**	**155 582**	**42 827**	**35 041**	**40 889**	**51 510**	**44 005**	**44 998**	**136 130**	**72 528**
Direct investment in the UK (UK liabilities = net credits)												
In:												
Monetary financial institutions (banks)	GPBQ	678	1 616	4 133	3 387	1 757	2 683	11 715	4 539	4 243	8 661	5 967
Insurance companies	HDQI	–138	1 763	2 492	1 304	312	876	1 959	–247	3 312	1 827	–665
Other financial intermediaries												
Securities dealers	HDRU	–1 188	836	1 919	938	706	212	1 735	2 956	1 404	14 892	8 245
Other	HFCL	9 865	–232	5 792	8 098	3 298	5 395	–5 220	–7 285	4 328	14 930	4 049
Total other financial intermediaries	HFDR	8 677	604	7 711	9 036	4 004	5 607	–3 485	–4 329	5 732	29 822	12 294
Private non-financial corporations	BCEC	35 837	51 083	66 230	23 621	10 709	7 610	21 019	97 882	71 602	57 840	34 865
Total	HJYU	**45 054**	**55 066**	**80 566**	**37 348**	**16 782**	**16 776**	**31 208**	**97 845**	**84 889**	**98 150**	**52 461**
Net transaction (net credits less net debits)												
In assets and liabilities of:												
Monetary financial institutions	LTMU	–293	588	755	–896	–1 068	741	–4 516	–4 994	–7 094	–1 557	–2 311
Insurance companies	LTMV	–1 107	3 898	326	1 560	–1 076	–2 162	–2 398	–1 701	–5 275	–6 447	778
Other financial intermediaries	LTMW	–2 999	–7 865	–2 005	4 568	–67	–8 251	–2 111	–6 718	3 610	6 745	11 515
Private non-financial corporations	LTMX	–23 826	–66 247	–72 871	–8 954	–15 150	–10 988	–10 029	68 997	48 440	–34 491	–27 892
Public corporations	HDND	–20	–280	–574	–201	–258	185	85	–155	2 003	–265	–1
Household sector[1]	AAQN	–487	–630	–647	–1 556	–640	–3 638	–1 333	–1 589	–1 793	–1 965	–2 156
Total	HJYV	**–28 732**	**–70 536**	**–75 016**	**–5 479**	**–18 259**	**–24 113**	**–20 302**	**53 840**	**39 891**	**–37 980**	**–20 067**

1 The household sector includes non-profit institutions serving households.

7.5 Portfolio investment

£ million

		1998	1999	2000	2001	2002	2003	2004	2005	2006	2007	2008
Portfolio investment abroad (UK assets = net debits)												
Transactions in equity securities (shares) by:												
Monetary financial Institutions (banks)	-VTWC	4 549	100	7 195	–1 287	–11 767	18 824	31 597	36 515	21 524	11 347	–67 277
Central Government	LOEQ	–	–	–	–	–	–	–	43	12	–8	16
Insurance companies and pension funds												
Insurance companies	-HBHM	1 015	3 111	–4 297	6 520	2 959	–3 354	6 116	19 601	1 727	12 117	1 828
Pension funds[1]	-HBHO	2 073	–518	–12 798	11 720	15 256	4 394	6 491	8 036	–417	–7 675	–11 089
Total insurance companies and pension funds	-HBRD	3 088	2 593	–17 095	18 240	18 215	1 040	12 607	27 637	1 310	4 442	–9 261
Other financial intermediaries												
Securities dealers	-HGLG	–7 634	5 783	13 673	24 128	–12 050	–796	9 734	–17 842	–6 505	14 821	17 974
Unit and Investment Trusts	-HBHQ	3 567	6 468	9 968	3 913	3 329	2 121	1 174	7 305	2 892	506	52
Other	-HBRC	–833	–1 300	–1 446	–1 077	–856	–1 563	–1 621	–1 668	–1 800	–2 898	–1 863
Total other financial intermediaries	-HBRE	–4 900	10 951	22 195	26 964	–9 577	–238	9 287	–12 205	–5 413	12 429	16 163
Private non-financial corporations	-XBNL	84	241	9 047	444	–52	17	–380	23	1 381	–1 314	–39
Household sector[2]	HALH	–108	570	–821	103	–8	41	3 536	9 310	783	1 305	–376
Total transactions in equity securities	-HBVI	2 713	14 455	20 521	44 464	–3 189	19 684	56 647	61 323	19 597	28 201	–60 774
Transactions in debt securities												
Transactions in bonds and notes by:												
Monetary financial institutions												
Banks	-VTWA	43 090	11 011	34 007	37 604	3 774	–11 215	57 131	62 455	100 499	40 445	–160 962
Building societies	RYWJ	1 417	1 099	2 464	854	–338	–1 498	770	282	1 739	2 374	–892
Total monetary financial institutions	-HPCP	44 507	12 110	36 471	38 458	3 436	–12 713	57 901	62 737	102 238	42 819	–161 854
Central Government	HQ5P	–	–	–	–	–	–	–	–	–	50	–50
Insurance companies and pension funds												
Insurance companies	-HBHN	11 615	7 103	5 363	8 200	8 535	1 618	1 522	3 280	12 777	12 699	7 853
Pension funds[1]	-HBHP	3 581	2 933	5 875	1 267	–3 604	1 732	3 980	3 779	11 310	24 433	7 491
Total insurance companies and pension funds	-HBRF	15 196	10 036	11 238	9 467	4 931	3 350	5 502	7 059	24 087	37 132	15 344
Other financial intermediaries												
Securities dealers	CGFO	–33 645	–28 883	–1 935	–19 589	–1 114	9 912	21 829	13 355	–24 941	–19 292	91 451
Unit and investment trusts	-HBHR	1 452	1 121	664	1 478	720	2 445	1 531	1 430	6 093	4 918	5 741
Other	-HBRG	–154	–38	–36	–57	–72	–76	–101	–119	–146	–209	–237
Total other financial intermediaries	-HBRH	–32 347	–27 800	–1 307	–18 168	–466	12 281	23 259	14 666	–18 994	–14 583	96 955
Private non-financial corporations	-XBNM	553	–1 299	1 179	566	300	1 292	197	–727	–1 621	673	2 135
Household sector[2]	HBRI	184	–380	256	88	88	88	88	88	88	88	88
Total transactions in bonds and notes	-HEPK	28 093	–7 333	47 837	30 411	8 289	4 298	86 947	83 823	105 798	66 179	–47 382
Transactions in Money Market Instruments												
Transactions in commercial paper by:												
Monetary financial institutions:												
Banks	-HBXH	4 111	9 728	–963	6 702	–3 981	7 584	–4 471	2 274	4 537	9 457	–16 111
Building societies	TAIH	–169	66	899	635	–564	–191	253	–60	19	–838	–179
Central government	-RUUR	–	–	–	458	467	–925	–1	–	–	2 390	–139
Insurance companies and pension funds	-HBVK	–1 558	243	–106	–159	333	70	602	1 419	–556	154	2 340
Other financial intermediaries	-HGIS	–815	504	–2 077	2 505	–602	2 579	615	1 341	4 081	–4 454	–1 330
Private non-financial corporations	-HBRL	–956	722	1 110	1 912	1 110	3 798	615	1 078	4 758	–9 820	–5 130
Total transactions in commercial paper	-HGLU	613	11 263	–1 137	12 053	–3 237	12 915	–2 387	6 052	12 839	–3 111	–20 549
Transactions in certificates of deposit by:												
Monetary financial institutions (Building societies)	TAIF	210	–71	409	37	563	39	–243	–175	765	–85	1 402
Other financial intermediaries	-RZUV	443	3 075	–2 067	–412	–1 416	–668	50	–68	–161	836	–1 317
Total transactions in certificates of deposit	HEPH	653	3 004	–1 658	–375	–853	–629	–193	–243	604	751	85
Total transactions in Money Market Instruments	-HHZM	1 266	14 267	–2 795	11 678	–4 090	12 286	–2 580	5 809	13 443	–2 360	–20 464
Total transactions in debt securities	-XBMW	29 359	6 934	45 042	42 089	4 199	16 584	84 367	89 632	119 241	63 819	–67 846
Total	-HHZC	**32 072**	**21 389**	**65 563**	**86 553**	**1 010**	**36 268**	**141 014**	**150 955**	**138 838**	**92 020**	**–128 620**

1 The pension funds data only covers self-administered funds, see glossary.   2 The household sector includes non-profit institutions serving households.

7.5 Portfolio investment
continued

£ million

Portfolio investment in the UK
(UK liabilities = net credits)

		1998	1999	2000	2001	2002	2003	2004	2005	2006	2007	2008
Transactions in equity securities (shares) issued by:												
Monetary financial Institutions (banks and building societies)	HBQG	–5 732	–3 294	–3 510	54	–1 276	714	–264	48	650	3 591	1 617
Other sectors[1]	HBQH	47 667	67 603	124 812	15 676	3 179	19 374	2 221	6 331	–11 214	8 579	42 428
Total transactions in equity securities	XBLW	41 935	64 309	121 302	15 730	1 903	20 088	1 957	6 379	–10 564	12 170	44 045
Transactions in debt securities												
Transactions in bonds and notes												
Issues by central government												
UK foreign currency bonds and notes	HEZP	–1 660	241	988	–3 342	–2 811	886	38	–32	–138	95	–1 499
Other central government bonds	HHJM	–	–	–	–	–	–	–	–	–	–	–
Transactions in British government stocks (gilts) by:												
Foreign central banks (exchange reserves)	AING	1 692	489	1 049	1 157	–1 245	–748	–2 339	384	4 212	2 662	9 523
Other foreign residents	VTWG	1 802	–6 017	–2 337	1 511	420	11 059	14 908	30 309	20 849	22 542	39 515
Total transactions in British government stocks	HEPC	3 494	–5 528	–1 288	2 668	–825	10 311	12 569	30 693	25 061	25 204	49 038
Total issues by central government	HBRX	1 834	–5 287	–300	–674	–3 636	11 197	12 607	30 661	24 923	25 299	47 539
Local authorities' bonds	HBQT	–	–	–	–	–	–	–	–	–	–	–
Public corporations' bonds	HCEW	–	–	–	–	–	–	–	–	–	–	–
Issues by monetary financial Institutions (banks and building societies)												
Bonds	HBRY	–1 154	6 587	1 886	511	4 885	15 129	13 214	18 828	17 072	26 411	45 734
European medium term notes and other medium-term paper:												
Issued by UK banks	HCEZ	1 881	4 244	891	3 425	1 706	12 117	16 525	19 240	26 148	34 587	–20 657
Issued by UK building societies	HCFC	–140	252	1 814	630	69	1 754	2 222	3 498	–113	1 910	–2 397
Total	HBRV	1 741	4 496	2 705	4 055	1 775	13 871	18 747	22 738	26 035	36 497	–23 054
Total monetary financial institutions	HMBD	587	11 083	4 591	4 566	6 660	29 000	31 961	41 566	43 107	62 908	22 680
Issues by other sectors[1]	HBRT	–3 597	20 502	5 871	1 587	15 210	47 198	40 774	58 619	53 148	82 223	142 377
Total transactions in bonds and notes	XBLY	–1 176	26 298	10 162	5 479	18 234	87 395	85 342	130 846	121 178	170 430	212 596
Transactions in Money Market Instruments												
Transactions in treasury bills (issued by central government)												
Sterling treasury bills	AARB	–820	637	–251	304	–180	2 150	1 974	–1 023	747	3 547	13 671
Euro treasury bills	HHNW	–913	–227	–	–	–	–	–	–	–	–	–
Total treasury bills	HHZO	–1 733	410	–251	304	–180	2 150	1 974	–1 023	747	3 547	13 671
Transactions in certificates of deposit (issued by UK monetary financial institutions)												
Issued by banks	HBRS	–16 985	11 500	34 653	19 911	4 080	–3 906	–1 388	–453	36 175	18 156	–28 839
Issued by building societies	HBHH	–25	–6	301	–50	264	952	531	–1 059	1 240	–164	–517
Total certificates of deposit	HBQX	–17 010	11 494	34 954	19 861	4 344	–2 954	–857	–1 512	37 415	17 992	–29 356
Transactions in commercial paper												
Issued by UK monetary financial Institutions												
Banks	HBHI	258	297	2 542	–600	14 950	–33	9 094	–3 568	5 034	1 951	–770
Building societies	HBHL	335	1 748	768	–182	–330	3 325	–259	556	3 609	–5 743	–2 733
Total monetary financial institutions	HBRU	593	2 045	3 310	–782	14 620	3 292	8 835	–3 012	8 643	–3 792	–3 503
Issued by other sectors[1]	HHZN	2 429	1 783	2 700	237	10 819	–4 323	93	–2 629	–3 499	2 926	3 133
Total transactions in commercial paper	HBQW	3 022	3 828	6 010	–545	25 439	–1 031	8 928	–5 641	5 144	–866	–370
Total transactions in Money Market Instruments	HHZE	–15 721	15 732	40 713	19 620	29 603	–1 835	10 045	–8 176	43 306	20 673	–16 055
Total transactions in debt securities	XBLX	–16 897	42 030	50 875	25 099	47 837	85 560	95 387	122 670	164 484	191 103	196 541
Total	HHZF	25 038	106 339	172 177	40 829	49 740	105 648	97 344	129 049	153 920	203 273	240 586

1 These series relate to non-governmental sectors other than monetary financial institutions.

7.5 Portfolio investment
continued

£ million

		1998	1999	2000	2001	2002	2003	2004	2005	2006	2007	2008
Net transactions (net credits less net debits)												
Equity securities (shares)	HBWV	39 222	49 854	100 781	−28 734	5 092	404	−54 690	−54 944	−30 161	−16 031	104 819
Debt securities												
Bonds and notes	LTMY	−29 269	33 631	−37 675	−24 932	9 945	83 097	−1 605	47 023	15 380	104 251	259 978
Money Market Instruments	LTMZ	−16 987	1 465	43 508	7 942	33 693	−14 121	12 625	−13 985	29 863	23 033	4 409
Total debt securities	HBWX	−46 256	35 096	5 833	−16 990	43 638	68 976	11 020	33 038	45 243	127 284	264 387
Total	HHZD	**−7 034**	**84 950**	**106 614**	**−45 724**	**48 730**	**69 380**	**−43 670**	**−21 906**	**15 082**	**111 253**	**369 206**

7.6 Portfolio investment
Sector analysis

£ million

		1998	1999	2000	2001	2002	2003	2004	2005	2006	2007	2008
Portfolio investment abroad (UK assets = net debits)												
Investment by:												
Monetary financial institutions												
Banks	-HBWF	51 750	20 839	40 239	43 019	−11 974	15 193	84 257	101 244	126 560	61 249	−244 350
Building societies	HEPI	1 458	1 094	3 772	1 526	−339	−1 650	780	47	2 523	1 451	331
Total monetary financial institutions	-HBRJ	53 208	21 933	44 011	44 545	−12 313	13 543	85 037	101 291	129 083	62 700	−244 019
Central government	LOFB	–	–	–	458	467	−925	−1	43	12	2 432	−173
Insurance companies and pension funds	-HBRO	16 726	12 872	−5 963	27 548	23 479	4 460	18 711	36 115	24 841	41 728	8 423
Other financial intermediaries	-HBRP	−37 619	−13 270	16 744	10 889	−12 061	13 954	33 211	3 734	−20 487	−5 772	110 471
Private non-financial corporations	-HBRQ	−319	−336	11 336	2 922	1 358	5 107	432	374	4 518	−10 461	−3 034
Household sector[1]	-HBRR	76	190	−565	191	80	129	3 624	9 398	871	1 393	−288
Total	-HHZC	**32 072**	**21 389**	**65 563**	**86 553**	**1 010**	**36 268**	**141 014**	**150 955**	**138 838**	**92 020**	**−128 620**
Portfolio investment in the UK (UK liabilities = net credits)												
Investment in securities issued by:												
Monetary financial institutions (banks and building societies)	CGPH	−21 562	21 328	39 345	23 699	24 348	30 052	39 675	37 090	89 815	80 699	−8 562
Central government	HBSO	101	−4 877	−551	−370	−3 816	13 347	14 581	29 638	25 670	28 846	61 210
Local authorities	HBQT	–	–	–	–	–	–	–	–	–	–	–
Public corporations	HCEW	–	–	–	–	–	–	–	–	–	–	–
Other sectors	CGPL	46 499	89 888	133 383	17 500	29 208	62 249	43 088	62 321	38 435	93 728	187 938
Total	HHZF	**25 038**	**106 339**	**172 177**	**40 829**	**49 740**	**105 648**	**97 344**	**129 049**	**153 920**	**203 273**	**240 586**
Net transactions (net credits less net debits)												
In assets and liabilities of:												
Monetary financial institutions	LTNA	−74 770	−605	−4 666	−20 846	36 661	16 509	−45 362	−64 201	−39 268	17 999	235 457
Central government	ZPOG	101	−4 877	−551	−828	−4 283	14 272	14 582	29 595	25 658	26 414	61 383
Local authorities	HBQT	–	–	–	–	–	–	–	–	–	–	–
Public corporations	HCEW	–	–	–	–	–	–	–	–	–	–	–
Other sectors	LTNB	67 635	90 432	111 831	−24 050	16 352	38 599	−12 890	12 700	28 692	66 840	72 366
Total	HHZD	**−7 034**	**84 950**	**106 614**	**−45 724**	**48 730**	**69 380**	**−43 670**	**−21 906**	**15 082**	**111 253**	**369 206**

1 The household sector includes non-profit institutions serving households.

7.7 Other investment

£ million

		1998	1999	2000	2001	2002	2003	2004	2005	2006	2007	2008
Other investment abroad (UK assets = net debits)												
Trade credit												
Long-term												
Central government	-XBMC	–	–	–	–	–	–	–	–	–	–	–
Other sectors[1]	-HCQK	–	–	–	–	–	–	–	–	–	–	–
Total long-term trade credit	-HBRZ	–	–	–	–	–	–	–	–	–	–	–
Short-term												
Other sectors[1]	-XBMF	–1 119	102	–42	–315	292	573	–336	–1 395	1 361	120	–158
Total trade credit	-XBMB	–1 119	102	–42	–315	292	573	–336	–1 395	1 361	120	–158
Loans												
Long-term												
Bank loans under ECGD guarantee	-HGBS	–7	–355	–1 476	187	–1 017	113	231	224	–467	–157	54
Inter-government loans by the UK	-HEUC	–176	–19	–27	–20	–19	–19	–15	–18	–13	–12	–75
Loans by Commonwealth Development Corporation (public corporations)	-HETB	47	25	2	–	–	–	–	–	–	–	–
Loans by the Export Credit Guarantee Department	CY93	–47	48	61	49	–186	–259	–176	–577	–1 335	–207	–316
Loans by specialist leasing companies[1]	-HGKU	–	–	–	–	–	–	–	–	–	–	–
Total long-term loans	-HBSG	–183	–301	–1 440	216	–1 222	–165	40	–371	–1 815	–376	–337
Short-term loans												
By monetary financial institutions												
By banks												
Sterling loans	NFBE	–620	2 590	1 896	4 796	4 736	460	6 888	20 215	22 120	26 218	5 838
Foreign currency loans	ZPON	2 211	14 632	53 028	43 294	12 778	70 529	105 145	114 591	97 718	200 311	–127 914
Total banks	HEQO	1 591	17 222	54 924	48 090	17 514	70 989	112 033	134 806	119 838	226 529	–122 076
By building societies	NFBG	–	–	–	1	3	2	3	2	–1	–1	4
Total monetary financial institutions	ZPOL	1 591	17 222	54 924	48 091	17 517	70 991	112 036	134 808	119 837	226 528	–122 072
By other sectors	-XBLN	–133	3	–	–	–	–	–	–3	–	5	2
Total short-term loans	VTUL	1 458	17 225	54 924	48 091	17 517	70 991	112 036	134 805	119 837	226 533	–122 070
Total loans	-XBMG	1 275	16 924	53 484	48 307	16 295	70 826	112 076	134 434	118 022	226 157	–122 407
Currency and deposits												
Transactions in foreign notes and coin												
Monetary financial institutions (banks)	TAAG	30	–63	–44	1	21	10	–2	–10	58	26	111
Other sectors[1]	-HETF	10	40	28	–4	33	20	46	24	62	10	–197
Total foreign notes and coin	HEOV	40	–23	–16	–3	54	30	44	14	120	36	–86
Deposits abroad by UK residents												
Deposits by monetary financial institutions												
Deposits by banks												
Sterling deposits	-HBQY	12 915	–12 201	19 480	7 488	–7 445	18 356	–2 731	34 535	47 040	110 582	–23 574
Foreign currency deposits	-HBQZ	11 767	–17 131	109 976	29 265	60 754	69 509	108 421	125 617	130 421	263 278	–121 919
Total deposits by UK banks	-XBMI	24 682	–29 332	129 456	36 753	53 309	87 865	105 690	160 152	177 461	373 860	–145 493
Deposits by building societies	TAID	–124	–145	610	–51	–567	–138	85	–2 279	127	1 519	–896
Total deposits by monetary financial institutions	HCES	24 558	–29 477	130 066	36 702	52 742	87 727	105 775	157 873	177 588	375 379	–146 389

1 These series relate to non-governmental sectors other than monetary financial institutions.

7.7 Other investment continued

£ million

Other investment abroad - *continued*

		1998	1999	2000	2001	2002	2003	2004	2005	2006	2007	2008
Currency and deposits - *continued*												
Deposits abroad by UK residents - *continued*												
Deposits by securities dealers	-HGTF	-6 117	45 920	47 567	58 756	-13 153	53 172	36 186	167 581	48 951	35 468	-338 084
Deposits by other UK residents[1]	-HBSI	11 085	7 740	10 322	27 325	13 907	47 914	70 661	43 095	50 155	109 164	23 505
Total deposits abroad by UK residents	-HBXV	29 526	24 183	187 955	122 783	53 496	188 813	212 622	368 549	276 694	520 011	-460 968
Total currency and deposits	-HBVN	29 566	24 160	187 939	122 780	53 550	188 843	212 666	368 563	276 814	520 047	-461 054
Other assets												
Central government subscriptions to international organisations												
International Development Association	-HEUB	202	211	237	200	319	108	185	378	468	460	770
Regional development banks	-HEUD	65	50	50	53	69	75	61	42	98	82	176
European Investment Bank (EIB)	-HEUE	–	–	–	–	–	–	–	–	–	–	–
Other subscriptions	-HEUF	2	41	3	3	21	51	37	52	214	159	-13
Total central government subscriptions	-HGLR	269	302	290	256	409	234	283	472	780	701	933
Short-term central government assets	-LOEL	28	106	50	-177	65	52	640	435	277	386	2 658
Total central government other assets	-LOES	297	408	340	79	474	286	923	907	1 057	1 087	3 591
Debt forgiveness (monetary financial institutions)[2]	-FJNF	–	–	–	–	–	–	–	–	–	–	–
Other sectors (excluding monetary financial institutions)												
Long-term assets	-HHZH	–	–	–	–	–	–	–	–	–	–	–
Short-term assets												
Public corporations assets abroad	-HBSR	–	–	–	–	–	–	–	–	–	–	–
Public corporations debt forgiveness	HMLW	-27	-49	-55	-188	-236	-127	-109	-1 249	-1 356	-76	–
Other[1]	-HBSK	–	–	–	–	–	–	–	–	–	–	–
Total short-term assets of other sectors	-HHZI	-27	-49	-55	-188	-236	-127	-109	-1 249	-1 356	-76	–
Total other sectors	-XBLP	-27	-49	-55	-188	-236	-127	-109	-1 249	-1 356	-76	–
Total other assets	-XBMK	270	359	285	-109	238	159	814	-342	-299	1 011	3 591
Total	-XBMM	29 992	41 545	241 666	170 663	70 375	260 401	325 220	501 260	395 898	747 335	-580 028

1 This series relates to non-governmental sectors other than monetary financial institutions.
2 This series also appears in the capital account (see Table 6.1).

7.7 Other investment
continued

£ million

		1998	1999	2000	2001	2002	2003	2004	2005	2006	2007	2008
Other investment in the UK (UK liabilities = net credits)												
Trade credit												
Long-term[1]	CGJF	–	–	–	–	–	–	–	–	–	–	–
Short-term[1]	XBLQ	–	–	–	–	–	–	–	–	–	–	–
Total trade credit	XBMO	–	–	–	–	–	–	–	–	–	–	–
Loans												
Long-term												
Drawings by:												
Central government	HBSP	–	–	–	–	–	–	–	–	–	–	–
Local authorities	HBSQ	9	17	–	–	–	–	–	–	–	–	–
Public corporations	HHYT	–	–	–	–	–	–	–	–	–	–	–
Other[1]	HIBY	–	–	–	–	–	–	–	–	–	–	–
Total long-term drawings	HBST	9	17	–	–	–	–	–	–	–	–	–
Repayments from:												
Central government	HBSW	–91	–105	–114	–45	–48	–45	–46	–65	7	–3	32
Local authorities	HBSX	–96	–123	–188	22	26	204	651	134	232	–42	361
Public corporations	HHYU	–5	–	–	–	–	–	283	–7	–12	–6	–9
Other[1]	HIBZ	–	–	–	–	–	–	–	–	–	–	–
Total long-term repayments	HBSY	–192	–228	–302	–23	–22	159	888	62	227	–51	384
Total long-term loans	HBSZ	–183	–211	–302	–23	–22	159	888	62	227	–51	384
Short-term loans to:												
Central government	HBTA	–	–	–	–	–	–	–	–	–	–	–
Local authorities	HBTB	–	–	–	–	–	–	–	–	–	–	–
Public corporations	HIAW	–	–	–	–	–	–	–	–	–	–	–
Securities dealers	HBTD	13 901	53 746	56 910	77 290	–34 313	31 054	71 239	208 816	–27 085	58 716	–335 515
Other[1]	HBSS	6 902	–6 864	–21 697	38 480	8 428	39 625	65 549	–1 861	59 202	–16 524	–13 130
Total short-term loans	HBTC	20 803	46 882	35 213	115 770	–25 885	70 679	136 788	206 955	32 117	42 192	–348 645
Total loans	XBMP	20 620	46 671	34 911	115 747	–25 907	70 838	137 676	207 017	32 344	42 141	–348 261
Currency and deposits												
Sterling notes and coin												
Notes (issued by Bank of England)	HLYV	98	77	67	–51	78	74	102	58	65	40	–31
Coins (issued by Royal Mint)	HMAT	11	8	8	–6	8	7	11	6	6	3	–4
Total notes and coin	AASD	109	85	75	–57	86	81	113	64	71	43	–35
Deposits from abroad with UK residents												
Deposits with monetary financial institutions												
Deposits with banks												
Sterling deposits	NWXP	13 609	19 212	32 466	16 297	10 992	22 840	26 775	45 858	56 878	216 324	–60 307
Foreign currency deposits	NFAS	37 454	–13 158	166 168	104 862	77 472	148 377	261 474	232 399	276 414	471 475	–516 330
Total deposits with banks	HBWA	51 062	6 054	198 634	121 159	88 464	171 216	288 249	278 257	333 292	687 799	–576 637
Deposits with building societies	NEWS	883	542	567	523	308	487	305	1 391	623	261	171
Total deposits with UK monetary financial institutions	HDKE	51 945	6 596	199 201	121 682	88 772	171 703	288 554	279 648	333 915	688 060	–576 466
Deposit liabilities of UK central government	HEUN	304	693	528	–178	–24	232	–877	–57	474	–299	–282
Total deposits from abroad with UK residents	HBXY	52 249	7 289	199 729	121 504	88 748	171 935	287 677	279 591	334 389	687 761	–576 748
Total currency and deposits	HMAO	52 358	7 374	199 804	121 447	88 834	172 016	287 790	279 655	334 460	687 804	–576 783

1 These series relate to non-governmental sectors other than monetary financial institutions.

7.7 Other investment
continued

£ million

		1998	1999	2000	2001	2002	2003	2004	2005	2006	2007	2008
Other investment in the UK - *continued*												
Other liabilities												
Long-term												
Net equity of foreign households in life insurance reserves and in pension funds	QZEP	−2	−2	−4	−5	−1	−12	−11	−55	−9	−37	−2
Prepayments of premiums and reserves against outstanding claims	NQMC	3	−602	942	−157	335	−1 371	1 324	2 675	4 423	−4 223	−5 259
Total long-term liabilities	VTUG	1	−604	938	−162	334	−1 383	1 313	2 620	4 414	−4 260	−5 261
Short-term	HJYF	138	−129	−90	526	−613	58	−158	158	57	245	175
Total other liabilities	XBMX	139	−733	848	364	−279	−1 325	1 155	2 778	4 471	−4 015	−5 086
Total	XBMN	**73 117**	**53 312**	**235 563**	**237 558**	**62 648**	**241 529**	**426 621**	**489 450**	**371 275**	**725 930**	**−930 130**
Net transactions (net credits less net debits)												
Trade credit	LTNC	1 119	−102	42	315	−292	−573	336	1 395	−1 361	−120	158
Loans	LTND	19 345	29 747	−18 573	67 440	−42 202	12	25 600	72 583	−85 678	−184 016	−225 854
Deposits	LTNE	22 792	−16 786	11 865	−1 333	35 284	−16 827	75 124	−88 908	57 646	167 757	−115 729
Other	LTNF	−131	−1 092	563	473	−517	−1 484	341	3 120	4 770	−5 026	−8 677
Total	HHYR	**43 125**	**11 767**	**−6 103**	**66 895**	**−7 727**	**−18 872**	**101 401**	**−11 810**	**−24 623**	**−21 405**	**−350 102**

7.8 Other investment
Sector analysis

£ million

		1998	1999	2000	2001	2002	2003	2004	2005	2006	2007	2008
Other investment abroad (UK assets = net debits)												
Investment by:												
Monetary financial institutions												
Banks	-HBSL	26 296	−12 528	182 860	85 031	69 827	158 977	217 952	295 172	296 890	600 258	−267 404
Building societies	HEQR	−124	−145	610	−50	−564	−136	88	−2 277	126	1 518	−892
Total monetary financial institutions	HCET	26 172	−12 673	183 470	84 981	69 263	158 841	218 040	292 895	297 016	601 776	−268 296
Central government	-HBSM	121	389	313	59	455	267	908	889	1 044	1 075	3 516
Public corporations	-HBSV	−27	24	8	−139	−422	−386	−285	−1 826	−2 691	−283	−316
Other sectors	-HBSN	3 726	53 805	57 875	85 762	1 079	101 679	106 557	209 302	100 529	144 767	−314 932
Total	-XBMM	29 992	41 545	241 666	170 663	70 375	260 401	325 220	501 260	395 898	747 335	−580 028
Other investment in the UK (UK liabilities = net credits)												
Investment in:												
Monetary financial institutions												
Banks	CGOT	51 160	6 131	198 701	121 108	88 542	171 290	288 351	278 315	333 357	687 839	−576 668
Building societies	NEWS	883	542	567	523	308	487	305	1 391	623	261	171
Total monetary financial institutions	HBWG	52 043	6 673	199 268	121 631	88 850	171 777	288 656	279 706	333 980	688 100	−576 497
Central government	HBWH	338	443	308	273	−722	310	−1 055	50	549	−36	−79
Local authorities	HBWJ	−87	−106	−188	22	26	204	651	134	232	−42	361
Public corporations	HBWL	−5	–	–	–	–	–	283	−7	−12	−6	−9
Other sectors	HBWM	20 828	46 302	36 175	115 632	−25 506	69 238	138 086	209 567	36 526	37 914	−353 906
Total	XBMN	73 117	53 312	235 563	237 558	62 648	241 529	426 621	489 450	371 275	725 930	−930 130
Net transactions (net credits less net debits)												
In assets and liabilities of:												
Monetary financial institutions												
Banks	LTNG	24 864	18 659	15 841	36 077	18 715	12 313	70 399	−16 857	36 467	87 581	−309 264
Building societies	LTNH	1 007	687	−43	573	872	623	217	3 668	497	−1 257	1 063
Total monetary financial institutions	LTNI	25 871	19 346	15 798	36 650	19 587	12 936	70 616	−13 189	36 964	86 324	−308 201
Central government	LTNJ	217	54	−5	214	−1 177	43	−1 963	−839	−495	−1 111	−3 595
Local authorities	HBWJ	−87	−106	−188	22	26	204	651	134	232	−42	361
Public corporations	LTNK	22	−24	−8	139	422	386	568	1 819	2 679	277	307
Other sectors	LTNL	17 102	−7 503	−21 700	29 870	−26 585	−32 441	31 529	265	−64 003	−106 853	−38 974
Total	HHYR	43 125	11 767	−6 103	66 895	−7 727	−18 872	101 401	−11 810	−24 623	−21 405	−350 102

7.9 Reserve assets
Central government sector
Net debits

£ million

		1998	1999	2000	2001	2002	2003	2004	2005	2006	2007	2008
Monetary gold	-HBOX	931	−412	−883	−786	−266	–	−2	–	−4	–	–
Special Drawing Rights	-HBOY	−16	38	−73	−22	26	−2	−35	−8	51	−50	−24
Reserve position in the Fund	-HBOZ	751	626	−478	633	469	−251	−558	−1 911	−225	−188	802
Foreign Exchange												
Currency and deposits												
With central banks	-HBPC	−1 822	239	−368	6	95	−79	33	28	−43	28	43
With other banks	-HBPD	−733	2 312	6	−900	−863	−586	−882	367	−403	−419	−41
Total currency and deposits	-HBPB	−2 555	2 551	−363	−892	−767	−664	−849	395	−447	−390	2
Securities												
Bonds and notes	-HBPG	−214	−3 105	5 418	−1 838	2 280	−390	1 551	370	−854	2 105	−1 035
Money market instruments	-HBPH	939	−337	244	−185	−2 043	−62	107	1 465	1 363	−265	−890
Total securities	-HBPE	725	−3 442	5 662	−2 023	237	−452	1 658	1 835	509	1 840	−1 925
Total foreign exchange	-HBPA	−1 830	−891	5 299	−2 915	−530	−1 116	809	2 230	62	1 450	−1 923
Other claims	-HBPI	–	–	50	5	−158	−190	−18	345	−310	−21	−193
Total	-LTCV	**−164**	**−639**	**3 915**	**−3 085**	**−459**	**−1 559**	**196**	**656**	**−426**	**1 191**	**−1 338**

Chapter 8

International investment position

Chapter 8: International investment position

Summary

The international investment position is the balance sheet of the stock of external assets and liabilities. Between 1966 and 1994 the UK's assets tended to exceed its liabilities, by up to a record £86.4 billion in 1986. But from 1995 to 2007, the UK recorded a net liability position in every year, reaching a record £352.6 billion in 2006. In 2008, the UK returned to a net asset position of £92.9 billion mainly due to exchange rate effects. The fall in the value of sterling against other major currencies increased the value of UK assets and liabilities denominated in foreign currencies. Since a higher proportion of UK assets than of UK liabilities are denominated in foreign currencies, the total value of UK assets held increased by more than did the total value of UK liabilities.

The value of UK assets and liabilities grew rapidly between 1996 and 2001, when they broadly doubled. This period corresponded with a surge in cross-border investment, much of it associated with merger and acquisition activity. In 2002 the level of assets and liabilities fell slightly as, although there was continued inward and outward investment, these flows were more than offset by revaluation changes resulting from the falls in the value of global equity markets. From 2003 the level of both UK external assets and liabilities increased strongly again, due to a rise in cross-border investment, revaluations in the value of equity prices and exchange rate effects. By 2008 external assets and liabilities were approximately double the levels seen in 2003.

Over half of all UK assets and UK liabilities at the end of 2008 were allocated to UK monetary financial institutions (MFIs - mostly banks). UK banks' liabilities have consistently exceeded their assets, their net liability position reaching a record £249.9 billion in the latest year. Central government liabilities exceeded their assets in every year from 1992, due to non-residents' holdings of British government stocks. These holdings have nearly quadrupled since 2002, resulting in central government having a net liability position of £186.4 billion at the end of 2008. Other sectors' (non-MFI private sector) assets have historically exceeded liabilities but they showed a net liability position from 1998 to 2001 and again from 2005, reaching a record net liability position of £112.9 billion in 2006 before returning to a net asset position in 2007 and 2008. The net asset position of other sectors was a record £530.5 billion in 2008.

UK assets include reserve assets held by central government. Reserves are mainly held in the form of foreign exchange – in particular bonds and notes. Reserve assets in 2008 accounted for 0.5 per cent of total UK assets, down from 5.8 per cent in 1980.

UK assets

The proportion of direct investment abroad remained fairly constant through much of the 1990s at around 12 to 14 per cent of total UK assets. Between 2000 and 2003 it increased to around 20 per cent, reflecting the high level of merger and acquisition activity by UK companies in those years. It has since declined to 15 per cent in 2008. Portfolio investment assets remained at around a third of total UK assets from 1993 until 2001. Since then they have declined to 25 per cent, with the drop in 2008 being due to the fall in world stock market prices and disinvestment by UK banks. From high proportions of total investment in the early 1980s (around 75 per cent), the proportion of other investment assets declined to 46 per cent of total assets in 1999, since when it has steadily increased to 60 per cent in 2008.

Figure 8.2
UK assets
£ billion

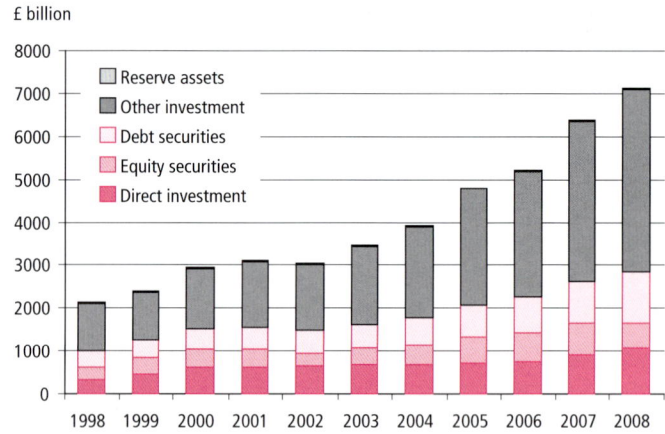

Figure 8.1
International Investment Position
£ billion

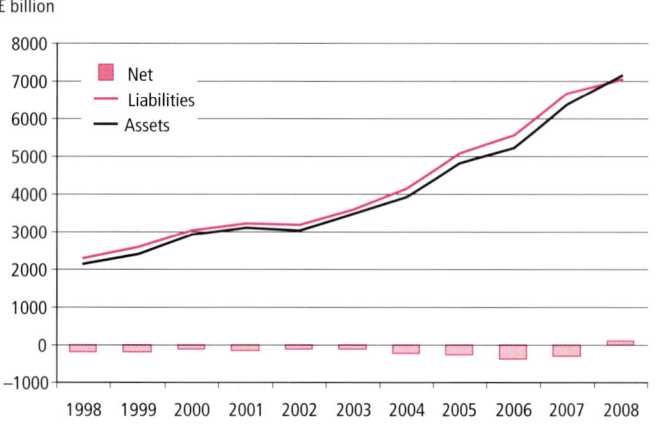

UK liabilities

Direct investment in the UK accounted for around 10 per cent of the total value of UK liabilities throughout the last decade. Portfolio investment increased from 22 per cent in 1992 to 36 per cent in 1999, before falling back to around 30 per cent from 2002, largely due to falls in the UK stock markets in 2001 and 2002 and the impact on the value of equity liabilities. Portfolio investment then increased to about 31 per cent of total liabilities in 2006 before dropping to 28 per cent in 2008 due to the effects of the global financial crisis and falls in stock market prices. Similarly to the asset position, the share of the value of other investment liabilities in the UK fell from around two-thirds in 1994 to 54 per cent in 1999. Since then it has increased, accounting for nearly 63 per cent of the total value of UK liabilities in 2008.

Figure 8.3
UK liabilities

£ billion

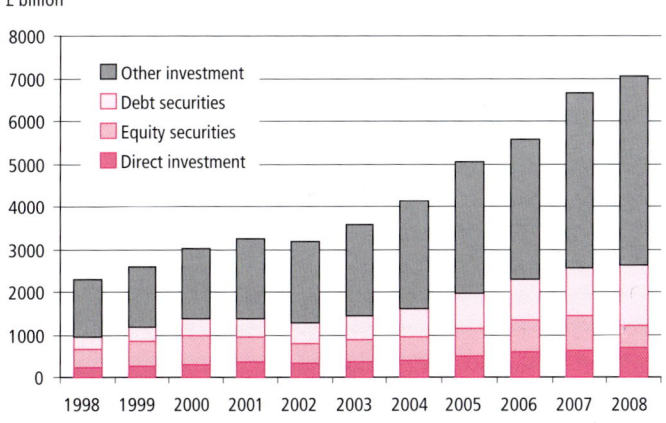

Direct investment

Direct investment assets have more than doubled over the last decade, to reach over £1 trillion for the first time at the end of 2008. Investments by UK private non-financial corporations (PNFCs) accounted for 76 per cent of UK direct investment assets at the end of 2008, while banks accounted for 7 per cent and other financial intermediaries a further 6 per cent. The value of PNFC's assets almost trebled between 1997 and 2000, reflecting the substantial foreign acquisitions by UK oil and telecom companies in that period. Since 2000, the value of PNFC assets has generally continued to rise, with a 20 per cent increase between 2007 and 2008.

Inward direct investment grew sharply in the late 1990s, with the total value of UK liabilities doubling between 1997 and 2001, and doubling again between 2002 and 2008. PNFCs' share of the value of total foreign direct investment liabilities fell from 84 per cent in 1992 to 75 per cent in 1997. Since then, the sector's contribution to direct investment liabilities has fluctuated between 74 and 80 per cent, standing at 75 per cent in 2008. Direct investment in UK banks increased to 9 per cent of total inward direct investment in 2004 following the merger and acquisition activity in that sector during the year, but since then has oscillated around the 8 per cent mark.

Portfolio investment

Between 1999 and 2008 UK portfolio investment assets more than doubled to £1,762.2 billion. The pattern of growth in equities has been more erratic than the growth in debt, as the value of equity securities assets is heavily influenced by changes in global equity prices. Between 2001 and 2002, the value of portfolio investment equity securities assets fell by 24 per cent to £305.9 billion. This mirrored the fall in world equity prices over the same period. There was a similar percentage fall in value between 2007 and 2008, to £569.1 billion, the result of a fall in world equity prices and disinvestment by UK banks and pension funds. The value of foreign debt securities held by UK investors nearly trebled between 1999 and 2008 – it increased by £252.3 billion in just one year between 2007 and 2008. UK banks held 63 per cent of total UK debt securities assets in 2007 before the financial crisis really began to take hold. At the end of 2008 they owned just 51 per cent, with other financial intermediaries increasing their share from 6 to 16 per cent, and insurance companies and pension funds increasing their share from 28 to 31 per cent. Prior to 2008, UK banks experienced

Figure 8.4
Direct investment

£ billion

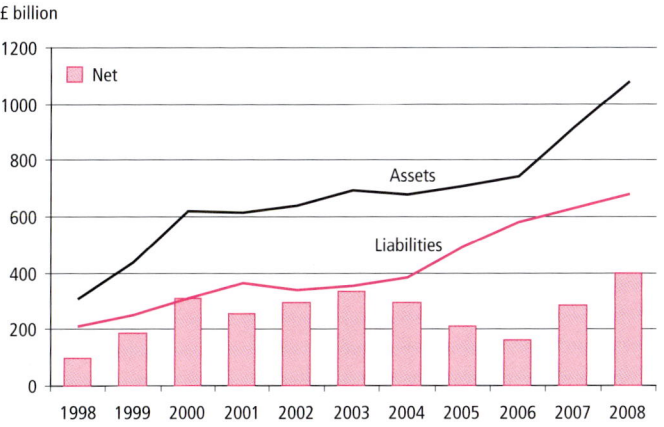

Figure 8.5
Portfolio investment

£ billion

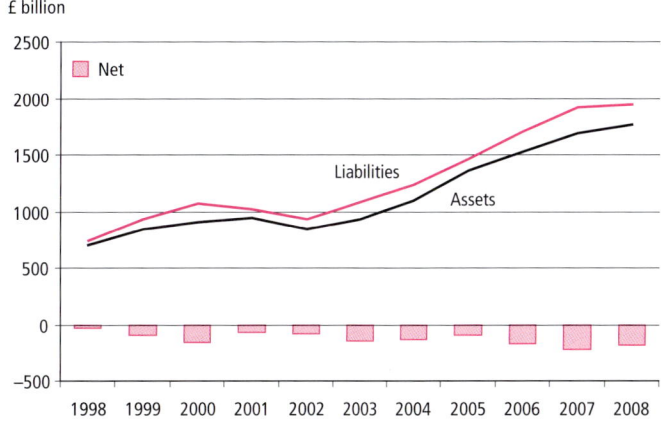

strong growth in their holdings of foreign equities rising from 1 per cent of total UK equity holdings in 2002 to 17 per cent at the end of 2007. In the wake of the global financial crisis, by the end of 2008, UK banks' holdings of foreign equities had reduced to 7 per cent of total equity. UK insurance companies, pension funds and other financial intermediaries hold the vast majority of UK equity securities assets.

The total value of UK portfolio investment liabilities increased in 2008 to £1,943.4 billion, due to continued foreign acquisitions of UK debt securities, particularly bonds and notes, which more than offset the decline in equity securities. This is in contrast to the last time equity prices fell, in 2001 and 2002, when the decline in equity securities drove an overall decline in portfolio investment. The fall in the value of portfolio investment liabilities in 2001 and 2002 mirrored the fall in the price of UK equity on the London stock exchange – which fell around 20 per cent in both 2001 and 2002.

Other investment

Other investment accounted for 60 per cent of total UK external assets in 2008, with the level of investment nearly quadrupling since 1999. UK banks' deposits and short-term loans to non-residents accounted for 75 per cent of total other investment abroad in 2008. This proportion has declined from around 90 per cent of total other investment in the late 1980s. The bulk of UK bank deposits abroad were in foreign currencies, only 13 per cent being held in sterling at the end of 2008.

Deposits from abroad held with UK banks represent the largest item in other investment liabilities. Although these have declined from over 90 per cent in the late 1980s, they have picked up to 81 per cent at the end of 2008. Of the £3,572.3 billion total deposits with UK banks in 2008, 15 per cent were held in sterling. The fall in the proportionate value of deposits with banks is largely the result of the increase in short-term loans to UK securities dealers and other non-bank sectors – increasing from £48.5 billion in 1990 to £825.0 billion at the end of 2008 after peaking at £954.0 billion in 2007.

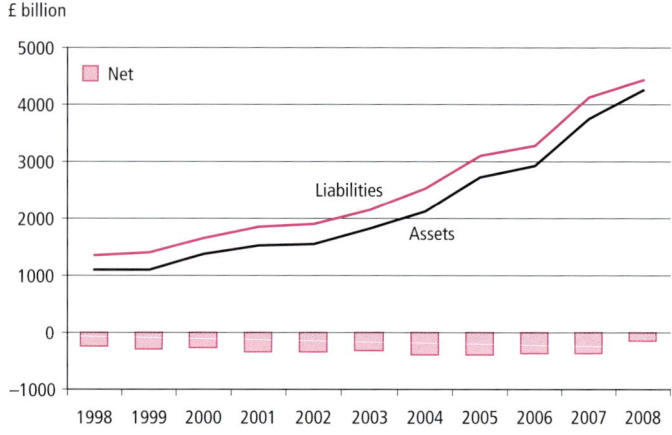

Figure **8.6**

Other investment

£ billion

8.1 International investment position Summary table

Balance sheets valued at end of year

£ billion

		1998	1999	2000	2001	2002	2003	2004	2005	2006	2007	2008
UK Assets												
Direct investment abroad												
Equity capital and reinvested earnings	CGMO	283.9	412.3	586.3	582.2	619.3	670.7	667.2	726.8	770.8	904.0	1 049.8
Other capital assets	HBUW	25.9	26.0	32.5	34.8	17.9	20.5	10.9	−20.9	−29.1	10.0	25.5
Total direct investment abroad	HBWD	309.8	438.3	618.8	616.9	637.2	691.1	678.1	705.9	741.7	913.9	1 075.2
Portfolio investment abroad												
Equity securities	HEPX	303.7	419.9	429.3	404.6	305.9	372.0	455.3	617.2	693.4	753.1	569.1
Debt securities	HHZX	400.2	418.4	476.8	532.8	538.1	563.9	636.8	743.8	837.7	940.8	1 193.1
Total portfolio investment abroad	HHZZ	703.8	838.3	906.1	937.4	844.0	935.8	1 092.1	1 360.9	1 531.1	1 693.8	1 762.2
Other investment abroad	HLXV	1 098.4	1 097.3	1 379.7	1 521.9	1 545.2	1 813.7	2 118.0	2 714.8	2 916.6	3 750.2	4 261.4
Reserve assets	LTEB	23.3	22.2	28.8	25.6	25.5	23.8	23.2	24.7	22.9	26.7	36.3
Total	HBQA	**2 135.4**	**2 396.1**	**2 933.4**	**3 101.9**	**3 051.9**	**3 464.5**	**3 911.4**	**4 806.3**	**5 212.3**	**6 384.6**	**7 135.0**
UK Liabilities												
Direct investment in the UK												
Equity capital and reinvested earnings	HBUY	159.8	192.3	240.6	259.7	229.2	245.7	267.9	368.7	433.0	511.9	570.9
Other capital liabilities	HBVC	53.8	57.9	69.8	103.7	111.4	109.9	115.5	125.5	145.3	118.3	105.7
Total direct investment in the UK	HBWI	213.6	250.2	310.4	363.5	340.6	355.5	383.3	494.2	578.3	630.2	676.7
Portfolio investment in the UK												
Equity securities	HLXX	449.1	614.2	673.7	584.1	442.7	527.1	574.7	659.3	780.0	818.2	549.8
Debt securities	HLXY	290.7	319.0	393.8	429.1	482.6	555.8	653.2	802.4	922.6	1 099.5	1 393.7
Total portfolio investment in the UK	HLXW	739.9	933.2	1 067.6	1 013.2	925.3	1 082.9	1 227.9	1 461.7	1 702.6	1 917.6	1 943.4
Other investment in the UK	HLYD	1 350.3	1 400.9	1 651.6	1 861.9	1 906.0	2 143.2	2 520.8	3 103.0	3 284.0	4 119.4	4 422.1
Total	HBQB	**2 303.8**	**2 584.3**	**3 029.5**	**3 238.5**	**3 171.9**	**3 581.6**	**4 132.1**	**5 058.9**	**5 564.8**	**6 667.2**	**7 042.1**
Net International Investment Position												
Direct investment												
Equity capital and reinvested earnings	HBSH	124.1	220.0	345.7	322.4	390.1	425.0	399.3	358.1	337.8	392.1	478.8
Other capital	CGKF	−27.9	−31.9	−37.3	−69.0	−93.5	−89.4	−104.6	−146.4	−174.4	−108.3	−80.3
Total net direct investment	HBWQ	96.2	188.1	308.4	253.5	296.6	335.6	294.7	211.7	163.4	283.8	398.6
Portfolio investment												
Equity securities	CGNE	−145.5	−194.3	−244.4	−179.4	−136.8	−155.1	−119.4	−42.1	−86.6	−65.1	19.3
Debt securities	CGNF	109.5	99.4	82.9	103.7	55.5	8.1	−16.4	−58.6	−84.9	−158.7	−200.6
Total net portfolio investment	CGNH	−36.0	−94.9	−161.5	−75.7	−81.3	−147.0	−135.8	−100.8	−171.5	−223.8	−181.3
Other investment	CGNG	−251.9	−303.6	−271.9	−339.9	−360.8	−329.5	−402.9	−388.2	−367.3	−369.2	−160.7
Reserve assets	LTEB	23.3	22.2	28.8	25.6	25.5	23.8	23.2	24.7	22.9	26.7	36.3
Total	HBQC	**−168.4**	**−188.2**	**−96.2**	**−136.5**	**−120.0**	**−117.2**	**−220.7**	**−252.6**	**−352.6**	**−282.5**	**92.9**
Allocations of Special Drawing Rights to the UK by the IMF	HEVP	1.6	1.6	1.7	1.7	1.6	1.6	1.5	1.6	1.5	1.5	2.0

8.2 International investment position
Summary table
Balance sheets valued at end of year

£ billion

		1998	1999	2000	2001	2002	2003	2004	2005	2006	2007	2008
UK Assets												
Monetary financial institutions												
Banks	CGNI	1 139.7	1 134.3	1 413.3	1 525.0	1 563.6	1 730.6	1 983.5	2 420.5	2 674.9	3 460.9	3 943.8
Building societies	VTXF	4.3	5.0	8.5	10.0	9.1	7.3	7.8	7.7	10.4	13.3	16.6
Total monetary financial institutions	CGNJ	1 144.0	1 139.3	1 421.8	1 535.0	1 572.6	1 737.9	1 991.2	2 428.3	2 685.3	3 474.3	3 960.4
Central government	CGNK	39.3	30.5	37.7	34.7	35.5	34.2	33.4	35.8	35.0	39.9	53.0
Public corporations	CGNL	4.2	4.5	4.6	3.8	4.2	4.2	4.7	3.4	1.7	1.8	1.6
Other sectors	CGNM	947.9	1 221.9	1 469.3	1 528.4	1 439.6	1 688.1	1 882.1	2 338.9	2 490.3	2 868.7	3 120.0
Total	HBQA	**2 135.4**	**2 396.1**	**2 933.4**	**3 101.9**	**3 051.9**	**3 464.5**	**3 911.4**	**4 806.3**	**5 212.3**	**6 384.6**	**7 135.0**
UK Liabilities												
UK Monetary financial institutions												
(banks and building societies)	HBYJ	1 184.2	1 199.3	1 486.6	1 623.8	1 707.1	1 893.3	2 180.0	2 582.4	2 817.9	3 695.0	4 210.3
Central government	CGOG	76.3	63.6	65.6	63.3	59.2	70.9	89.3	115.2	141.2	167.6	239.4
Local authorities	CGOH	1.2	1.1	0.8	0.8	0.9	1.1	1.7	1.9	2.1	2.1	2.5
Public corporations	CGOI	–	–	–	–	–	–	0.5	0.4	0.4	0.4	0.4
Other sectors	HCON	1 042.2	1 320.3	1 476.6	1 550.5	1 404.7	1 616.3	1 860.6	2 359.0	2 603.2	2 802.1	2 589.5
Total	HBQB	**2 303.8**	**2 584.3**	**3 029.5**	**3 238.5**	**3 171.9**	**3 581.6**	**4 132.1**	**5 058.9**	**5 564.8**	**6 667.2**	**7 042.1**
Net International Investment Position												
Monetary financial institutions												
(banks and building societies)	HDIJ	–40.2	–60.0	–64.8	–88.8	–134.5	–155.4	–188.8	–154.1	–132.7	–220.7	–249.9
Central government	CGOK	–37.0	–33.1	–27.9	–28.6	–23.7	–36.7	–55.9	–79.4	–106.2	–127.7	–186.4
Local authorities	-CGOH	–1.2	–1.1	–0.8	–0.8	–0.9	–1.1	–1.7	–1.9	–2.1	–2.1	–2.5
Public corporations	CGOL	4.2	4.5	4.6	3.8	4.2	4.2	4.2	2.9	1.3	1.4	1.2
Other sectors	HDKB	–94.2	–98.5	–7.3	–22.1	34.8	71.8	21.5	–20.1	–112.9	66.5	530.5
Total	HBQC	**–168.4**	**–188.2**	**–96.2**	**–136.5**	**–120.0**	**–117.2**	**–220.7**	**–252.6**	**–352.6**	**–282.5**	**92.9**

8.3 Direct investment
Balance sheets valued at end of year

£ billion

		1998	1999	2000	2001	2002	2003	2004	2005	2006	2007	2008
Direct investment abroad (UK assets)												
Equity capital and reinvested earnings												
Ordinary share capital and reinvested earnings	CVWF	271.9	399.8	570.6	565.7	600.4	646.1	636.6	689.5	727.3	855.1	995.5
Holdings of property	HCHP	12.0	12.5	15.7	16.5	18.9	24.6	30.6	37.3	43.5	48.9	54.3
Total equity capital and reinvested earnings	CGMO	283.9	412.3	586.3	582.2	619.3	670.7	667.2	726.8	770.8	904.0	1 049.8
Other capital												
Claims on affiliated enterprises												
Debt securities issued by affiliated enterprises	CVWG	6.3	8.8	28.1	31.0	31.8	31.9	15.4	18.0	18.0	19.7	23.6
Other claims on affiliated enterprises												
Inter-company balance	CVOK	66.1	71.4	80.7	88.8	103.1	105.2	131.7	137.4	132.3	171.1	246.5
Branch indebtedness balance	CVOP	10.4	10.2	7.9	12.4	11.4	11.1	12.8	8.2	14.8	18.2	25.8
Total claims on affiliated enterprises	CGLS	82.8	90.3	116.8	132.2	146.3	148.2	159.9	163.6	165.1	209.0	295.8
Liabilities to affiliated enterprises												
Inter-company balance	-CVOL	-53.2	-61.8	-79.1	-93.2	-124.6	-122.4	-144.9	-179.5	-190.2	-194.1	-264.5
Branch indebtedness balance	-CVOQ	-3.7	-2.5	-5.2	-4.2	-3.9	-5.3	-4.1	-5.0	-4.0	-4.9	-5.9
Total liabilities to affiliated enterprises	-HHDJ	-56.9	-64.4	-84.3	-97.4	-128.4	-127.7	-149.0	-184.5	-194.2	-199.0	-270.4
Total other capital assets	HBUW	25.9	26.0	32.5	34.8	17.9	20.5	10.9	-20.9	-29.1	10.0	25.5
Total	HBWD	**309.8**	**438.3**	**618.8**	**616.9**	**637.2**	**691.1**	**678.1**	**705.9**	**741.7**	**913.9**	**1 075.2**
Direct investment in the UK (UK liabilities)												
Equity capital and reinvested earnings												
Share capital and reinvested earnings												
Quoted share capital and reinvested earnings[1]	CVVB	–	–	–	–	20.7	25.8	35.6	73.6	39.8	42.8	67.0
Unquoted share capital and reinvested earnings	CVVC	149.0	180.7	227.1	245.6	192.6	204.0	214.5	276.8	373.0	444.2	479.2
Total share capital and reinvested earnings	HBUX	149.0	180.7	227.1	245.6	213.3	229.8	250.1	350.4	412.8	487.0	546.2
Holdings of UK property	HCQM	10.9	11.7	13.5	14.1	15.9	15.9	17.8	18.4	20.2	24.8	24.7
Total equity capital and reinvested earnings	HBUY	159.8	192.3	240.6	259.7	229.2	245.7	267.9	368.7	433.0	511.9	570.9
Other capital												
Liabilities to direct investors												
Debt securities issued by affiliated enterprises	CVVD	6.6	7.0	11.0	17.5	17.3	16.0	20.4	28.3	39.6	38.7	42.5
Other liabilities to direct investors												
Inter-company balance	CVVJ	78.4	96.0	103.8	133.1	147.0	142.2	147.6	165.7	166.6	147.6	154.7
Branch indebtedness balance	CVVM	8.1	6.8	8.5	9.4	8.7	10.7	8.5	8.5	16.0	9.9	8.2
Total liabilities to direct investors	HBVB	93.2	109.8	123.2	160.0	173.0	168.9	176.5	202.5	222.2	196.3	205.4
Claims on direct investors												
Inter-company balance	-CVVI	-39.2	-51.8	-51.3	-53.4	-60.5	-55.6	-58.6	-72.7	-73.0	-77.3	-98.8
Branch indebtedness balance	-CVVL	-0.2	-0.1	-2.1	-2.9	-1.1	-3.5	-2.4	-4.3	-3.9	-0.7	-0.9
Total claims on direct investors	-HBVA	-39.4	-51.9	-53.4	-56.3	-61.6	-59.0	-61.0	-77.0	-76.9	-78.0	-99.7
Total other capital liabilities	HBVC	53.8	57.9	69.8	103.7	111.4	109.9	115.5	125.5	145.3	118.3	105.7
Total	HBWI	**213.6**	**250.2**	**310.4**	**363.5**	**340.6**	**355.5**	**383.3**	**494.2**	**578.3**	**630.2**	**676.7**
Net international investment position (UK assets less UK liabilities)												
Equity capital												
Ordinary share capital and reinvested earnings	LTNM	123.0	219.1	343.5	320.0	387.1	416.3	386.5	339.1	314.4	368.0	449.3
Holdings of property	LTNN	1.1	0.9	2.2	2.4	3.0	8.7	12.8	18.9	23.3	24.1	29.5
Total equity capital and reinvested earnings	HBSH	124.1	220.0	345.7	322.4	390.1	425.0	399.3	358.1	337.8	392.1	478.8
Total other capital	CGKF	-27.9	-31.9	-37.3	-69.0	-93.5	-89.4	-104.6	-146.4	-174.4	-108.3	-80.3
Total	HBWQ	**96.2**	**188.1**	**308.4**	**253.5**	**296.6**	**335.6**	**294.7**	**211.7**	**163.4**	**283.8**	**398.6**

1 Prior to 2002 holdings of quoted share capital were included in series CVVC

8.4 Direct investment Sector analysis
Balance sheets valued at end of year

£ billion

		1998	1999	2000	2001	2002	2003	2004	2005	2006	2007	2008
Direct investment abroad (UK assets)												
By:												
Monetary financial institutions (banks)	CVKH	9.9	11.7	18.1	25.5	27.7	27.6	39.1	47.5	60.3	70.5	78.8
Insurance companies	DPYH	22.0	21.2	24.3	22.8	22.0	24.9	27.1	27.7	38.8	47.5	53.7
Other financial intermediaries	CVWH	26.9	26.8	34.9	37.8	42.0	44.2	32.0	32.2	35.8	65.2	67.7
Private non-financial corporations	CVLX	239.5	366.7	527.9	515.8	527.5	569.9	549.4	561.9	564.5	682.8	822.3
Public corporations	CVOF	0.8	1.1	1.7	0.8	1.5	1.4	1.7	0.8	0.3	0.5	0.3
Household sector[1]	AQHH	10.7	10.8	12.0	14.3	16.5	23.2	28.7	35.7	41.9	47.3	52.5
Total	HBWD	**309.8**	**438.3**	**618.8**	**616.9**	**637.2**	**691.1**	**678.1**	**705.9**	**741.7**	**913.9**	**1 075.2**
Direct investment in the UK (UK liabilities)												
In:												
Monetary financial institutions (banks)	CVJW	20.3	19.8	26.0	27.2	28.1	30.1	34.2	38.6	42.8	51.5	57.5
Insurance companies	CVSM	9.4	13.7	11.7	13.0	14.1	19.4	18.8	17.5	25.0	21.6	20.8
Other financial intermediaries												
Securities dealers	CVTC	7.2	8.2	9.5	11.0	11.9	12.4	14.3	18.3	15.9	23.3	30.9
Other	CVTS	8.1	7.4	15.8	27.3	29.1	30.3	31.9	26.3	46.4	56.8	60.6
Total other financial intermediaries	CVUI	15.2	15.6	25.2	38.3	41.0	42.7	46.2	44.6	62.4	80.1	91.6
Private non-financial corporations	CVKW	168.7	201.2	247.4	284.9	257.3	263.3	284.1	393.6	448.0	477.0	506.8
Total	HBWI	**213.6**	**250.2**	**310.4**	**363.5**	**340.6**	**355.5**	**383.3**	**494.2**	**578.3**	**630.2**	**676.7**
Net international investment position (UK assets less UK liabilities)												
Monetary financial institutions	LTNO	−10.5	−8.1	−8.0	−1.7	−0.5	−2.5	4.9	8.9	17.5	19.0	21.3
Insurance companies	LTNP	12.6	7.6	12.6	9.8	7.9	5.4	8.3	10.2	13.7	25.9	32.9
Other financial intermediares	LTNQ	11.7	11.2	9.7	−0.5	1.0	1.4	−14.2	−12.4	−26.5	−14.8	−23.9
Private non-financial corporations	LTNR	70.8	165.5	280.4	230.8	270.2	306.6	265.2	168.3	116.5	205.8	315.5
Public corporations	CVOF	0.8	1.1	1.7	0.8	1.5	1.4	1.7	0.8	0.3	0.5	0.3
Household sector[1]	AQHH	10.7	10.8	12.0	14.3	16.5	23.2	28.7	35.7	41.9	47.3	52.5
Total	HBWQ	**96.2**	**188.1**	**308.4**	**253.5**	**296.6**	**335.6**	**294.7**	**211.7**	**163.4**	**283.8**	**398.6**

1 The household sector includes non-profit institutions serving households.

8.5 Portfolio investment
Balance sheets valued at end of year

£ billion

		1998	1999	2000	2001	2002	2003	2004	2005	2006	2007	2008
Portfolio investment abroad (UK assets)												
Investment in equity securities (shares) by:												
Monetary financial Institutions (banks)	VTWF	8.8	6.8	19.7	14.3	2.7	20.8	53.0	86.2	109.2	127.0	41.7
Central Government	LOER	–	–	–	–	–	–	–	0.2	0.2	0.2	0.2
Insurance companies and pension funds												
Insurance companies	CGPB	77.3	115.7	100.7	106.2	82.1	79.1	91.4	132.0	150.2	178.6	148.5
Pension funds[1]	ZPOR	108.9	148.3	135.5	127.9	104.4	125.7	140.3	192.1	202.0	178.6	138.2
Total insurance companies and pension funds	CGPV	186.2	264.0	236.2	234.1	186.5	204.9	231.7	324.0	352.1	357.2	286.6
Other financial intermediaries												
Securities dealers	HCEA	27.0	38.3	49.3	46.8	22.9	32.4	46.3	33.9	31.3	50.2	60.7
Unit and Investment Trusts	CGSN	69.0	93.6	99.1	88.0	77.3	94.1	100.0	131.0	151.6	167.0	138.3
Other	CGTV	–	–	–	–	–	–	–	–	–	1.0	1.0
Total other financial intermediaries	HDIG	96.0	131.8	148.4	134.8	100.2	126.5	146.2	164.9	182.9	218.2	200.1
Private non-financial corporations	XBNN	0.7	1.1	10.0	8.9	6.5	7.8	7.9	9.3	11.6	11.3	8.9
Household sector[2]	HFLX	11.9	16.1	15.0	12.5	10.0	12.0	16.5	32.6	37.3	39.1	31.5
Total investment in equity securities	HEPX	303.7	419.9	429.3	404.6	305.9	372.0	455.3	617.2	693.4	753.1	569.1
Investment in debt securities												
Investment in bonds and notes by:												
Monetary financial institutions												
Banks	VTWJ	224.8	239.0	282.8	312.9	326.0	318.2	349.5	403.2	466.9	539.5	548.9
Building societies	HPEG	3.0	4.1	5.8	6.7	6.3	4.8	5.6	5.9	7.6	10.0	12.3
Total monetary financial institutions	HPCO	227.8	243.1	288.7	319.6	332.3	323.1	355.0	409.1	474.5	549.5	561.3
Central Government	HQ5O	–	–	–	–	–	–	–	–	–	0.1	–
Insurance companies and pension funds												
Insurance companies	CGTU	41.4	37.8	39.8	55.9	62.9	64.5	77.0	80.5	103.6	114.7	161.5
Pension funds[1]	JIRX	23.9	36.4	44.2	49.9	45.7	53.9	64.6	87.0	107.9	141.7	199.7
Total insurance companies and pension funds	HBUM	65.3	74.1	84.0	105.8	108.6	118.3	141.7	167.6	211.4	256.4	361.2
Other financial intermediaries												
Securities dealers	HCDZ	68.1	45.6	45.2	34.9	31.1	38.7	57.3	73.8	40.6	17.9	133.5
Unit and investment trusts	HBXZ	4.7	5.8	6.8	8.4	7.7	10.7	13.4	20.6	29.8	34.1	53.7
Other	HCNA	–	–	–	–	–	–	–	–	–	–	–
Total other financial intermediaries	HCOR	72.8	51.4	52.1	43.3	38.8	49.4	70.7	94.4	70.4	52.0	187.2
Private non-financial corporations	XBNK	1.4	0.4	1.6	2.0	2.2	3.5	3.7	3.0	1.3	2.0	4.3
Household sector[2]	HCJC	7.1	6.9	7.5	7.6	7.8	7.7	7.7	7.7	7.5	7.6	8.5
Total investment in bonds and notes	HEPW	374.4	376.0	433.8	478.3	489.6	502.0	578.8	681.7	765.2	867.5	1 122.5
Investment in Money Market Instruments												
Investment in commercial paper by:												
Monetary financial institutions												
Banks	HBMW	21.3	31.3	33.2	39.7	32.3	40.6	35.2	37.9	40.4	52.4	54.2
Building societies	TAIG	0.2	0.2	1.1	1.8	1.2	1.0	1.0	1.0	1.0	0.2	–
Central government	LSPI	–	–	–	0.5	0.9	–	–	–	–	2.4	2.3
Insurance companies and pension funds	HBXX	1.1	1.4	1.3	1.1	1.4	1.5	2.1	3.5	3.0	3.1	5.5
Other financial intermediaries	HGRJ	1.1	4.1	2.2	4.7	4.2	7.2	7.9	6.8	10.1	6.3	4.5
Private non-financial corporations	HFBN	1.2	1.9	3.0	4.9	6.0	9.8	10.4	11.4	16.2	6.4	1.3
Total investment in commercial paper	HGRK	24.8	38.9	40.8	52.6	46.0	60.0	56.5	60.7	70.6	70.7	67.6
Investment in certificates of deposit by:												
Monetary financial institutions (Building societies)	TAIE	0.2	0.1	0.6	0.6	1.2	1.2	0.8	0.6	1.4	1.3	2.9
Other financial intermediaries	CDHB	0.8	3.4	1.6	1.2	1.4	0.7	0.7	0.7	0.5	1.3	0.1
Total transactions in certificates of deposit	VTWN	1.0	3.6	2.2	1.8	2.5	1.9	1.5	1.3	1.9	2.6	3.0
Total investment in Money Market Instruments	HLYR	25.8	42.5	43.0	54.5	48.5	61.9	58.0	62.0	72.5	73.3	70.6
Total investment in debt securities	HHZX	400.2	418.4	476.8	532.8	538.1	563.9	636.8	743.8	837.7	940.8	1 193.1
Total	HHZZ	703.8	838.3	906.1	937.4	844.0	935.8	1 092.1	1 360.9	1 531.1	1 693.8	1 762.2

1 The pension funds data only covers self-administered funds, see glossary.   2 The household sector includes non-profit institutions serving households.

8.5 Portfolio investment
Balance sheets valued at end of year
continued

£ billion

Portfolio investment in the UK
(UK liabilities)

		1998	1999	2000	2001	2002	2003	2004	2005	2006	2007	2008
Investment in equity securities (shares) issued by:												
Monetary financial Institutions (banks and building societies)	HBQD	12.2	11.0	6.6	5.6	3.2	4.5	4.6	5.3	7.0	10.8	8.0
Other sectors[1]	HBQE	436.9	603.2	667.1	578.5	439.5	522.6	570.1	654.0	773.0	807.4	541.7
Total investment in equity securities	HLXX	449.1	614.2	673.7	584.1	442.7	527.1	574.7	659.3	780.0	818.2	549.8
Investment in debt securities												
Investment in bonds and notes												
Issues by central government												
UK foreign currency bonds and notes	HEWE	5.1	4.7	6.5	3.3	0.9	1.6	1.5	1.7	1.5	1.5	–
Investment in British government stocks by:												
Foreign central banks (exchange reserves)	HCCH	18.0	16.7	18.1	18.7	17.3	15.9	21.0	21.0	25.2	28.7	35.7
Other foreign residents	HEQF	50.9	39.6	37.8	37.8	38.2	48.6	61.3	88.0	108.8	128.0	180.7
Total investment in British government stocks	HEWD	68.8	56.2	55.9	56.5	55.5	64.5	82.3	109.0	134.0	156.7	216.4
Total issues by central government	HHGF	73.9	60.9	62.4	59.9	56.4	66.1	83.8	110.7	135.5	158.2	216.4
Local authorities' bonds	HHGG	–	–	–	–	–	–	–	–	–	–	–
Public corporations' bonds	HEWM	–	–	–	–	–	–	–	–	–	–	–
Issues by monetary financial Institutions (banks and building societies)												
Bonds	HMBL	28.6	33.6	39.0	41.6	51.4	68.0	83.0	105.9	119.3	137.2	159.3
European medium term notes and other medium-term paper:												
Issued by UK banks	HCFA	27.7	33.5	35.8	39.2	40.4	49.5	64.5	85.6	105.0	155.2	188.3
Issued by UK building societies	HCFD	1.1	1.2	2.6	3.3	3.2	4.2	6.4	9.9	9.9	11.7	11.9
Total	HHGI	28.9	34.7	38.4	42.5	43.6	53.7	70.9	95.5	114.9	166.9	200.2
Total monetary financial institutions	HMBF	57.4	68.3	77.4	84.1	95.0	121.7	154.0	201.3	234.1	304.1	359.5
Issues by other sectors[1]	HHGJ	89.0	104.6	121.3	129.5	160.1	211.7	258.3	329.3	371.3	427.1	562.8
Total investment in bonds and notes	HLXZ	220.4	233.8	261.1	273.4	311.5	399.5	496.1	641.3	740.8	889.5	1 138.7
Investment in Money Market Instruments												
Investment in treasury bills (issued by central government)												
Sterling treasury bills	ACQJ	0.1	0.1	–	0.1	0.2	1.9	3.8	2.8	3.5	7.2	20.9
Euro treasury bills	HHNX	0.2	–	–	–	–	–	–	–	–	–	–
Total treasury bills	HLYU	0.3	0.1	–	0.1	0.2	1.9	3.8	2.8	3.5	7.2	20.9
Investment in certificates of deposit (issued by monetary financial institutions)												
Issued by UK banks	HHGK	41.6	53.9	92.8	115.0	108.4	96.2	87.9	95.1	114.6	137.9	148.5
Issued by UK building societies	HHGL	0.3	0.5	0.5	0.4	0.6	1.7	2.2	1.1	2.1	3.3	2.8
Total certificates of deposit	HHGM	42.0	54.4	93.3	115.4	108.9	97.8	90.1	96.2	116.7	141.2	151.3
Investment in commercial paper												
Issued by UK monetary financial Institutions												
UK banks	HHGN	11.4	10.1	14.7	14.9	28.9	27.0	35.1	33.9	35.6	38.6	50.9
Building societies	HHGO	1.0	2.7	2.9	2.8	2.4	5.7	5.5	6.0	9.7	3.9	2.0
Total monetary financial institutions	HHGP	12.4	12.8	17.7	17.7	31.4	32.8	40.6	39.9	45.2	42.5	52.9
Issued by other sectors[1]	HLYQ	15.6	17.8	21.7	22.5	30.6	23.7	22.5	22.2	16.3	19.1	29.9
Total investment in commercial paper	HHGR	28.0	30.6	39.4	40.2	62.0	56.5	63.2	62.1	61.5	61.6	82.8
Total investment in Money Market Instruments	HLYB	70.3	85.2	132.7	155.7	171.1	156.3	157.1	161.1	181.8	210.0	255.0
Total investment in debt securities	HLXY	290.7	319.0	393.8	429.1	482.6	555.8	653.2	802.4	922.6	1 099.5	1 393.7
Total	HLXW	**739.9**	**933.2**	**1 067.6**	**1 013.2**	**925.3**	**1 082.9**	**1 227.9**	**1 461.7**	**1 702.6**	**1 917.6**	**1 943.4**

1 These series relate to non-governmental sectors other than monetary financial institutions.

8.5 Portfolio investment
Balance sheets valued at end of year
continued

£ billion

		1998	1999	2000	2001	2002	2003	2004	2005	2006	2007	2008
Net international investment position (UK assets less UK liabilities)												
Equity securities	CGNE	−145.5	−194.3	−244.4	−179.4	−136.8	−155.1	−119.4	−42.1	−86.6	−65.1	19.3
Debt securities												
Bonds and notes	LTNS	154.0	142.1	172.7	204.9	178.1	102.5	82.7	40.4	24.4	−22.0	−16.2
Money market instruments	LTNT	−44.5	−42.7	−89.8	−101.2	−122.6	−94.4	−99.1	−99.1	−109.3	−136.7	−184.4
Total debt securities	CGNF	109.5	99.4	82.9	103.7	55.5	8.1	−16.4	−58.6	−84.9	−158.7	−200.6
Total	**CGNH**	**−36.0**	**−94.9**	**−161.5**	**−75.7**	**−81.3**	**−147.0**	**−135.8**	**−100.8**	**−171.5**	**−223.8**	**−181.3**

8.6 Portfolio investment
Sector analysis
Balance sheets valued at end of year

£ billion

		1998	1999	2000	2001	2002	2003	2004	2005	2006	2007	2008
Portfolio investment abroad (UK assets)												
Investment by:												
Monetary financial institutions												
Banks	HBRW	254.8	277.1	335.8	367.0	361.0	379.6	437.6	527.3	616.5	718.9	644.9
Building societies	VTWM	3.4	4.5	7.5	9.0	8.7	7.0	7.4	7.5	10.0	11.5	15.3
Total monetary financial institutions	HHGQ	258.2	281.6	343.2	376.0	369.7	386.7	445.0	534.8	626.5	730.3	660.1
Central government	LOFC	–	–	–	0.5	0.9	–	–	0.2	0.2	2.6	2.5
Insurance companies and pension funds	HHHH	252.7	339.5	321.4	341.0	296.5	324.7	375.4	495.1	566.6	616.7	653.3
Other financial intermediaries	HHNH	170.7	190.8	204.3	184.0	144.5	183.7	225.5	266.8	263.8	277.7	391.8
Private non-financial corporations	AIMH	3.2	3.4	14.7	15.8	14.6	21.0	21.9	23.7	29.2	19.7	14.5
Household sector[1]	AINA	19.0	23.0	22.4	20.2	17.7	19.7	24.2	40.3	44.8	46.7	39.9
Total	**HHZZ**	**703.8**	**838.3**	**906.1**	**937.4**	**844.0**	**935.8**	**1 092.1**	**1 360.9**	**1 531.1**	**1 693.8**	**1 762.2**
Portfolio investment in the UK (UK liabilities)												
Investment in securities issued by:												
Monetary financial institutions (banks and building societies)	CGPC	124.0	146.5	195.0	222.8	238.6	256.8	289.3	342.7	403.1	498.6	571.7
Central government	HHGS	74.3	61.1	62.4	60.0	56.5	68.0	87.6	113.4	139.0	165.4	237.1
Local authorities	HHGG	–	–	–	–	–	–	–	–	–	–	–
Public corporations	HEWM	–	–	–	–	–	–	–	–	–	–	–
Other sectors	CGPG	541.6	725.6	810.2	730.5	630.2	758.0	851.0	1 005.5	1 160.5	1 253.6	1 134.4
Total	**HLXW**	**739.9**	**933.2**	**1 067.6**	**1 013.2**	**925.3**	**1 082.9**	**1 227.9**	**1 461.7**	**1 702.6**	**1 917.6**	**1 943.4**
Net international investment position (UK assets less UK liabilities)												
Monetary financial institutions	LTNU	134.2	135.1	148.3	153.2	131.1	129.8	155.7	192.1	223.4	231.7	88.4
Central government	ZPOH	−74.3	−61.1	−62.4	−59.5	−55.6	−68.0	−87.6	−113.3	−138.8	−162.8	−234.8
Local authorities	HHGG	–	–	–	–	–	–	–	–	–	–	–
Public corporations	-HEWM	–	–	–	–	–	–	–	–	–	–	–
Other sectors	LTNV	−96.0	−169.0	−247.3	−169.5	−156.7	−208.8	−203.9	−179.6	−256.2	−292.7	−34.9
Total	**CGNH**	**−36.0**	**−94.9**	**−161.5**	**−75.7**	**−81.3**	**−147.0**	**−135.8**	**−100.8**	**−171.5**	**−223.8**	**−181.3**

1 The household sector includes non-profit institutions serving households.

8.7 Other investment
Balance sheets valued at end of year

£ billion

		1998	1999	2000	2001	2002	2003	2004	2005	2006	2007	2008
Other investment abroad (UK assets)												
Trade credit												
Long-term												
Central government	ZPOC	8.2	–	–	–	–	–	–	–	–	–	–
Other sectors[1]	HCLK	0.5	–	–	–	–	–	–	–	–	–	–
Total long-term trade credit	HHGU	8.7	–	–	–	–	–	–	–	–	–	–
Short-term												
Other sectors[1]	HLXU	1.4	0.5	0.4	0.1	0.4	1.0	0.6	–0.7	0.6	0.7	0.6
Total trade credit	HLXP	10.1	0.5	0.4	0.1	0.4	1.0	0.6	–0.7	0.6	0.7	0.6
Loans												
Long-term												
Bank loans under ECGD guarantee	HCFQ	6.0	6.0	4.8	5.1	3.8	3.7	3.7	4.1	3.3	3.2	4.4
Inter-government loans by the UK and other central government assets	HCFN	0.3	0.3	0.2	0.2	0.2	0.2	0.2	0.2	0.1	0.1	0.1
Loans by Commonwealth Development Corporation (public corporations)	HEWZ	1.1	1.1	0.5	0.4	0.4	0.4	0.3	0.3	0.3	0.3	0.3
Loans by the Export Credit Guarantee Department	CY94	2.3	2.4	2.4	2.6	2.4	2.4	2.6	2.2	1.1	1.0	1.0
Loans by specialist leasing companies[1]	HGIH	–	–	–	–	–	–	–	–	–	–	–
Total long-term loans	HFAX	9.7	9.7	8.0	8.3	6.8	6.6	6.8	6.8	4.9	4.6	5.8
Short-term												
By monetary financial institutions												
By banks												
Sterling loans	NLHN	23.4	26.1	27.5	32.2	37.4	40.2	47.4	66.9	87.7	113.1	116.2
Foreign currency loans	ZPOO	180.0	189.1	252.4	290.9	290.9	358.3	448.9	575.1	621.3	842.8	1 010.0
Total banks	HEQS	203.3	215.2	279.9	323.0	328.4	398.4	496.3	642.0	709.1	955.9	1 126.2
By building societies	NLHP	–	–	–	–	–	–	–	–	–	–	–
Total monetary financial institutions	ZPOM	203.3	215.2	279.9	323.0	328.4	398.4	496.3	642.0	709.1	955.9	1 126.2
By other sectors	HLXI	0.6	0.5	0.5	0.5	0.5	0.5	0.5	0.5	0.5	0.5	1.3
Total short-term loans	VTUM	203.9	215.8	280.5	323.6	328.9	399.0	496.9	642.6	709.6	956.4	1 127.5
Total loans	HLXQ	213.6	225.5	288.5	331.9	335.7	405.6	503.7	649.4	714.5	961.1	1 133.2
Currency and deposits												
Foreign notes and coin												
Monetary financial institutions (banks)	TAAF	0.2	0.1	0.1	0.1	0.1	0.1	0.1	0.1	0.2	0.2	0.4
Other sectors[1]	CGML	0.3	0.4	0.4	0.4	0.4	0.5	0.5	0.5	0.5	0.6	0.6
Total foreign notes and coin	HEOX	0.5	0.5	0.5	0.5	0.5	0.6	0.6	0.6	0.7	0.8	0.9
Deposits abroad by UK residents												
Deposits by monetary financial institutions												
Deposits by banks												
Sterling deposits	HFBB	89.2	77.2	96.5	103.8	96.2	114.6	111.7	145.9	193.0	302.9	277.8
Foreign currency deposits	HFBG	576.3	546.9	678.2	700.6	746.5	806.6	894.9	1 053.5	1 092.6	1 409.4	1 811.5
Total deposits by UK banks	HLXL	665.5	624.1	774.6	804.4	842.7	921.2	1 006.6	1 199.4	1 285.6	1 712.3	2 089.2
Deposits by building societies	TAIC	0.9	0.5	1.0	0.9	0.4	0.2	0.3	0.2	0.3	1.9	1.3
Total deposits by monetary financial institutions	VTWL	666.4	624.6	775.6	805.3	843.0	921.4	1 006.9	1 199.7	1 286.0	1 714.1	2 090.6
Deposits by securities dealers	HGUX	111.5	152.2	206.1	261.9	242.0	289.7	315.7	497.4	504.8	555.7	354.8
Deposits by other UK residents[1]	HHGW	88.4	85.3	98.9	112.3	112.4	183.9	279.3	356.5	397.6	502.8	662.0
Total deposits abroad	HBXS	866.3	862.2	1 080.6	1 179.5	1 197.4	1 395.0	1 602.0	2 053.5	2 188.3	2 772.7	3 107.4
Total currency and deposits	HBVS	866.8	862.6	1 081.1	1 180.0	1 198.0	1 395.6	1 602.6	2 054.1	2 189.0	2 773.5	3 108.4

1 These series relate to non-governmental sectors other than monetary financial institutions.

8.7 Other investment
Balance sheets valued at end of year
continued

£ billion

		1998	1999	2000	2001	2002	2003	2004	2005	2006	2007	2008
Other investment abroad - *continued* (UK assets)												
Other assets													
Central government assets												
Central government subscriptions to international organisations												
International Development Association	HEXS	4.5	4.7	5.0	5.2	5.5	5.6	5.8	6.2	6.6	7.2	7.9
Regional development banks	HEXW	1.0	1.0	1.1	1.1	1.2	1.3	1.3	1.4	1.5	1.5	1.7
European Investment Bank (EIB)	HEXX	0.4	0.4	0.4	0.4	0.4	0.4	0.4	0.4	0.4	0.4	0.4
Other subscriptions	HEXZ	0.3	0.4	0.4	0.4	0.4	0.4	0.5	0.5	0.7	0.9	0.9
Total central government subscriptions	HLXO	6.2	6.5	6.8	7.1	7.5	7.7	8.0	8.5	9.2	10.0	11.0
Other long-term central government assets	XBJL	–	–	–	–	–	–	–	–	–	–	–
Other short-term central government assets	LOEM	1.2	1.5	1.8	1.7	2.3	2.5	1.9	2.4	2.6	3.0	5.7
Total central government	LOET	7.4	8.0	8.6	8.8	9.8	10.2	10.0	10.9	11.9	13.0	16.7
Other sectors assets												
Long-term assets[1]	HLXM	–	–	–	–	–	–	–	–	–	–	–
Short-term assets												
Public corporations assets abroad	HGJM	–	–	–	–	–	–	–	–	–	–	–
Other[1]	HHGY	0.5	0.8	1.1	1.1	1.4	1.3	1.1	1.1	0.6	1.9	2.5
Total short-term assets	HLXJ	0.5	0.8	1.1	1.1	1.4	1.3	1.1	1.1	0.6	1.9	2.5
Total other sectors	HLXN	0.5	0.8	1.1	1.1	1.4	1.3	1.1	1.1	0.6	1.9	2.5
Total other assets	HLXS	7.9	8.8	9.7	10.0	11.2	11.5	11.0	12.0	12.5	14.9	19.2
Total	HLXV	1 098.4	1 097.3	1 379.7	1 521.9	1 545.2	1 813.7	2 118.0	2 714.8	2 916.6	3 750.2	4 261.4

1 These series relate to non-governmental sectors other than monetary financial institutions.

8.7 Other investment
Balance sheets valued at end of year
continued

£ billion

		1998	1999	2000	2001	2002	2003	2004	2005	2006	2007	2008
Other investment in the UK (UK liabilities)												
Trade credit												
Long-term [1]	HBWC	1.5	–	–	–	–	–	–	–	–	–	–
Short-term [1]	HCGB	1.2	1.0	1.1	1.1	1.0	0.9	0.9	1.0	0.8	0.8	1.1
Total trade credit	HLYL	2.7	1.0	1.1	1.1	1.0	0.9	0.9	1.0	0.8	0.8	1.1
Loans												
Long-term loans to:												
Central government	HHGZ	0.4	0.4	0.6	0.5	0.4	0.2	0.1	0.1	–	–	–
Local authorities	HHHA	1.2	1.1	0.8	0.8	0.9	1.1	1.7	1.9	2.1	2.1	2.5
Public corporations	HHHB	–	–	–	–	–	–	0.4	0.4	0.4	0.4	0.4
Other [1]	AQBX	–	–	–	–	–	–	–	–	–	–	–
Total long-term loans	HHHC	1.6	1.4	1.4	1.3	1.2	1.3	2.3	2.4	2.5	2.5	2.9
Short-term loans to:												
Central government	HHHD	–	–	–	–	–	–	–	–	–	–	–
Local authorities	HHHE	–	–	–	–	–	–	–	–	–	–	–
Securities dealers	HHHF	209.3	271.7	314.1	388.6	356.1	382.5	444.5	668.1	600.1	679.9	515.0
Other [1]	HHHG	79.7	76.9	55.5	82.8	91.7	138.6	203.0	214.1	287.0	274.1	310.0
Total short-term loans	HHHJ	289.1	348.6	369.6	471.3	447.7	521.1	647.5	882.1	887.1	954.0	825.0
Total loans	HLYI	290.7	350.0	371.0	472.6	449.0	522.4	649.8	884.5	889.6	956.5	827.9
Currency and deposits												
Sterling notes and coin												
Notes (issued by Bank of England)	HLVG	0.9	1.0	1.0	1.0	1.1	1.1	1.2	1.3	1.4	1.4	1.4
Coins (issued by Royal Mint)	HLVH	0.1	0.1	0.1	0.1	0.1	0.1	0.1	0.1	0.2	0.2	0.2
Total notes and coin	APME	1.0	1.1	1.1	1.1	1.2	1.3	1.4	1.4	1.5	1.5	1.5
Deposits from abroad with UK residents												
Deposits with monetary financial institutions												
Deposits with banks												
Sterling deposits	NLCZ	147.2	167.5	200.5	215.9	228.0	251.7	279.6	331.3	389.0	604.6	540.8
Foreign currency deposits	NLDA	886.7	859.4	1 060.0	1 152.4	1 206.5	1 348.1	1 570.0	1 861.6	1 974.2	2 531.0	3 031.5
Total deposits with banks	CGEH	1 033.9	1 026.9	1 260.4	1 368.2	1 434.5	1 599.8	1 849.6	2 192.9	2 363.2	3 135.6	3 572.3
Deposits with building societies	NLDB	4.9	5.2	4.1	4.6	4.9	5.4	5.6	6.9	7.5	7.8	7.5
Total deposits with UK monetary financial institutions	HDKG	1 038.9	1 032.1	1 264.6	1 372.9	1 439.4	1 605.3	1 855.2	2 199.8	2 370.7	3 143.4	3 579.8
Deposit liabilities of UK central government	HEYH	0.6	1.3	1.8	1.7	1.6	1.9	1.0	0.9	1.4	1.1	0.8
Total deposits from abroad with UK residents	HBYA	1 039.5	1 033.4	1 266.4	1 374.5	1 441.0	1 607.1	1 856.2	2 200.7	2 372.1	3 144.5	3 580.6
Total currency and deposits	HLVI	1 040.5	1 034.5	1 267.5	1 375.6	1 442.2	1 608.4	1 857.6	2 202.1	2 373.6	3 146.1	3 582.2
Other liabilities												
Long-term												
Net equity of foreign households in life insurance reserves and in pension funds	VTUE	0.2	0.2	0.2	0.2	0.2	0.2	0.2	0.2	0.2	0.2	0.2
Prepayments of premiums and reserves against oustanding claims	NQLR	15.0	14.1	10.8	10.7	12.6	10.2	11.5	14.2	18.6	14.4	9.2
Total long-term liabilities[1]	VTUF	15.2	14.3	11.0	10.9	12.9	10.4	11.7	14.4	18.8	14.6	9.4
Short-term[1]	HBMV	1.3	1.1	1.1	1.6	1.0	1.0	0.9	1.0	1.1	1.3	1.5
Total other liabilities	HLYM	16.5	15.4	12.0	12.5	13.8	11.4	12.6	15.5	19.9	16.0	10.9
Total	HLYD	**1 350.3**	**1 400.9**	**1 651.6**	**1 861.9**	**1 906.0**	**2 143.2**	**2 520.8**	**3 103.0**	**3 284.0**	**4 119.4**	**4 422.1**

1 These series relate to non-governmental sectors other than monetary financial institutions.

8.7 Other investment
Balance sheets valued at end of year
continued

£ billion

		1998	1999	2000	2001	2002	2003	2004	2005	2006	2007	2008
Net international investment position (UK assets less UK liabilities)												
Trade credit	LTNW	7.4	−0.5	−0.7	−1.0	−0.6	0.1	−0.2	−1.7	−0.2	−0.1	−0.6
Loans	LTNX	−77.1	−124.5	−82.5	−140.7	−113.3	−116.8	−146.1	−235.1	−175.1	4.6	305.3
Currency and deposits	LTNY	−173.7	−171.9	−186.5	−195.7	−244.2	−212.8	−254.9	−148.0	−184.6	−372.6	−473.8
Other	LTNZ	−8.5	−6.7	−2.3	−2.5	−2.7	0.1	−1.6	−3.5	−7.4	−1.0	8.3
Total	CGNG	**−251.9**	**−303.6**	**−271.9**	**−339.9**	**−360.8**	**−329.5**	**−402.9**	**−388.2**	**−367.3**	**−369.2**	**−160.7**

8.8 Other investment
Sector analysis
Balance sheets valued at end of year

£ billion

		1998	1999	2000	2001	2002	2003	2004	2005	2006	2007	2008
Other investment abroad (UK assets)												
Investment by:												
Monetary financial institutions												
Banks	CGEI	875.0	845.4	1 059.5	1 132.6	1 174.9	1 323.4	1 506.8	1 845.7	1 998.1	2 671.6	3 220.1
Building societies	HEQT	0.9	0.5	1.0	0.9	0.4	0.2	0.3	0.2	0.4	1.9	1.4
Total monetary financial institutions	VTXD	875.9	845.9	1 060.5	1 133.5	1 175.3	1 323.6	1 507.1	1 845.9	1 998.5	2 673.4	3 221.5
Central government	CGEN	15.9	8.3	8.9	9.1	10.0	10.4	10.1	11.0	12.1	13.2	16.7
Public corporations	CGEO	3.4	3.4	2.9	3.0	2.8	2.8	2.9	2.5	1.4	1.3	1.3
Other sectors	CGGH	203.2	239.7	307.4	376.3	357.1	476.8	597.8	855.3	904.6	1 062.3	1 021.8
Total	HLXV	**1 098.4**	**1 097.3**	**1 379.7**	**1 521.9**	**1 545.2**	**1 813.7**	**2 118.0**	**2 714.8**	**2 916.6**	**3 750.2**	**4 261.4**
Other investment in the UK (UK liabilities)												
Investment in:												
Monetary financial institutions												
Banks	CGOV	1 034.8	1 027.9	1 261.5	1 369.2	1 435.5	1 601.0	1 850.8	2 194.1	2 364.5	3 137.0	3 573.7
Building societies	NLDB	4.9	5.2	4.1	4.6	4.9	5.4	5.6	6.9	7.5	7.8	7.5
Total monetary financial institutions	CGHB	1 039.8	1 033.1	1 265.6	1 373.9	1 440.5	1 606.4	1 856.4	2 201.0	2 372.0	3 144.8	3 581.2
Central government	CGHG	2.1	2.5	3.2	3.4	2.6	2.8	1.7	1.8	2.3	2.2	2.1
Local authorities	CGHX	1.2	1.1	0.8	0.8	0.9	1.1	1.7	1.9	2.1	2.1	2.5
Public corporations	ZPOX	–	–	–	–	–	–	0.5	0.4	0.4	0.4	0.4
Other sectors	CGNC	307.3	364.3	382.1	483.8	462.1	532.8	660.5	897.9	907.2	969.8	835.9
Total	HLYD	**1 350.3**	**1 400.9**	**1 651.6**	**1 861.9**	**1 906.0**	**2 143.2**	**2 520.8**	**3 103.0**	**3 284.0**	**4 119.4**	**4 422.1**
Net international investment position (UK assets less UK liabilities)												
Monetary financial institutions												
Banks	LTOA	−159.8	−182.4	−202.0	−236.6	−260.6	−277.6	−344.1	−348.5	−366.4	−465.5	−353.5
Building societies	LTOB	−4.1	−4.7	−3.1	−3.7	−4.6	−5.2	−5.3	−6.7	−7.2	−5.9	−6.1
Total monetary financial institutions	LTOC	−163.9	−187.1	−205.1	−240.3	−265.1	−282.8	−349.4	−355.1	−373.6	−471.4	−359.7
Central government	LTOD	13.9	5.7	5.7	5.7	7.4	7.6	8.4	9.3	9.8	11.0	14.6
Local authorities	-CGHX	−1.2	−1.1	−0.8	−0.8	−0.9	−1.1	−1.7	−1.9	−2.1	−2.1	−2.5
Public corporations	LTOE	3.4	3.4	2.9	3.0	2.8	2.8	2.5	2.1	1.0	0.9	0.9
Other sectors	LTOF	−104.1	−124.6	−74.6	−107.4	−104.9	−56.0	−62.6	−42.6	−2.5	92.5	185.9
Total	CGNG	**−251.9**	**−303.6**	**−271.9**	**−339.9**	**−360.8**	**−329.5**	**−402.9**	**−388.2**	**−367.3**	**−369.2**	**−160.7**

8.9 Reserve assets
Central government sector
Balance sheets valued at end of year

£ billion

		1998	1999	2000	2001	2002	2003	2004	2005	2006	2007	2008
Monetary gold	HCGD	4.0	3.7	2.9	2.2	2.1	2.3	2.3	3.0	3.2	4.2	6.0
Special drawing rights	HCGE	0.3	0.3	0.2	0.2	0.2	0.2	0.2	0.2	0.2	0.2	0.3
Reserve position in the Fund	HCGF	2.6	3.3	2.9	3.5	3.8	3.5	2.9	1.0	0.7	0.5	1.6
Foreign exchange												
Currency and deposits												
With central banks	CGDE	0.8	0.4	0.1	0.1	0.2	0.1	0.1	0.1	0.1	0.1	0.4
With other banks	CGDF	2.6	5.0	3.7	2.8	1.9	1.3	0.3	0.8	0.4	0.4	0.4
Total currency and deposits	CGDD	3.4	5.5	3.7	2.9	2.1	1.4	0.4	1.0	0.5	0.5	0.9
Securities												
Bonds and notes	CGDH	10.9	7.6	16.7	14.4	16.8	16.2	17.1	17.5	15.3	18.2	24.4
Money market instruments	CGDL	2.1	1.8	2.3	2.2	0.2	0.2	0.3	1.7	3.0	3.1	3.1
Total securities	CGDG	13.0	9.5	19.0	16.6	17.0	16.4	17.4	19.2	18.3	21.3	27.5
Total foreign exchange	HCGG	16.4	14.9	22.7	19.4	19.1	17.7	17.8	20.2	18.8	21.7	28.4
Other claims	CGDM	–	–	0.1	0.4	0.2	–	0.1	0.4	–	0.1	–
Total	**LTEB**	**23.3**	**22.2**	**28.8**	**25.6**	**25.5**	**23.8**	**23.2**	**24.7**	**22.9**	**26.7**	**36.3**

Other titles from the
Office for National Statistics

www.palgrave.com/ons/

8.10 External debt statement
End of period

£ billion

		2000	2001	2002	2003	2004	2005	2006	2007	2008
General Government										
Short-term										
Money market instruments	HLYU	–	0.1	0.2	1.9	3.8	2.8	3.5	7.2	20.9
Currency and deposits	HLVH	0.1	0.1	0.1	0.1	0.1	0.1	0.2	0.2	0.2
Other liabilities	VTZZ	1.8	1.7	1.6	1.9	1.0	0.9	1.4	1.1	0.8
Total short-term	ZAVF	2.0	1.9	1.9	3.9	4.9	3.8	5.1	8.5	21.9
Long-term										
Bonds and notes issued by central government	HHGF	62.4	59.9	56.4	66.1	83.8	110.7	135.5	158.2	216.4
Loans										
to central government	HHGZ	0.6	0.5	0.4	0.2	0.1	0.1	–	–	–
to local authorities	HHHA	0.8	0.8	0.9	1.1	1.7	1.9	2.1	2.1	2.5
Total long-term	ZAVG	63.7	61.2	57.6	67.4	85.7	112.6	137.6	160.2	218.9
Total General Government liabilities	ZAVH	65.7	63.0	59.5	71.4	90.6	116.4	142.6	168.7	240.8
Monetary Authorities										
Short-term										
Money market instruments	VTZS	0.2	1.4	2.8	3.5	3.4	3.6	2.4	2.5	3.3
Currency and deposits	VTZT	5.2	3.8	5.5	6.8	9.9	13.0	14.6	21.0	38.2
Total short-term	VTZY	5.5	5.2	8.3	10.3	13.3	16.5	17.0	23.5	41.6
Long-term										
Bonds and notes	VTZU	–	–	–	–	–	–	–	–	–
Total long-term	VTZV	–	–	–	–	–	–	–	–	–
Total Monetary Authorities liabilities	VTZW	5.5	5.2	8.3	10.3	13.3	16.5	17.0	23.5	41.6
Banks										
Short-term										
Money market instruments										
Banks	ZAVC	107.3	128.5	134.5	119.7	119.7	125.4	147.9	174.0	196.1
Building societies	ZAVD	3.4	3.2	3.0	7.4	7.7	7.2	11.8	7.2	4.8
Total money market instruments	ZAUX	110.7	131.7	137.5	127.1	127.4	132.6	159.6	181.2	200.9
Currency and deposits										
Banks	VTZX	1 255.2	1 364.4	1 429.0	1 593.1	1 839.7	2 179.9	2 348.5	3 114.6	3 534.1
Building societies	NLDB	4.1	4.6	4.9	5.4	5.6	6.9	7.5	7.8	7.5
Total short-term	ZAVI	1 370.0	1 500.7	1 571.4	1 725.6	1 972.7	2 319.4	2 515.7	3 303.6	3 742.5
Long-term										
Bonds and notes	HMBF	77.4	84.1	95.0	121.7	154.0	201.3	234.1	304.1	359.5
Total long-term	ZPOK	77.4	84.1	95.0	121.7	154.0	201.3	234.1	304.1	359.5
Total Banks liabilities	ZAVA	1 447.4	1 584.8	1 666.5	1 847.3	2 126.7	2 520.7	2 749.8	3 607.8	4 101.9
Other sectors										
Short-term										
Money market instruments	HLYQ	21.7	22.5	30.6	23.7	22.5	22.2	16.3	19.1	29.9
Loans	ZLBY	369.6	471.3	447.7	521.1	647.5	882.1	887.1	954.0	825.0
Trade credits	HCGB	1.1	1.1	1.0	0.9	0.9	1.0	0.8	0.8	1.1
Other liabilities	LSYR	1.1	1.6	1.0	1.0	0.9	1.0	1.1	1.3	1.5
Total short-term liabilities	ZAVB	393.5	496.6	480.3	546.8	671.7	906.3	905.3	975.3	857.5
Long-term										
Bond and notes	HHGJ	121.3	129.5	160.1	211.7	258.3	329.3	371.3	427.1	562.8
Loans	ZLBZ	–	–	–	–	0.4	0.4	0.4	0.4	0.4
Trade credits	HBWC	–	–	–	–	–	–	–	–	–
Other liabilities	VTUF	11.0	10.9	12.9	10.4	11.7	14.4	18.8	14.6	9.4
Total long-term liabilities	ZAUQ	132.3	140.3	173.0	222.1	270.5	344.2	390.5	442.2	572.6
Total other sectors liabilities	ZAUR	525.8	636.9	653.3	768.9	942.2	1 250.5	1 295.8	1 417.5	1 430.1
Direct investment										
Debt liabilities to affiliated enterprises	HHDJ	84.3	97.4	128.4	127.7	149.0	184.5	194.2	199.0	270.4
Debt liabilities to direct investors	HBVB	123.2	160.0	173.0	168.9	176.5	202.5	222.2	196.3	205.4
Total liabilities to direct investors	ZAUY	207.5	257.4	301.4	296.6	325.5	387.0	416.4	395.3	475.8
GROSS EXTERNAL DEBT	ZAUS	2 251.9	2 547.4	2 689.0	2 994.5	3 498.3	4 291.1	4 621.7	5 612.7	6 290.2

FD Financial derivatives[1]
Balance sheets valued at end of year

£ billion

		2000	2001	2002	2003	2004	2005	2006	2007	2008
Financial derivatives assets										
UK banks										
Sterling	ZPNP	49.8	43.5	56.7	44.1	46.1	51.3	62.9	84.2	180.2
Foreign currency	ZPNQ	340.6	481.0	626.2	579.3	663.3	768.8	790.9	1 294.0	3 859.9
Total UK banks	ZPNA	390.5	524.5	682.8	623.4	709.4	820.1	853.7	1 378.1	4 040.2
Other Financial Intermediaries										
UK securities dealers										
Sterling	RUVI	3.2	13.2	16.2	10.6	11.5	15.0	28.6	38.6	83.7
Foreign currency	RUVJ	52.6	51.9	70.9	144.0	104.7	186.5	234.5	400.6	849.4
Total UK securities dealers	RVAP	55.7	65.1	87.1	154.7	116.2	201.5	263.1	439.2	933.1
Other[2]	D4AG	0.5	0.6	0.7	1.1	0.4	0.5	0.2	1.9	..
Total Other Financial Intermediaries	D4AH	56.2	65.7	87.8	155.8	116.6	202.1	263.3	441.1	..
Insurance companies and pension funds										
Insurance companies[3]	D4AE	0.7	1.0	0.8	0.2	–	–	–	0.3	..
Pension funds[4]	GOJU	0.8	0.8	0.7	0.6	3.0	2.7	6.0	8.7	..
Total insurance companies and pension funds	D4AF	1.5	1.7	1.5	0.8	3.0	2.6	6.0	8.9	..
Total UK assets	ZPNC	448.2	592.0	772.1	780.0	828.9	1 024.8	1 123.0	1 828.2	..
Financial derivative liabilities										
UK banks										
Sterling	ZPNR	48.2	43.8	57.1	32.4	36.3	66.3	62.4	82.3	258.2
Foreign currency	ZPNS	351.8	485.8	631.5	600.0	678.8	764.8	828.1	1 309.9	3 657.0
Total UK banks	ZPNB	400.0	529.6	688.7	632.4	715.0	831.1	890.5	1 392.2	3 915.3
Other Financial Intermediaries										
UK securities dealers										
Sterling	RUXE	4.3	13.6	17.2	14.0	14.0	18.2	23.6	40.2	86.3
Foreign currency	RUXF	46.5	50.2	73.7	150.0	112.2	183.1	234.4	392.5	740.8
Total UK securities dealers	RVAV	50.9	63.8	90.9	163.9	126.2	201.3	258.0	432.6	827.1
Other[2]	D4AK	0.1	–	0.1	0.7	0.1	0.1	–	1.8	..
Total Other Financial Intermediaries	D4AL	51.0	63.8	91.0	164.6	126.3	201.4	258.0	434.5	..
Insurance companies and pension funds										
Insurance companies[3]	D4AI	0.3	0.2	0.5	0.2	0.1	–	–	0.4	..
Pension funds[4]	GKGR	0.6	0.7	0.4	0.4	3.1	2.8	7.0	11.3	..
Total insurance companies and pension funds	D4AJ	0.9	0.9	0.9	0.7	3.2	2.8	7.0	11.6	..
Total UK liabilities	ZPND	451.9	594.3	780.6	797.7	844.6	1 035.3	1 155.5	1 838.3	..
Net international investment position										
Banks	ZPNE	–9.5	–5.1	–5.8	–9.0	–5.6	–11.0	–36.8	–14.1	124.9
Other Financial Intermediaries										
Securities dealers	ZPNF	4.9	1.3	–3.8	–9.2	–10.0	0.2	5.1	6.6	106.0
Other[2]	D4AP	0.3	0.6	0.6	0.4	0.3	0.4	0.1	0.1	..
Total Other Financial Intermediaries	D4AQ	5.2	1.9	–3.2	–8.8	–9.8	0.6	5.3	6.7	..
Insurance companies and pension funds										
Insurance companies[3]	D4AM	0.4	0.8	0.3	–	–0.1	–0.1	–	–0.1	..
Pension funds[4]	D4AN	0.2	–	0.3	0.1	–0.1	–0.1	–1.0	–2.6	..
Total insurance companies and pension funds	D4AO	0.6	0.8	0.6	0.1	–0.3	–0.2	–1.0	–2.7	..
Total	ZPNG	–3.7	–2.4	–8.5	–17.7	–15.7	–10.6	–32.5	–10.1	..

1 The data in this table are not included in the main aggregates of the UK's international investment position as the data are developmental. Work is continuing to validate and improve the estimates and to obtain more information on the type of derivatives traded. An article assessing the current position can be found at http://www.statistics.gov.uk/articles/economic_trends/ET618Sem.pdf .
2 Includes unit and investment trusts and open-ended investment companies, finance leasing companies, credit grantors, factoring companies and building societies.
3 Includes both general and long-term insurance.
4 Includes self-administered pension funds only.

Geographical breakdown

Part 3

Chapter 9

Geographical breakdown of current account

The tables appearing in this chapter show a geographical breakdown of the current account. The data cover 66 individual countries as well as international organisations. These estimates are generally less firmly based than the world totals, and data for earlier years are less reliable than recent figures. In some cases estimates are unavailable for the first few years.

Changes to the pattern of trading associated with Missing Trader Intra-Community (MTIC) fraud can make it difficult to analyse trade by country as changes in the impact of activity associated with this fraud (which includes carousel fraud) affect both imports and exports. Originally, most carousel chains only involved EU member states. From 2004 in particular, some carousel chains included non-EU countries, for example, Dubai and Switzerland. However, the MTIC trade adjustments are added to the EU import estimates as it is this part of the chain that is not generally recorded. For more information, see the methodological notes relating to chapter 2.

Data are presented as if the EU expanded to 27 countries on 1 January 1999.

Current account by region

Current account surpluses were recorded with the Americas and Australasia & Oceania in all years from 1992 when data became available. The current account surplus with the Americas narrowed from £26.5 billion in 2007 to £8.8 billion in 2008. In contrast, the UK has consistently recorded a current account deficit with Europe, rising to a record £54.2 billion in 2006, but narrowing to £18.4 billion in 2008. There was a surplus with Asia for the years 1994 to 1997 but a deficit in all years since then. The current account deficit with Asia widened to £15.4 billion in 2008, with imports of goods from China at £23.1 billion, £4.4 billion higher than in 2007.

In 2008, around half of the value of current account credit and debit transactions was with the 27 European Union (EU) member states. EU countries accounted for over 80 per cent of current account credits and debits with Europe. By component, trade in goods accounted for 39 per cent of the value of current account credits and 52 per cent of the value of debits with Europe, with income accounting for around 37 per cent of credits and 28 per cent of debits.

The Americas accounted for around a quarter of total credits and a fifth of total debits in 2008. Income and goods transactions together accounted for 71 per cent of credits and 81 per cent of debits with the Americas. The United States of America (USA) was the most significant country, representing over three-quarters of total current account credits and debits in the region.

Figure 9.2

Current account by continent, 2008

£ billion

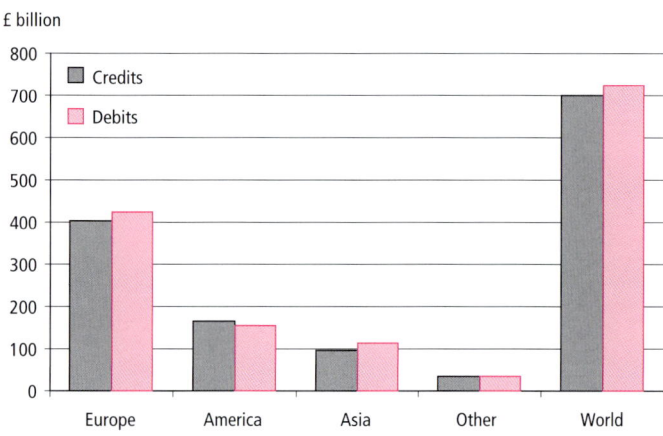

Asia accounted for 14 per cent of UK current account credits in 2008, down from 17 per cent in 1997, when the region accounted for a higher proportion of total income credits. Similarly, Asia has accounted for a lower proportion of total UK debits in recent years, also due to income, but this proportion has increased from 14 per cent to 16 per cent between 2006 and 2008. This is due to imports of goods, which at £68.8 billion represented 61 percent of the total debits with the region in 2008. While Japan remains the UK's largest current account partner country in Asia, transactions with China have grown the fastest in recent years – between 2000 and 2008, though exports of goods to China increased by £3.6 billion to £5.1 billion, imports of goods from China increased by £18.3 billion to £23.1 billion.

The current account with Africa was in surplus up to 1999, with the first deficit being recorded in 2000. In 2006 the deficit increased to £3.5 billion, but has narrowed to £2.2 billion in 2008. These deficits have been mainly driven by higher imports of goods to the UK.

Figure 9.1

Current account

Credits less debits

£ billion

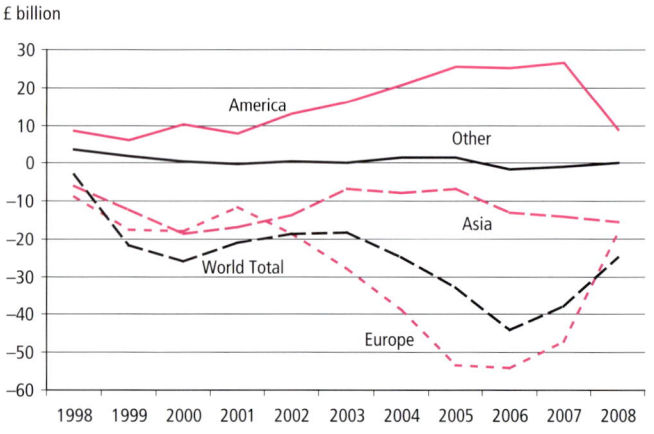

Current account with EU27, USA and Japan

Except for 2001, a current account deficit has been recorded with the EU27 in every year from 1999 when data became available. Broadly speaking, surpluses on the income account have been offset by deficits on the other components of the current account, notably trade in goods. From 2004, trade in services has been in surplus for four of the last five years. Though the income surplus declined over the same period, it rose sharply in 2008 to £28.5 billion, compared to a surplus of £1.5 billion in 2007. As a result, between 2007 and 2008, the current account deficit with the EU narrowed by £33.3 billion to £6.8 billion.

Figure 9.3
Current account with the European Union
Credits less debits
£ billion

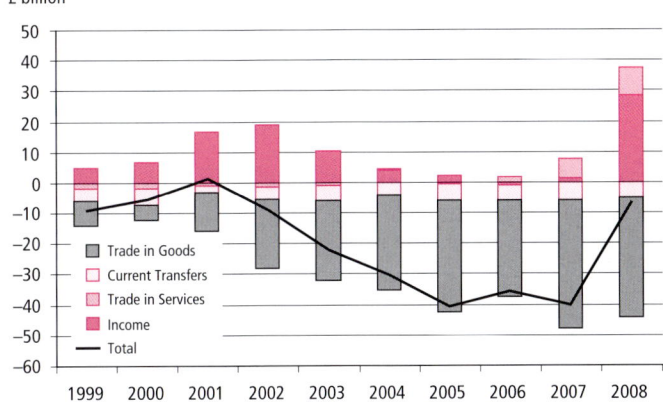

The current account deficit with the EU narrowed from £8.8 billion in 1999 to a surplus of £1.1 billion in 2001 before increasing rapidly to a record deficit of £40.6 billion in 2005, and falling sharply in 2008 to a deficit of £6.8 billion.

The trade in goods and services deficit with the EU decreased to £30.1 billion in 2008, largely due to higher exports of goods to Germany and the Netherlands. Net income received from the EU grew from £5.1 billion in 1999 to £18.7 billion in 2002, falling back to £1.5 billion in 2007, but rising to £28.5 billion in 2008. The deficit on current transfers has remained relatively stable since 1999, typically at between £4 billion and £6 billion. The main components of current transfers are payments to, and receipts from, EU institutions.

The USA is consistently the single largest counterpart country within the UK's balance of payments, representing 18 per cent of current account credits and 17 per cent of debits in 2008. There has been a current account surplus with the USA in all years for which data are available. Prior to 2000 these were typically between £1 billion and £5 billion, whereas more

Figure 9.4
Current account with the USA
Credits less debits
£ billion

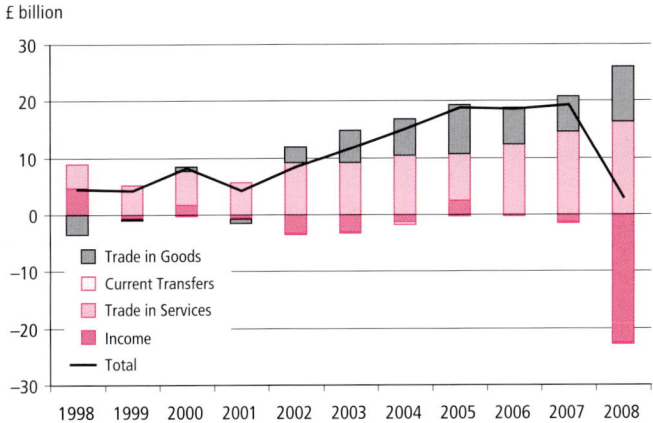

recent years have seen significantly higher surpluses, peaking in 2007 at £19.3 billion, but falling back significantly to £3.1 billion in 2008. Compared to 2007, the deficit on income widened by £21.3 billion to £22.5 billion in 2008, offset by a £9.5 billion surplus on trade in goods and a £16.5 billion surplus on trade in services.

The UK has recorded a current account deficit with Japan in every year for which data are available, peaking at £7.2 billion in 2000. The deficit narrowed to £2.5 billion in 2008.

Figure 9.5
Current account: largest five surpluses in 2008
£ billion

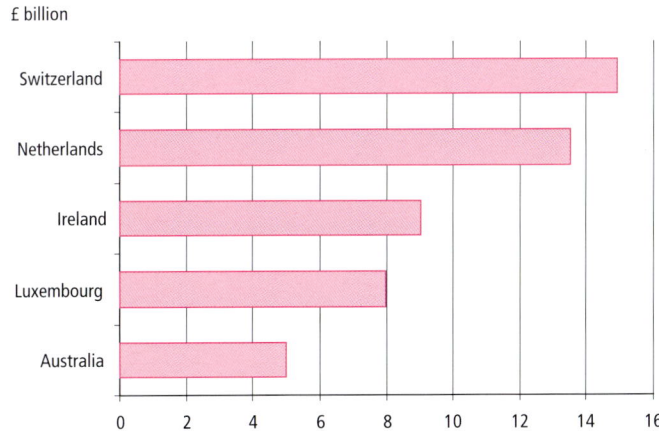

When ranking individual countries by the size of the current account balance in 2008, the largest surpluses were recorded with: Switzerland (£14.9 billion), the Netherlands (£13.5 billion), Ireland (£9.0 billion), Luxembourg (£8.0 billion) and Australia (£5.0 billion).

The surpluses with Switzerland, the Netherlands and Luxembourg are driven mainly by a surplus on income. The surplus with Ireland is because of a surplus on trade in goods and services, and the surplus with Australia is largely due to surpluses on income and trade in services.

Figure 9.6

Current account: largest five deficits in 2008

£ billion

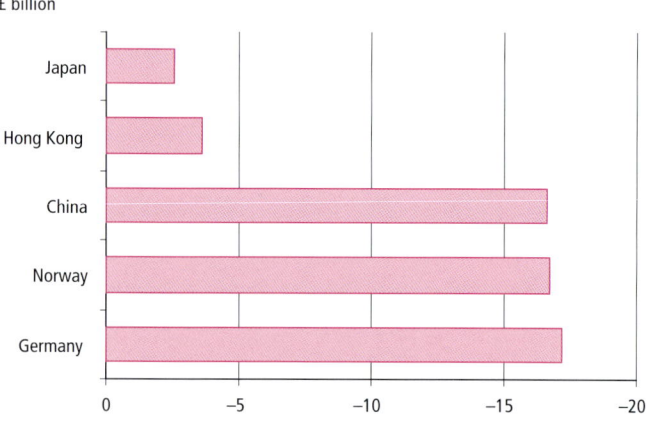

When ranking individual countries by the size of the current account balance in 2008, the largest deficits were recorded with: Germany (£17.2 billion), Norway (£16.7 billion), China (£16.6 billion), Hong Kong (£3.6 billion) and Japan (£2.5 billion).

The current account deficits with Germany, Norway, China, Hong Kong and Japan are all mainly a result of deficits on trade in goods.

Chapter 9: Geographical breakdown of current account

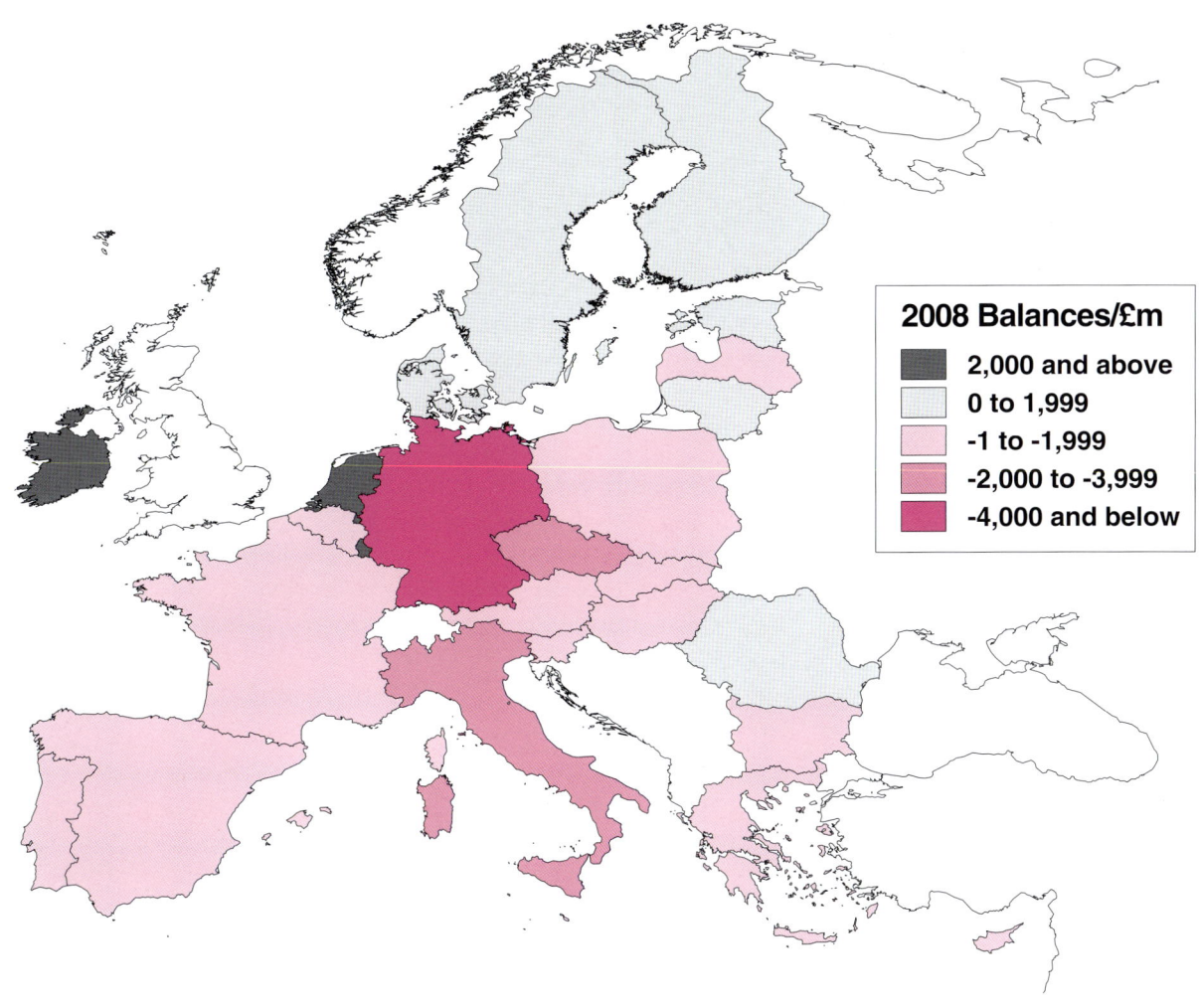

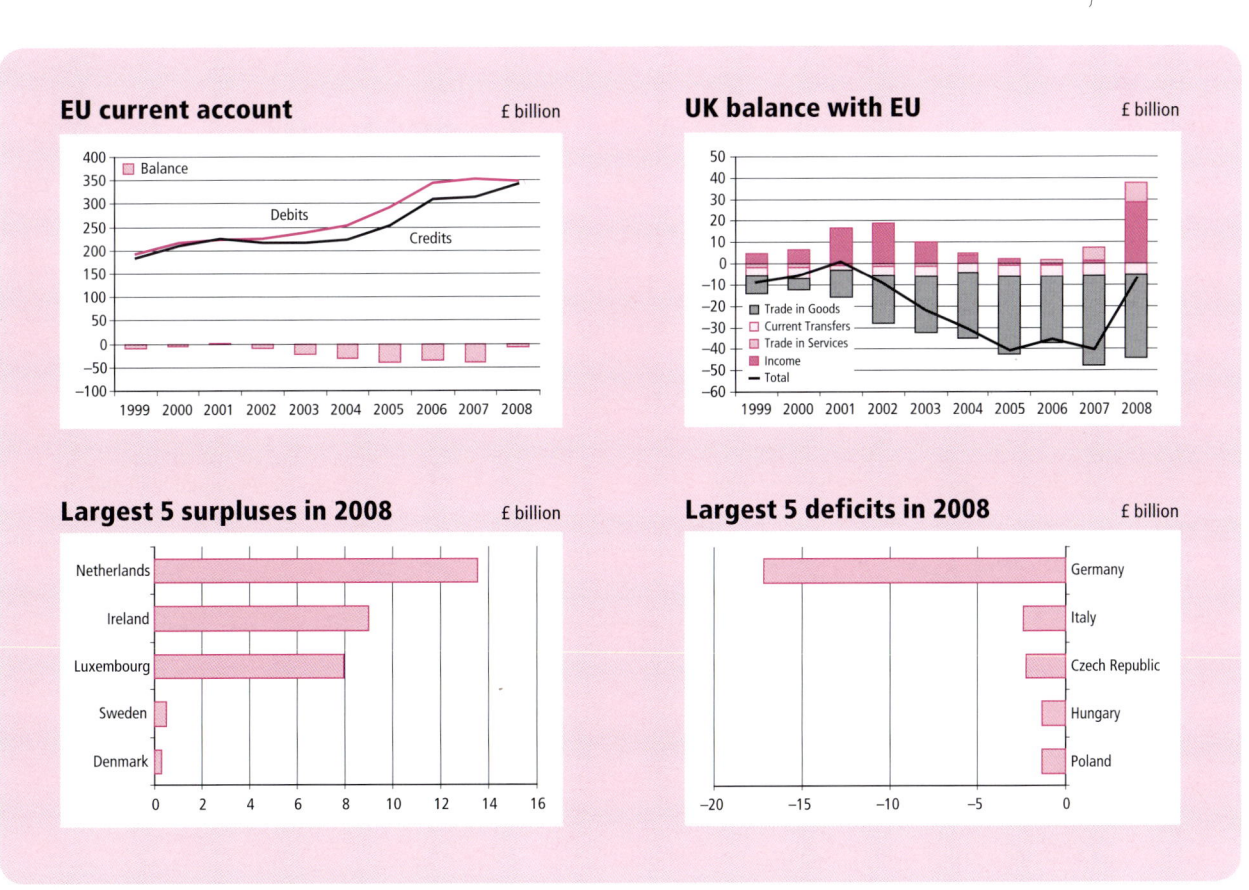

Chapter 9: Geographical breakdown of current account

The Pink Book: 2009 edition

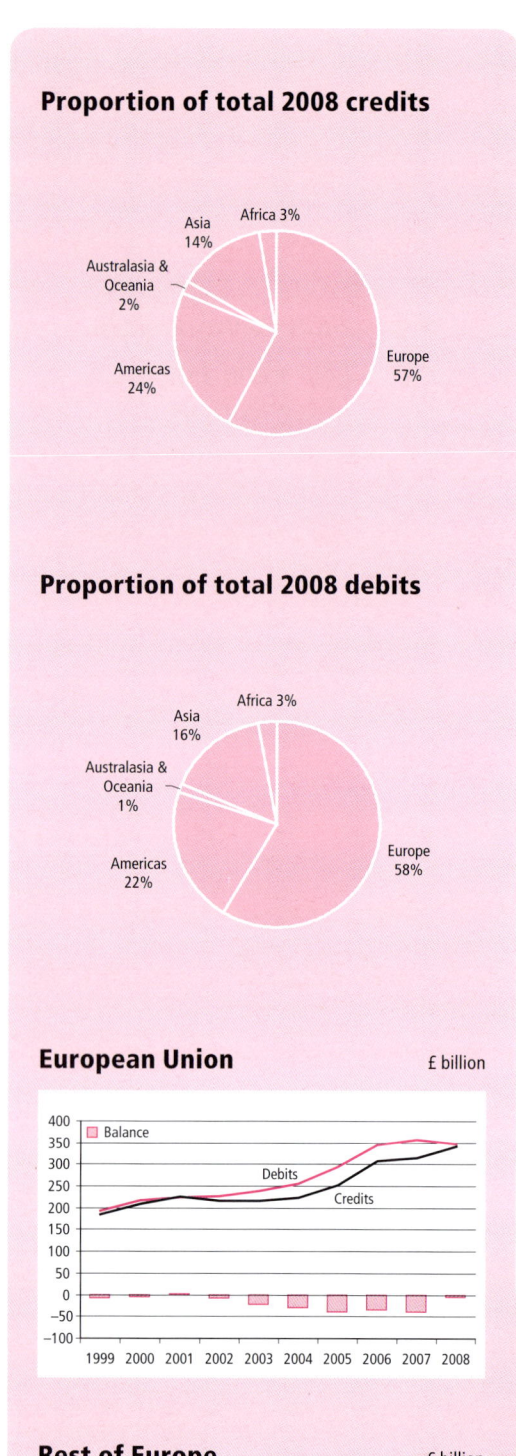

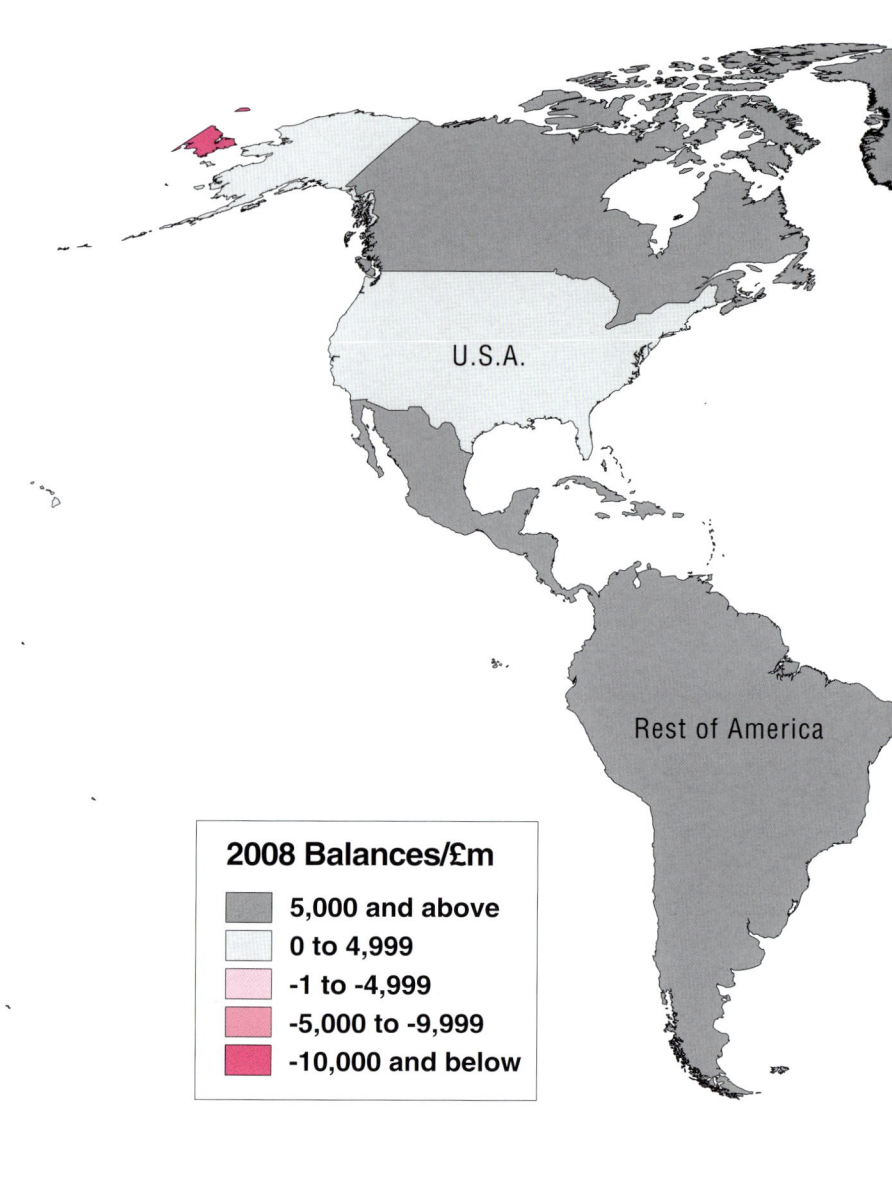

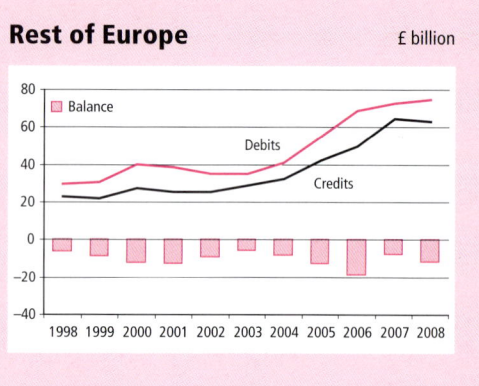

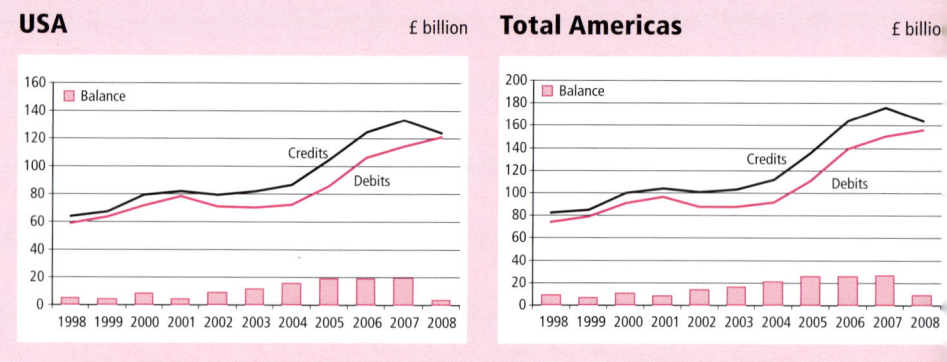

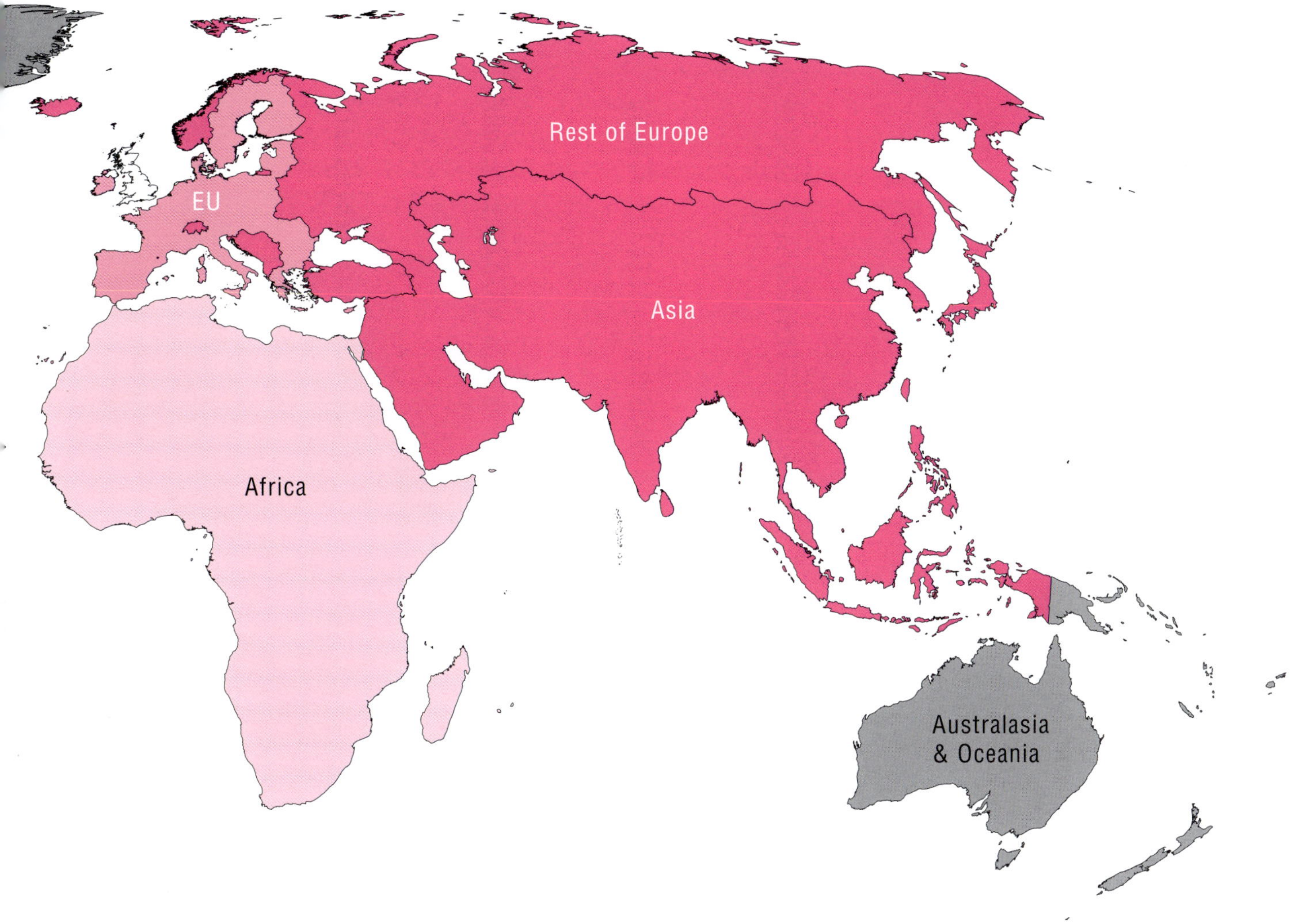

The Pink Book: 2009 edition Chapter 9: Geographical breakdown of current account

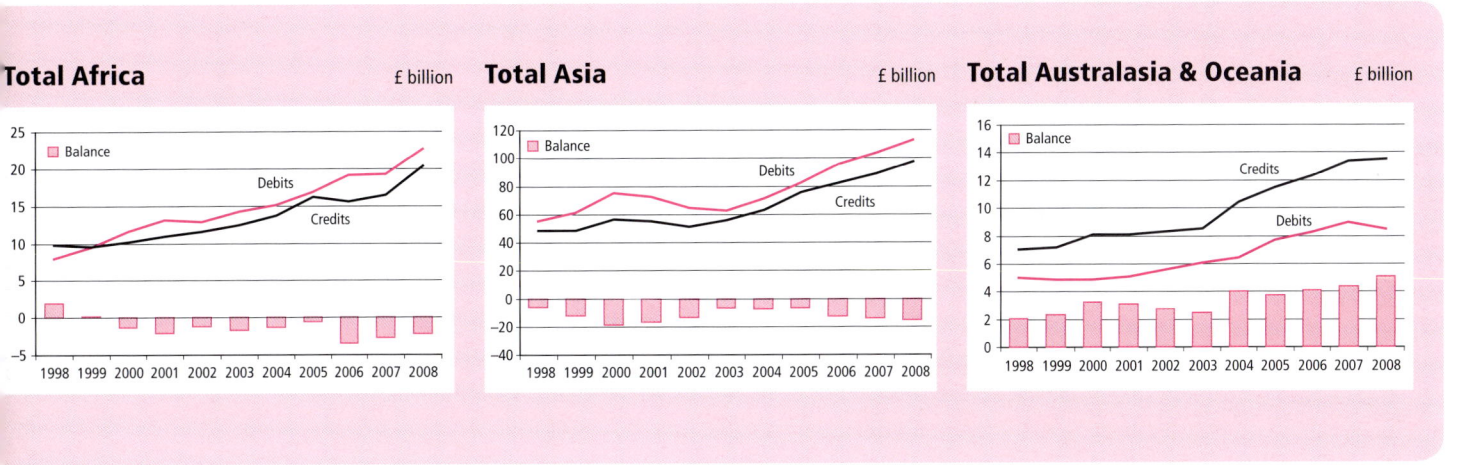

9.1 Current account
Summary transactions in 2008

£ million

	Trade in goods	Trade in services	Income	Current transfers	Current account
Credits					
Europe					
European Union (EU)					
Austria	1 464	718	962	34	3 178
Belgium	13 353	3 648	5 755	214	22 970
Bulgaria	253	183	26	14	476
Cyprus	527	586	534	3	1 650
Czech Republic	1 536	415	41	18	2 010
Denmark	2 579	2 426	1 867	38	6 910
Estonia	220	43	9	–	272
Finland	1 900	1 139	1 001	18	4 058
France	18 057	9 683	18 693	294	46 727
Germany	27 899	11 815	18 185	448	58 347
Greece	1 651	1 201	1 586	45	4 483
Hungary	1 008	455	183	12	1 658
Ireland	19 011	8 449	14 737	172	42 369
Italy	9 332	4 479	6 292	143	20 246
Latvia	167	86	–22	5	236
Lithuania	281	270	–1	13	563
Luxembourg	202	2 077	15 633	14	17 926
Malta	441	168	134	4	747
Netherlands	19 812	9 731	20 530	306	50 379
Poland	2 993	1 031	653	123	4 800
Portugal	1 635	724	1 239	18	3 616
Romania	752	272	209	8	1 241
Slovak Republic	455	290	139	18	902
Slovenia	222	84	86	–	392
Spain	10 182	5 522	8 469	128	24 301
Sweden	5 187	2 316	3 242	93	10 838
European Central Bank	–	–	–	–	–
EU Institutions	–	679	573	8 578	9 830
Total EU27	141 119	68 490	120 755	10 761	341 125
European Free Trade Association (EFTA)					
Iceland	187	225	1 144	34	1 590
Liechtenstein	9	68	26	2	105
Norway	2 847	2 478	2 691	77	8 093
Switzerland	4 654	7 083	12 697	70	24 504
Total EFTA	7 697	9 854	16 558	183	34 292
Other Europe					
Albania	16	25	5	–	46
Belarus	95	14	7	–	116
Croatia	217	109	70	8	404
Russia	4 264	2 188	2 680	20	9 151
Turkey	2 560	648	895	32	4 135
Ukraine	611	223	219	8	1 061
Serbia and Montenegro	132	33	25	4	194
Other	558	4 754	8 368	36	13 716
Total Europe	**157 269**	**86 337**	**149 582**	**11 052**	**404 240**
Americas					
Argentina	317	144	357	9	827
Brazil	1 689	594	1 253	14	3 550
Canada	3 251	2 851	4 387	224	10 713
Chile	264	177	764	9	1 214
Colombia	163	89	294	14	560
Mexico	902	345	784	24	2 055
United States of America	35 351	36 173	49 994	2 197	123 715
Uruguay	66	24	12	–	102
Venezuela	282	70	165	10	527
Other Central American Countries	1 019	4 755	14 728	186	20 688
Other	253	300	161	12	726
Total Americas	**43 557**	**45 522**	**72 899**	**2 699**	**164 677**
Asia					
China	5 072	2 471	993	15	8 551
Hong Kong	3 668	2 121	4 519	33	10 341
India	4 125	1 827	2 117	17	8 086
Indonesia	384	297	247	19	947
Iran	438	256	98	3	795
Israel	1 337	549	144	33	2 063
Japan	3 897	4 991	9 008	112	18 008
Malaysia	1 130	535	643	20	2 328
Pakistan	472	321	192	6	991
Philippines	245	229	305	9	788
Saudi Arabia	2 189	2 633	760	463	6 045
Singapore	2 813	3 458	4 157	17	10 445
South Korea	2 543	1 080	1 679	8	5 310
Taiwan	888	694	549	8	2 139
Thailand	756	333	220	5	1 314
Residual Gulf Arabian Countries	6 026	3 653	2 240	165	12 084
Other Near & Middle Eastern Countries	1 011	574	1 509	280	3 374
Other	842	1 576	1 155	47	3 620
Total Asia	**37 836**	**27 598**	**30 535**	**1 260**	**97 229**
Australasia & Oceania					
Australia	3 092	4 016	4 464	205	11 777
New Zealand	385	456	553	57	1 451
Other	103	142	68	3	316
Total Australasia & Oceania	**3 580**	**4 614**	**5 085**	**265**	**13 544**
Africa					
Egypt	942	690	470	4	2 106
Morocco	516	77	28	2	623
South Africa	2 654	1 580	2 551	82	6 867
Other North Africa	805	602	298	10	1 715
Other	3 943	3 330	1 763	48	9 084
Total Africa	**8 860**	**6 279**	**5 110**	**146**	**20 395**
International Organisations	–	49	476	–	525
World Total	**251 102**	**170 399**	**263 703**	**15 422**	**700 626**

9.1 Current account
Summary transactions in 2008
continued

£ million

	Trade in goods	Trade in services	Income	Current transfers	Current account
Debits					
Europe					
European Union (EU)					
Austria	2 329	957	969	33	4 288
Belgium	16 441	2 624	4 675	81	23 821
Bulgaria	206	397	58	2	663
Cyprus	157	1 178	417	29	1 781
Czech Republic	3 561	476	200	21	4 258
Denmark	3 912	1 113	1 531	50	6 606
Estonia	144	60	14	–	218
Finland	2 764	395	878	17	4 054
France	23 046	9 842	14 468	387	47 743
Germany	44 521	10 093	20 463	447	75 524
Greece	664	2 261	2 378	71	5 374
Hungary	2 521	335	117	12	2 985
Ireland	12 252	4 185	16 276	640	33 353
Italy	14 099	4 955	3 435	182	22 671
Latvia	374	71	15	2	462
Lithuania	348	89	34	3	474
Luxembourg	825	599	8 526	8	1 781
Malta	138	379	316	29	862
Netherlands	25 829	3 749	7 054	209	36 841
Poland	4 295	1 261	489	66	6 111
Portugal	1 736	1 909	799	51	4 495
Romania	758	208	39	5	1 010
Slovak Republic	1 623	112	63	1	1 799
Slovenia	314	65	32	–	411
Spain	10 717	10 707	3 817	206	25 447
Sweden	6 789	1 344	2 167	40	10 340
European Central Bank	–	2	–	–	2
EU Institutions	–	5	3 064	13 329	16 398
Total EU27	180 363	59 371	92 294	15 921	347 949
European Free Trade Association (EFTA)					
Iceland	457	85	–1 382	3	–837
Liechtenstein	33	8	115	2	158
Norway	21 599	1 150	1 987	94	24 830
Switzerland	5 253	2 582	1 622	119	9 576
Total EFTA	27 342	3 825	2 342	218	33 727
Other Europe					
Albania	–	24	3	9	36
Belarus	106	20	21	–	147
Croatia	91	228	47	11	377
Russia	6 907	1 102	1 891	31	9 931
Turkey	4 874	1 470	259	38	6 641
Ukraine	150	234	311	24	719
Serbia and Montenegro	89	63	19	35	206
Other	335	1 248	21 131	230	22 944
Total Europe	**220 257**	**67 585**	**118 318**	**16 517**	**422 677**
Americas					
Argentina	561	128	14	20	723
Brazil	2 611	348	68	26	3 053
Canada	5 786	1 497	282	399	7 964
Chile	580	52	99	14	745
Colombia	686	33	33	21	773
Mexico	787	448	204	29	1 468
United States of America	25 848	19 703	72 466	2 615	120 632
Uruguay	118	6	9	1	134
Venezuela	600	38	76	11	725
Other Central American Countries	1 349	3 084	14 010	481	18 924
Other	371	178	158	49	756
Total Americas	**39 297**	**25 515**	**87 419**	**3 666**	**155 897**
Asia					
China	23 107	1 272	620	151	25 150
Hong Kong	8 057	1 050	4 630	176	13 913
India	4 478	2 229	344	912	7 963
Indonesia	1 183	123	37	120	1 463
Iran	70	45	118	23	256
Israel	1 153	302	219	44	1 718
Japan	8 512	3 635	8 280	130	20 557
Malaysia	1 869	241	371	66	2 547
Pakistan	628	400	66	313	1 407
Philippines	626	192	63	42	923
Saudi Arabia	672	564	2 109	60	3 405
Singapore	3 995	1 347	3 413	123	8 878
South Korea	3 498	401	402	9	4 310
Taiwan	2 591	357	311	8	3 267
Thailand	2 419	677	202	45	3 343
Residual Gulf Arabian Countries	2 331	2 056	2 227	246	6 860
Other Near & Middle Eastern Countries	428	222	269	58	977
Other	3 185	968	410	1 090	5 653
Total Asia	**68 802**	**16 081**	**24 091**	**3 616**	**112 590**
Australasia & Oceania					
Australia	2 380	2 051	1 963	379	6 773
New Zealand	744	377	125	115	1 361
Other	165	86	65	15	331
Total Australasia & Oceania	**3 289**	**2 514**	**2 153**	**509**	**8 465**
Africa					
Egypt	638	747	237	34	1 656
Morocco	436	389	43	11	879
South Africa	4 725	899	1 156	405	7 185
Other North Africa	2 296	460	589	18	3 363
Other	4 239	1 687	9 549	2 420	9 549
Total Africa	**12 334**	**4 182**	**3 228**	**2 888**	**22 632**
International Organisations	–	43	1 537	1 836	3 416
World total	**343 979**	**115 920**	**236 763**	**29 032**	**725 694**

9.1 Current account
Summary transactions in 2008
continued

£ million

	Trade in goods	Trade in services	Income	Current transfers	Current account
Balances					
Europe					
European Union(EU)					
Austria	−865	−239	−7	1	−1 110
Belgium	−3 088	1 024	1 080	133	−851
Bulgaria	47	−214	−32	12	−187
Cyprus	370	−592	117	−26	−131
Czech Republic	−2 025	−61	−159	−3	−2 248
Denmark	−1 333	1 313	336	−12	304
Estonia	76	−17	−5	–	54
Finland	−864	744	123	1	4
France	−4 989	−159	4 225	−93	−1 016
Germany	−16 622	1 722	−2 278	1	−17 177
Greece	987	−1 060	−792	−26	−891
Hungary	−1 513	120	66	–	−1 327
Ireland	6 759	4 264	−1 539	−468	9 016
Italy	−4 767	−476	2 857	−39	−2 425
Latvia	−207	15	−37	3	−226
Lithuania	−67	181	−35	10	89
Luxembourg	−623	1 478	7 107	6	7 968
Malta	303	−211	−182	−25	−115
Netherlands	−6 017	5 982	13 476	97	13 538
Poland	−1 302	−230	164	57	−1 311
Portugal	−101	−1 185	440	−33	−879
Romania	−6	64	170	3	231
Slovak Republic	−1 168	178	76	17	−897
Slovenia	−92	19	54	–	−19
Spain	−535	−5 185	4 652	−78	−1 146
Sweden	−1 602	972	1 075	53	498
European Central Bank	–	−2	–	–	−2
EU Institutions	–	674	−2 491	−4 751	−6 568
Total EU27	−39 244	9 119	28 461	−5 160	−6 824
European Free Trade Association (EFTA)					
Iceland	−270	140	2 526	31	2 427
Liechtenstein	−24	60	−89	–	−53
Norway	−18 752	1 328	704	−17	−16 737
Switzerland	−599	4 501	11 075	−49	14 928
Total EFTA	−19 645	6 029	14 216	−35	565
Other Europe					
Albania	16	1	2	−9	10
Belarus	−11	−6	−14	–	−31
Croatia	126	−119	23	−3	27
Russia	−2 643	1 085	789	−11	−780
Turkey	−2 314	−822	636	−6	−2 506
Ukraine	461	−11	−92	−16	342
Serbia and Montenegro	43	−30	6	−31	−12
Other	223	3 506	−12 763	−194	−9 228
Total Europe	**−62 988**	**18 752**	**31 264**	**−5 465**	**−18 437**
Americas					
Argentina	−244	16	343	−11	104
Brazil	−922	246	1 185	−12	497
Canada	−2 535	1 354	4 105	−175	2 749
Chile	−316	125	665	−5	469
Colombia	−523	56	261	−7	−213
Mexico	115	−103	580	−5	587
USA	9 503	16 470	−22 472	−418	3 083
Uruguay	−52	18	3	−1	−32
Venezuela	−318	32	89	−1	−198
Other Central American Countries	−330	1 671	718	−295	1 764
Other America	−118	122	3	−37	−30
Total Americas	**4 260**	**20 007**	**−14 520**	**−967**	**8 780**
Asia					
China	−18 035	1 198	373	−136	−16 599
Hong Kong	−4 389	1 071	−111	−143	−3 572
India	−353	−402	1 773	−895	123
Indonesia	−799	174	210	−101	−516
Iran	368	211	−20	−20	539
Israel	184	247	−75	−11	345
Japan	−4 615	1 356	728	−18	−2 549
Malaysia	−739	294	272	−46	−219
Pakistan	−156	−79	126	−307	−416
Philippines	−381	37	242	−33	−135
Saudi Arabia	1 517	2 069	−1 349	403	2 640
Singapore	−1 182	2 111	744	−106	1 567
South Korea	−955	679	1 277	−1	1 000
Taiwan	−1 703	337	238	–	−1 128
Thailand	−1 663	−344	18	−40	−2 029
Residual Gulf Arabian Countries	3 695	1 597	13	−81	5 224
Other Near & Middle Eastern Countries	583	352	1 240	222	2 397
Other	−2 343	608	745	−1 043	−2 033
Total Asia	**−30 966**	**11 517**	**6 444**	**−2 356**	**−15 361**
Australasia & Oceania					
Australia	712	1 965	2 501	−174	5 004
New Zealand	−359	79	428	−58	90
Other	−62	56	3	−12	−15
Total Australasia & Oceania	**291**	**2 100**	**2 932**	**−244**	**5 079**
Africa					
Egypt	304	−57	233	−30	450
Morocco	80	−312	−15	−9	−256
South Africa	−2 071	681	1 395	−323	−318
Other North Africa	−1 491	142	−291	−8	−1 648
Other	−296	1 643	560	−2 372	−465
Total Africa	**−3 474**	**2 097**	**1 882**	**−2 742**	**−2 237**
International Organisations	–	6	−1 061	−1 836	−2 891
World total	**−92 877**	**54 479**	**26 940**	**−13 610**	**−25 068**

9.2 Current account

£ million

		1998	1999	2000	2001	2002	2003	2004	2005	2006	2007	2008
Credits												
Europe												
European Union (EU)												
Austria	CUGP	2 196	2 178	2 323	2 347	2 409	2 485	2 379	2 790	3 155	3 243	3 178
Belgium and Luxembourg	CTFH	14 537	15 419	19 089	19 251	19 147	19 585	21 139	25 194	33 419	35 331	40 896
of which Belgium	AA2Q	..	12 940	14 741	14 615	15 003	15 779	16 055	17 853	20 660	21 514	22 970
Luxembourg	AA2U	..	2 479	4 348	4 636	4 144	3 806	5 084	7 341	12 759	13 817	17 926
Bulgaria	ZWVI	116	165	166	250	289	296	323	350	405	408	476
Cyprus[1]	AA2R	..	499	615	591	631	612	735	791	1 644	1 334	1 650
Czech Republic	LEPQ	1 014	1 015	1 226	1 460	1 367	1 474	1 540	1 586	1 959	2 167	2 010
Denmark	LEQR	4 210	4 015	4 624	4 666	4 665	4 441	4 557	5 325	7 779	6 576	6 910
Estonia	ZWVK	86	70	110	105	127	125	144	166	541	347	272
Finland	LEUD	2 453	2 442	3 035	3 153	2 877	2 981	2 858	2 960	3 556	4 227	4 058
France	LEUM	26 968	28 209	31 834	34 335	32 062	32 292	33 665	37 798	50 962	47 783	46 727
Germany	LEQI	34 465	35 025	39 998	42 305	39 509	37 374	39 869	44 363	51 763	53 242	58 347
Greece	LEUV	2 459	2 900	3 128	2 876	2 754	2 933	2 982	3 188	3 258	3 595	4 483
Hungary	BFKO	756	872	1 268	1 139	1 328	1 417	1 690	1 809	1 468	1 683	1 658
Ireland	BFLV	15 069	16 463	19 162	22 365	23 783	22 537	25 512	30 874	34 937	40 289	42 369
Italy	BFOD	18 100	15 931	17 649	17 769	16 438	16 632	16 637	17 721	19 141	20 318	20 246
Latvia	ZWVM	114	95	118	118	120	143	142	204	483	426	236
Lithuania	ZWVN	127	115	157	191	185	236	198	294	364	456	563
Malta[1]	AA2V	..	295	314	323	338	387	831	357	474	108	747
Netherlands	BFQF	25 471	27 385	32 861	36 414	34 816	34 504	28 825	31 452	40 618	43 138	50 379
Poland	BFRY	1 561	1 553	1 732	1 966	2 059	2 280	2 399	3 000	4 378	4 167	4 800
Portugal	BFSH	2 663	2 785	2 788	2 887	2 845	2 819	3 077	3 318	3 999	3 212	3 616
Romania	ZWVO	286	330	445	492	584	703	865	851	920	1 096	1 241
Slovak Republic	ZWVP	169	187	247	277	265	301	300	423	489	647	902
Slovenia	ZWVQ	164	222	233	299	303	293	315	270	302	316	392
Spain	LEST	11 490	11 847	13 214	13 116	13 259	14 221	15 799	19 520	23 439	23 300	24 301
Sweden	BFTI	7 325	7 120	8 025	7 984	7 568	7 374	8 447	9 146	10 457	10 623	10 838
European Central Bank	ZWVF	–	–	3	12	3	–	–	–	–	3	–
EU Institutions	CSFH	5 611	6 847	5 932	8 287	7 106	7 950	8 454	9 092	9 255	8 520	9 830
Total EU27	G97O	..	183 984	210 296	224 978	216 837	216 395	223 682	252 842	309 165	316 555	341 125
European Free Trade Association (EFTA)												
Iceland	BFNH	274	256	334	285	263	304	345	469	637	1 413	1 590
Liechtenstein	BFPE	64	77	90	73	68	64	83	61	100	141	105
Norway	BFQO	4 590	3 927	4 131	3 866	3 912	4 076	4 371	6 059	6 123	8 057	8 093
Switzerland	LEOY	8 862	9 934	13 178	12 375	11 631	11 983	12 189	16 051	18 807	23 131	24 504
Total EFTA	CTFQ	13 790	14 194	17 733	16 598	15 874	16 427	16 988	22 640	25 667	32 742	34 292
Other Europe												
Albania	ZWVG	8	15	9	28	25	16	34	24	29	33	46
Belarus	ZWVH	33	30	64	37	43	49	59	69	74	92	116
Croatia	ZWVJ	131	133	127	149	180	234	219	238	296	297	404
Russia	BFSQ	1 668	1 039	1 378	1 912	2 239	2 727	3 648	5 363	6 784	7 820	9 151
Turkey	BFUJ	2 204	1 974	2 672	1 986	2 011	2 436	2 691	3 223	3 929	4 259	4 135
Ukraine	ZWVR	247	173	200	234	502	399	332	496	906	944	1 061
Serbia and Montenegro	BFWC	63	71	138	94	93	111	86	107	163	185	194
Other[1]	LEVW	4 895	4 152	4 988	4 457	4 693	6 469	8 152	10 055	11 884	18 246	13 716
Total Europe	LERA	200 449	205 765	237 605	250 473	242 497	245 263	255 891	295 057	358 897	381 173	404 240
Americas												
Argentina	ZWVT	1 099	717	969	834	328	414	588	561	906	830	827
Brazil	LENO	2 125	1 441	1 659	1 800	1 837	1 656	1 874	2 318	2 510	2 880	3 550
Canada	LEOP	5 958	6 004	7 306	7 373	6 581	7 001	7 601	8 501	10 538	11 172	10 713
Chile	ZWVU	501	395	477	441	451	519	1 064	1 452	1 175	1 304	1 214
Colombia	ZWVV	310	271	491	493	421	491	615	648	562	480	560
Mexico	BFPN	1 118	1 359	1 417	1 300	1 626	1 396	1 734	1 802	2 185	2 102	2 055
United States of America	BFVB	63 738	67 451	79 289	82 242	79 359	81 853	86 877	104 561	124 569	133 424	123 715
Uruguay	ZWVW	102	82	80	66	55	99	41	64	91	71	102
Venezuela	ZWVX	287	273	225	610	602	342	567	739	686	479	527
Other Central American Countries	JISS	6 856	6 393	8 003	8 319	8 871	9 194	10 343	14 775	20 271	22 860	20 688
Other	LEVE	579	448	476	401	382	406	764	298	416	624	726
Total Americas	LESK	82 673	84 834	100 392	103 880	100 513	103 315	112 068	135 719	163 909	176 226	164 677
Asia												
China	LEPH	1 389	1 945	2 234	2 861	2 663	3 260	4 278	5 076	5 670	6 590	8 551
Hong Kong	BFJR	5 800	5 195	5 422	5 249	4 800	5 482	7 006	8 667	9 436	10 299	10 341
India	BFMY	2 158	2 373	3 116	2 964	3 050	3 679	3 853	4 808	5 732	6 276	8 086
Indonesia	BFKX	845	729	762	752	714	888	801	844	1 171	779	947
Iran	ZWWA	453	376	469	647	622	741	743	820	814	679	795
Israel	BFMP	1 483	1 914	2 042	1 962	1 938	1 839	1 884	2 044	1 965	1 964	2 063
Japan	BFOM	12 862	13 930	16 246	14 875	12 447	12 966	13 277	15 300	17 357	17 352	18 008
Malaysia	BFPW	1 606	1 772	1 811	1 832	1 887	2 116	2 272	2 362	2 161	2 290	2 328
Pakistan	BFRP	569	594	517	647	604	684	825	1 185	1 280	995	991
Philippines	BFRG	549	476	643	730	602	686	627	632	649	786	788
Saudi Arabia	BFSZ	5 226	4 370	4 703	4 426	4 072	4 831	4 859	4 651	5 310	5 807	6 045
Singapore	BFTR	3 999	4 253	5 465	5 348	4 462	4 799	6 133	8 198	9 002	10 257	10 445
South Korea	BFOV	1 540	1 680	2 178	2 203	2 674	2 602	3 203	3 649	4 029	4 351	5 310
Taiwan	BFUS	1 291	1 318	1 565	1 473	1 576	1 629	2 011	2 208	2 176	2 294	2 139
Thailand	BFUA	695	788	1 004	1 067	981	1 140	1 194	1 207	866	1 238	1 314
Residual Gulf Arabian Countries	JITT	5 285	4 549	5 360	5 167	4 888	5 542	6 780	10 396	9 369	9 539	12 084
Other Near & Middle Eastern Countries	ZWWC	1 023	984	1 107	1 316	1 166	1 284	1 572	1 888	2 434	3 096	3 374
Other	LEWF	1 920	1 430	1 813	1 746	1 783	1 638	1 903	1 899	3 144	4 344	3 620
Total Asia	LETC	48 693	48 676	56 457	55 264	50 928	55 806	63 221	75 834	82 565	88 936	97 229
Australasia & Oceania												
Australia	CWBG	5 581	5 910	6 961	6 883	6 934	7 056	8 987	9 913	10 696	11 743	11 777
New Zealand	BFQX	1 002	1 127	986	1 104	1 204	1 286	1 252	1 367	1 382	1 367	1 451
Other	LEVN	474	135	151	147	188	211	215	184	260	248	316
Total Australasia & Oceania	LETU	7 057	7 172	8 098	8 134	8 326	8 553	10 454	11 464	12 338	13 358	13 544
Africa												
Egypt	ZWWE	529	863	1 045	1 053	1 016	962	1 192	1 260	1 502	1 846	2 106
Morocco	ZWWF	424	434	499	481	438	425	411	332	434	402	623
South Africa	BFWU	3 329	3 489	3 673	4 085	4 724	4 862	6 053	7 514	5 893	6 318	6 867
Other North Africa	JIRU	845	573	794	802	681	1 016	919	-2 484	-84	1 240	1 715
Other	LEWO	4 718	4 206	4 172	4 565	4 751	5 168	5 150	9 646	7 887	6 682	9 084
Total Africa	LERS	9 845	9 565	10 183	10 986	11 609	12 433	13 725	16 268	15 632	16 488	20 395
International Organisations	CTEY	407	424	501	578	560	539	503	583	625	670	525
World total	HBOE	349 124	356 436	413 236	429 317	414 434	425 909	455 874	534 934	633 974	676 851	700 626

1 Cyprus and Malta are included within Other Europe before 1999.

9.2 Current account
continued

£ million

Debits

		1998	1999	2000	2001	2002	2003	2004	2005	2006	2007	2008
Europe												
European Union (EU)												
Austria	CUGW	2 423	2 348	2 501	3 111	3 802	4 093	3 760	4 138	4 804	4 549	4 288
Belgium and Luxembourg	CTFI	15 774	16 151	17 435	18 997	19 895	20 319	22 121	24 845	30 138	30 721	33 779
of which Belgium	AA34	..	13 389	14 438	15 537	16 293	16 402	17 174	19 421	21 336	22 295	23 821
Luxembourg	AA38	..	2 762	2 997	3 460	3 602	3 917	4 947	5 424	8 802	8 426	9 958
Bulgaria	ZWWL	196	166	189	188	251	246	339	460	518	664	663
Cyprus[1]	AA35	..	1 068	1 270	1 486	1 383	1 476	1 459	1 714	2 968	1 783	1 781
Czech Republic	LEPR	819	839	1 108	1 418	1 592	1 842	1 811	2 464	3 730	3 645	4 258
Denmark	LEQS	3 637	3 873	4 440	4 531	5 239	5 201	5 372	6 786	8 917	6 170	6 606
Estonia	ZWWN	214	236	373	321	347	302	432	423	2 179	377	218
Finland	LEUE	2 879	2 976	3 569	3 710	3 351	3 310	2 947	3 291	4 068	3 827	4 054
France	LEUN	29 910	32 681	34 108	35 002	34 481	36 715	38 937	44 140	51 994	50 416	47 743
Germany	LEQJ	37 078	39 847	44 947	44 160	44 572	49 798	54 097	63 445	70 471	79 006	75 524
Greece	LEUW	2 156	2 587	3 019	3 119	3 004	3 123	3 272	3 811	4 430	5 178	5 374
Hungary	BFKP	725	856	868	887	1 039	1 303	1 797	2 181	2 748	2 973	2 985
Ireland	BFLW	12 943	13 420	15 971	18 949	20 611	17 968	19 896	23 422	26 370	30 930	33 353
Italy	BFOE	15 785	15 064	15 408	16 035	15 757	17 255	18 348	20 001	20 387	22 162	22 671
Latvia	ZWWP	362	336	466	471	516	559	740	791	931	764	462
Lithuania	ZWWQ	209	215	289	278	321	311	299	371	393	444	474
Malta[1]	AA39	..	382	410	461	467	514	556	582	555	713	862
Netherlands	BFQG	19 781	22 785	30 775	30 663	26 439	27 256	29 772	33 361	43 320	49 351	36 841
Poland	BFRZ	1 043	1 039	1 334	1 588	1 619	1 928	2 350	3 292	5 122	5 452	6 111
Portugal	BFSI	2 904	3 077	3 050	3 077	3 288	3 728	3 761	3 949	5 176	4 049	4 495
Romania	ZWWR	336	366	464	561	658	793	949	1 023	1 098	1 180	1 010
Slovak Republic	ZWWS	191	195	214	211	253	291	316	498	1 085	1 473	1 799
Slovenia	ZWWT	196	186	197	206	238	221	232	274	817	395	411
Spain	LESU	13 023	13 438	14 020	16 224	18 493	20 152	20 102	24 992	27 835	25 863	25 447
Sweden	BFTJ	6 126	6 940	7 234	6 903	6 543	6 747	7 319	8 113	9 202	8 741	10 340
European Central Bank	ZWWI	–	1	1	1	1	–	–	–	–	–	2
EU Institutions	CSFI	11 153	11 755	12 211	11 325	11 789	12 997	13 153	15 069	15 395	15 861	16 398
Total EU27	G97F	..	192 827	215 871	223 883	225 949	238 448	254 137	293 436	344 651	356 687	347 949
European Free Trade Association (EFTA)												
Iceland	BFNI	309	319	453	335	347	365	468	519	810	862	–837
Liechtenstein	BFPF	163	115	146	125	75	94	76	93	151	201	158
Norway	BFQP	4 103	4 249	6 754	6 863	7 229	7 885	10 103	14 440	17 622	18 138	24 830
Switzerland	LEOZ	12 361	14 805	18 763	16 064	13 019	11 701	11 488	15 141	18 351	20 416	9 576
Total EFTA	CTFR	16 936	19 488	26 116	23 387	20 670	20 045	22 135	30 193	36 934	39 617	33 727
Other Europe												
Albania	ZWWJ	115	48	41	28	26	24	27	15	20	36	36
Belarus	ZWWK	97	67	65	37	44	30	77	288	737	624	147
Croatia	ZWWM	273	122	135	157	153	155	167	249	320	338	377
Russia	BFSR	1 712	1 677	2 207	2 717	2 562	3 114	4 483	6 848	9 084	9 175	9 931
Turkey	BFUK	1 859	1 855	2 134	2 425	2 995	3 513	4 191	4 740	5 316	6 091	6 641
Ukraine	ZWWU	150	141	137	169	201	207	292	386	471	708	719
Serbia and Montenegro	BFWD	99	93	141	110	100	110	108	124	193	208	206
Other[1]	LEVX	8 293	7 090	8 670	9 303	8 368	7 478	9 194	12 091	15 367	16 314	22 944
Total Europe	LERB	209 397	223 408	255 517	262 216	261 068	273 124	294 811	348 370	413 093	429 798	422 677
Americas												
Argentina	ZWWW	344	334	378	370	313	317	351	391	500	529	723
Brazil	LENP	1 308	1 233	1 478	1 703	1 743	1 770	1 888	2 213	2 420	2 567	3 053
Canada	LEOQ	4 625	5 413	6 896	6 316	6 560	6 395	7 766	8 024	10 042	9 556	7 964
Chile	ZWWX	458	401	506	558	541	485	586	609	650	678	745
Colombia	ZWWY	331	273	331	414	287	278	326	375	423	451	773
Mexico	BFPO	747	812	1 160	1 360	941	883	869	883	956	1 094	1 468
United States of America	BFVC	58 937	63 182	71 124	78 009	70 872	70 255	71 762	85 597	105 970	114 142	120 632
Uruguay	ZWWZ	45	55	62	54	74	56	54	72	91	95	134
Venezuela	ZWXA	186	210	282	253	259	177	264	463	731	641	725
Other Central American Countries	JIST	6 137	5 869	7 191	6 373	5 242	6 005	7 270	10 900	16 385	19 341	18 924
Other	LEVF	965	880	883	696	558	476	475	545	628	621	756
Total Americas	LESL	74 083	78 662	90 291	96 106	87 390	87 097	91 611	110 072	138 796	149 715	155 897
Asia												
China	LEPI	3 283	3 915	5 563	6 575	7 587	9 078	11 321	14 137	16 637	20 725	25 150
Hong Kong	BFJS	6 948	8 549	10 112	9 777	8 215	7 615	8 019	9 257	10 921	12 443	13 913
India	BFMZ	2 686	2 848	3 173	3 529	3 423	3 682	4 385	5 495	6 576	7 528	7 963
Indonesia	BFKY	1 100	1 210	1 345	1 408	1 266	1 293	1 156	1 183	1 333	1 198	1 463
Iran	ZWXD	168	169	323	361	182	181	213	234	361	313	256
Israel	BFMQ	1 282	1 438	1 553	1 547	1 309	1 280	1 342	1 570	1 762	1 824	1 718
Japan	BFON	17 461	18 650	23 401	21 019	17 050	13 895	15 453	17 943	20 209	20 397	20 557
Malaysia	BFPX	2 380	2 463	2 907	2 451	2 102	2 163	2 409	2 332	2 686	2 518	2 547
Pakistan	BFRQ	753	812	876	931	1 174	1 164	1 241	1 251	1 365	1 316	1 407
Philippines	BFRH	1 019	1 188	1 482	1 321	1 110	920	821	938	1 060	1 006	923
Saudi Arabia	BFTA	2 220	2 057	2 441	2 560	2 406	2 150	2 362	2 959	3 080	2 938	3 405
Singapore	BFTS	4 081	4 832	5 556	5 142	4 310	4 625	5 653	7 082	8 059	8 955	8 878
South Korea	BFOW	2 541	3 033	3 728	3 152	3 045	2 786	3 198	3 649	3 753	3 874	4 310
Taiwan	BFUT	2 446	2 874	3 865	3 133	2 684	2 500	2 723	2 815	2 919	3 264	3 267
Thailand	BFUB	1 671	1 704	2 163	2 291	2 196	2 259	2 508	2 499	2 866	3 001	3 343
Residual Gulf Arabian Countries	JITU	2 268	2 285	2 970	3 294	2 771	3 078	3 697	4 461	5 697	6 323	6 860
Other Near & Middle Eastern Countries	ZWXF	419	489	580	586	559	536	533	729	1 383	966	977
Other	LEWG	2 242	2 397	3 023	3 072	3 155	3 274	4 014	4 097	4 868	4 909	5 653
Total Asia	LETD	54 968	60 913	75 061	72 149	64 544	62 479	71 048	82 631	95 535	103 498	112 590
Australasia & Oceania												
Australia	CWBO	3 863	3 776	3 701	3 844	4 354	4 804	4 988	6 200	6 388	7 323	6 773
New Zealand	BFQY	1 004	918	983	1 016	1 025	1 050	1 190	1 295	1 300	1 291	1 361
Other	LEVO	137	187	188	186	195	205	235	209	567	365	331
Total Australasia & Oceania	LETV	5 004	4 881	4 872	5 046	5 574	6 059	6 413	7 704	8 255	8 979	8 465
Africa												
Egypt	ZWXH	718	787	1 050	1 074	920	936	1 016	1 201	1 682	1 525	1 656
Morocco	ZWXI	511	565	606	624	620	605	680	633	723	889	879
South Africa	BFWV	2 461	3 169	4 081	4 463	4 394	4 975	5 368	6 369	6 600	5 609	7 185
Other North Africa	JIRV	770	681	1 208	1 063	984	956	1 192	1 553	2 429	2 846	3 363
Other	LEWP	3 429	4 190	4 581	5 884	5 873	6 720	6 802	7 089	7 720	8 442	9 549
Total Africa	LERT	7 889	9 392	11 526	13 108	12 791	14 192	15 058	16 845	19 154	19 311	22 632
International Organisations	CTEZ	962	1 034	1 756	1 793	1 724	1 265	1 833	2 144	2 963	3 261	3 416
World total	HBOF	352 303	378 290	439 023	450 419	433 091	444 216	480 791	567 775	677 816	714 561	725 694

1 Cyprus and Malta are included in Other Europe before 1999.

9.2 Current account
continued

£ million

Balances		1998	1999	2000	2001	2002	2003	2004	2005	2006	2007	2008
Europe												
European Union (EU)												
Austria	CUGX	-227	-170	-178	-764	-1 393	-1 608	-1 381	-1 348	-1 649	-1 306	-1 110
Belgium and Luxembourg	CTFJ	-1 237	-732	1 654	254	-748	-734	-982	349	3 281	4 610	7 117
of which Belgium	AA4H	..	-449	303	-922	-1 290	-623	-1 119	-1 568	-676	-781	-851
Luxembourg	AA4L	..	-283	1 351	1 176	542	-111	137	1 917	3 957	5 391	7 968
Bulgaria	ZWXO	-80	-1	-23	62	38	50	-16	-110	-113	-256	-187
Cyprus[1]	AA4I	..	-569	-655	-895	-752	-864	-724	-923	-1 324	-449	-131
Czech Republic	LEPS	195	176	118	42	-225	-368	-271	-878	-1 771	-1 478	-2 248
Denmark	LEQT	573	142	184	135	-574	-760	-815	-1 461	-1 138	406	304
Estonia	ZWXQ	-128	-166	-263	-216	-220	-177	-288	-257	-1 638	-30	54
Finland	LEUF	-426	-534	-534	-557	-474	-329	-89	-331	-512	400	4
France	LEUO	-2 942	-4 472	-2 274	-667	-2 419	-4 423	-5 272	-6 342	-1 032	-2 633	-1 016
Germany	LEQK	-2 613	-4 822	-4 949	-1 855	-5 063	-12 424	-14 228	-19 082	-18 708	-25 764	-17 177
Greece	LEUX	303	313	109	-243	-250	-190	-290	-623	-1 172	-1 583	-891
Hungary	BFKQ	31	16	400	252	289	114	-107	-372	-1 280	-1 290	-1 327
Ireland	BFLX	2 126	3 043	3 191	3 416	3 172	4 569	5 616	7 452	8 567	9 359	9 016
Italy	BFOF	2 315	867	2 241	1 734	681	-623	-1 711	-2 280	-1 246	-1 844	-2 425
Latvia	ZWXS	-248	-241	-348	-353	-396	-416	-598	-587	-448	-338	-226
Lithuania	ZWXT	-82	-100	-132	-87	-136	-75	-101	-77	-29	12	89
Malta[1]	AA4M	..	..	-87	-96	-138	-129	-127	275	-225	-81	-605	-115
Netherlands	BFQH	5 690	4 600	2 086	5 751	8 377	7 248	-947	-1 909	-2 702	-6 213	13 538
Poland	BFSA	518	514	398	378	440	352	49	-292	-744	-1 285	-1 311
Portugal	BFSJ	-241	-292	-262	-190	-443	-909	-684	-631	-1 177	-837	-879
Romania	ZWXU	-50	-36	-19	-69	-74	-90	-84	-172	-178	-84	231
Slovak Republic	ZWXV	-22	-8	33	66	12	10	-16	-75	-596	-826	-897
Slovenia	ZWXW	-32	36	36	93	65	72	83	-4	-515	-79	-19
Spain	LESV	-1 533	-1 591	-806	-3 108	-5 234	-5 931	-4 303	-5 472	-4 396	-2 563	-1 146
Sweden	BFTK	1 199	180	791	1 081	1 025	627	1 128	1 033	1 255	1 882	498
European Central Bank	ZWXL	–	-1	2	11	2	–	–	–	–	3	-2
EU Institutions	CSFJ	-5 542	-4 908	-6 279	-3 038	-4 683	-5 047	-4 699	-5 977	-6 140	-7 341	-6 568
Total EU27	G977	..	-8 843	-5 575	1 095	-9 112	-22 053	-30 455	-40 594	-35 486	-40 130	-6 824
European Free Trade Association (EFTA)												
Iceland	BFNJ	-35	-63	-119	-50	-84	-61	-123	-50	-173	551	2 427
Liechtenstein	BFPG	-99	-38	-56	-52	-7	-30	7	-32	-51	-60	-53
Norway	BFQQ	487	-322	-2 623	-2 997	-3 317	-3 809	-5 732	-8 381	-11 499	-10 081	-16 737
Switzerland	LEPA	-3 499	-4 871	-5 585	-3 689	-1 388	282	701	910	456	2 715	14 928
Total EFTA	CTFS	-3 146	-5 294	-8 383	-6 789	-4 796	-3 618	-5 147	-7 553	-11 267	-6 875	565
Other Europe												
Albania	ZWXM	-107	-33	-32	–	-1	-8	7	9	9	-3	10
Belarus	ZWXN	-64	-37	-1	–	-1	19	-18	-219	-663	-532	-31
Croatia	ZWXP	-142	11	-8	-8	27	79	52	-11	-24	-41	27
Russia	BFSS	-44	-638	-829	-805	-323	-387	-835	-1 485	-2 300	-1 355	-780
Turkey	BFUL	345	119	538	-439	-984	-1 077	-1 500	-1 517	-1 387	-1 832	-2 506
Ukraine	ZWXX	97	32	63	65	301	192	40	110	435	236	342
Serbia and Montenegro	BFWE	-36	-22	-3	-16	-7	1	-22	-17	-30	-23	-12
Other[1]	LEVY	-3 398	-2 938	-3 682	-4 846	-3 675	-1 009	-1 042	-2 036	-3 483	1 932	-9 228
Total Europe	LERC	-8 948	-17 643	-17 912	-11 743	-18 571	-27 861	-38 920	-53 313	-54 196	-48 625	-18 437
Americas												
Argentina	ZWXZ	755	383	591	464	15	97	237	170	406	301	104
Brazil	LENQ	817	208	181	97	94	-114	-14	105	90	313	497
Canada	LEOR	1 333	591	410	1 057	21	606	-165	477	496	1 616	2 749
Chile	ZWYA	43	-6	-29	-117	-90	34	478	843	525	626	469
Colombia	ZWYB	-21	-2	160	79	134	213	289	273	139	29	-213
Mexico	BFPP	371	547	257	-60	685	513	865	919	1 229	1 008	587
United States of America	BFVD	4 801	4 269	8 165	4 233	8 487	11 598	15 115	18 964	18 599	19 282	3 083
Uruguay	ZWYC	57	27	18	12	-19	43	-13	-8	–	-24	-32
Venezuela	ZWYD	101	63	-57	357	343	165	303	276	-45	-162	-198
Other Central American Countries	JISU	719	524	812	1 946	3 629	3 189	3 073	3 875	3 886	3 519	1 764
Other	LEVG	-386	-432	-407	-295	-176	-70	289	-247	-212	3	-30
Total Americas	LESM	8 590	6 172	10 101	7 774	13 123	16 218	20 457	25 647	25 113	26 511	8 780
Asia												
China	LEPJ	-1 894	-1 970	-3 329	-3 714	-4 924	-5 818	-7 043	-9 061	-10 967	-14 135	-16 599
Hong Kong	BFJT	-1 148	-3 354	-4 690	-4 528	-3 415	-2 133	-1 013	-590	-1 485	-2 114	-3 572
India	BFNA	-528	-475	-57	-565	-373	-3	-532	-687	-844	-1 252	123
Indonesia	BFKZ	-255	-481	-583	-656	-552	-405	-355	-339	-162	-419	-516
Iran	ZWYG	285	207	146	286	440	560	530	586	453	366	539
Israel	BFMR	201	476	489	415	629	559	542	474	203	140	345
Japan	BFOO	-4 599	-4 720	-7 155	-6 144	-4 603	-929	-2 176	-2 643	-2 852	-3 045	-2 549
Malaysia	BFPY	-774	-691	-1 096	-619	-215	-47	-137	30	-525	-228	-219
Pakistan	BFRR	-184	-218	-359	-284	-570	-480	-416	-66	-85	-321	-416
Philippines	BFRI	-470	-712	-839	-591	-508	-234	-194	-306	-411	-220	-135
Saudi Arabia	BFTB	3 006	2 313	2 262	1 866	1 666	2 681	2 497	1 692	2 230	2 869	2 640
Singapore	BFTT	-82	-579	-91	206	152	174	480	1 116	943	1 302	1 567
South Korea	BFOX	-1 001	-1 353	-1 550	-949	-371	-184	5	–	276	477	1 000
Taiwan	BFUU	-1 155	-1 556	-2 300	-1 660	-1 108	-871	-712	-607	-743	-970	-1 128
Thailand	BFUC	-976	-916	-1 159	-1 224	-1 215	-1 119	-1 314	-1 292	-2 000	-1 763	-2 029
Residual Gulf Arabian Countries	JITV	3 017	2 264	2 390	1 873	2 117	2 464	3 083	5 935	3 672	3 216	5 224
Other Near & Middle Eastern Countries	ZWYI	604	495	527	730	607	748	1 039	1 159	1 051	2 130	2 397
Other	LEWH	-322	-967	-1 210	-1 326	-1 372	-1 636	-2 111	-2 198	-1 724	-565	-2 033
Total Asia	LETE	-6 275	-12 237	-18 604	-16 885	-13 616	-6 673	-7 827	-6 797	-12 970	-14 562	-15 361
Australasia & Oceania												
Australia	CWJK	1 718	2 134	3 260	3 039	2 580	2 252	3 999	3 713	4 308	4 420	5 004
New Zealand	BFQZ	-2	209	3	88	179	236	62	72	82	76	90
Other	LEVP	337	-52	-37	-39	-7	6	-20	-25	-307	-117	-15
Total Australasia & Oceania	LETW	2 053	2 291	3 226	3 088	2 752	2 494	4 041	3 760	4 083	4 379	5 079
Africa												
Egypt	ZWYK	-189	76	-5	-21	96	26	176	59	-180	321	450
Morocco	ZWYL	-87	-131	-107	-143	-182	-180	-269	-301	-289	-487	-256
South Africa	BFWW	868	320	-408	-378	330	-113	685	1 145	-707	709	-318
Other North Africa	JIRW	75	-108	-414	-261	-303	60	-273	-4 037	-2 513	-1 606	-1 648
Other	LEWQ	1 289	16	-409	-1 319	-1 122	-1 552	-1 652	2 557	167	-1 760	-465
Total Africa	LERU	1 956	173	-1 343	-2 122	-1 182	-1 759	-1 333	-577	-3 522	-2 823	-2 237
International Organisations	CTFA	-555	-610	-1 255	-1 215	-1 164	-726	-1 330	-1 561	-2 338	-2 591	-2 891
World total	HBOG	-3 179	-21 854	-25 787	-21 102	-18 657	-18 307	-24 917	-32 841	-43 842	-37 710	-25 068

1 Cyprus and Malta are included in Other Europe before 1999.

Chapter 9: Geographical breakdown of current account

9.3 Trade in goods and services

£ million

		1998	1999	2000	2001	2002	2003	2004	2005	2006	2007	2008
Exports												
Europe												
European Union (EU)												
Austria	LGHT	1 541	1 567	1 551	1 633	1 691	1 688	1 528	1 852	2 243	1 989	2 182
Belgium and Luxembourg	LGHU	10 467	11 641	12 799	12 387	13 371	14 587	14 378	15 057	18 801	16 549	19 280
of which Belgium	A7RS	..	11 110	12 190	11 660	12 565	13 632	13 209	13 991	15 993	14 741	17 001
Luxembourg	A7RV	..	531	609	727	806	955	1 169	1 066	2 808	1 808	2 279
Bulgaria	ZWLR	95	117	127	157	209	221	233	314	354	372	436
Cyprus[1]	A7RT	..	393	460	426	491	552	659	672	1 318	1 044	1 113
Czech Republic	LGIN	897	886	1 095	1 260	1 212	1 247	1 307	1 415	1 874	1 922	1 951
Denmark	LGHV	3 099	3 039	3 495	3 657	4 103	3 708	3 634	3 839	6 027	4 527	5 005
Estonia	ZWLX	73	65	108	97	121	117	135	152	530	337	263
Finland	LGHW	1 971	2 015	2 426	2 490	2 274	2 371	2 321	2 371	2 943	3 144	3 039
France	LGHX	20 712	21 779	24 020	25 327	24 778	25 145	25 175	26 374	35 929	26 435	27 740
Germany	LGHY	25 976	26 222	29 471	30 848	29 561	28 665	29 886	32 176	37 524	35 360	39 714
Greece	LGHZ	1 744	2 023	2 087	1 965	1 999	2 076	2 151	2 299	2 241	2 237	2 852
Hungary	XUXI	581	624	819	817	968	1 082	1 306	1 393	1 270	1 411	1 463
Ireland	LGIA	12 179	13 368	15 223	17 493	19 710	17 540	19 723	22 846	24 272	25 237	27 460
Italy	LGIB	11 038	10 644	11 122	11 305	11 524	11 632	11 812	12 490	13 196	13 367	13 811
Latvia	ZWMF	102	93	114	117	115	142	141	196	460	390	253
Lithuania	ZWME	123	111	148	183	181	232	197	279	342	432	551
Malta[1]	A7RW	..	255	263	267	289	333	338	311	408	491	609
Netherlands	LGIC	16 247	17 797	19 724	19 513	18 720	19 007	18 732	19 628	24 219	23 532	29 543
Poland	LGIO	1 465	1 441	1 585	1 634	1 710	1 873	1 922	2 452	3 713	3 379	4 024
Portugal	LGID	2 178	2 296	2 096	2 064	2 048	1 997	2 258	2 328	2 939	2 128	2 359
Romania	ZWMH	262	286	425	414	508	606	746	774	802	920	1 024
Slovak Republic	ZWMJ	127	145	196	246	231	273	270	358	386	572	745
Slovenia	ZWMI	142	166	185	198	230	204	215	232	272	279	306
Spain	LGIE	8 967	9 642	10 558	10 615	11 102	11 821	12 049	14 429	16 754	15 093	15 704
Sweden	LGIF	5 767	5 473	5 829	5 587	5 350	5 523	6 066	6 344	7 232	7 004	7 503
European Central Bank	ZWLL	–	–	3	12	3	–	–	–	–	3	–
EU Institutions	LGIG	228	232	248	544	544	515	578	600	604	625	679
Total EU27	GC8Q	..	132 320	146 177	151 256	153 043	153 157	157 760	171 181	206 653	188 779	209 609
European Free Trade Association (EFTA)												
Iceland	LGII	206	189	266	213	195	213	256	314	376	381	412
Liechtenstein	LGIJ	26	36	43	33	45	43	59	42	63	100	77
Norway	LGIK	3 874	3 136	3 049	2 789	3 145	3 214	3 464	4 022	4 068	5 243	5 325
Switzerland	LGIL	5 380	5 465	5 845	6 984	7 047	7 415	7 201	9 837	9 789	10 249	11 737
Total EFTA	LGIM	9 486	8 826	9 203	10 018	10 432	10 885	10 980	14 215	14 296	15 973	17 551
Other Europe												
Albania	ZWLP	8	15	9	28	25	16	34	24	29	31	41
Belarus	ZWLS	33	30	64	36	36	42	59	64	71	85	109
Croatia	ZWMC	118	118	110	122	149	189	169	164	242	256	326
Russia	LGIP	1 373	829	1 083	1 363	1 562	2 153	2 367	2 992	3 731	5 101	6 451
Turkey	LGIQ	1 900	1 599	2 151	1 548	1 659	2 041	2 271	2 669	2 983	3 031	3 208
Ukraine	ZWMK	231	170	199	231	484	371	279	376	486	655	834
Serbia and Montenegro	ZWMN	63	68	135	92	90	105	87	93	131	169	165
Other[1]	ZWLM	1 718	1 348	1 438	1 345	1 639	2 213	2 464	2 997	3 463	3 694	5 312
Total Europe	LGIS	140 911	145 323	160 569	166 039	169 119	171 172	176 470	194 775	232 085	217 774	243 606
Americas												
Argentina	ZWLQ	670	460	474	459	210	217	320	266	322	361	461
Brazil	LGIT	1 326	1 117	1 125	1 200	1 201	1 160	1 096	1 203	1 416	1 555	2 283
Canada	LGIU	3 560	3 929	4 884	4 842	4 650	4 834	5 118	5 029	5 928	5 850	6 102
Chile	ZWLT	296	221	211	235	202	202	217	238	310	366	441
Colombia	ZWLU	242	155	157	245	169	205	205	183	204	217	252
Mexico	LGIV	681	798	942	969	969	959	983	943	1 144	1 143	1 247
United States of America	LGIW	37 134	42 364	48 823	48 730	51 142	52 974	54 584	55 518	61 513	65 238	71 524
Uruguay	ZWML	79	75	64	53	35	90	42	52	58	50	90
Venezuela	ZWMM	314	273	305	424	405	245	289	330	307	321	352
Other Central American Countries	ZWLW	2 265	2 131	2 398	2 288	2 899	3 097	3 608	4 153	4 496	4 646	5 774
Other	ZWLZ	493	396	378	379	304	326	295	344	389	487	553
Total Americas	LGIY	47 060	51 919	59 761	59 825	62 186	64 309	66 757	68 259	76 087	80 234	89 079
Asia												
China	LGIZ	1 163	1 667	1 917	2 300	2 217	2 813	3 645	4 195	4 763	5 407	7 543
Hong Kong	LGJA	3 658	3 381	3 714	3 777	3 417	3 676	3 758	4 433	4 154	4 366	5 789
India	LGJB	1 730	1 971	2 611	2 447	2 390	3 006	3 233	3 957	4 331	4 616	5 952
Indonesia	LGJC	568	550	596	518	498	617	587	553	598	541	681
Iran	ZWMD	413	336	416	603	582	696	684	667	637	555	694
Israel	LGJD	1 388	1 822	1 961	1 868	1 857	1 729	1 793	1 908	1 763	1 739	1 886
Japan	LGJE	5 876	6 526	7 141	7 231	7 427	7 615	8 088	8 203	8 411	8 439	8 888
Malaysia	LGJF	1 221	1 328	1 297	1 405	1 281	1 451	1 545	1 552	1 375	1 428	1 665
Pakistan	LGJG	471	517	383	507	413	474	574	891	847	743	793
Philippines	LGJH	394	365	456	570	457	518	441	417	340	361	474
Saudi Arabia	LGJI	4 540	3 642	3 926	3 672	3 361	4 139	4 141	3 775	4 335	4 672	4 822
Singapore	LGJJ	2 182	2 757	2 711	2 886	2 611	3 235	3 867	4 716	5 197	5 795	6 271
South Korea	LGJK	1 158	1 360	1 746	1 690	1 966	1 942	2 394	2 412	2 600	2 870	3 623
Taiwan	LGJL	1 102	1 116	1 296	1 170	1 218	1 279	1 465	1 520	1 495	1 596	1 582
Thailand	LGJM	617	670	776	813	736	906	956	896	859	931	1 089
Residual Gulf Arabian Countries	ZWMA	3 652	3 292	3 689	3 863	3 952	4 688	5 794	8 936	7 372	7 288	9 679
Other Near & Middle Eastern Countries	ZWMB	644	612	624	820	767	893	1 113	1 191	1 403	1 233	1 585
Other	ZWLN	1 784	1 250	1 454	1 448	1 237	1 398	1 566	1 686	2 099	2 961	2 418
Total Asia	LGJO	32 561	33 162	36 714	37 587	36 386	41 075	45 644	51 908	52 579	55 541	65 434
Australasia & Oceania												
Australia	LGJP	3 644	3 763	4 287	4 262	3 940	4 312	4 748	5 284	5 307	5 735	7 108
New Zealand	LGJQ	657	678	606	610	586	650	797	826	767	797	841
Other	LGJR	89	99	127	137	152	179	173	144	191	164	245
Total Australasia & Oceania	LGJS	4 390	4 540	5 020	5 009	4 678	5 141	5 718	6 254	6 265	6 696	8 194
Africa												
Egypt	ZWLY	609	822	778	792	689	697	989	916	1 040	1 293	1 632
Morocco	ZWMG	405	406	468	450	396	401	307	395	367	593	
South Africa	LGJT	2 454	2 406	2 389	2 663	2 606	2 856	2 955	3 204	3 540	3 698	4 234
Other North Africa	ZWLV	732	504	684	664	700	874	828	858	897	984	1 407
Other	ZWLO	4 115	3 569	3 385	3 771	3 691	4 074	3 982	4 253	4 950	4 871	7 273
Total Africa	LGJV	8 315	7 707	7 704	8 340	8 081	8 907	9 155	9 538	10 822	11 213	15 139
International Organisations	LGJW	47	40	51	64	85	73	52	60	41	45	49
World total	KTMW	233 284	242 691	269 819	276 866	280 536	290 677	303 796	330 794	377 879	371 503	421 501

1 Cyprus and Malta are included in Other Europe before 1999.

9.3 Trade in goods and services
continued

£ million

Imports

		1998	1999	2000	2001	2002	2003	2004	2005	2006	2007	2008
Europe												
European Union (EU)												
Austria	LGJY	1 872	1 909	1 887	2 394	3 084	3 436	3 110	3 331	3 677	3 315	3 286
Belgium and Luxembourg	LGJZ	11 281	11 879	12 602	13 959	15 237	15 411	16 207	17 609	20 827	18 563	20 489
of which Belgium	A8EO	..	11 578	12 287	13 475	14 273	14 439	14 909	16 389	17 680	17 401	19 065
Luxembourg	A8ER	..	301	315	484	964	972	1 298	1 220	3 147	1 162	1 424
Bulgaria	ZWNX	103	105	123	153	212	228	324	423	448	573	603
Cyprus[1]	A8EP	..	952	1 093	1 302	1 224	1 339	1 285	1 477	2 625	1 360	1 335
Czech Republic	LGKS	701	726	970	1 296	1 500	1 749	1 717	2 351	3 520	3 452	4 037
Denmark	LGKA	2 667	2 980	3 304	3 577	4 341	4 182	4 209	5 334	7 479	4 461	5 025
Estonia	ZWOD	155	194	342	310	345	299	426	416	2 169	358	204
Finland	LGKB	2 547	2 670	3 169	3 325	3 073	2 977	2 621	2 784	3 477	3 037	3 159
France	LGKC	23 700	25 097	26 175	27 655	28 639	28 651	28 645	30 938	35 948	31 689	32 888
Germany	LGKD	28 969	31 569	33 167	35 431	37 842	39 247	41 818	46 889	50 551	52 800	54 614
Greece	LGKE	1 414	1 834	2 076	2 362	2 462	2 592	2 606	2 704	2 801	2 889	2 925
Hungary	ZWOJ	617	757	778	836	975	1 271	1 765	2 134	2 687	2 848	2 856
Ireland	LGKF	9 600	10 877	12 522	14 478	15 492	12 497	13 183	13 848	14 257	15 274	16 437
Italy	LGKG	12 106	12 038	12 370	12 862	13 813	14 910	15 747	16 978	16 958	18 071	19 054
Latvia	ZWOM	295	286	431	459	504	554	731	769	914	742	445
Lithuania	ZWOL	147	163	253	251	305	310	289	345	358	399	437
Malta[1]	A8ES	..	323	349	400	406	464	502	520	455	492	517
Netherlands	LGKH	15 525	16 211	18 406	18 523	19 523	20 012	21 548	24 011	25 870	26 374	29 578
Poland	LGKT	797	851	1 089	1 366	1 452	1 769	2 134	2 877	4 578	4 865	5 556
Portugal	LGKI	2 618	2 827	2 756	2 741	2 969	3 333	3 325	3 459	4 488	3 205	3 645
Romania	ZWOO	244	304	400	525	606	770	917	972	1 031	1 108	966
Slovak Republic	ZWOQ	103	130	166	191	238	281	294	437	908	1 372	1 735
Slovenia	ZWOP	112	118	151	166	196	193	203	249	793	362	379
Spain	LGKJ	10 953	11 899	12 636	14 591	17 036	18 225	18 224	20 917	22 074	20 503	21 424
Sweden	LGKK	4 900	5 426	5 781	5 500	5 157	5 701	6 266	6 777	7 330	6 478	8 133
European Central Bank	ZWNR	–	–	1	1	1	1	–	–	–	–	2
EU Institutions	LGKL	10	6	3	5	14	17	4	4	2	–	5
Total EU27	GCU9	..	142 132	153 000	164 659	176 646	180 418	188 100	208 553	236 225	224 590	239 734
European Free Trade Association (EFTA)												
Iceland	LGKN	297	307	440	325	331	342	412	417	500	506	542
Liechtenstein	LGKO	53	30	28	32	23	36	22	17	43	56	41
Norway	LGKP	3 965	4 045	6 099	6 170	6 524	7 133	9 265	13 052	15 454	15 308	22 749
Switzerland	LGKQ	6 231	6 879	7 118	6 131	6 271	5 553	5 277	6 237	6 733	7 539	7 835
Total EFTA	LGKR	10 546	11 261	13 685	12 658	13 149	13 064	14 976	19 723	22 730	23 409	31 167
Other Europe												
Albania	ZWNV	1	7	7	9	15	17	20	8	13	23	24
Belarus	ZWNY	25	21	36	22	34	26	73	279	729	607	126
Croatia	ZWOI	77	60	68	106	115	123	137	193	243	234	319
Russia	LGKU	1 588	1 461	1 684	2 265	2 246	2 757	4 005	5 558	6 461	6 160	8 009
Turkey	LGKV	1 665	1 728	1 971	2 238	2 868	3 407	4 061	4 548	5 035	5 797	6 344
Ukraine	ZWOR	64	56	78	104	168	117	150	186	201	304	384
Serbia and Montenegro	ZWOU	41	45	45	61	63	75	76	85	137	145	152
Other[1]	ZWNS	2 243	888	1 289	1 267	1 415	1 378	1 262	1 367	1 624	1 702	1 583
Total Europe	LGKX	147 686	157 659	171 863	183 389	196 719	201 382	212 860	240 500	273 398	262 971	287 842
Americas												
Argentina	ZWNW	268	265	256	283	291	300	334	370	466	506	689
Brazil	LGKY	1 023	1 066	1 288	1 510	1 616	1 653	1 762	2 002	2 168	2 346	2 959
Canada	LGKZ	3 390	4 002	5 114	4 856	4 653	4 666	5 242	5 319	6 294	7 174	7 283
Chile	ZWNZ	372	370	486	512	508	457	546	559	557	570	632
Colombia	ZWOA	259	226	270	342	247	255	300	338	345	391	719
Mexico	LGLA	554	620	896	1 078	841	802	776	745	718	945	1 235
United States of America	LGLB	36 516	37 366	42 043	43 773	39 145	38 188	37 825	38 816	42 580	44 482	45 551
Uruguay	ZWOS	59	44	42	45	70	47	46	65	75	76	124
Venezuela	ZWOT	155	190	253	202	218	147	233	420	623	530	638
Other Central American Countries	ZWOC	1 758	1 862	2 517	2 022	2 078	2 414	2 981	2 961	4 053	3 766	4 433
Other	ZWOF	431	504	534	443	383	353	347	394	414	392	549
Total Americas	LGLD	44 785	46 515	53 699	55 066	50 050	49 282	50 392	51 989	58 293	61 178	64 812
Asia												
China	LGLE	3 035	3 650	5 118	6 116	7 222	8 805	10 949	13 657	16 034	19 717	24 379
Hong Kong	LGLF	4 906	5 529	6 488	6 360	6 185	6 215	6 481	7 360	8 174	8 152	9 107
India	LGLG	1 936	2 099	2 315	2 633	2 620	2 911	3 375	4 087	4 714	5 648	6 707
Indonesia	LGLH	958	1 081	1 206	1 249	1 142	1 172	1 018	936	1 095	1 037	1 306
Iran	ZWOK	57	54	73	65	62	74	102	76	131	107	115
Israel	LGLI	1 082	1 211	1 291	1 253	1 082	1 074	1 153	1 251	1 260	1 348	1 455
Japan	LGLJ	10 368	10 420	11 878	10 896	9 528	9 824	9 812	10 925	10 597	10 830	12 147
Malaysia	LGLK	2 145	2 147	2 515	2 130	1 924	2 037	2 230	2 084	2 147	1 915	2 110
Pakistan	LGLL	534	606	663	701	870	905	985	959	996	925	1 028
Philippines	LGLM	919	1 071	1 361	1 237	1 044	868	764	854	914	870	818
Saudi Arabia	LGLN	1 242	1 309	1 530	1 576	1 979	1 779	1 936	2 279	1 927	1 337	1 236
Singapore	LGLO	2 665	2 709	2 731	2 462	2 387	3 097	4 040	4 557	4 618	5 146	5 342
South Korea	LGLP	2 330	2 919	3 557	2 935	2 913	2 749	3 329	3 317	3 318	3 412	3 899
Taiwan	LGLQ	2 327	2 745	3 718	2 933	2 568	2 378	2 543	2 536	2 556	2 756	2 948
Thailand	LGLR	1 572	1 598	1 987	2 065	2 071	2 159	2 401	2 331	2 605	2 705	3 096
Residual Gulf Arabian Countries	ZWOG	1 233	1 267	1 523	1 689	1 836	2 277	2 652	3 029	3 455	3 628	4 387
Other Near & Middle Eastern Countries	ZWOH	159	219	243	288	340	328	318	432	983	554	650
Other	ZWNT	1 652	1 696	2 227	2 200	2 276	2 629	3 138	2 923	3 502	3 527	4 153
Total Asia	LGLT	39 120	42 330	50 424	48 788	48 049	51 281	57 226	63 593	69 026	73 614	84 883
Australasia & Oceania												
Australia	LGLU	2 327	2 384	2 734	3 027	3 118	3 265	3 257	3 967	3 910	4 264	4 431
New Zealand	LGLV	744	814	808	829	859	899	1 018	1 093	1 039	1 105	1 121
Other	LGLW	150	151	149	114	129	153	184	178	197	147	251
Total Australasia & Oceania	LGLX	3 221	3 349	3 691	3 970	4 106	4 317	4 459	5 238	5 146	5 516	5 803
Africa												
Egypt	ZWOE	394	484	701	773	729	782	839	887	1 265	1 136	1 385
Morocco	ZWON	468	520	568	586	594	584	659	595	612	818	825
South Africa	LGLY	1 838	2 116	3 081	3 439	3 369	3 870	4 180	4 953	4 925	4 008	5 624
Other North Africa	ZWOB	612	551	1 022	864	851	834	1 066	1 284	1 901	2 130	2 756
Other	ZWNU	1 904	2 600	2 664	3 940	4 102	4 311	4 564	4 559	4 786	5 022	5 926
Total Africa	LGMA	5 216	6 271	8 036	9 602	9 645	10 381	11 308	12 278	13 489	13 114	16 516
International Organisations	LGMB	66	56	80	62	40	29	37	43	57	57	43
World total	KTMX	240 094	256 180	287 793	300 878	308 609	316 672	336 282	373 641	419 409	416 450	459 899

1 Cyprus and Malta are included in Other Europe before 1999.

9.3 Trade in goods and services
continued

£ million

		1998	1999	2000	2001	2002	2003	2004	2005	2006	2007	2008
Balances												
Europe												
European Union (EU)												
Austria	LGMD	-331	-342	-336	-761	-1 393	-1 748	-1 582	-1 479	-1 434	-1 326	-1 104
Belgium and Luxembourg	LGME	-814	-238	197	-1 572	-1 866	-824	-1 829	-2 552	-2 026	-2 014	-1 209
of which Belgium	A8HC	..	-468	-97	-1 815	-1 708	-807	-1 700	-2 398	-1 687	-2 660	-2 064
Luxembourg	A8HF	..	230	294	243	-158	-17	-129	-154	-339	646	855
Bulgaria	ZWSK	-8	12	4	4	-3	-7	-91	-109	-94	-201	-167
Cyprus[1]	A8HD	..	-559	-633	-876	-733	-787	-626	-805	-1 307	-316	-222
Czech Republic	LGMX	196	160	125	-36	-288	-502	-410	-936	-1 646	-1 530	-2 086
Denmark	LGMF	432	59	191	80	-238	-474	-575	-1 495	-1 452	66	-20
Estonia	ZWSQ	-82	-129	-234	-213	-224	-182	-291	-264	-1 639	-21	59
Finland	LGMG	-576	-655	-743	-835	-799	-606	-300	-413	-534	107	-120
France	LGMH	-2 988	-3 318	-2 155	-2 328	-3 861	-3 506	-3 470	-4 564	-19	-5 254	-5 148
Germany	LGMI	-2 993	-5 347	-3 696	-4 583	-8 281	-10 582	-11 932	-14 713	-13 027	-17 440	-14 900
Greece	LGMJ	330	189	11	-397	-463	-516	-455	-405	-560	-652	-73
Hungary	ZWSW	-36	-133	41	-19	-7	-189	-459	-741	-1 417	-1 437	-1 393
Ireland	LGMK	2 579	2 491	2 701	3 015	4 218	5 043	6 540	8 998	10 015	9 963	11 023
Italy	LGML	-1 068	-1 394	-1 248	-1 557	-2 289	-3 278	-3 935	-4 488	-3 762	-4 704	-5 243
Latvia	ZWSZ	-193	-193	-317	-342	-389	-412	-590	-573	-454	-352	-192
Lithuania	ZWSY	-24	-52	-105	-68	-124	-78	-92	-66	-16	33	114
Malta[1]	A8HG	..	-68	-86	-133	-117	-131	-164	-209	-47	-1	92
Netherlands	LGMM	722	1 586	1 318	990	-803	-1 005	-2 816	-4 383	-1 651	-2 842	-35
Poland	LGMY	668	590	496	268	258	104	-212	-425	-865	-1 486	-1 532
Portugal	LGMN	-440	-531	-660	-677	-921	-1 336	-1 067	-1 131	-1 549	-1 077	-1 286
Romania	ZWTB	18	-18	25	-111	-98	-164	-171	-198	-229	-188	58
Slovak Republic	ZWTD	24	15	30	55	-7	-8	-24	-79	-522	-800	-990
Slovenia	ZWTC	30	48	34	32	34	11	12	-17	-521	-83	-73
Spain	LGMO	-1 986	-2 257	-2 078	-3 976	-5 934	-6 404	-6 175	-6 488	-5 320	-5 410	-5 720
Sweden	LGMP	867	47	48	87	193	-178	-200	-433	-98	526	-630
European Central Bank	ZWSE	–	-1	2	11	2	–	–	–	–	3	-2
EU Institutions	LGMQ	218	226	245	539	530	498	574	596	602	625	674
Total EU27	GD6Q	..	-9 812	-6 823	-13 403	-23 603	-27 261	-30 340	-37 372	-29 572	-35 811	-30 125
European Free Trade Association (EFTA)												
Iceland	LGMS	-91	-118	-174	-112	-136	-129	-156	-103	-124	-125	-130
Liechtenstein	LGMT	-27	6	15	1	22	7	37	25	20	44	36
Norway	LGMU	-91	-909	-3 050	-3 381	-3 379	-3 919	-5 801	-9 030	-11 386	-10 065	-17 424
Switzerland	LGMV	-851	-1 414	-1 273	853	776	1 862	1 924	3 600	3 056	2 710	3 902
Total EFTA	LGMW	-1 060	-2 435	-4 482	-2 640	-2 717	-2 179	-3 996	-5 508	-8 434	-7 436	-13 616
Other Europe												
Albania	ZWSI	7	8	2	19	10	-1	14	16	16	8	17
Belarus	ZWSL	8	9	28	14	2	16	-14	-215	-658	-522	-17
Croatia	ZWSV	41	58	42	16	34	66	32	-29	-1	22	7
Russia	LGMZ	-215	-632	-601	-902	-684	-604	-1 638	-2 566	-2 730	-1 059	-1 558
Turkey	LGNA	235	-129	180	-690	-1 209	-1 366	-1 790	-1 879	-2 052	-2 766	-3 136
Ukraine	ZWTE	167	114	121	127	316	254	129	190	285	351	450
Serbia and Montenegro	ZWTH	22	23	90	31	27	30	11	8	-6	24	13
Other[1]	ZWSF	-525	460	149	78	224	835	1 202	1 630	1 839	1 992	3 729
Total Europe	LGNC	-6 775	-12 336	-11 294	-17 350	-27 600	-30 210	-36 390	-45 725	-41 313	-45 197	-44 236
Americas												
Argentina	ZWSJ	402	195	218	176	-81	-83	-14	-104	-144	-145	-228
Brazil	LGND	303	51	-163	-310	-415	-493	-666	-799	-752	-791	-676
Canada	LGNE	170	-73	-230	-14	-3	168	-124	-290	-366	-1 324	-1 181
Chile	ZWSM	-76	-149	-275	-277	-306	-255	-329	-321	-247	-204	-191
Colombia	ZWSN	-17	-71	-113	-97	-78	-50	-95	-155	-141	-174	-467
Mexico	LGNF	127	178	46	-109	128	157	207	198	426	198	12
United States of America	LGNG	618	4 998	6 780	4 957	11 997	14 786	16 759	16 702	18 933	20 756	25 973
Uruguay	ZWTF	20	31	22	8	-35	43	-4	-13	-17	-26	-34
Venezuela	ZWTG	159	83	52	222	187	98	56	-90	-316	-209	-286
Other Central American Countries	ZWSP	507	269	-119	266	821	683	627	1 192	443	880	1 341
Other	ZWSS	62	-108	-156	-64	-79	-27	-52	-50	-25	95	4
Total Americas	LGNI	2 275	5 404	6 062	4 759	12 136	15 027	16 365	16 270	17 794	19 056	24 267
Asia												
China	LGNJ	-1 872	-1 983	-3 201	-3 816	-5 005	-5 992	-7 304	-9 462	-11 271	-14 310	-16 836
Hong Kong	LGNK	-1 248	-2 148	-2 774	-2 583	-2 768	-2 539	-2 723	-2 927	-4 020	-3 786	-3 318
India	LGNL	-206	-128	296	-186	-230	95	-142	-130	-383	-1 032	-755
Indonesia	LGNM	-390	-531	-610	-731	-644	-555	-431	-383	-497	-496	-625
Iran	ZWSX	356	282	343	538	520	622	582	591	506	448	579
Israel	LGNN	306	611	670	615	775	655	640	657	503	391	431
Japan	LGNO	-4 492	-3 894	-4 737	-3 665	-2 101	-2 209	-1 724	-2 722	-2 186	-2 391	-3 259
Malaysia	LGNP	-924	-819	-1 218	-725	-643	-586	-685	-532	-772	-487	-445
Pakistan	LGNQ	-63	-89	-280	-194	-457	-431	-411	-68	-149	-182	-235
Philippines	LGNR	-525	-706	-905	-667	-587	-350	-323	-437	-574	-509	-344
Saudi Arabia	LGNS	3 298	2 333	2 396	2 096	1 382	2 360	2 205	1 496	2 408	3 335	3 586
Singapore	LGNT	-483	48	-20	424	224	138	-173	159	579	649	929
South Korea	LGNU	-1 172	-1 559	-1 811	-1 245	-947	-807	-935	-905	-718	-542	-276
Taiwan	LGNV	-1 225	-1 629	-2 422	-1 763	-1 350	-1 099	-1 078	-1 016	-1 061	-1 161	-1 366
Thailand	LGNW	-955	-928	-1 211	-1 252	-1 335	-1 253	-1 445	-1 435	-1 746	-1 774	-2 007
Residual Gulf Arabian Countries	ZWST	2 419	2 025	2 166	2 174	2 116	2 411	3 142	5 907	3 917	3 660	5 292
Other Near & Middle Eastern Countries	ZWSU	485	393	381	532	427	565	795	759	420	679	935
Other	ZWSG	132	-446	-773	-752	-1 039	-1 231	-1 572	-1 237	-1 403	-566	-1 735
Total Asia	LGNY	-6 559	-9 168	-13 710	-11 201	-11 663	-10 206	-11 582	-11 685	-16 447	-18 073	-19 449
Australasia & Oceania												
Australia	LGNZ	1 317	1 379	1 553	1 235	822	1 047	1 491	1 317	1 397	1 471	2 677
New Zealand	LGOA	-87	-136	-202	-219	-273	-249	-221	-267	-272	-308	-280
Other	LGOB	-61	-52	-22	23	23	26	-11	-34	-6	17	-6
Total Australasia & Oceania	LGOC	1 169	1 191	1 329	1 039	572	824	1 259	1 016	1 119	1 180	2 391
Africa												
Egypt	ZWSR	215	338	77	19	-40	-85	150	29	-225	157	247
Morocco	ZWTA	-63	-114	-100	-136	-198	-178	-258	-288	-217	-451	-232
South Africa	LGOD	616	290	-692	-776	-763	-1 014	-1 225	-1 749	-1 385	-310	-1 390
Other North Africa	ZWSO	120	-47	-338	-200	-151	40	-238	-426	-1 004	-1 146	-1 349
Other	ZWSH	2 211	969	721	-169	-411	-237	-582	-306	164	-151	1 347
Total Africa	LGOF	3 099	1 436	-332	-1 262	-1 564	-1 474	-2 153	-2 740	-2 667	-1 901	-1 377
International Organisations	LGOG	-19	-16	-29	2	45	44	15	17	-16	-12	6
World total	KTMY	-6 810	-13 489	-17 974	-24 012	-28 073	-25 995	-32 486	-42 847	-41 530	-44 947	-38 398

1 Cyprus and Malta are included in Other Europe before 1999.

9.4 Trade in goods

£ million

		1998	1999	2000	2001	2002	2003	2004	2005	2006	2007	2008
Exports												
Europe												
European Union (EU)												
Austria	QBRY	1 190	1 168	1 146	1 224	1 265	1 264	1 095	1 332	1 699	1 376	1 464
Belgium and Luxembourg	QBSB	8 445	9 241	10 322	9 893	10 552	11 374	10 510	11 394	15 082	12 122	13 555
of which Belgium	QDOH	..	9 117	10 102	9 609	10 182	11 073	10 249	11 182	13 418	11 851	13 353
Luxembourg	QDOK	..	124	220	284	370	301	261	212	1 664	271	202
Bulgaria	QAMF	81	76	85	122	134	154	155	220	237	202	253
Cyprus[1]	QDNZ	..	259	311	291	272	317	324	359	960	415	527
Czech Republic	QDLF	698	733	927	1 075	1 031	1 003	978	1 080	1 526	1 401	1 536
Denmark	QBSE	2 057	2 054	2 315	2 267	2 729	2 180	2 042	2 314	3 715	2 182	2 579
Estonia	QAMN	68	51	96	83	100	95	106	115	472	228	220
Finland	QBSH	1 434	1 354	1 471	1 611	1 442	1 493	1 363	1 514	1 872	1 958	1 900
France	QDJA	16 449	16 907	18 577	19 249	18 757	18 885	18 562	19 931	28 693	18 103	18 057
Germany	QDJD	20 590	20 464	22 789	23 655	22 064	20 805	21 668	23 025	27 602	24 699	27 899
Greece	QDJG	1 045	1 206	1 251	1 156	1 234	1 286	1 408	1 367	1 469	1 350	1 651
Hungary	QDLI	486	486	613	612	750	856	934	834	855	863	1 008
Ireland	QDJJ	9 604	10 783	12 372	13 835	15 422	12 224	14 134	16 294	17 480	17 801	19 011
Italy	QDJM	8 608	7 831	8 429	8 404	8 506	8 603	8 400	8 790	9 494	9 189	9 332
Latvia	QAMO	86	69	84	84	77	113	92	103	393	145	167
Lithuania	QAMP	116	96	131	137	149	189	142	167	238	311	281
Malta[1]	QDOC	..	189	206	215	228	260	259	240	319	362	441
Netherlands	QDJP	12 983	13 632	15 167	14 599	14 011	13 597	12 029	12 716	16 522	15 115	19 812
Poland	QDLL	1 178	1 169	1 299	1 297	1 318	1 462	1 417	1 653	2 705	2 372	2 993
Portugal	QDJT	1 722	1 712	1 660	1 579	1 518	1 453	1 580	1 698	2 374	1 481	1 635
Romania	QAMQ	233	242	381	341	432	509	609	647	637	668	752
Slovak Republic	QAMR	103	114	157	203	201	237	224	259	272	382	455
Slovenia	QAMS	136	140	157	160	182	161	163	169	200	205	222
Spain	QDJW	7 171	7 526	8 302	8 363	8 490	8 943	9 100	10 677	12 295	9 979	10 182
Sweden	QDJZ	4 392	4 035	4 211	3 951	3 873	3 823	4 356	4 588	5 246	4 904	5 187
European Central Bank	QARP	–	–	–	–	–	–	–	–	–	–	–
EU Institutions	EOAY	–	–	–	–	–	–	–	–	–	–	–
Total EU27	LGCJ	..	101 537	112 459	114 406	114 737	111 286	111 650	121 486	152 357	127 813	141 119
European Free Trade Association (EFTA)												
Iceland	QDKW	158	159	193	150	131	141	167	179	188	198	187
Liechtenstein	EPOW	4	2	6	3	2	3	6	2	20	3	9
Norway	QDKZ	2 658	1 999	2 018	1 813	1 696	1 886	1 939	2 211	2 125	2 697	2 847
Switzerland	QDLC	2 892	2 768	3 061	3 496	3 080	2 786	2 842	4 985	4 189	3 808	4 654
Total EFTA	EPOT	5 712	4 928	5 278	5 461	4 909	4 816	4 954	7 377	6 522	6 706	7 697
Other Europe												
Albania	QAMC	8	12	7	23	19	10	12	16	16	20	16
Belarus	QAME	32	27	37	33	32	38	53	57	62	72	95
Croatia	QAMM	106	80	72	88	94	138	125	118	144	159	217
Russia	QDLO	929	532	668	893	981	1 420	1 465	1 869	2 063	2 893	4 264
Turkey	QDLR	1 562	1 198	1 800	1 150	1 287	1 638	1 903	2 160	2 426	2 283	2 560
Ukraine	QAMT	166	147	156	202	182	245	224	279	338	449	611
Serbia and Montenegro	QAMW	43	29	32	51	62	65	66	58	88	105	132
Other[1]	BOQE	604	133	196	185	134	176	214	249	326	291	558
Total Europe	EPLM	108 037	108 623	120 705	122 492	122 437	119 832	120 666	133 669	164 342	140 791	157 269
Americas												
Argentina	QAOM	458	293	288	264	127	134	178	167	217	234	317
Brazil	QDLU	899	739	775	808	880	825	789	836	918	1 108	1 689
Canada	QATH	2 147	2 532	3 487	3 203	3 107	3 239	3 340	3 277	3 894	3 291	3 251
Chile	QAMG	171	115	115	132	115	123	134	150	184	191	264
Colombia	QAML	175	107	101	105	83	108	118	117	134	142	163
Mexico	QDLX	516	577	675	681	704	687	629	638	747	801	902
United States of America	J8V9	21 427	24 475	29 549	29 519	28 452	28 997	28 794	31 095	32 287	32 274	35 351
Uruguay	QAMU	68	66	57	48	30	30	32	39	41	36	66
Venezuela	QAMV	242	205	222	314	306	143	190	234	236	259	282
Other Central American Countries	BOQQ	785	922	979	684	690	712	619	677	855	874	1 019
Other	BOQT	244	161	158	160	153	166	147	153	167	187	253
Total Americas	EPLO	27 132	30 192	36 406	35 919	34 647	35 164	34 970	37 383	39 680	39 397	43 557
Asia												
China	QDMA	860	1 211	1 468	1 709	1 493	1 924	2 366	2 811	3 264	3 860	5 072
Hong Kong	QDMD	2 671	2 312	2 673	2 683	2 411	2 481	2 630	3 087	2 864	2 726	3 668
India	QDMG	1 242	1 450	2 058	1 772	1 755	2 284	2 234	2 798	2 693	2 968	4 125
Indonesia	QDMJ	369	385	404	313	324	452	397	366	311	289	384
Iran	QAON	320	237	292	434	397	471	442	452	423	392	438
Israel	QDMM	1 079	1 295	1 516	1 357	1 428	1 359	1 386	1 352	1 308	1 257	1 337
Japan	QAMJ	3 127	3 300	3 672	3 673	3 583	3 710	3 863	3 900	4 109	3 866	3 897
Malaysia	QDMP	677	934	907	1 029	877	1 028	991	1 088	877	975	1 130
Pakistan	QDMS	228	221	207	229	240	291	343	461	488	423	472
Philippines	QDMV	301	239	273	392	352	377	315	279	242	251	245
Saudi Arabia	QDMY	2 605	1 481	1 557	1 525	1 388	1 819	1 611	1 559	1 644	1 857	2 189
Singapore	QDNB	1 598	1 597	1 625	1 592	1 445	1 582	1 708	2 078	2 318	2 467	2 813
South Korea	QDNE	666	949	1 350	1 262	1 461	1 468	1 481	1 677	1 746	1 914	2 543
Taiwan	QDNH	867	865	1 015	875	848	897	950	939	911	957	888
Thailand	QDNK	386	463	582	594	529	572	637	638	567	613	756
Residual Gulf Arabian Countries	BOQW	2 640	2 258	2 586	2 749	2 620	3 353	4 027	6 951	5 074	4 490	6 026
Other Near & Middle Eastern Countries	QARJ	466	406	393	481	499	632	774	744	970	765	1 011
Other	BORB	771	592	644	564	510	600	607	580	677	1 516	842
Total Asia	EPLP	20 873	20 195	23 222	23 232	22 159	25 300	26 762	31 760	30 486	31 586	37 836
Australasia & Oceania												
Australia	QDNN	2 188	2 155	2 699	2 298	2 114	2 289	2 455	2 580	2 488	2 630	3 092
New Zealand	QDNQ	336	324	305	309	311	348	418	415	373	364	385
Other	EGIZ	42	38	43	42	55	64	43	81	70	56	103
Total Australasia & Oceania	EPLQ	2 566	2 517	3 047	2 649	2 480	2 701	2 916	3 076	2 931	3 050	3 580
Africa												
Egypt	QDNT	505	539	498	452	463	458	667	543	577	686	942
Morocco	QAOO	348	359	407	368	346	358	340	261	306	294	516
South Africa	QDNW	1 520	1 281	1 413	1 534	1 597	1 766	1 874	2 073	2 184	2 244	2 654
Other North Africa	BORU	440	386	419	445	478	587	540	484	494	514	805
Other	BOQH	2 635	2 074	1 819	2 000	1 917	2 154	2 139	2 359	2 633	2 296	3 943
Total Africa	EPLN	5 448	4 639	4 556	4 799	4 800	5 323	5 560	5 720	6 194	6 034	8 860
International Organisations	EPLR	–	–	–	–	–	–	–	–	–	–	–
World total	LQAD	164 056	166 166	187 936	189 093	186 524	188 320	190 874	211 608	243 633	220 858	251 102

1 Cyprus and Malta are included in Other Europe before 1999.

9.4 Trade in goods
continued

£ million

Imports

		1998	1999	2000	2001	2002	2003	2004	2005	2006	2007	2008
Europe												
European Union (EU)												
Austria	QBRZ	1 411	1 453	1 410	1 888	2 396	2 776	2 354	2 461	2 786	2 488	2 329
Belgium and Luxembourg	QBSC	9 831	10 156	10 927	12 159	13 201	13 205	13 846	15 155	18 183	15 820	17 266
of which Belgium	QDOI	..	10 079	10 795	11 859	12 449	12 481	12 906	14 238	15 558	15 127	16 441
Luxembourg	QDOL	..	77	132	300	752	724	940	917	2 625	693	825
Bulgaria	QAMZ	74	69	85	101	116	124	150	169	208	239	206
Cyprus[1]	QDOA	..	186	208	243	247	251	205	272	1 445	193	157
Czech Republic	QDLG	555	580	802	1 097	1 250	1 412	1 291	1 883	2 987	2 983	3 561
Denmark	QBSF	2 156	2 341	2 630	2 922	3 595	3 399	3 357	4 393	6 439	3 444	3 912
Estonia	QAND	150	188	309	283	327	264	379	363	2 100	226	144
Finland	QBTG	2 328	2 365	2 765	2 965	2 791	2 663	2 336	2 431	3 118	2 619	2 764
France	QDJB	17 956	18 410	18 644	20 127	20 798	20 389	20 133	21 984	26 376	21 896	23 046
Germany	QDJE	25 095	26 812	28 462	30 192	32 442	33 667	35 381	39 169	42 660	44 565	44 521
Greece	QDJH	363	408	459	476	555	613	637	703	790	640	664
Hungary	QDLJ	535	668	683	710	846	1 120	1 579	1 860	2 348	2 377	2 521
Ireland	QDJK	7 802	8 705	10 261	12 141	13 176	9 920	10 131	10 411	10 770	11 338	12 252
Italy	QDJN	9 744	9 383	9 514	9 860	10 675	11 481	12 184	12 673	12 775	13 316	14 099
Latvia	QANE	290	274	406	439	485	525	693	725	833	605	374
Lithuania	QANF	140	158	247	235	268	285	270	273	274	299	348
Malta[1]	QDOD	..	127	126	144	168	185	184	177	161	179	138
Netherlands	QDJQ	13 408	13 768	15 380	15 395	16 143	16 692	18 196	20 436	22 275	23 079	25 829
Poland	QDLM	653	676	905	1 166	1 265	1 545	1 835	2 320	3 622	3 695	4 295
Portugal	QDJU	1 790	1 822	1 735	1 625	1 761	1 966	1 928	2 018	3 054	1 506	1 736
Romania	QANG	222	253	336	448	522	679	786	803	861	938	758
Slovak Republic	QANH	71	102	136	177	211	259	261	370	815	1 273	1 623
Slovenia	QANI	100	104	122	149	173	169	169	201	740	318	314
Spain	QDJX	5 738	5 966	6 141	7 360	9 190	9 247	9 120	11 450	12 144	10 489	10 717
Sweden	QDKA	4 361	4 648	4 951	4 671	4 330	4 568	5 118	5 463	5 985	5 274	6 789
European Central Bank	QARQ	–	–	–	–	–	–	–	–	–	–	–
EU Institutions	EOBS	–	–	–	–	–	–	–	–	–	–	–
Total EU27	LGDB	..	109 622	117 644	126 973	136 931	137 404	142 523	158 163	183 749	169 799	180 363
European Free Trade Association (EFTA)												
Iceland	QDKX	251	282	365	281	289	296	355	346	402	415	457
Liechtenstein	EPOX	20	23	22	25	22	25	18	13	37	37	33
Norway	QDLA	3 440	3 546	5 563	5 523	5 258	6 423	8 495	12 077	14 453	14 316	21 599
Switzerland	QDLD	4 755	5 341	5 485	4 544	4 595	3 759	3 447	3 884	4 372	4 746	5 253
Total EFTA	EPOU	8 466	9 192	11 435	10 373	10 164	10 503	12 315	16 320	19 264	19 514	27 342
Other Europe												
Albania	QAMX	–	1	2	–	2	3	–	–	–	–	–
Belarus	QAMY	20	20	34	18	31	22	72	271	710	584	106
Croatia	QANC	40	39	41	51	68	50	54	54	67	75	91
Russia	QDLP	1 406	1 324	1 496	2 047	1 950	2 454	3 506	5 010	5 740	5 248	6 907
Turkey	QDLS	1 103	1 204	1 450	1 669	2 164	2 619	3 250	3 510	3 946	4 632	4 874
Ukraine	QANJ	50	47	64	71	143	94	108	91	125	129	150
Serbia and Montenegro	QANM	30	14	23	23	30	34	38	42	64	74	89
Other[1]	BOQF	407	172	177	271	261	283	265	325	303	324	335
Total Europe	EPMM	116 295	121 635	132 366	141 496	151 744	153 466	162 131	183 786	213 968	200 379	220 257
Americas												
Argentina	QAOP	198	190	181	209	236	252	265	283	351	414	561
Brazil	QDLV	883	910	1 114	1 279	1 365	1 477	1 545	1 740	1 905	2 061	2 611
Canada	QATI	2 519	3 026	4 009	3 664	3 563	3 664	4 194	4 157	4 954	5 793	5 786
Chile	QANA	329	328	451	464	460	414	474	478	519	502	580
Colombia	QANB	199	191	231	311	212	223	277	298	299	354	686
Mexico	QDLY	366	395	613	680	505	490	411	446	444	582	787
United States of America	J8VA	24 929	24 613	28 838	30 270	25 742	23 326	22 525	22 530	25 830	26 095	25 848
Uruguay	QANK	53	40	36	36	47	43	41	58	63	69	118
Venezuela	QANL	115	144	207	160	183	113	207	386	593	493	600
Other Central American Countries	BOQR	712	871	1 044	616	766	1 000	1 100	1 189	1 380	1 117	1 349
Other	BOQU	266	289	278	295	259	223	237	224	290	232	371
Total Americas	EPMO	30 569	30 997	37 002	37 984	33 338	31 225	31 276	31 789	36 628	37 712	39 297
Asia												
China	QDMB	2 816	3 384	4 826	5 741	6 726	8 342	10 390	12 962	15 237	18 734	23 107
Hong Kong	QDME	4 391	4 909	5 917	5 754	5 561	5 500	5 761	6 602	7 338	6 939	8 057
India	QDMH	1 382	1 426	1 651	1 816	1 804	2 093	2 287	2 781	3 121	3 809	4 478
Indonesia	QDMK	854	931	1 081	1 128	1 006	875	918	839	958	925	1 183
Iran	QAOQ	32	33	30	28	33	29	41	34	70	63	70
Israel	QDMN	875	996	1 025	939	880	861	920	1 002	965	1 045	1 153
Japan	QAMK	9 124	9 118	10 214	9 080	8 079	8 085	8 109	8 669	7 857	7 885	8 512
Malaysia	QDMQ	1 892	1 961	2 288	1 939	1 731	1 867	2 022	1 813	1 895	1 684	1 869
Pakistan	QDMT	340	318	363	421	472	519	554	487	511	512	628
Philippines	QDMW	855	983	1 155	1 155	944	713	655	712	742	717	626
Saudi Arabia	QDMZ	791	783	977	933	677	715	1 158	1 714	1 232	821	672
Singapore	QDNC	2 343	2 348	2 395	2 067	1 959	2 672	3 379	3 828	3 756	4 247	3 995
South Korea	QDNF	2 201	2 784	3 416	2 756	2 728	2 563	3 083	3 063	3 069	3 073	3 498
Taiwan	QDNI	2 217	2 626	3 561	2 784	2 385	2 198	2 341	2 226	2 339	2 418	2 591
Thailand	QDNL	1 264	1 291	1 602	1 607	1 550	1 646	1 760	1 719	1 922	2 012	2 419
Residual Gulf Arabian Countries	BOQX	847	833	1 109	1 138	1 225	1 516	1 725	2 012	2 198	2 080	2 331
Other Near & Middle Eastern Countries	QARK	81	135	118	133	189	177	110	233	763	386	428
Other	BORD	1 117	1 217	1 596	1 665	1 719	1 984	2 238	2 077	2 479	2 695	3 185
Total Asia	EPMP	33 422	36 076	43 324	41 084	39 668	42 355	47 451	52 773	56 452	60 045	68 802
Australasia & Oceania												
Australia	QDNO	1 363	1 338	1 543	1 776	1 688	1 789	1 868	2 100	2 107	2 245	2 380
New Zealand	QDNR	517	565	544	542	522	552	584	592	600	667	744
Other	HFKF	124	122	124	94	96	125	130	130	120	100	165
Total Australasia & Oceania	EPMQ	2 004	2 025	2 211	2 412	2 306	2 466	2 582	2 822	2 827	3 012	3 289
Africa												
Egypt	QDNU	277	255	411	406	416	432	495	349	662	538	638
Morocco	QAOR	349	383	454	439	453	443	510	420	373	435	436
South Africa	QDNX	1 351	1 636	2 553	2 841	2 685	2 949	3 272	3 937	3 904	3 060	4 725
Other North Africa	BORW	280	333	699	515	588	568	736	935	1 617	1 720	2 296
Other	BOQJ	1 322	1 877	1 892	3 127	3 031	3 023	3 321	3 386	3 514	3 711	4 239
Total Africa	EPMN	3 579	4 484	6 009	7 328	7 173	7 415	8 334	9 027	10 070	9 464	12 334
International Organisations	EPMR	–	–	–	–	–	–	–	–	–	–	–
World total	LQBL	185 869	195 217	220 912	230 305	234 229	236 927	251 774	280 197	319 945	310 612	343 979

1 Cyprus and Malta are included in Other Europe before 1999.

9.4 Trade in goods
continued

£ million

Balances

		1998	1999	2000	2001	2002	2003	2004	2005	2006	2007	2008
Europe												
European Union (EU)												
Austria	QBSA	−221	−285	−264	−664	−1 131	−1 512	−1 259	−1 129	−1 087	−1 112	−865
Belgium and Luxembourg	QBSD	−1 386	−915	−605	−2 266	−2 649	−1 831	−3 336	−3 761	−3 101	−3 698	−3 711
of which Belgium	QDOJ	..	−962	−693	−2 250	−2 267	−1 408	−2 657	−3 056	−2 140	−3 276	−3 088
Luxembourg	QDOM	..	47	88	−16	−382	−423	−679	−705	−961	−422	−623
Bulgaria	QANP	7	7	–	21	18	30	5	51	29	−37	47
Cyprus[1]	QDOB	..	73	103	48	25	66	119	87	−485	222	370
Czech Republic	QDLH	143	153	125	−22	−219	−409	−313	−803	−1 461	−1 582	−2 025
Denmark	QBSG	−99	−287	−315	−655	−866	−1 219	−1 315	−2 079	−2 724	−1 262	−1 333
Estonia	QANT	−82	−137	−213	−200	−227	−169	−273	−248	−1 628	2	76
Finland	QBTL	−894	−1 011	−1 294	−1 354	−1 349	−1 170	−973	−917	−1 246	−661	−864
France	QDJC	−1 507	−1 503	−67	−878	−2 041	−1 504	−1 571	−2 053	2 317	−3 793	−4 989
Germany	QDJF	−4 505	−6 348	−5 673	−6 537	−10 378	−12 862	−13 713	−16 144	−15 058	−19 866	−16 622
Greece	QDJI	682	798	792	680	679	673	771	664	679	710	987
Hungary	QDLK	−49	−182	−70	−98	−96	−264	−645	−1 026	−1 493	−1 514	−1 513
Ireland	QDJL	1 802	2 078	2 111	1 694	2 246	2 304	4 003	5 883	6 710	6 463	6 759
Italy	QDJO	−1 136	−1 552	−1 085	−1 456	−2 169	−2 878	−3 784	−3 883	−3 281	−4 127	−4 767
Latvia	QANU	−204	−205	−322	−355	−408	−412	−601	−622	−440	−460	−207
Lithuania	QANV	−24	−62	−116	−98	−119	−96	−128	−106	−36	12	−67
Malta[1]	QDOE	..	62	80	71	60	75	75	63	158	183	303
Netherlands	QDJR	−425	−136	−213	−796	−2 132	−3 095	−6 167	−7 720	−5 753	−7 964	−6 017
Poland	QDLN	525	493	394	131	53	−83	−418	−667	−917	−1 323	−1 302
Portugal	QDJV	−68	−110	−75	−46	−243	−513	−348	−320	−680	−25	−101
Romania	QAOD	11	−11	45	−107	−90	−170	−177	−156	−224	−270	−6
Slovak Republic	QAOG	32	12	21	26	−10	−22	−37	−111	−543	−891	−1 168
Slovenia	QAOH	36	36	35	11	9	−8	−6	−32	−540	−113	−92
Spain	QDJY	1 433	1 560	2 161	1 003	−700	−304	−20	−773	151	−510	−535
Sweden	QDKV	31	−613	−740	−720	−457	−745	−762	−875	−739	−370	−1 602
European Central Bank	QARR	–	–	–	–	–	–	–	–	–	–	–
EU Institutions	EOCM	–	–	–	–	–	–	–	–	–	–	–
Total EU27	LGCF	..	−8 085	−5 185	−12 567	−22 194	−26 118	−30 873	−36 677	−31 392	−41 986	−39 244
European Free Trade Association (EFTA)												
Iceland	QDKY	−93	−123	−172	−131	−158	−155	−188	−167	−214	−217	−270
Liechtenstein	EPOY	−16	−21	−16	−22	−20	−22	−12	−11	−17	−34	−24
Norway	QDLB	−782	−1 547	−3 545	−3 710	−3 562	−4 537	−6 556	−9 866	−12 328	−11 619	−18 752
Switzerland	QDLE	−1 863	−2 573	−2 424	−1 048	−1 515	−973	−605	1 101	−183	−938	−599
Total EFTA	EPOV	−2 754	−4 264	−6 157	−4 912	−5 255	−5 687	−7 361	−8 943	−12 742	−12 808	−19 645
Other Europe												
Albania	QANN	8	11	5	23	17	7	12	16	16	20	16
Belarus	QANO	12	7	3	15	1	16	−19	−214	−648	−512	−11
Croatia	QANS	66	41	31	37	26	88	71	64	77	84	126
Russia	QDLQ	−477	−792	−828	−1 154	−969	−1 034	−2 041	−3 141	−3 677	−2 355	−2 643
Turkey	QDLT	459	−6	350	−519	−877	−981	−1 347	−1 350	−1 520	−2 349	−2 314
Ukraine	QAOI	116	100	92	131	39	151	116	188	213	320	461
Serbia and Montenegro	QAOL	13	15	9	28	32	31	28	16	24	31	43
Other[1]	BOQG	197	−39	19	−86	−127	−107	−51	−76	23	−33	223
Total Europe	EPNM	−8 258	−13 012	−11 661	−19 004	−29 307	−33 634	−41 465	−50 117	−49 626	−59 588	−62 988
Americas												
Argentina	QAOS	260	103	107	55	−109	−118	−87	−116	−134	−180	−244
Brazil	QDLW	16	−171	−339	−471	−485	−652	−756	−904	−987	−953	−922
Canada	QBRV	−372	−494	−522	−461	−456	−425	−854	−880	−1 060	−2 502	−2 535
Chile	QANQ	−158	−213	−336	−332	−345	−291	−340	−328	−335	−311	−316
Colombia	QANR	−24	−84	−130	−206	−129	−115	−159	−181	−165	−212	−523
Mexico	QDLZ	150	182	62	1	199	197	218	192	303	219	115
United States of America	J8VB	−3 502	−139	711	−751	2 710	5 670	6 269	8 565	6 457	6 179	9 503
Uruguay	QAOJ	15	26	21	12	−17	−13	−9	−19	−22	−33	−52
Venezuela	QAOK	127	61	15	154	123	30	−17	−152	−357	−234	−318
Other Central American Countries	BOQS	73	51	−65	68	−76	−288	−481	−512	−525	−243	−330
Other	BOQV	−22	−128	−120	−135	−106	−57	−90	−71	−123	−45	−118
Total Americas	EPNO	−3 437	−805	−596	−2 065	1 309	3 939	3 694	5 594	3 052	1 685	4 260
Asia												
China	QDMC	−1 956	−2 173	−3 358	−4 032	−5 233	−6 418	−8 024	−10 151	−11 973	−14 874	−18 035
Hong Kong	QDMF	−1 720	−2 597	−3 244	−3 071	−3 150	−3 019	−3 131	−3 515	−4 474	−4 213	−4 389
India	QDMI	−140	24	407	−44	−49	191	−53	17	−428	−841	−353
Indonesia	QDML	−485	−546	−677	−815	−682	−423	−521	−473	−647	−636	−799
Iran	QAOT	288	204	262	406	364	442	401	418	353	329	368
Israel	QDMO	204	299	491	418	548	498	466	350	343	212	184
Japan	QBRR	−5 997	−5 818	−6 542	−5 407	−4 496	−4 375	−4 246	−4 769	−3 748	−4 019	−4 615
Malaysia	QDMR	−1 215	−1 027	−1 381	−910	−854	−839	−1 031	−725	−1 018	−709	−739
Pakistan	QDMU	−112	−97	−156	−192	−232	−228	−211	−26	−23	−89	−156
Philippines	QDMX	−554	−744	−882	−763	−592	−336	−340	−433	−500	−466	−381
Saudi Arabia	QDNA	1 814	698	580	592	711	1 104	453	−155	412	1 036	1 517
Singapore	QDND	−745	−751	−770	−475	−514	−1 090	−1 671	−1 750	−1 438	−1 780	−1 182
South Korea	QDNG	−1 535	−1 835	−2 066	−1 494	−1 267	−1 095	−1 602	−1 386	−1 323	−1 159	−955
Taiwan	QDNJ	−1 350	−1 761	−2 546	−1 909	−1 537	−1 301	−1 391	−1 287	−1 428	−1 461	−1 703
Thailand	QDNM	−878	−1 184	−1 020	−1 013	−1 021	−1 074	−1 123	−1 081	−1 355	−1 399	−1 663
Residual Gulf Arabian Countries	BORA	1 793	1 425	1 477	1 611	1 395	1 837	2 302	4 939	2 876	2 410	3 695
Other Near & Middle Eastern Countries	QARL	385	271	275	348	310	455	664	511	207	379	583
Other	BORE	−346	−625	−952	−1 101	−1 209	−1 384	−1 631	−1 497	−1 802	−1 179	−2 343
Total Asia	EPNP	−12 549	−15 881	−20 102	−17 852	−17 509	−17 055	−20 689	−21 013	−25 966	−28 459	−30 966
Australasia & Oceania												
Australia	QDNP	825	817	1 156	522	426	500	587	480	381	385	712
New Zealand	QDNS	−181	−241	−239	−233	−211	−204	−166	−177	−227	−303	−359
Other	HFKK	−82	−84	−81	−52	−41	−61	−87	−49	−50	−44	−62
Total Australasia & Oceania	EPNQ	562	492	836	237	174	235	334	254	104	38	291
Africa												
Egypt	QDNV	228	284	87	46	47	26	172	194	−85	148	304
Morocco	QAOU	−1	−24	−47	−71	−107	−85	−170	−159	−67	−141	80
South Africa	QDNY	169	−355	−1 140	−1 307	−1 088	−1 183	−1 398	−1 864	−1 720	−816	−2 071
Other North Africa	BORX	160	53	−280	−70	−110	19	−196	−451	−1 123	−1 206	−1 491
Other	BOQK	1 313	197	−73	−1 127	−1 114	−869	−1 182	−1 027	−881	−1 415	−296
Total Africa	EPNN	1 869	155	−1 453	−2 529	−2 373	−2 092	−2 774	−3 307	−3 876	−3 430	−3 474
International Organisations	EPNR	–	–	–	–	–	–	–	–	–	–	–
World total	LQCT	−21 813	−29 051	−32 976	−41 212	−47 705	−48 607	−60 900	−68 589	−76 312	−89 754	−92 877

1 Cyprus and Malta are included in Other Europe before 1999.

9.5 Trade in services

£ million

		1998	1999	2000	2001	2002	2003	2004	2005	2006	2007	2008
Exports												
Europe												
European Union (EU)												
Austria	FYVC	351	399	405	409	426	424	433	520	544	613	718
Belgium and Luxembourg	FYVD	2 022	2 400	2 477	2 494	2 819	3 213	3 868	3 663	3 719	4 427	5 725
of which Belgium	A7RX	..	1 993	2 088	2 051	2 383	2 559	2 960	2 809	2 575	2 890	3 648
Luxembourg	A7S2	..	407	389	443	436	654	908	854	1 144	1 537	2 077
Bulgaria	ZWKO	14	41	42	35	75	67	78	94	117	170	183
Cyprus[1]	A7RY	..	134	149	135	219	235	335	313	358	629	586
Czech Republic	FYVW	199	153	168	185	181	244	329	335	348	521	415
Denmark	FYVE	1 042	985	1 180	1 390	1 374	1 528	1 592	1 525	2 312	2 345	2 426
Estonia	ZWKU	5	14	12	14	21	22	29	37	58	109	43
Finland	FYVF	537	661	955	879	832	878	958	857	1 071	1 186	1 139
France	FYVG	4 263	4 872	5 443	6 078	6 021	6 260	6 613	6 443	7 236	8 332	9 683
Germany	FYVH	5 386	5 758	6 682	7 193	7 497	7 860	8 218	9 151	9 922	10 661	11 815
Greece	FYVI	699	817	836	809	765	790	743	932	772	887	1 201
Hungary	GYWV	95	138	206	205	218	226	372	559	415	548	455
Ireland	FYVJ	2 575	2 585	2 851	3 658	4 288	5 316	5 589	6 552	6 792	7 436	8 449
Italy	FYVK	2 430	2 813	2 693	2 901	3 018	3 029	3 412	3 700	3 702	4 178	4 479
Latvia	ZWLC	16	24	30	33	38	29	49	93	67	245	86
Lithuania	ZWLB	7	15	17	46	32	43	55	112	104	121	270
Malta[1]	A7S3	..	66	57	52	61	73	79	71	89	129	168
Netherlands	FYVL	3 264	4 165	4 557	4 914	4 709	5 410	6 703	6 912	7 697	8 417	9 731
Poland	FYVX	287	272	286	337	392	411	505	799	1 008	1 007	1 031
Portugal	FYVM	456	584	436	485	530	544	678	630	565	647	724
Romania	ZWLE	29	44	44	73	76	97	137	127	165	252	272
Slovak Republic	ZWLG	24	31	39	43	30	36	46	99	114	190	290
Slovenia	ZWLF	6	26	28	38	48	43	52	63	72	74	84
Spain	FYVN	1 796	2 116	2 256	2 252	2 612	2 878	2 949	3 752	4 459	5 114	5 522
Sweden	FYVO	1 375	1 438	1 618	1 636	1 477	1 700	1 710	1 756	1 986	2 100	2 316
European Central Bank	KNWZ	–	–	3	12	3	–	–	–	–	3	–
EU Institutions	FYVP	228	232	248	544	544	515	578	600	604	625	679
Total EU27	GC8R	..	30 783	33 718	36 850	38 306	41 871	46 110	49 695	54 296	60 966	68 490
European Free Trade Association (EFTA)												
Iceland	FYVR	48	30	73	63	64	72	89	135	188	183	225
Liechtenstein	FYVS	22	34	37	30	43	40	53	40	43	97	68
Norway	FYVT	1 216	1 137	1 031	976	1 449	1 328	1 525	1 811	1 943	2 546	2 478
Switzerland	FYVU	2 488	2 697	2 784	3 488	3 967	4 629	4 359	4 852	5 600	6 441	7 083
Total EFTA	FYVV	3 774	3 898	3 925	4 557	5 523	6 069	6 026	6 838	7 774	9 267	9 854
Other Europe												
Albania	ZWKM	–	3	2	5	6	6	22	8	13	11	25
Belarus	ZWKP	1	3	27	3	4	4	6	7	9	13	14
Croatia	ZWKZ	12	38	38	34	55	51	44	46	98	97	109
Russia	FYVY	444	297	415	470	581	733	902	1 123	1 668	2 208	2 188
Turkey	FYVZ	338	401	351	398	372	403	368	509	557	748	648
Ukraine	ZWLH	65	23	43	29	302	126	55	97	148	206	223
Serbia and Montenegro	ZWLK	20	39	103	41	28	40	21	35	43	64	33
Other[1]	ZWKJ	1 114	1 215	1 242	1 160	1 505	2 037	2 250	2 748	3 137	3 403	4 754
Total Europe	FYWB	32 874	36 700	39 864	43 547	46 682	51 340	55 804	61 106	67 743	76 983	86 337
Americas												
Argentina	ZWKN	212	167	186	195	83	83	142	99	105	127	144
Brazil	FYWC	427	378	350	392	321	335	307	367	498	447	594
Canada	FYWD	1 413	1 397	1 397	1 639	1 543	1 595	1 778	1 752	2 034	2 559	2 851
Chile	ZWKQ	125	106	96	103	87	79	83	88	126	175	177
Colombia	ZWKR	67	48	56	140	86	97	87	66	70	75	89
Mexico	FYWE	165	221	267	288	265	272	354	305	397	342	345
United States of America	FYWF	15 707	17 889	19 274	19 211	22 690	23 977	25 790	24 423	29 226	32 964	36 173
Uruguay	ZWLI	11	9	7	5	5	60	10	13	17	14	24
Venezuela	ZWLJ	72	68	83	110	99	102	99	96	71	62	70
Other Central American Countries	ZWKT	1 480	1 209	1 419	1 604	2 209	2 385	2 989	3 476	3 641	3 772	4 755
Other	ZWKW	249	235	220	219	151	160	148	191	222	300	300
Total Americas	FYWH	19 928	21 727	23 355	23 906	27 539	29 145	31 787	30 876	36 407	40 837	45 522
Asia												
China	FYWI	303	456	449	591	724	889	1 279	1 384	1 499	1 547	2 471
Hong Kong	FYWJ	987	1 069	1 041	1 094	1 006	1 195	1 128	1 346	1 290	1 640	2 121
India	FYWK	488	521	553	675	635	722	999	1 159	1 638	1 648	1 827
Indonesia	FYWL	199	165	192	205	174	165	190	187	287	252	297
Iran	ZWLA	93	99	124	169	185	225	242	215	214	163	256
Israel	FYWM	309	527	445	511	429	370	407	556	455	482	549
Japan	FYWN	2 749	3 226	3 469	3 558	3 844	3 905	4 225	4 303	4 302	4 573	4 991
Malaysia	FYWO	544	394	390	376	404	423	554	464	498	453	535
Pakistan	FYWP	243	296	176	278	173	183	231	430	359	320	321
Philippines	FYWQ	93	126	183	178	105	141	126	138	98	110	229
Saudi Arabia	FYWR	1 935	2 161	2 369	2 147	1 973	2 320	2 530	2 216	2 691	2 815	2 633
Singapore	FYWS	584	1 160	1 086	1 294	1 166	1 653	2 159	2 638	2 879	3 328	3 458
South Korea	FYWT	492	411	396	428	505	474	913	735	854	956	1 080
Taiwan	FYWU	235	251	281	295	370	382	515	581	584	639	694
Thailand	FYWV	231	207	194	219	207	334	319	258	292	318	333
Residual Gulf Arabian Countries	ZWKX	1 012	1 034	1 103	1 114	1 332	1 335	1 767	1 985	2 298	2 798	3 653
Other Near & Middle Eastern Countries	ZWKY	178	206	231	339	268	261	339	447	433	468	574
Other Asian Countries	ZWKK	1 013	658	810	884	727	798	959	1 106	1 422	1 445	1 576
Total Asia	FYWX	11 688	12 967	13 492	14 355	14 227	15 775	18 882	20 148	22 093	23 955	27 598
Australasia & Oceania												
Australia	FYWY	1 456	1 608	1 588	1 964	1 826	2 023	2 293	2 704	2 819	3 105	4 016
New Zealand	FYWZ	321	354	301	301	275	302	379	411	394	433	456
Other	FYXA	47	61	84	95	97	115	130	63	121	108	142
Total Australasia & Oceania	FYXB	1 824	2 023	1 973	2 360	2 198	2 440	2 802	3 178	3 334	3 646	4 614
Africa												
Egypt	ZWKV	104	283	280	340	226	239	322	373	463	607	690
Morocco	ZWLD	57	47	61	82	50	48	61	46	89	73	77
South Africa	FYXC	934	1 125	976	1 129	1 009	1 090	1 081	1 131	1 356	1 454	1 580
Other North Africa	ZWKS	292	118	265	219	222	287	288	374	403	470	602
Other	ZWKL	1 480	1 495	1 566	1 771	1 774	1 920	1 843	1 894	2 317	2 575	3 330
Total Africa	FYXE	2 867	3 068	3 148	3 541	3 281	3 584	3 595	3 818	4 628	5 179	6 279
International Organisations	FYXF	47	40	51	64	85	73	52	60	41	45	49
World total	KTMQ	69 228	76 525	81 883	87 773	94 012	102 357	112 922	119 186	134 246	150 645	170 399

1 Cyprus and Malta are included in Other Europe before 1999.

9.5 Trade in services
continued

£ million

		1998	1999	2000	2001	2002	2003	2004	2005	2006	2007	2008
Imports												
Europe												
European Union (EU)												
Austria	GGOR	461	456	477	506	688	660	756	870	891	827	957
Belgium and Luxembourg	GGOS	1 450	1 723	1 675	1 800	2 036	2 206	2 361	2 454	2 644	2 743	3 223
of which Belgium	A8ET	..	1 499	1 492	1 616	1 824	1 958	2 003	2 151	2 122	2 274	2 624
Luxembourg	A8EW	..	224	183	184	212	248	358	303	522	469	599
Bulgaria	ZWMU	29	36	38	52	96	104	174	254	240	334	397
Cyprus[1]	A8EU	..	766	885	1 059	977	1 088	1 080	1 205	1 180	1 167	1 178
Czech Republic	GGPL	146	146	168	199	250	337	426	468	533	469	476
Denmark	GGOT	511	639	674	655	746	783	852	941	1 040	1 017	1 113
Estonia	ZWNA	5	6	33	27	18	35	47	53	69	132	60
Finland	GGOU	219	305	404	360	282	314	285	353	359	418	395
France	GGOV	5 744	6 687	7 531	7 528	7 841	8 262	8 512	8 954	9 572	9 793	9 842
Germany	GGOW	3 874	4 757	4 705	5 239	5 400	5 580	6 437	7 720	7 891	8 235	10 093
Greece	GGOX	1 051	1 426	1 617	1 886	1 907	1 979	1 969	2 001	2 011	2 249	2 261
Hungary	GYXH	82	89	95	126	129	151	186	274	339	471	335
Ireland	GGOY	1 798	2 172	2 261	2 337	2 316	2 577	3 052	3 437	3 487	3 936	4 185
Italy	GGOZ	2 362	2 655	2 856	3 002	3 138	3 429	3 563	4 305	4 183	4 755	4 955
Latvia	ZWNI	5	12	25	20	19	29	38	44	81	137	71
Lithuania	ZWNH	7	5	6	16	37	25	19	72	84	100	89
Malta[1]	A8EX	..	196	223	256	238	279	318	343	294	313	379
Netherlands	GGPA	2 117	2 443	3 026	3 128	3 380	3 320	3 352	3 575	3 595	3 295	3 749
Poland	GGPM	144	175	184	200	187	224	299	557	956	1 170	1 261
Portugal	GGPB	828	1 005	1 021	1 116	1 208	1 367	1 397	1 441	1 434	1 699	1 909
Romania	ZWNK	22	51	64	77	84	91	131	169	170	170	208
Slovak Republic	ZWNM	32	28	30	14	27	22	33	67	93	99	112
Slovenia	ZWNL	12	14	29	17	23	24	34	48	53	44	65
Spain	GGPC	5 215	5 933	6 495	7 231	7 846	8 978	9 104	9 467	9 930	10 014	10 707
Sweden	GGPD	539	778	830	829	827	1 133	1 148	1 314	1 345	1 204	1 344
European Central Bank	KOFJ	–	1	1	1	1	–	–	–	–	–	2
EU Institutions	GGPE	10	6	3	5	14	17	4	4	2	–	5
Total EU27	GCV2	..	32 510	35 356	37 686	39 715	43 014	45 577	50 390	52 476	54 791	59 371
European Free Trade Association (EFTA)												
Iceland	GGPG	46	25	75	44	42	46	57	71	98	91	85
Liechtenstein	GGPH	33	7	6	7	1	11	4	4	6	19	8
Norway	GGPI	525	499	536	647	1 266	710	770	975	1 001	992	1 150
Switzerland	GGPJ	1 476	1 538	1 633	1 587	1 676	1 794	1 830	2 353	2 361	2 793	2 582
Total EFTA	GGPK	2 080	2 069	2 250	2 285	2 985	2 561	2 661	3 403	3 466	3 895	3 825
Other Europe												
Albania	ZWMS	1	6	5	9	13	14	20	8	13	23	24
Belarus	ZWMV	5	1	2	4	3	4	1	8	19	23	20
Croatia	ZWNF	37	21	27	55	47	73	83	139	176	159	228
Russia	GGPN	182	137	188	218	296	303	499	548	721	912	1 102
Turkey	GGPO	562	524	521	569	704	788	811	1 038	1 089	1 165	1 470
Ukraine	ZWNN	14	9	14	33	25	23	42	95	76	175	234
Serbia and Montenegro	ZWNQ	11	31	22	38	33	41	38	43	73	71	63
Other[1]	ZWMP	1 836	716	1 112	996	1 154	1 095	997	1 042	1 321	1 378	1 248
Total Europe	GGPQ	31 391	36 024	39 497	41 893	44 975	47 916	50 729	56 714	59 430	62 592	67 585
Americas												
Argentina	ZWMT	70	75	75	74	55	48	69	87	115	92	128
Brazil	GGPR	140	156	174	231	251	176	217	262	263	285	348
Canada	GGPS	871	976	1 105	1 192	1 090	1 002	1 048	1 162	1 340	1 381	1 497
Chile	ZWMW	43	42	35	48	48	43	72	81	38	68	52
Colombia	ZWMX	60	35	39	31	35	32	23	40	46	37	33
Mexico	GGPT	188	225	283	398	336	312	365	299	274	363	448
United States of America	GGPU	11 587	12 753	13 205	13 503	13 403	14 862	15 300	16 286	16 750	18 387	19 703
Uruguay	ZWNO	6	4	6	9	23	4	5	7	12	7	6
Venezuela	ZWNP	40	46	46	42	35	34	26	34	30	37	38
Other Central American Countries	ZWMZ	1 046	991	1 473	1 406	1 312	1 414	1 881	1 772	2 673	2 649	3 084
Other	ZWNC	165	215	256	148	124	130	110	170	124	160	178
Total Americas	GGPW	14 216	15 518	16 697	17 082	16 712	18 057	19 116	20 200	21 665	23 466	25 515
Asia												
China	GGPX	219	266	292	375	496	463	559	695	797	983	1 272
Hong Kong	GGPY	515	620	571	606	624	715	720	758	836	1 213	1 050
India	GGPZ	554	673	664	817	816	818	1 088	1 306	1 593	1 839	2 229
Indonesia	GGQA	104	150	125	121	136	297	100	97	137	112	123
Iran	ZWNG	25	21	43	37	29	45	61	42	61	44	45
Israel	GGQB	207	215	266	314	202	213	233	249	295	303	302
Japan	GGQC	1 244	1 302	1 664	1 816	1 449	1 739	1 703	2 257	2 740	2 945	3 635
Malaysia	GGQD	253	186	227	191	193	170	208	271	252	231	241
Pakistan	GGQE	194	288	300	280	398	386	431	472	485	413	400
Philippines	GGQF	64	88	206	82	100	155	109	142	172	153	192
Saudi Arabia	GGQG	451	526	553	643	1 302	1 064	778	565	695	516	564
Singapore	GGQH	322	361	336	395	428	425	661	729	862	899	1 347
South Korea	GGQI	129	135	141	179	185	186	246	254	249	339	401
Taiwan	GGQJ	110	119	157	149	183	180	202	310	217	338	357
Thailand	GGQK	308	307	385	458	521	513	641	612	683	693	677
Residual Gulf Arabian Countries	ZWND	386	434	414	551	611	761	927	1 017	1 257	1 548	2 056
Other Near & Middle Eastern Countries	ZWNE	78	84	125	155	151	151	208	199	220	168	222
Other	ZWMQ	535	479	631	535	557	645	900	846	1 023	832	968
Total Asia	GGQM	5 698	6 254	7 100	7 704	8 381	8 926	9 775	10 820	12 574	13 569	16 081
Australasia & Oceania												
Australia	GGQN	964	1 046	1 191	1 251	1 430	1 476	1 389	1 867	1 803	2 019	2 051
New Zealand	GGQO	227	249	264	287	337	347	434	501	439	438	377
Other	GGQP	26	29	25	20	33	28	54	48	77	47	86
Total Australasia & Oceania	GGQQ	1 217	1 324	1 480	1 558	1 800	1 851	1 877	2 416	2 319	2 504	2 514
Africa												
Egypt	ZWNB	117	229	290	367	313	350	344	538	603	598	747
Morocco	ZWNJ	119	137	114	147	141	141	149	175	239	383	389
South Africa	GGQR	487	480	528	598	684	921	908	1 016	1 021	948	899
Other North Africa	ZWMY	332	218	323	349	263	266	330	349	284	410	460
Other	ZWMR	582	723	772	813	1 071	1 288	1 243	1 173	1 272	1 311	1 687
Total Africa	GGQT	1 637	1 787	2 027	2 274	2 472	2 966	2 974	3 251	3 419	3 650	4 182
International Organisations	GGQU	66	56	80	62	40	29	37	43	57	57	43
World total	KTMR	54 225	60 963	66 881	70 573	74 380	79 745	84 508	93 444	99 464	105 838	115 920

1 Cyprus and Malta are included in Other Europe before 1999.

9.5 Trade in services
continued

£ million

		1998	1999	2000	2001	2002	2003	2004	2005	2006	2007	2008
Balances												
Europe												
European Union (EU)												
Austria	GGQW	−110	−57	−72	−97	−262	−236	−323	−350	−347	−214	−239
Belgium and Luxembourg	GGQX	572	677	802	694	783	1 007	1 507	1 209	1 075	1 684	2 502
of which Belgium	A8HH	..	494	596	435	559	601	957	658	453	616	1 024
Luxembourg	A8HK	..	183	206	259	224	406	550	551	622	1 068	1 478
Bulgaria	ZWTO	−15	5	4	−17	−21	−37	−96	−160	−123	−164	−214
Cyprus[1]	A8HI	..	−632	−736	−924	−758	−853	−745	−892	−822	−538	−592
Czech Republic	GGRQ	53	7	–	−14	−69	−93	−97	−133	−185	52	−61
Denmark	GGQY	531	346	506	735	628	745	740	584	1 272	1 328	1 313
Estonia	ZWTU	–	8	−21	−13	3	−13	−18	−16	−11	−23	−17
Finland	GGQZ	318	356	551	519	550	564	673	504	712	768	744
France	GGRA	−1 481	−1 815	−2 088	−1 450	−1 820	−2 002	−1 899	−2 511	−2 336	−1 461	−159
Germany	GGRB	1 512	1 001	1 977	1 954	2 097	2 280	1 781	1 431	2 031	2 426	1 722
Greece	GGRC	−352	−609	−781	−1 077	−1 142	−1 189	−1 226	−1 069	−1 239	−1 362	−1 060
Hungary	GYXT	13	49	111	79	89	75	186	285	76	77	120
Ireland	GGRD	777	413	590	1 321	1 972	2 739	2 537	3 115	3 305	3 500	4 264
Italy	GGRE	68	158	−163	−101	−120	−400	−151	−605	−481	−577	−476
Latvia	ZWUC	11	12	5	13	19	–	11	49	−14	108	15
Lithuania	ZWUB	–	10	11	30	−5	18	36	40	20	21	181
Malta[1]	A8HL	..	−130	−166	−204	−177	−206	−239	−272	−205	−184	−211
Netherlands	GGRF	1 147	1 722	1 531	1 786	1 329	2 090	3 351	3 337	4 102	5 122	5 982
Poland	GGRR	143	97	102	137	205	187	206	242	52	−163	−230
Portugal	GGRG	−372	−421	−585	−631	−678	−823	−719	−811	−869	−1 052	−1 185
Romania	ZWUE	7	−7	−20	−4	−8	6	6	−42	−5	82	64
Slovak Republic	ZWUG	−8	3	9	29	3	14	13	32	21	91	178
Slovenia	ZWUF	−6	12	−1	21	25	19	18	15	19	30	19
Spain	GGRH	−3 419	−3 817	−4 239	−4 979	−5 234	−6 100	−6 155	−5 715	−5 471	−4 900	−5 185
Sweden	GGRI	836	660	788	807	650	567	562	442	641	896	972
European Central Bank	ZWTI	–	−1	2	11	2	–	–	–	–	3	−2
EU Institutions	GGRJ	218	226	245	539	530	498	574	596	602	625	674
Total EU27	GD6R	..	−1 727	−1 638	−836	−1 409	−1 143	533	−695	1 820	6 175	9 119
European Free Trade Association (EFTA)												
Iceland	GGRL	2	5	−2	19	22	26	32	64	90	92	140
Liechtenstein	GGRM	−11	27	31	23	42	29	49	36	37	78	60
Norway	GGRN	691	638	495	329	183	618	755	836	942	1 554	1 328
Switzerland	GGRO	1 012	1 159	1 151	1 901	2 291	2 835	2 529	2 499	3 239	3 648	4 501
Total EFTA	GGRP	1 694	1 829	1 675	2 272	2 538	3 508	3 365	3 435	4 308	5 372	6 029
Other Europe												
Albania	ZWTM	−1	−3	−3	−4	−7	−8	2	–	–	−12	1
Belarus	ZWTP	−4	2	25	−1	1	–	5	−1	−10	−10	−6
Croatia	ZWTZ	−25	17	11	−21	8	−22	−39	−93	−78	−62	−119
Russia	GGRS	262	160	227	252	285	430	403	575	947	1 296	1 085
Turkey	GGRT	−224	−123	−170	−171	−332	−385	−443	−529	−532	−417	−822
Ukraine	ZWUH	51	14	29	−4	277	103	13	2	72	31	−11
Serbia and Montenegro	ZWUK	9	8	81	3	−5	−1	−17	−8	−30	−7	−30
Other[1]	ZWTJ	−722	499	130	164	351	942	1 253	1 706	1 816	2 025	3 506
Total Europe	GGRV	1 483	676	367	1 654	1 707	3 424	5 075	4 392	8 313	14 391	18 752
Americas												
Argentina	ZWTN	142	92	111	121	28	35	73	12	−10	35	16
Brazil	GGRW	287	222	176	161	70	159	90	105	235	162	246
Canada	GGRX	542	421	292	447	453	593	730	590	694	1 178	1 354
Chile	ZWTQ	82	64	61	55	39	36	11	7	88	107	125
Colombia	ZWTR	7	13	17	109	51	65	64	26	24	38	56
Mexico	GGRY	−23	−4	−16	−110	−71	−40	−11	6	123	−21	−103
United States of America	GGRZ	4 120	5 136	6 069	5 708	9 287	9 115	10 490	8 137	12 476	14 577	16 470
Uruguay	ZWUI	5	5	1	−4	−18	56	5	6	5	7	18
Venezuela	ZWUJ	32	22	37	68	64	68	73	62	41	25	32
Other Central American Countries	ZWTT	434	218	−54	198	897	971	1 108	1 704	968	1 123	1 671
Other	ZWTW	84	20	−36	71	27	30	38	21	98	140	122
Total Americas	GGSB	5 712	6 209	6 658	6 824	10 827	11 088	12 671	10 676	14 742	17 371	20 007
Asia												
China	GGSC	84	190	157	216	228	426	720	689	702	564	1 198
Hong Kong	GGSD	472	449	470	488	382	480	408	588	454	427	1 071
India	GGSE	−66	−152	−111	−142	−181	−96	−89	−147	45	−191	−402
Indonesia	GGSF	95	15	67	84	38	−132	90	90	150	140	174
Iran	ZWUA	68	78	81	132	156	180	181	173	153	119	211
Israel	GGSG	102	312	179	197	227	157	174	307	160	179	247
Japan	GGSH	1 505	1 924	1 805	1 742	2 395	2 166	2 522	2 047	1 562	1 628	1 356
Malaysia	GGSI	291	208	163	185	211	253	346	193	246	222	294
Pakistan	GGSJ	49	8	−124	−2	−225	−203	−200	−42	−126	−93	−79
Philippines	GGSK	29	38	−23	96	5	−14	17	−4	−74	−43	37
Saudi Arabia	GGSL	1 484	1 635	1 816	1 504	671	1 256	1 752	1 651	1 996	2 299	2 069
Singapore	GGSM	262	799	750	899	738	1 228	1 498	1 909	2 017	2 429	2 111
South Korea	GGSN	363	276	255	249	320	288	667	481	605	617	679
Taiwan	GGSO	125	132	124	146	187	202	313	271	367	301	337
Thailand	GGSP	−77	−100	−191	−239	−314	−179	−322	−354	−391	−375	−344
Residual Gulf Arabian Countries	ZWTX	626	600	689	563	721	574	840	968	1 041	1 250	1 597
Other Near & Middle Eastern Countries	ZWTY	100	122	106	184	117	110	131	248	213	300	352
Other	ZWTK	478	179	179	349	170	153	59	260	399	613	608
Total Asia	GGSR	5 990	6 713	6 392	6 651	5 846	6 849	9 107	9 328	9 519	10 386	11 517
Australasia & Oceania												
Australia	GGSS	492	562	397	713	396	547	904	837	1 016	1 086	1 965
New Zealand	GGST	94	105	37	14	−62	−45	−55	−90	−45	−5	79
Other	GGSU	21	32	59	75	64	87	76	15	44	61	56
Total Australasia & Oceania	GGSV	607	699	493	802	398	589	925	762	1 015	1 142	2 100
Africa												
Egypt	ZWTV	−13	54	−10	−27	−87	−111	−22	−165	−140	9	−57
Morocco	ZWUD	−62	−90	−53	−65	−91	−93	−88	−129	−150	−310	−312
South Africa	GGSW	447	645	448	531	325	169	173	115	335	506	681
Other North Africa	ZWTS	−40	−100	−58	−130	−41	21	−42	25	119	60	142
Other	ZWTL	898	772	794	958	703	632	600	721	1 045	1 264	1 643
Total Africa	GGSY	1 230	1 281	1 121	1 267	809	618	621	567	1 209	1 529	2 097
International Organisations	GGSZ	−19	−16	−29	2	45	44	15	17	−16	−12	6
World total	KTMS	15 003	15 562	15 002	17 200	19 632	22 612	28 414	25 742	34 782	44 807	54 479

1 Cyprus and Malta are included in Other Europe before 1999.

9.6 Income

£ million

Credits

		1998	1999	2000	2001	2002	2003	2004	2005	2006	2007	2008
Europe												
European Union (EU)												
Austria	CUGY	621	577	742	683	685	746	815	900	867	1 220	962
Belgium and Luxembourg	CTFK	3 820	3 542	6 066	6 647	5 529	4 766	6 515	9 874	14 351	18 550	21 388
of which Belgium	AA2K	..	1 611	2 342	2 753	2 208	1 930	2 619	3 620	4 429	6 556	5 755
Luxembourg	AA2O	..	1 931	3 724	3 894	3 321	2 836	3 896	6 254	9 922	11 994	15 633
Bulgaria	ZWYR	21	48	37	93	72	74	89	28	41	21	26
Cyprus[1]	AA2L	..	105	153	163	137	56	72	115	317	287	534
Czech Republic	LEPT	113	125	125	198	152	195	210	155	48	228	41
Denmark	LEQU	1 064	943	1 101	979	521	705	883	1 441	1 691	2 015	1 867
Estonia	ZWYT	13	5	2	8	6	8	9	14	11	10	9
Finland	LEUG	464	411	585	648	587	517	520	572	589	1 065	1 001
France	LEUP	5 901	6 139	7 535	8 680	6 948	6 954	8 158	11 105	14 654	21 073	18 693
Germany	LEQL	8 024	8 383	10 136	11 065	9 504	8 330	9 526	11 688	13 683	17 439	18 185
Greece	LEUY	655	834	1 002	871	707	817	782	834	958	1 315	1 586
Hungary	BFKR	175	248	448	321	352	334	383	411	192	260	183
Ireland	BFLY	2 698	2 965	3 824	4 710	3 918	4 884	5 619	7 862	10 463	14 892	14 737
Italy	BFOG	6 890	5 165	6 426	6 347	4 791	4 900	4 647	5 051	5 709	6 822	6 292
Latvia	ZWYU	8	–	2	–	–	–	–	1	19	32	–22
Lithuania	ZWYV	4	4	9	7	4	4	1	8	9	10	–1
Malta[1]	AA2P	..	39	51	55	48	53	491	44	64	–386	134
Netherlands	BFQI	8 904	9 280	12 814	16 586	15 722	15 205	9 740	11 447	16 044	19 287	20 530
Poland	BFSB	91	108	144	329	335	400	440	441	535	666	653
Portugal	BFSK	466	471	664	808	776	807	797	970	1 032	1 066	1 239
Romania	ZWYW	22	42	20	78	65	96	117	70	109	168	209
Slovak Republic	ZWYX	37	38	51	29	31	28	30	52	41	58	139
Slovenia	ZWYY	22	56	48	101	68	89	99	37	26	36	86
Spain	LESW	2 402	2 100	2 564	2 403	2 052	2 314	3 623	4 954	6 511	8 082	8 469
Sweden	BFTL	1 449	1 554	2 108	2 307	2 121	1 767	2 273	2 695	3 104	3 529	3 242
European Central Bank	ZWYO	–	–	–	–	–	–	–	–	–	–	–
EU Institutions	CSFK	280	224	370	468	657	747	522	516	533	516	573
Total EU27	GNF6	..	43 406	57 027	64 584	55 788	54 796	56 361	71 285	91 601	118 263	120 755
European Free Trade Association (EFTA)												
Iceland	BFNQ	32	32	35	38	33	27	55	121	221	998	1 144
Liechtenstein	BFPH	34	39	45	39	21	20	23	19	32	40	26
Norway	BFQR	632	727	1 022	1 017	687	796	832	1 950	1 948	2 743	2 691
Switzerland	LEPB	3 379	4 395	7 274	5 326	4 504	4 505	4 903	6 109	8 863	12 820	12 697
Total EFTA	CTFT	4 077	5 193	8 376	6 420	5 245	5 348	5 813	8 199	11 064	16 601	16 558
Other Europe												
Albania	ZWYP	–	–	–	–	–	–	–	–	–	2	5
Belarus	ZWYQ	–	–	–	–	7	–	–	4	3	7	7
Croatia	ZWYS	9	13	15	26	29	43	48	74	45	32	70
Russia	BFST	269	193	285	537	661	563	1 262	2 347	3 001	2 702	2 680
Turkey	BFUM	268	344	493	408	318	365	383	515	883	1 196	895
Ukraine	ZWYZ	16	3	–	3	18	21	34	118	418	281	219
Serbia and Montenegro	BFWF	–	1	1	1	1	1	–2	14	27	13	25
Other[1]	LEVZ	3 146	2 792	3 540	3 085	3 038	4 240	5 679	7 044	8 391	14 510	8 368
Total Europe	LERD	51 929	51 945	69 737	75 064	65 105	65 377	69 578	89 600	115 433	153 605	149 582
Americas												
Argentina	ZWZB	410	247	487	365	107	190	260	290	566	463	357
Brazil	LENR	776	309	524	586	620	429	766	1 103	1 055	1 314	1 253
Canada	LEOS	2 093	1 867	2 248	2 334	1 722	2 007	2 240	3 205	4 332	5 133	4 387
Chile	ZWZC	190	166	259	196	240	310	838	1 204	836	931	764
Colombia	ZWZD	41	100	320	224	235	261	395	450	321	252	294
Mexico	BFPQ	404	540	457	312	629	416	724	827	939	939	784
United States of America	BFVE	24 503	23 744	29 284	31 117	26 524	27 662	30 744	44 857	59 552	65 948	49 994
Uruguay	ZWZE	23	7	16	13	20	9	–1	12	31	21	12
Venezuela	ZWZF	–48	–14	–88	176	185	89	265	394	350	151	165
Other Central American Countries	JISP	4 331	4 106	5 465	5 886	5 791	5 962	6 521	10 364	15 242	18 059	14 728
Other	LEVH	67	41	90	12	65	67	456	–61	–5	129	161
Total Americas	LESN	32 790	31 113	39 062	41 221	36 138	37 402	43 208	62 645	83 219	93 340	72 899
Asia												
China	LEPK	206	265	308	551	433	438	620	869	869	1 172	993
Hong Kong	BFJU	2 065	1 756	1 659	1 418	1 343	1 777	3 211	4 198	5 233	5 911	4 519
India	BFNB	411	385	490	494	635	660	593	821	1 323	1 643	2 117
Indonesia	BFLP	238	159	149	215	192	227	196	273	496	224	247
Iran	ZWZG	36	38	50	42	37	43	56	149	168	122	98
Israel	BFMS	42	56	52	63	46	77	59	102	151	198	144
Japan	BFOP	6 812	7 291	9 008	7 535	4 890	5 256	5 065	6 960	8 663	8 822	9 008
Malaysia	BFPZ	356	423	497	404	585	617	706	789	747	845	643
Pakistan	BFRS	93	72	131	136	187	181	247	291	420	247	192
Philippines	BFRJ	136	100	179	150	134	161	177	205	291	419	305
Saudi Arabia	BFTC	195	227	292	260	223	193	237	386	464	656	760
Singapore	BFTU	1 797	1 482	2 745	2 447	1 836	1 551	2 243	3 454	3 774	4 447	4 157
South Korea	BFOY	363	306	423	501	688	650	787	1 209	1 370	1 477	1 679
Taiwan	BFUV	174	194	262	293	343	328	534	673	652	692	549
Thailand	BFUD	70	112	223	249	236	228	230	301	14	303	220
Residual Gulf Arabian Countries	JITQ	1 454	1 087	1 509	1 139	764	686	809	1 281	1 763	2 084	2 240
Other Near & Middle Eastern Countries	ZWZH	85	67	189	197	104	97	166	398	719	1 573	1 509
Other	LEWI	71	123	305	236	502	202	296	172	974	1 338	1 155
Total Asia	LETF	14 604	14 143	18 471	16 330	13 178	13 372	16 232	22 531	28 063	32 173	30 535
Australasia & Oceania												
Australia	CXAT	1 724	1 974	2 516	2 452	2 791	2 579	3 995	4 361	5 163	5 813	4 464
New Zealand	BFRA	276	391	327	436	560	585	391	481	546	515	553
Other	LEVQ	381	33	21	8	33	30	36	35	62	81	68
Total Australasia & Oceania	LETX	2 381	2 398	2 864	2 896	3 384	3 194	4 422	4 877	5 771	6 409	5 085
Africa												
Egypt	ZWZJ	–81	37	264	259	323	239	196	335	442	549	470
Morocco	ZWZK	15	26	29	30	40	17	8	24	32	33	28
South Africa	BFWX	748	990	1 203	1 334	2 035	1 937	3 002	4 205	2 232	2 561	2 551
Other North Africa	JIRR	98	58	100	128	–32	122	77	–3 357	–998	246	298
Other	LEWR	547	599	754	758	1 018	1 059	1 125	5 348	2 836	1 761	1 763
Total Africa	LERV	1 327	1 710	2 350	2 509	3 384	3 374	4 408	6 555	4 544	5 150	5 110
International Organisations	CTFB	360	384	450	514	475	466	451	523	584	625	476
World total	HMBQ	103 391	101 693	132 934	138 534	121 664	123 185	138 311	186 740	237 622	291 302	263 703

1 Cyprus and Malta are included in Other Europe before 1999.

9.6 Income
continued

£ million

Debits

		1998	1999	2000	2001	2002	2003	2004	2005	2006	2007	2008
Europe												
European Union (EU)												
Austria	CUGZ	535	422	591	696	694	632	621	773	1 088	1 204	969
Belgium and Luxembourg	CTFL	4 416	4 202	4 755	4 945	4 560	4 803	5 800	7 143	9 223	12 080	13 201
of which Belgium	AA2W	..	1 750	2 081	1 980	1 933	1 869	2 164	2 953	3 590	4 824	4 675
Luxembourg	AA32	..	2 452	2 674	2 965	2 627	2 934	3 636	4 190	5 633	7 256	8 526
Bulgaria	ZWZP	93	53	54	27	25	11	11	33	60	86	58
Cyprus[1]	AA2X	..	106	159	165	132	111	142	202	305	391	417
Czech Republic	LEPU	104	92	129	113	81	81	81	99	191	177	200
Denmark	LEQV	920	852	1 099	922	862	989	1 121	1 398	1 376	1 669	1 531
Estonia	ZWZR	59	42	31	11	2	2	2	3	6	15	14
Finland	LEUH	320	296	378	371	264	320	309	490	567	775	878
France	LEUQ	5 960	7 283	7 665	7 059	5 509	7 797	9 972	12 851	15 615	18 389	14 468
Germany	LEQM	7 795	7 997	11 486	8 441	6 364	10 235	11 878	16 101	19 440	25 849	20 463
Greece	LEUZ	692	719	894	712	496	485	607	1 042	1 562	2 225	2 378
Hungary	BFKS	90	82	74	39	45	22	21	35	46	112	117
Ireland	BFLZ	2 543	2 154	2 978	4 029	4 643	4 965	6 154	8 963	11 484	15 070	16 276
Italy	BFOH	3 423	2 873	2 905	3 034	1 794	2 214	2 423	2 816	3 179	3 931	3 435
Latvia	ZWZS	63	44	33	11	10	4	8	22	10	21	15
Lithuania	ZWZT	62	44	35	12	2	1	2	17	31	41	34
Malta[1]	AA33	..	50	46	44	43	31	32	39	76	195	316
Netherlands	BFQJ	4 119	6 416	12 182	11 996	6 738	7 117	8 048	9 145	17 299	22 812	7 054
Poland	BFSC	190	153	187	176	117	107	160	356	477	527	489
Portugal	BFSL	260	219	246	300	279	354	390	443	630	798	799
Romania	ZWZU	78	52	50	25	32	13	20	39	49	60	39
Slovak Republic	ZWZV	78	58	43	17	9	7	21	55	176	100	63
Slovenia	ZWZW	83	60	46	35	38	28	28	24	20	32	32
Spain	LESX	1 925	1 375	1 259	1 507	1 316	1 776	1 707	3 903	5 562	5 174	3 817
Sweden	BFTM	1 169	1 459	1 420	1 369	1 347	1 011	1 010	1 295	1 816	2 232	2 167
European Central Bank	ZWZM	–	–	–	–	–	–	–	–	–	–	–
EU Institutions	CSFL	878	1 225	1 489	1 763	1 678	1 495	1 644	1 967	2 368	2 801	3 064
Total EU27	G97L	..	38 328	50 234	47 819	37 080	44 611	52 212	69 254	92 656	116 766	92 294
European Free Trade Association (EFTA)												
Iceland	BFNR	8	10	9	8	10	21	54	101	303	354	–1 382
Liechtenstein	BFPI	106	83	116	92	50	57	53	76	103	144	115
Norway	BFQS	63	122	599	634	642	698	766	1 311	2 074	2 749	1 987
Switzerland	LEPC	6 031	7 841	11 551	9 842	6 624	6 058	6 090	8 758	11 431	12 779	1 622
Total EFTA	CTFU	6 208	8 056	12 275	10 576	7 326	6 834	6 963	10 246	13 911	16 026	2 342
Other Europe												
Albania	ZWZN	112	39	28	10	–1	–	–	–	3	4	3
Belarus	ZWZO	70	42	29	9	–1	1	2	7	8	17	21
Croatia	ZWZQ	188	58	59	46	32	27	24	45	61	90	47
Russia	BFSU	20	146	433	397	293	308	418	1 228	2 521	2 960	1 891
Turkey	BFUN	156	94	135	153	86	74	86	144	210	260	259
Ukraine	ZWZX	63	43	29	11	18	62	101	158	248	378	311
Serbia and Montenegro	BFWG	58	40	29	11	6	5	5	10	23	31	19
Other[1]	LEWA	5 909	6 080	7 255	7 887	6 797	5 911	7 764	10 544	13 548	14 386	21 131
Total Europe	LERE	48 639	52 926	70 506	66 919	51 636	57 833	67 575	91 636	123 189	150 918	118 318
Americas												
Argentina	ZWZZ	55	57	106	70	4	3	1	6	8	8	14
Brazil	LENS	244	130	154	148	70	82	88	170	190	191	68
Canada	LEOT	874	1 129	1 517	1 180	1 592	1 453	2 156	2 299	3 341	2 037	282
Chile	ZXAA	67	18	8	35	20	18	27	36	60	97	99
Colombia	ZXAB	38	22	38	43	18	9	5	16	37	43	33
Mexico	BFPR	152	163	239	260	69	60	65	105	135	126	204
United States of America	BFVF	20 263	24 241	27 660	31 683	29 836	30 618	32 092	42 310	59 628	67 106	72 466
Uruguay	ZXAC	–15	10	19	8	3	8	7	6	13	18	9
Venezuela	ZXAD	12	9	20	40	28	21	17	27	78	103	76
Other Central American Countries	JISQ	3 756	3 552	4 245	3 950	2 738	3 226	3 833	7 429	11 526	15 137	14 010
Other	LEVI	375	289	269	157	79	59	60	83	146	173	158
Total Americas	LESO	25 821	29 620	34 275	37 574	34 457	35 557	38 351	52 487	75 162	85 039	87 419
Asia												
China	LEPL	139	167	363	373	240	196	236	343	447	864	620
Hong Kong	BFJV	1 949	2 897	3 507	3 296	1 897	1 274	1 391	1 742	2 570	4 140	4 630
India	BFNC	343	327	369	362	246	268	389	697	1 126	1 081	344
Indonesia	BFLQ	39	54	85	114	73	54	55	65	77	63	37
Iran	ZXAE	91	96	230	279	101	90	90	135	202	184	118
Israel	BFMT	149	192	229	258	185	171	149	276	441	441	219
Japan	BFOQ	6 930	8 106	11 428	10 019	7 390	3 972	5 509	6 870	9 328	9 464	8 280
Malaysia	BFQA	192	254	347	277	129	80	126	187	459	546	371
Pakistan	BFRT	61	55	69	68	71	76	60	81	118	125	66
Philippines	BFRK	48	81	91	51	31	19	20	44	98	98	63
Saudi Arabia	BFTD	957	711	870	942	376	323	374	631	1 086	1 548	2 109
Singapore	BFTV	1 374	2 046	2 749	2 604	1 835	1 438	1 504	2 407	3 320	3 699	3 413
South Korea	BFOZ	189	97	160	204	111	27	–154	303	376	457	402
Taiwan	BFUW	104	116	140	189	101	113	168	264	334	502	311
Thailand	BFUE	81	83	147	196	85	69	70	118	209	255	202
Residual Gulf Arabian Countries	JITR	945	928	1 373	1 522	847	608	720	1 090	1 879	2 398	2 227
Other Near & Middle Eastern Countries	ZXAF	214	214	270	221	142	135	124	201	305	339	269
Other	LEWJ	307	401	392	334	270	116	136	320	402	436	410
Total Asia	LETG	14 112	16 825	22 819	21 309	14 130	9 029	10 967	15 774	22 777	26 640	24 091
Australasia & Oceania												
Australia	CXCM	1 200	1 172	750	577	961	1 275	1 386	1 834	2 120	2 714	1 963
New Zealand	BFRB	178	51	109	112	86	72	80	101	150	81	125
Other	LEVR	–38	5	28	62	43	30	25	4	342	198	65
Total Australasia & Oceania	LETY	1 340	1 228	887	751	1 090	1 377	1 491	1 939	2 612	2 993	2 153
Africa												
Egypt	ZXAH	324	275	325	278	164	128	141	275	370	352	237
Morocco	ZXAI	34	35	30	31	18	12	12	29	96	60	43
South Africa	BFWY	421	826	743	738	716	792	842	1 052	1 286	1 249	1 156
Other North Africa	JIRS	115	106	176	186	119	96	106	248	507	700	589
Other	LEWS	539	548	649	624	408	322	344	521	843	1 119	1 203
Total Africa	LERW	1 433	1 790	1 923	1 857	1 425	1 350	1 445	2 125	3 102	3 480	3 228
International Organisations	CTFC	243	347	562	699	640	516	620	915	1 187	1 458	1 537
World total	HMBR	91 588	102 736	130 972	129 109	103 378	105 662	120 466	164 885	228 049	270 527	236 763

1 Cyprus and Malta are included in Other Europe before 1999.

9.6 Income
continued

£ million

		1998	1999	2000	2001	2002	2003	2004	2005	2006	2007	2008
Balances												
Europe												
European Union (EU)												
Austria	CUHA	86	155	151	−13	−9	114	194	127	−221	16	−7
Belgium and Luxembourg	CTFM	−596	−660	1 311	1 702	969	−37	715	2 731	5 128	6 470	8 187
of which Belgium	AA3A	..	−139	261	773	275	61	455	667	839	1 732	1 080
Luxembourg	AA3E	..	−521	1 050	929	694	−98	260	2 064	4 289	4 738	7 107
Bulgaria	ZXAN	−72	−5	−17	66	47	63	78	−5	−19	−65	−32
Cyprus[1]	AA3B	..	−1	−6	−2	5	−55	−70	−87	12	−104	117
Czech Republic	LEPV	9	33	−4	85	71	114	129	56	−143	51	−159
Denmark	LEQW	144	91	2	57	−341	−284	−238	43	315	346	336
Estonia	ZXAP	−46	−37	−29	−3	4	6	7	11	5	−5	−5
Finland	LEUI	144	115	207	277	323	197	211	82	22	290	123
France	LEUR	−59	−1 144	−130	1 621	1 439	−843	−1 814	−1 746	−961	2 684	4 225
Germany	LEQN	229	386	−1 350	2 624	3 140	−1 905	−2 352	−4 413	−5 757	−8 410	−2 278
Greece	LEVA	−37	115	108	159	211	332	175	−208	−604	−910	−792
Hungary	BFKT	85	166	374	282	307	312	362	376	146	148	66
Ireland	BFML	155	811	846	681	−725	−81	−535	−1 101	−1 021	−178	−1 539
Italy	BFOI	3 467	2 292	3 521	3 313	2 997	2 686	2 224	2 235	2 530	2 891	2 857
Latvia	ZXAQ	−55	−44	−31	−11	−10	−4	−8	−21	9	11	−37
Lithuania	ZXAR	−58	−40	−26	−5	2	3	−1	−9	−22	−31	−35
Malta[1]	AA3F	..	−11	5	11	5	22	459	5	−12	−581	−182
Netherlands	BFQK	4 785	2 864	632	4 590	8 984	8 088	1 692	2 302	−1 255	−3 525	13 476
Poland	BFSD	−99	−45	−43	153	218	293	280	85	58	139	164
Portugal	BFSM	206	252	418	508	497	453	407	527	402	268	440
Romania	ZXAS	−56	−10	−30	53	33	83	97	31	60	108	170
Slovak Republic	ZXAT	−41	−20	8	12	22	21	9	−3	−135	−42	76
Slovenia	ZXAU	−61	−4	2	66	30	61	71	13	6	4	54
Spain	LESY	477	725	1 305	896	736	538	1 916	1 051	949	2 908	4 652
Sweden	BFTN	280	95	688	938	774	756	1 263	1 400	1 288	1 297	1 075
European Central Bank	ZXAK	−	−	−	−	−	−	−	−	−	−	−
EU Institutions	CSFM	−598	−1 001	−1 119	−1 295	−1 021	−748	−1 122	−1 451	−1 835	−2 285	−2 491
Total EU27	G97D	..	5 078	6 793	16 765	18 708	10 185	4 149	2 031	−1 055	1 497	28 461
European Free Trade Association (EFTA)												
Iceland	BFNU	24	22	26	30	23	6	1	20	−82	644	2 526
Liechtenstein	BFPJ	−72	−44	−71	−53	−29	−37	−30	−57	−71	−104	−89
Norway	BFQT	569	605	423	383	45	98	66	639	−126	−6	704
Switzerland	LEPD	−2 652	−3 446	−4 277	−4 516	−2 120	−1 553	−1 187	−2 649	−2 568	41	11 075
Total EFTA	CTFV	−2 131	−2 863	−3 899	−4 156	−2 081	−1 486	−1 150	−2 047	−2 847	575	14 216
Other Europe												
Albania	ZXAL	−112	−39	−28	−10	1	−	−	−	−3	−2	2
Belarus	ZXAM	−70	−42	−29	−9	8	−1	−2	−3	−5	−10	−14
Croatia	ZXAO	−179	−45	−44	−20	−3	16	24	29	−16	−58	23
Russia	BFSV	249	47	−148	140	368	255	844	1 119	480	−258	789
Turkey	BFUO	112	250	358	255	232	291	297	371	673	936	636
Ukraine	ZXAV	−47	−40	−29	−8	−	−41	−67	−40	170	−97	−92
Serbia and Montenegro	BFWH	−58	−39	−28	−10	−5	−4	−7	4	4	−18	6
Other[1]	LEWB	−2 763	−3 288	−3 715	−4 802	−3 759	−1 671	−2 085	−3 500	−5 157	124	−12 763
Total Europe	LERF	3 290	−981	−769	8 145	13 469	7 544	2 003	−2 036	−7 756	2 687	31 264
Americas												
Argentina	ZXAX	355	190	381	295	103	187	259	284	558	455	343
Brazil	LENT	532	179	370	438	550	347	678	933	865	1 123	1 185
Canada	LEOU	1 219	738	731	1 154	130	554	84	906	991	3 096	4 105
Chile	ZXAY	123	148	251	161	220	292	811	1 168	776	834	665
Colombia	ZXAZ	3	78	282	181	217	252	390	434	284	209	261
Mexico	BFPS	252	377	218	52	560	356	659	722	804	813	580
United States of America	BFVG	4 240	−497	1 624	−566	−3 312	−2 956	−1 348	2 547	−76	−1 158	−22 472
Uruguay	ZXBA	38	−3	−3	5	17	1	−8	6	18	3	3
Venezuela	ZXBB	−60	−23	−108	136	157	68	248	367	272	48	89
Other Central American Countries	JISR	575	554	1 220	1 936	3 053	2 736	2 688	2 935	3 716	2 922	718
Other	LEVJ	−308	−248	−179	−145	−14	8	396	−144	−151	−44	3
Total Americas	LESP	6 969	1 493	4 787	3 647	1 681	1 845	4 857	10 158	8 057	8 301	−14 520
Asia												
China	LEPM	67	98	−55	178	193	242	384	526	422	308	373
Hong Kong	BFJW	116	−1 141	−1 848	−1 878	−554	503	1 820	2 456	2 663	1 771	−111
India	BFND	68	58	121	132	389	392	204	124	197	562	1 773
Indonesia	BFLR	199	105	64	101	119	173	141	208	419	161	210
Iran	ZXBC	−55	−58	−180	−237	−64	−47	−34	14	−34	−62	−20
Israel	BFMU	−107	−136	−177	−195	−139	−94	−90	−174	−290	−243	−75
Japan	BFOR	−118	−815	−2 420	−2 484	−2 500	1 284	−444	90	−665	−642	728
Malaysia	BFQB	164	169	150	127	456	537	580	602	288	299	272
Pakistan	BFRU	32	17	62	68	116	105	187	210	302	122	126
Philippines	BFRL	88	19	88	99	103	142	157	161	193	321	242
Saudi Arabia	BFTE	−762	−484	−578	−682	−153	−130	−137	−245	−622	−892	−1 349
Singapore	BFTW	423	−564	−4	−157	1	113	739	1 047	454	748	744
South Korea	BFPA	174	209	263	297	577	623	941	906	994	1 020	1 277
Taiwan	BFUX	70	78	122	104	242	215	366	409	318	190	238
Thailand	BFUF	−11	29	76	53	151	159	160	183	−223	48	18
Residual Gulf Arabian Countries	JITS	509	159	136	−383	−83	78	89	191	−116	−314	13
Other Near & Middle Eastern Countries	ZXBD	−129	−147	−81	−24	−38	−38	42	197	414	1 234	1 240
Other	LEWK	−236	−278	−87	−98	232	86	160	−148	572	902	745
Total Asia	LETH	492	−2 682	−4 348	−4 979	−952	4 343	5 265	6 757	5 286	5 533	6 444
Australasia & Oceania												
Australia	CYAA	524	802	1 766	1 875	1 830	1 304	2 609	2 527	3 043	3 099	2 501
New Zealand	BFRC	98	340	218	324	474	513	311	380	396	434	428
Other	LEVS	419	28	−7	−54	−10	−	11	31	−280	−117	3
Total Australasia & Oceania	LETZ	1 041	1 170	1 977	2 145	2 294	1 817	2 931	2 938	3 159	3 416	2 932
Africa												
Egypt	ZXBF	−405	−238	−61	−19	159	111	55	60	72	197	233
Morocco	ZXBG	−19	−9	−1	−1	22	5	−4	−5	−64	−27	−15
South Africa	BFWZ	327	164	460	596	1 319	1 145	2 160	3 153	946	1 312	1 395
Other North Africa	JIRT	−17	−48	−76	−58	−151	26	−29	−3 605	−1 505	−454	−291
Other	LEWT	8	51	105	134	610	737	781	4 827	1 993	642	560
Total Africa	LERX	−106	−80	427	652	1 959	2 024	2 963	4 430	1 442	1 670	1 882
International Organisations	CTFD	117	37	−112	−185	−165	−50	−169	−392	−603	−833	−1 061
World total	HMBP	11 803	−1 043	1 962	9 425	18 286	17 523	17 845	21 855	9 573	20 775	26 940

1 Cyprus and Malta are included in Other Europe before 1999.

9.7 Current transfers

£ million

		1998	1999	2000	2001	2002	2003	2004	2005	2006	2007	2008
Credits												
Europe												
European Union (EU)												
Austria	GXVQ	34	34	30	31	33	51	36	38	45	34	34
Belgium and Luxembourg	GXVR	250	236	224	217	247	232	246	263	267	232	228
of which Belgium	A7PL	..	219	209	202	230	217	227	242	238	217	214
Luxembourg	A7PO	..	17	15	15	17	15	19	21	29	15	14
Bulgaria	KOLZ	–	–	2	–	8	1	1	8	10	15	14
Cyprus[1]	A7PM	..	1	2	2	3	4	4	4	9	3	3
Czech Republic	GXWK	4	4	6	2	3	32	23	16	37	17	18
Denmark	GXVS	47	33	28	30	41	28	40	45	61	34	38
Estonia	LWMG	–	–	–	–	–	–	–	–	–	–	–
Finland	GXVT	18	16	24	15	16	93	17	17	24	18	18
France	GXVU	355	291	279	328	336	193	332	319	379	275	294
Germany	GXVV	465	420	391	392	444	379	457	499	556	443	448
Greece	GXVW	60	43	39	40	48	40	49	55	59	43	45
Hungary	HZXT	–	–	1	1	8	1	1	5	6	12	12
Ireland	GXVX	192	130	115	162	155	113	170	166	202	160	172
Italy	GXVY	172	122	101	117	123	100	178	180	236	129	143
Latvia	LWWC	4	2	2	1	5	1	1	7	4	4	5
Lithuania	LYTR	–	–	–	1	–	–	–	7	13	14	13
Malta[1]	A7PP	..	1	–	1	1	1	2	2	2	3	4
Netherlands	GXVZ	320	308	323	315	374	292	353	377	355	319	306
Poland	GXWL	5	4	3	3	14	7	37	107	130	122	123
Portugal	GXWA	19	18	28	15	21	15	22	20	28	18	18
Romania	HZXV	2	2	–	–	11	1	2	7	9	8	8
Slovak Republic	HZXX	5	4	–	2	3	–	–	13	62	17	18
Slovenia	HZXY	–	–	–	–	5	–	1	1	4	1	–
Spain	GXWB	121	105	92	98	105	86	127	137	174	125	128
Sweden	GXWC	109	93	88	90	97	84	108	107	121	90	93
European Central Bank	KNWK	–	–	–	–	–	–	–	–	–	–	–
EU Institutions	GXWD	5 103	6 391	5 314	7 275	5 905	6 688	7 354	7 976	8 118	7 379	8 578
Total EU27	GC84	..	8 258	7 092	9 138	8 006	8 442	9 561	10 376	10 911	9 515	10 761
European Free Trade Association (EFTA)												
Iceland	GXWF	36	35	33	34	35	64	34	34	40	34	34
Liechtenstein	GXWG	4	2	2	1	2	1	1	–	5	1	2
Norway	GXWH	84	64	60	60	80	66	75	87	107	71	77
Switzerland	GXWI	103	74	59	65	80	63	85	105	155	62	70
Total EFTA	GXWJ	227	175	154	160	197	194	195	226	307	168	183
Other Europe												
Albania	HZXP	–	–	–	–	–	–	–	–	–	–	–
Belarus	HZXQ	–	–	–	1	–	7	–	1	–	–	–
Croatia	HZXR	4	2	2	1	2	2	2	–	9	9	8
Russia	GXWM	26	17	10	12	16	11	19	24	52	17	20
Turkey	GXWN	36	31	28	30	34	30	37	39	63	32	32
Ukraine	HZYA	–	–	1	–	–	7	19	2	2	8	8
Serbia and Montenegro	LTVE	–	2	2	1	2	5	1	–	5	3	4
Other[1]	HKJF	31	12	10	27	16	16	9	14	30	42	36
Total Europe	GXWP	7 609	8 497	7 299	9 370	8 273	8 714	9 843	10 682	11 379	9 794	11 052
Americas												
Argentina	HZYJ	19	10	8	10	11	7	8	5	18	6	9
Brazil	GXWQ	23	15	10	14	16	11	12	12	39	11	14
Canada	GXWR	305	208	174	197	209	160	243	267	278	189	224
Chile	HZYL	15	8	7	10	9	7	9	10	29	7	9
Colombia	HZYM	27	16	14	24	17	25	15	15	37	11	14
Mexico	GXWS	33	21	18	19	28	21	27	32	102	20	24
United States of America	GXWT	2 101	1 343	1 182	2 395	1 693	1 217	1 549	4 186	3 504	2 238	2 197
Uruguay	HZYN	–	–	–	–	–	–	–	–	2	–	–
Venezuela	HZYO	21	14	8	10	12	8	13	15	29	7	10
Other Central American Countries	HZYG	260	156	140	145	181	135	214	258	533	155	186
Other	HZYI	19	11	8	10	13	13	13	15	32	8	12
Total Americas	GXWV	2 823	1 802	1 569	2 834	2 189	1 604	2 103	4 815	4 603	2 652	2 699
Asia												
China	GXWW	20	13	9	10	13	9	13	12	38	11	15
Hong Kong	GXWX	77	58	49	54	40	29	37	36	49	22	33
India	GXWY	17	17	15	23	25	13	27	30	78	17	17
Indonesia	GXWZ	39	20	17	19	24	44	18	18	77	14	19
Iran	HZYQ	4	2	3	2	3	2	3	4	9	2	3
Israel	GXXA	53	36	29	31	35	33	32	34	51	27	33
Japan	GXXB	174	113	97	109	130	95	124	137	283	91	112
Malaysia	GXXC	29	21	17	23	21	48	21	21	39	17	20
Pakistan	GXXD	5	5	3	4	4	29	4	3	13	5	6
Philippines	GXXE	19	11	8	10	11	7	9	10	18	6	9
Saudi Arabia	GXXF	491	501	485	494	488	499	481	490	511	479	463
Singapore	GXXG	20	14	9	15	15	13	23	28	31	15	17
South Korea	GXXH	19	14	9	12	20	10	22	28	59	4	8
Taiwan	GXXI	15	8	7	10	15	22	12	15	29	6	8
Thailand	GXXJ	8	6	5	5	9	6	8	10	21	4	5
Residual Gulf Arabian Countries	HZYS	179	170	162	165	172	168	177	179	234	167	165
Other Near & Middle Eastern Countries	HZYU	294	305	294	299	295	294	293	299	312	290	280
Other	HZVR	65	57	54	62	44	38	41	41	71	45	47
Total Asia	GXXL	1 528	1 371	1 272	1 347	1 364	1 359	1 345	1 395	1 923	1 222	1 260
Australasia & Oceania												
Australia	GXXM	213	173	158	169	203	165	244	268	226	195	205
New Zealand	GXXN	69	58	53	58	58	51	64	60	69	55	57
Other	GXXO	4	3	3	2	3	2	6	5	7	3	3
Total Australasia & Oceania	GXXP	286	234	214	229	264	218	314	333	302	253	265
Africa												
Egypt	LZDN	1	4	3	2	4	26	7	9	20	4	4
Morocco	HICY	4	2	2	1	2	2	2	1	7	2	2
South Africa	GXXQ	127	93	81	88	83	69	96	105	121	59	82
Other North Africa	HICX	15	11	10	10	13	20	14	15	17	10	10
Other	HZUI	56	38	33	36	42	35	43	45	101	50	48
Total Africa	GXXS	203	148	129	137	144	152	162	175	266	125	146
International Organisations	GXXT	–	–	–	–	–	–	–	–	–	–	–
World total	KTND	12 449	12 052	10 483	13 917	12 234	12 047	13 767	17 400	18 473	14 046	15 422

1 Cyprus and Malta are included in Other Europe before 1999.

9.7 Current transfers
continued

£ million

		1998	1999	2000	2001	2002	2003	2004	2005	2006	2007	2008
Debits												
Europe												
European Union (EU)												
Austria	GXXV	16	17	23	21	24	25	29	34	39	30	33
Belgium and Luxembourg	GXXW	77	70	78	93	98	105	114	93	88	78	89
of which Belgium	A8BV	..	61	70	82	87	94	101	79	66	70	81
Luxembourg	A8BY	..	9	8	11	11	11	13	14	22	8	8
Bulgaria	LTQA	–	8	12	8	14	7	4	4	10	5	2
Cyprus[1]	A8BW	..	10	18	19	27	26	32	35	38	32	29
Czech Republic	GXYP	14	21	9	9	11	12	13	14	19	16	21
Denmark	GXXX	50	41	37	32	36	30	42	54	62	40	50
Estonia	LWQY	–	–	–	–	–	1	4	4	4	4	–
Finland	GXXY	12	10	22	14	14	13	17	17	24	15	17
France	GXXZ	250	301	268	288	333	267	320	351	431	338	387
Germany	GXYA	314	281	294	288	366	316	401	455	480	357	447
Greece	GXYB	50	34	49	45	46	46	59	65	67	64	71
Hungary	HIEC	18	17	16	12	19	10	11	12	15	13	12
Ireland	GXYC	800	389	471	442	476	506	559	611	629	586	640
Italy	GXYD	256	153	133	139	150	131	178	207	250	160	182
Latvia	LYON	4	6	2	1	2	1	1	–	7	1	2
Lithuania	LYYJ	–	8	1	15	14	–	8	9	4	4	3
Malta[1]	A8BZ	..	9	15	17	18	19	22	23	24	26	29
Netherlands	GXYE	137	158	187	144	178	127	176	205	151	165	209
Poland	GXYQ	56	35	58	46	50	52	56	59	67	60	66
Portugal	GXYF	26	31	48	36	40	41	46	47	58	46	51
Romania	HIEE	14	10	14	11	20	10	12	12	18	12	5
Slovak Republic	HIEG	10	7	5	3	6	3	1	6	1	1	1
Slovenia	HIEH	1	8	–	5	4	–	1	1	4	1	–
Spain	GXYG	145	164	125	126	141	151	171	172	199	186	206
Sweden	GXYH	57	55	33	34	39	35	43	41	56	31	40
European Central Bank	KOEJ	–	–	–	–	–	–	–	–	–	–	–
EU Institutions	GXYI	10 265	10 524	10 719	9 557	10 097	11 485	11 505	13 098	13 025	13 060	13 329
Total EU27	GCR2	..	12 367	12 637	11 405	12 223	13 419	13 825	15 629	15 770	15 331	15 921
European Free Trade Association (EFTA)												
Iceland	GXYK	4	2	4	2	6	2	2	1	7	2	3
Liechtenstein	GXYL	4	2	2	1	2	1	1	–	5	1	2
Norway	GXYM	75	82	56	59	63	54	72	77	94	81	94
Switzerland	GXYN	99	85	94	91	124	90	121	146	187	98	119
Total EFTA	GXYO	182	171	156	153	195	147	196	224	293	182	218
Other Europe												
Albania	HIDY	2	2	6	9	12	7	7	7	4	9	9
Belarus	HIDZ	2	4	–	6	11	3	2	2	–	–	–
Croatia	HIEA	8	4	8	5	6	5	6	11	16	14	11
Russia	GXYR	104	70	90	55	23	49	60	62	102	55	31
Turkey	GXYS	38	33	28	34	41	32	44	48	71	34	38
Ukraine	HIEJ	23	42	30	54	15	28	41	42	22	26	24
Serbia and Montenegro	LWHC	–	8	67	38	31	30	27	29	33	32	35
Other[1]	HZWJ	141	122	126	149	156	189	168	180	195	226	230
Total Europe	GXYU	13 072	12 823	13 148	11 908	12 713	13 909	14 376	16 234	16 506	15 909	16 517
Americas												
Argentina	HIES	21	12	16	17	18	14	16	15	26	15	20
Brazil	GXYV	41	37	36	45	57	35	38	41	62	30	26
Canada	GXYW	361	282	265	280	315	276	368	406	407	345	399
Chile	HIEU	19	13	12	11	13	10	13	14	33	11	14
Colombia	HIEV	34	25	23	29	22	14	21	21	41	17	21
Mexico	GXYX	41	29	25	22	31	21	28	33	103	23	29
United States of America	GXYY	2 158	1 575	1 421	2 553	1 891	1 449	1 845	4 471	3 762	2 554	2 615
Uruguay	HIEW	1	1	1	1	1	1	1	1	3	1	1
Venezuela	HIEX	19	11	9	11	13	9	14	16	30	8	11
Other Central American Countries	HIEP	623	455	429	401	426	365	456	510	806	438	481
Other	HIER	159	87	80	96	96	64	68	68	68	56	49
Total Americas	GXZA	3 477	2 527	2 317	3 466	2 883	2 258	2 868	5 596	5 341	3 498	3 666
Asia												
China	GXZB	109	98	82	86	125	77	136	137	156	144	151
Hong Kong	GXZC	93	123	117	121	133	126	147	155	177	151	176
India	GXZD	407	422	489	534	557	503	621	711	736	799	912
Indonesia	GXZE	103	75	54	45	51	67	83	182	161	98	120
Iran	HIEZ	20	19	20	17	19	17	21	23	28	22	23
Israel	GXZF	51	35	33	36	42	35	40	43	61	35	44
Japan	GXZG	163	124	95	104	132	99	132	148	284	103	130
Malaysia	GXZH	43	62	45	44	49	46	53	61	80	57	66
Pakistan	GXZI	158	151	144	162	233	183	196	211	251	266	313
Philippines	GXZJ	52	36	30	33	35	33	37	40	48	38	42
Saudi Arabia	GXZK	21	37	41	42	51	48	52	49	67	53	60
Singapore	GXZL	42	77	76	76	88	90	109	118	121	110	123
South Korea	GXZM	22	17	11	13	21	10	23	29	59	5	9
Taiwan	GXZN	15	13	7	11	15	9	12	15	29	6	8
Thailand	GXZO	18	23	29	30	40	31	37	50	52	41	45
Residual Gulf Arabian Countries	HIFB	90	90	74	83	88	193	325	342	363	297	246
Other Near & Middle Eastern Countries	HIFD	46	56	67	77	77	73	91	96	95	73	58
Other	HZWN	283	300	404	538	609	529	740	854	964	946	1 090
Total Asia	GXZQ	1 736	1 758	1 818	2 052	2 365	2 169	2 855	3 264	3 732	3 244	3 616
Australasia & Oceania												
Australia	GXZR	336	220	217	240	275	264	345	399	358	345	379
New Zealand	GXZS	82	53	66	75	80	79	92	101	111	105	115
Other	GXZT	25	31	11	10	23	22	26	27	28	20	15
Total Australasia & Oceania	GXZU	443	304	294	325	378	365	463	527	497	470	509
Africa												
Egypt	LZIF	–	28	24	23	27	26	36	39	47	37	34
Morocco	HIYZ	9	10	8	7	8	9	9	9	15	11	11
South Africa	GXZV	202	227	257	286	309	313	346	364	389	352	405
Other North Africa	HIYX	43	24	10	13	14	26	20	21	21	16	18
Other	HZUA	986	1 042	1 268	1 320	1 363	2 087	1 894	2 009	2 091	2 301	2 420
Total Africa	GXZX	1 240	1 331	1 567	1 649	1 721	2 461	2 305	2 442	2 563	2 717	2 888
International Organisations	GXZY	653	631	1 114	1 032	1 044	720	1 176	1 186	1 719	1 746	1 836
World total	KTNE	20 621	19 374	20 258	20 432	21 104	21 882	24 043	29 249	30 358	27 584	29 032

1 Cyprus and Malta are included in Other Europe before 1999.

9.7 Current transfers
continued

£ million

Balances

		1998	1999	2000	2001	2002	2003	2004	2005	2006	2007	2008
Europe												
European Union (EU)												
Austria	GZDU	18	17	7	10	9	26	7	4	6	4	1
Belgium and Luxembourg	GZDV	173	166	146	124	149	127	132	170	179	154	139
of which Belgium	A8H2	..	158	139	120	143	123	126	163	172	147	133
Luxembourg	A8H5	..	8	7	4	6	4	6	7	7	7	6
Bulgaria	ZWRH	–	–8	–10	–8	–6	–6	–3	4	–	10	12
Cyprus[1]	A8H3	..	–9	–16	–17	–24	–22	–28	–31	–29	–29	–26
Czech Republic	GZCJ	–10	–17	–3	–7	–8	20	10	2	18	1	–3
Denmark	GZDW	–3	–8	–9	–2	5	–2	–2	–9	–1	–6	–12
Estonia	ZWRN	–	–	–	–	–	–1	–4	–4	–4	–4	–
Finland	GZDX	6	6	2	1	2	80	–	–	–	3	1
France	GZDY	105	–10	11	40	3	–74	12	–32	–52	–63	–93
Germany	GZDZ	151	139	97	104	78	63	56	44	76	86	1
Greece	GZEA	10	9	–10	–5	2	–6	–10	–10	–8	–21	–26
Hungary	GYWH	–18	–17	–15	–11	–11	–9	–10	–7	–9	–1	–
Ireland	GZEB	–608	–259	–356	–280	–321	–393	–389	–445	–427	–426	–468
Italy	GZEC	–84	–31	–32	–22	–27	–31	–	–27	–14	–31	–39
Latvia	ZWRV	–	–4	–	–	3	–	–	7	–3	3	3
Lithuania	ZWRU	–	–8	–1	–14	–14	–	–8	–2	9	10	10
Malta[1]	A8H6	..	–8	–15	–16	–17	–18	–20	–21	–22	–23	–25
Netherlands	GZED	183	150	136	171	196	165	177	172	204	154	97
Poland	GZCK	–51	–31	–55	–43	–36	–45	–19	48	63	62	57
Portugal	GZEE	–7	–13	–20	–21	–19	–26	–24	–27	–30	–28	–33
Romania	ZWRX	–12	–8	–14	–11	–9	–9	–10	–5	–9	–4	3
Slovak Republic	ZWRZ	–5	–3	–5	–1	–3	–3	–1	7	61	16	17
Slovenia	ZWRY	–1	–8	–	–5	1	–	–	–	–	–	–
Spain	GZEF	–24	–59	–33	–28	–36	–65	–44	–35	–25	–61	–78
Sweden	GYRO	52	38	55	56	58	49	65	66	65	59	53
European Central Bank	ZWRB	–	–	–	–	–	–	–	–	–	–	–
EU Institutions	GYRP	–5 162	–4 133	–5 405	–2 282	–4 192	–4 797	–4 151	–5 122	–4 907	–5 681	–4 751
Total EU27	GD6K	..	–4 109	–5 545	–2 267	–4 217	–4 977	–4 264	–5 253	–4 859	–5 816	–5 160
European Free Trade Association (EFTA)												
Iceland	GXEL	32	33	29	32	29	62	32	33	33	32	31
Liechtenstein	GXEM	–	–	–	–	–	–	–	–	–	–	–
Norway	GXEN	9	–18	4	1	17	12	3	10	13	–10	–17
Switzerland	GZCH	4	–11	–35	–26	–44	–27	–36	–41	–32	–36	–49
Total EFTA	GZCI	45	4	–2	7	2	47	–1	2	14	–14	–35
Other Europe												
Albania	ZWRF	–2	–2	–6	–9	–12	–7	–7	–7	–4	–9	–9
Belarus	ZWRI	–2	–4	–	–5	–11	4	–2	–1	–	–	–
Croatia	ZWRS	–4	–2	–6	–4	–4	–3	–4	–11	–7	–5	–3
Russia	GZCL	–78	–53	–80	–43	–7	–38	–41	–38	–50	–38	–11
Turkey	GZCM	–2	–2	–	–4	–7	–2	–7	–9	–8	–2	–6
Ukraine	ZWSA	–23	–42	–29	–54	–15	–21	–22	–40	–20	–18	–16
Serbia and Montenegro	ZWSD	–	–6	–65	–37	–29	–25	–26	–29	–28	–29	–31
Other[1]	ZWRC	–110	–110	–116	–122	–140	–173	–159	–166	–165	–184	–194
Total Europe	GZCO	–5 463	–4 326	–5 849	–2 538	–4 440	–5 195	–4 533	–5 552	–5 127	–6 115	–5 465
Americas												
Argentina	ZWRG	–2	–2	–8	–7	–7	–7	–8	–10	–8	–9	–11
Brazil	GZCP	–18	–22	–26	–31	–41	–24	–26	–29	–23	–19	–12
Canada	GZCQ	–56	–74	–91	–83	–106	–116	–125	–139	–129	–156	–175
Chile	ZWRJ	–4	–5	–5	–1	–4	–3	–4	–4	–4	–4	–5
Colombia	ZWRK	–7	–9	–9	–5	–5	11	–6	–6	–4	–6	–7
Mexico	GZCR	–8	–8	–7	–3	–3	–	–1	–1	–1	–3	–5
United States of America	GZCS	–57	–232	–239	–158	–198	–232	–296	–285	–258	–316	–418
Uruguay	ZWSB	–1	–1	–1	–1	–1	–1	–1	–1	–1	–1	–1
Venezuela	ZWSC	2	3	–1	–1	–1	–1	–1	–1	–1	–1	–1
Other Central American Countries	ZWRM	–363	–299	–289	–256	–245	–230	–242	–252	–273	–283	–295
Other	ZWRP	–140	–76	–72	–86	–83	–51	–55	–53	–36	–48	–37
Total Americas	GZCU	–654	–725	–748	–632	–694	–654	–765	–781	–738	–846	–967
Asia												
China	GZCV	–89	–85	–73	–76	–112	–68	–123	–125	–118	–133	–136
Hong Kong	GZCW	–16	–65	–68	–67	–93	–97	–110	–119	–128	–129	–143
India	GZCX	–390	–405	–474	–511	–532	–490	–594	–681	–658	–782	–895
Indonesia	GZCY	–64	–55	–37	–26	–27	–23	–65	–164	–84	–84	–101
Iran	ZWRT	–16	–17	–17	–15	–16	–15	–18	–19	–19	–20	–20
Israel	GZCZ	2	1	–4	–5	–7	–2	–8	–9	–10	–8	–11
Japan	GZDA	11	–11	2	5	–2	–4	–8	–11	–1	–12	–18
Malaysia	GZDB	–14	–41	–28	–21	–28	2	–32	–40	–41	–40	–46
Pakistan	GZDC	–153	–146	–141	–158	–229	–154	–192	–208	–238	–261	–307
Philippines	GZDD	–33	–25	–22	–23	–24	–26	–28	–30	–30	–32	–33
Saudi Arabia	GZDE	470	464	444	452	437	451	429	441	444	426	403
Singapore	GZDF	–22	–63	–67	–61	–73	–77	–86	–90	–90	–95	–106
South Korea	GZDG	–3	–3	–2	–1	–1	–	–1	–1	–	–1	–1
Taiwan	GZDH	–	–5	–	–1	–	13	–	–	–	–	–
Thailand	GZDI	–10	–17	–24	–25	–31	–25	–29	–40	–31	–37	–40
Residual Gulf Arabian Countries	ZWRQ	89	80	88	82	84	–25	–148	–163	–129	–130	–81
Other Near & Middle Eastern Countries	ZWRR	248	249	227	222	218	221	202	203	217	217	222
Other	ZWRD	–218	–243	–350	–476	–565	–491	–699	–813	–893	–901	–1 043
Total Asia	GZDK	–208	–387	–546	–705	–1 001	–810	–1 510	–1 869	–1 809	–2 022	–2 356
Australasia & Oceania												
Australia	GZDL	–123	–47	–59	–71	–72	–99	–101	–131	–132	–150	–174
New Zealand	GZDM	–13	5	–13	–17	–22	–28	–28	–41	–42	–50	–58
Other	GZDN	–21	–28	–8	–8	–20	–20	–20	–22	–21	–17	–12
Total Australasia & Oceania	GZDO	–157	–70	–80	–96	–114	–147	–149	–194	–195	–217	–244
Africa												
Egypt	ZWRO	1	–24	–21	–21	–23	–	–29	–30	–27	–33	–30
Morocco	ZWRW	–5	–8	–6	–6	–6	–7	–7	–8	–8	–9	–9
South Africa	GZDP	–75	–134	–176	–198	–226	–244	–250	–259	–268	–293	–323
Other North Africa	ZWRL	–28	–13	–	–3	–1	–6	–6	–6	–4	–6	–8
Other	ZWRE	–930	–1 004	–1 235	–1 284	–1 321	–2 052	–1 851	–1 964	–1 990	–2 251	–2 372
Total Africa	GZDR	–1 037	–1 183	–1 438	–1 512	–1 577	–2 309	–2 143	–2 267	–2 297	–2 592	–2 742
International Organisations	GZDS	–653	–631	–1 114	–1 032	–1 044	–720	–1 176	–1 186	–1 719	–1 746	–1 836
World total	KTNF	–8 172	–7 322	–9 775	–6 515	–8 870	–9 835	–10 276	–11 849	–11 885	–13 538	–13 610

1 Cyprus and Malta are included in Other Europe before 1999.

9.8 Current account
Transactions with Europe and USA[1,2]

£ million

		2000	2001	2002	2003	2004	2005	2006	2007	2008
Credits										
Exports of goods										
EMU members	QATL	102 295	104 405	104 109	100 868	100 819	109 765	136 333	114 537	126 143
EU members	LGCJ	112 459	114 406	114 737	111 286	111 650	121 486	152 357	127 813	141 119
Total Europe	EPLM	120 705	122 492	122 437	119 832	120 666	133 669	164 342	140 791	157 269
USA	J8V9	29 549	29 519	28 452	28 997	28 794	31 095	32 287	32 274	35 351
Exports of services										
EMU members	J5Z5	29 867	32 352	33 878	36 989	40 676	43 658	47 112	52 923	60 314
EU members	GC8R	33 718	36 850	38 306	41 871	46 110	49 695	54 296	60 966	68 490
Total Europe	FYWB	39 864	43 547	46 682	51 340	55 804	61 106	67 743	76 983	86 337
USA	FYWF	19 274	19 211	22 690	23 977	25 790	24 423	29 226	32 964	36 173
Income										
EMU members	IV9S	52 661	59 796	51 503	50 466	51 434	65 505	85 309	110 806	113 975
EU members	GNF6	57 027	64 584	55 788	54 796	56 361	71 285	91 601	118 263	120 755
Total Europe	LERD	69 737	75 064	65 105	65 377	69 578	89 600	115 433	153 605	149 582
USA	BFVE	29 284	31 117	26 524	27 662	30 744	44 857	59 552	65 948	49 994
Current transfers										
EMU members	J5YF	1 648	1 735	1 914	1 599	1 994	2 091	2 402	1 820	1 859
EU members	GC84	7 092	9 138	8 006	8 442	9 561	10 376	10 911	9 515	10 761
Total Europe	GXWP	7 299	9 370	8 273	8 714	9 843	10 682	11 379	9 794	11 052
USA	GXWT	1 182	2 395	1 693	1 217	1 549	4 186	3 504	2 238	2 197
TOTAL CREDITS										
EMU members	IV9V	186 471	198 288	191 404	189 922	194 923	221 019	271 156	280 086	302 291
EU members	G97O	210 296	224 978	216 837	216 395	223 682	252 842	309 165	316 555	341 125
Total Europe	LERA	237 605	250 473	242 497	245 263	255 891	295 057	358 897	381 173	404 240
USA	BFVB	79 289	82 242	79 359	81 853	86 877	104 561	124 569	133 424	123 715
Debits										
Imports of goods										
EMU members	QBRM	106 282	114 901	123 927	123 483	127 065	139 911	158 092	149 719	157 455
EU members	LGDB	117 644	126 973	136 931	137 404	142 523	158 163	183 749	169 799	180 363
Total Europe	EPMM	132 366	141 496	151 744	153 466	162 131	183 786	213 968	200 379	220 257
USA	J8VA	28 838	30 270	25 742	23 326	22 525	22 530	25 830	26 095	25 848
Imports of services										
EMU members	J63A	33 236	35 480	37 308	40 085	42 253	46 240	47 617	49 587	54 012
EU members	GCV2	35 356	37 686	39 715	43 014	45 577	50 390	52 476	54 791	59 371
Total Europe	GGPQ	39 497	41 893	44 975	47 916	50 729	56 714	59 430	62 592	67 585
USA	GGPU	13 205	13 503	13 403	14 862	15 300	16 286	16 750	18 387	19 703
Income										
EMU members	IV9T	45 633	43 351	32 879	40 875	48 132	63 990	86 226	109 028	84 566
EU members	G97L	50 234	47 819	37 080	44 611	52 212	69 254	92 656	116 766	92 294
Total Europe	LERE	70 506	66 919	51 636	57 833	67 575	91 636	123 189	150 918	118 318
USA	BFVF	27 660	31 683	29 836	30 618	32 092	42 310	59 628	67 106	72 466
Current transfers										
EMU members	J62B	1 736	1 680	1 921	1 776	2 126	2 322	2 483	2 085	2 391
EU members	GCR2	12 637	11 405	12 223	13 419	13 825	15 629	15 770	15 331	15 921
Total Europe	GXYU	13 148	11 908	12 713	13 909	14 376	16 234	16 506	15 909	16 517
USA	GXYY	1 421	2 553	1 891	1 449	1 845	4 471	3 762	2 554	2 615
TOTAL DEBITS										
EMU members	IV9W	186 887	195 412	196 035	206 219	219 576	252 463	294 418	310 419	298 424
EU members	G97F	215 871	223 883	225 949	238 448	254 137	293 436	344 651	356 687	347 949
Total Europe	LERB	255 517	262 216	261 068	273 124	294 811	348 370	413 093	429 798	422 677
USA	BFVC	71 124	78 009	70 872	70 255	71 762	85 597	105 970	114 142	120 632
Balances										
Trade in goods										
EMU members	QBRX	−3 987	−10 496	−19 818	−22 615	−26 246	−30 146	−21 759	−35 182	−31 312
EU members	LGCF	−5 185	−12 567	−22 194	−26 118	−30 873	−36 677	−31 392	−41 986	−39 244
Total Europe	EPNM	−11 661	−19 004	−29 307	−33 634	−41 465	−50 117	−49 626	−59 588	−62 988
USA	J8VB	711	−751	2 710	5 670	6 269	8 565	6 457	6 179	9 503
Trade in services										
EMU members	J64N	−3 369	−3 128	−3 430	−3 096	−1 577	−2 582	−505	3 336	6 302
EU members	GD6R	−1 638	−836	−1 409	−1 143	533	−695	1 820	6 175	9 119
Total Europe	GGRV	367	1 654	1 707	3 424	5 075	4 392	8 313	14 391	18 752
USA	GGRZ	6 069	5 708	9 287	9 115	10 490	8 137	12 476	14 577	16 470
Income										
EMU members	IV9U	7 028	16 445	18 624	9 591	3 302	1 515	−917	1 778	29 409
EU members	G97D	6 793	16 765	18 708	10 185	4 149	2 031	−1 055	1 497	28 461
Total Europe	LERF	−769	8 145	13 469	7 544	2 003	−2 036	−7 756	2 687	31 264
USA	BFVG	1 624	−566	−3 312	−2 956	−1 348	2 547	−76	−1 158	−22 472
Current transfers										
EMU members	J64F	−88	55	−7	−177	−132	−231	−81	−265	−532
EU members	GD6K	−5 545	−2 267	−4 217	−4 977	−4 264	−5 253	−4 859	−5 816	−5 160
Total Europe	GZCO	−5 849	−2 538	−4 440	−5 195	−4 533	−5 552	−5 127	−6 115	−5 465
USA	GZCS	−239	−158	−198	−232	−296	−285	−258	−316	−418
CURRENT BALANCE										
EMU members	IV9X	−416	2 876	−4 631	−16 297	−24 653	−31 444	−23 262	−30 333	3 867
EU members	G977	−5 575	1 095	−9 112	−22 053	−30 455	−40 594	−35 486	−40 130	−6 824
Total Europe	LERC	−17 912	−11 743	−18 571	−27 861	−38 920	−53 313	−54 196	−48 625	−18 437
USA	BFVD	8 165	4 233	8 487	11 598	15 115	18 964	18 599	19 282	3 083

1 EMU Members: Austria, Belgium, Cyprus, Finland, France, Germany, Greece, Irish Republic, Italy, Luxembourg, Malta, Netherlands, Portugal, Slovakia, Slovenia and Spain.
2 EU and Europe include transactions with European Union institutions.

9.9 UK official transactions with institutions of the EU

£ million

		1998	1999	2000	2001	2002	2003	2004	2005	2006	2007	2008
Credits												
Exports of services												
UK charge for collecting duties and levies(net)[1]	QWUE	212	208	217	525	487	489	543	565	583	603	660
Current transfers												
Other sectors												
Agricultural Guarantee Fund[2]	EBGL	2 935	2 781	2 571	2 336	2 381	2 691	3 315	3 408	3 219	2 952	3 108
European Social Fund	HDIZ	783	434	659	370	412	427	433	900	1 305	795	608
European Coal & Steel Community Grant	FJKP	1	–	–	1	–	–	2	–	–	–	–
Central government												
Fontainebleau abatement	FKKL	1 377	3 171	2 084	4 560	3 099	3 560	3 592	3 655	3 570	3 523	4 862
Other EU receipts	GCSD	7	5	–	8	13	10	12	13	24	109	–
Capital transfers												
Other sectors												
Agricultural Fund for Regional Development[3]	FJXL	56	47	82	26	–	2	49	80	50	150	417
European Regional Development Fund	HBZA	357	285	989	543	296	622	1 062	1 402	618	707	972
Other capital transfers from EU Institutions[2]	EBGO	43	–	–	322	–	–	–	–	–	–	–
Total credits	GCSL	5 771	6 931	6 602	8 691	6 688	7 801	9 008	10 023	9 369	8 839	10 627
Debits												
Current transfers												
Other sectors												
Customs duties and agricultural levies [4]	FJWD	2 076	2 024	2 086	2 069	1 919	1 937	2 145	2 237	2 329	2 412	2 636
Sugar levies [4]	GTBA	42	46	44	31	25	18	25	24	–	–	–
European Coal & Steel Community production levy [4]	GTBB	–	–	–	–	–	–	–	–	–	–	–
VAT based contribution [5]	HCML	3 758	3 920	4 104	3 624	2 720	2 775	1 764	1 980	2 165	2 293	2 255
VAT adjustment [5]	FSVL	470	–109	100	–49	88	–35	25	19	2	26	15
Central government												
GNP fourth resource[6]	HCSO	3 516	4 403	4 243	3 859	5 259	6 622	7 565	8 597	8 358	7 996	8 628
GNP adjustments[6]	HCSM	404	229	136	–1	76	150	–16	135	163	327	–205
Total GNP based fourth own resource contribution	NMFH	*3 920*	*4 632*	*4 379*	*3 858*	*5 335*	*6 772*	*7 549*	*8 732*	*8 521*	*8 323*	*8 423*
Inter-government agreements	HCBW	–	–	–	–	–	–	–	–	–	–	–
EU non-budget (miscellaneous)	HRTM	–	–	–	–	–	–	–	–	–	–	–
Other current transfers to EU institutions	GVEG	–1	11	6	24	10	18	–3	106	8	6	–
Total debits	GCSM	10 265	10 524	10 719	9 557	10 097	11 485	11 505	13 098	13 025	13 060	13 329
Balance (UK net contribution to the EU)	BLZS	–4 494	–3 593	–4 117	–866	–3 409	–3 684	–2 497	–3 075	–3 656	–4 221	–2 702

1 Before 1989 this is netted off the VAT contribution but cannot be identified separately.
2 Other capital transfers from EU institutions are included indistinguishably with Agricultural Guarantee Fund receipts before 1996.
3 Up to 2006 this series includes the European Agricultural Guidance Fund.
4 EU traditional own resource.
5 Third own resource contribution.
6 Fourth own resource contribution.

9.10 Trade in services
By type of service 2007

£ million

	Transportation	Travel	Communications	Construction	Insurance	Financial	Computer and information	Royalties and license fees	Other business services	Personal, cultural and recreational	Government	Total services
Exports												
European Union (EU27) total	7 469	8 995	2 397	399	650	17 226	3 831	2 250	16 211	731	807	60 966
Belgium	417	271	50	13	19	805	161	51	1 083	15	5	2 890
Luxembourg	3	24	50	..	11	888	..	3	516	..	–	1 537
Denmark	1 000	260	39	..	29	364	72	55	483	31	..	2 345
France	869	1 243	275	28	122	2 908	484	181	2 155	46	21	8 332
Germany	898	1 384	484	21	101	3 735	875	259	2 755	113	36	10 661
Ireland	755	1 059	290	263	66	1 434	945	544	1 993	79	8	7 436
Italy	503	829	324	4	105	1 140	173	195	787	109	9	4 178
Netherlands	907	605	264	8	62	2 457	376	280	3 432	18	8	8 417
Russia	119	289	35	14	17	1 065	35	53	546	25	10	2 208
Spain	1 343	983	258	19	35	1 435	141	83	753	52	12	5 114
Switzerland	302	395	50	–	57	2 099	..	263	2 359	26	..	6 441
Turkey	81	204	27	..	14	220	36	20	129	8	..	748
Argentina	21	24	16	..	9	14	2	7	25	..	..	127
Brazil	83	155	20	..	17	..	19	20	48	1	6	447
Canada	357	596	50	3	221	670	47	50	518	17	30	2 559
Chile	35	61	5	..	12	5	–	3	..	..	10	175
Mexico	64	45	9	..	32	81	5	25	75	..	..	342
United States of America	3 463	2 778	708	39	3 286	9 396	1 353	2 176	8 930	490	345	32 964
China	534	476	27	4	13	229	16	52	180	4	12	1 547
Hong Kong	336	209	31	1	23	659	27	30	287	34	3	1 640
India	409	393	42	4	19	246	51	63	324	26	71	1 648
Iran	9	39	7	..	3	32	..	4	53	..	..	163
Japan	472	254	..	..	95	2 534	55	352	723	44	4	4 573
Malaysia	41	117	15	..	13	115	13	21	104	7	..	453
Philippines	30	24	..	..	9	12	..	4	16	1	1	110
Saudi Arabia	100	176	33	8	15	221	21	7	2 225	..	..	2 815
Singapore	494	108	23	..	23	427	24	..	535	..	1	3 328
South Korea	237	135	10	..	7	260	23	61	213	..	..	956
Taiwan	100	88	5	–	10	299	8	16	90	..	..	639
Thailand	50	76	16	..	7	83	6	8	57	..	5	318
Australia	665	715	90	22	137	598	82	90	663	35	8	3 105
South Africa	289	257	53	9	36	296	89	80	302	32	11	1 454
Other	2 736	5 020	..	..	728	..	..	..	..	..	..	30 975
Global total	17 722	19 292	4 263	996	5 353	43 874	7 081	7 555	40 511	1 878	2 120	150 645
Imports												
European Union (EU27) total	11 186	20 718	1 728	480	561	4 778	1 296	1 698	10 124	305	1 917	54 791
Belgium	387	453	49	4	45	480	51	70	693	14	28	2 274
Luxembourg	38	48	..	..	..	170	4	82	122	..	..	469
Denmark	531	123	18	19	15	63	32	30	169	12	5	1 017
France	1 781	4 024	247	20	90	569	205	..	2 015	25	..	9 793
Germany	955	889	602	119	131	1 400	412	232	2 141	37	1 317	8 235
Ireland	576	1 038	146	137	56	787	211	65	867	..	..	3 936
Italy	1 252	1 873	195	12	38	..	40	..	845	..	48	4 755
Netherlands	698	672	119	78	72	379	113	167	968	4	25	3 295
Russia	146	110	29	..	14	..	7	10	440	..	10	912
Spain	2 409	6 236	164	9	30	246	69	8	681	16	146	10 014
Switzerland	388	649	29	2	14	359	141	290	883	35	3	2 793
Turkey	307	738	22	..	14	25	–	2	49	..	..	1 165
Argentina	11	54	..	–	..	..	..	1	18	..	..	92
Brazil	50	97	10	..	6	..	..	..	61	..	8	285
Canada	233	565	40	3	18	126	19	67	256	4	50	1 381
Chile	14	47	..	–	..	..	..	..	..	..	..	68
Mexico	49	250	9	–	2	10	..	3	33	..	..	363
United States of America	1 922	3 804	374	27	102	3 740	787	2 028	4 506	439	658	18 387
China	301	285	52	..	52	35	13	2	204	..	7	983
Hong Kong	140	161	32	..	20	519	6	4	317	..	4	1 213
India	346	834	80	1	11	62	252	2	237	..	..	1 839
Iran	13	16	..	–	..	..	..	..	..	–	1	44
Japan	210	144	24	–	22	791	8	563	1 174	..	..	2 945
Malaysia	49	117	13	–	..	12	2	..	27	..	3	231
Philippines	42	67	11	–	..	1	..	..	22	..	–	153
Saudi Arabia	31	88	6	..	..	15	..	..	..	1	2	516
Singapore	89	49	20	2	14	181	32	12	482	6	12	899
South Korea	53	39	5	..	8	..	8	..	135	..	2	339
Taiwan	49	7	..	..	7	..	..	..	101	..	1	338
Thailand	113	500	16	..	..	13	..	..	37	..	2	693
Australia	292	834	53	9	7	210	21	205	284	99	5	2 019
South Africa	159	469	28	..	8	42	11	..	216	..	3	948
Other	5 179	10 412	..	..	..	..	..	..	..	..	..	23 444
Global total	18 813	35 692	3 620	805	1 022	12 130	2 664	5 053	21 990	952	3 097	105 838

Symbols used in this table:
 .. Indicates that data might be disclosive and have therefore been omitted
 - Indicates that the data is nil or less than £500,000

9.11 Trade in services
By type of service 2008

£ million

	Trans-port-ation	Travel	Commun-ications	Cons-truction	Insu-rance	Finan-cial	Computer and infor-mation	Royal-ties and license fees	Other busi-ness services	Personal, cultural and recrea-tional	Govern-ment	Total services
Exports												
European Union (EU27) total	8 175	9 499	2 524	361	1 118	20 697	3 640	2 605	18 182	774	915	68 490
Belgium	488	252	55	..	35	1 111	182	42	1 435	12	..	3 648
Luxembourg	10	25	11	1	16	1 282	..	..	644	..	–	2 077
Denmark	894	237	35	3	51	363	87	86	614	51	5	2 426
France	1 000	1 344	232	29	215	3 869	461	189	2 249	65	30	9 683
Germany	1 056	1 346	565	18	181	4 462	829	263	2 948	104	43	11 815
Ireland	816	1 029	332	196	120	1 861	940	757	2 359	26	13	8 449
Italy	601	831	351	3	177	1 141	196	269	785	112	13	4 479
Netherlands	1 034	761	263	71	98	2 930	298	283	3 876	98	19	9 731
Russia	137	196	41	8	32	1 116	49	47	532	19	10	2 187
Spain	1 516	921	317	4	58	1 451	187	134	818	99	17	5 522
Switzerland	352	421	65	2	101	2 087	..	336	2 781	33	..	7 083
Turkey	91	125	25	..	24	170	33	23	133	14	..	648
Argentina	16	29	..	–	21	17	..	7	25	..	4	144
Brazil	96	152	24	..	32	98	13	12	141	..	5	594
Canada	434	524	40	..	376	809	55	50	514	17	..	2 851
Chile	36	14	7	..	21	15	4	3	67	..	..	177
Mexico	74	49	9	..	54	83	4	20	46	..	..	345
United States of America	3 977	2 264	712	65	4 493	11 110	1 429	2 055	9 151	615	302	36 173
China	1 063	516	31	..	26	385	19	52	339	15	..	2 471
Hong Kong	398	209	..	..	54	921	38	37	369	56	3	2 121
India	468	455	60	6	28	246	54	49	375	13	73	1 827
Iran	15	109	12	..	6	22	..	..	73	..	..	256
Japan	585	205	..	..	178	2 718	45	360	832	25	4	4 991
Malaysia	54	121	14	1	26	125	19	26	136	10	3	535
Philippines	64	25	..	–	21	13	..	4	26	61	1	229
Saudi Arabia	124	266	54	..	26	405	23	10	1 698	8	..	2 633
Singapore	705	121	24	..	36	648	51	..	703	..	–	3 458
South Korea	287	129	12	1	19	281	23	62	259	..	..	1 080
Taiwan	133	99	..	..	19	273	9	16	..	..	21	694
Thailand	52	57	12	..	12	96	9	6	63	..	5	333
Australia	914	753	73	..	207	1 022	88	117	743	..	8	4 016
South Africa	422	224	57	1	85	242	100	85	319	33	12	1 580
Other	2 968	5 789	..	..	1 188	11 456	..	..	..	..	..	36 143
Global total	20 880	19 598	4 639	1 127	8 036	52 828	7 040	7 361	44 697	2 091	2 102	170 399
Imports												
European Union (EU27) total	11 754	21 812	1 883	151	552	6 042	1 369	1 365	11 303	314	2 826	59 371
Belgium	479	466	62	1	45	700	42	82	705	6	36	2 624
Luxembourg	46	101	14	..	3	198	..	127	103	..	..	599
Denmark	590	111	19	..	..	94	23	48	184	15	9	1 113
France	1 759	4 203	221	14	93	736	207	160	2 289	31	129	9 842
Germany	1 037	942	658	5	126	1 771	465	301	2 621	46	2 121	10 093
Ireland	585	1 097	185	76	..	833	207	103	985	13	..	4 185
Italy	1 337	1 823	236	9	37	..	42	102	917	48	..	4 955
Netherlands	699	627	163	26	71	588	118	315	1 024	89	29	3 749
Russia	170	158	27	..	18	..	9	..	536	..	9	1 102
Spain	2 498	6 613	141	–	28	339	95	27	743	16	207	10 707
Switzerland	420	541	32	–	14	451	181	167	743	30	3	2 582
Turkey	324	997	25	..	13	34	..	4	57	..	..	1 470
Argentina	11	80	..	..	..	6	..	..	22	..	..	128
Brazil	57	140	8	..	7	..	7	..	65	..	7	348
Canada	248	546	47	..	16	164	57	94	290	..	25	1 497
Chile	16	25	..	..	..	..	..	..	..	..	1	52
Mexico	52	339	11	..	..	12	..	..	24	..	3	448
United States of America	2 134	3 726	401	..	94	3 844	973	2 541	4 729	417	..	19 703
China	312	306	43	1	61	205	11	6	318	..	..	1 272
Hong Kong	157	171	33	..	21	311	7	..	343	..	..	1 050
India	451	856	113	7	12	55	257	12	449	7	10	2 229
Iran	14	20	..	–	..	..	..	–	..	–	1	45
Japan	327	123	32	–	22	1 060	8	900	1 154	..	..	3 635
Malaysia	52	109	13	–	..	13	4	..	43	..	..	241
Philippines	66	68	14	..	..	1	..	..	30	–	–	192
Saudi Arabia	36	130	8	..	..	11	..	–	..	..	2	564
Singapore	121	74	28	..	12	260	6	10	790	6	..	1 347
South Korea	52	39	7	..	9	149	..	..	132	..	2	401
Taiwan	42	20	..	–	9	..	27	..	121	..	1	357
Thailand	113	496	15	..	..	12	..	..	28	..	2	677
Australia	308	805	46	..	11	198	..	212	302	100	2	2 051
South Africa	182	384	31	..	25	46	8	8	206	..	3	899
Other	5 681	11 120	..	..	..	..	..	..	..	..	..	25 763
Global total	20 376	37 256	4 122	904	1 073	14 209	3 055	5 500	24 404	959	4 062	115 920

Symbols used in this table:
.. Indicates that data might be disclosive and have therefore been omitted
- Indicates that the data is nil or less than £500,000

9.12 Trade in goods and services
Top fifty UK trading partners

Exports				Imports			
Goods (£251bn in 2008)		Services (£170bn in 2008)		Goods (£344bn in 2008)		Services (£116bn in 2008)	
	08 07		08 07		08 07		08 07
USA[1]	1 1	USA[1]	1 1	Germany	1 1	USA[1]	1 1
Germany	2 2	Germany	2 2	USA[1]	2 2	Spain	2 2
Netherlands	3 5	Netherlands	3 3	Netherlands	3 3	Germany	3 4
Ireland	4 4	France	4 4	China	4 5	France	4 3
France	5 3	Ireland	5 5	France	5 4	Italy	5 5
Belgium	6 6	Switzerland	6 6	Norway	6 7	Ireland	6 6
Spain	7 7	Spain	7 7	Belgium	7 6	Netherlands	7 7
Italy	8 8	Japan	8 8	Italy	8 8	Japan	8 8
Sweden	9 9	Italy	9 9	Ireland	9 9	Belgium	9 10
China	10 11	The Channel Islands	10 13	Spain	10 10	Switzerland	10 9
Switzerland	11 12	Australia	11 11	Japan	11 11	Greece	11 11
Russia	12 15	Belgium	12 12	Hong Kong	12 12	India	12 13
India	13 14	Singapore	13 10	Russia	13 15	Australia	13 12
Japan	14 10	Canada	14 15	Sweden	14 14	Portugal	14 14
United Arab Emirates[2]	15 17	Saudi Arabia	15 14	Canada	15 13	Canada	15 15
Hong Kong	16 16	Norway	16 16	Switzerland	16 16	Turkey	16 21
Canada	17 13	China	17 23	Turkey	17 17	Bermuda	17 16
Australia	18 19	Denmark	18 17	South Africa	18 23	Singapore	18 29
Poland	19 21	Sweden	19 19	India	19 19	Sweden	19 18
Norway	20 18	Russia	20 18	Poland	20 20	China	20 26
Singapore	21 20	Cayman Islands	21 20	Singapore	21 18	Poland	21 19
South Africa	22 23	Hong Kong	22 22	Denmark	22 21	United Arab Emirates[2]	22 23
Denmark	23 24	Luxembourg	23 24	Czech Republic	23 24	Cyprus	23 20
Turkey	24 22	India	24 21	South Korea	24 22	Norway	24 25
South Korea	25 26	United Arab Emirates[2]	25 26	Finland	25 25	Denmark	25 24
Saudi Arabia	26 27	South Africa	26 25	Brazil	26 30	Russia	26 28
Finland	27 25	Nigeria	27 32	Taiwan	27 27	Hong Kong	27 17
Brazil	28 33	Greece	28 31	Hungary	28 28	The Channel Islands	28 22
Greece	29 31	Finland	29 27	Thailand	29 31	Austria	29 30
Portugal	30 28	British Virgin Islands	30 33	Australia	30 29	South Africa	30 27
Czech Republic	31 29	South Korea	31 29	Austria	31 26	Egypt	31 32
Nigeria	32 34	Poland	32 28	Malaysia	32 32	Thailand	32 31
Austria	33 30	Kazakhstan	33 30	Portugal	33 33	Luxembourg	33 35
Israel	34 32	Bermuda	34 34	Slovakia	34 35	Barbados	34 37
Malaysia	35 35	Portugal	35 36	Indonesia	35 40	Saudi Arabia	35 33
Hungary	36 38	Austria	36 39	Israel	36 36	Nigeria	36 –
Egypt	37 40	Taiwan	37 37	Kuwait	37 44	Czech Republic	37 35
Mexico	38 39	Egypt	38 40	Vietnam	38 41	Mexico	38 43
Taiwan	39 36	Turkey	39 35	Libya	39 –	South Korea	39 44
Thailand	40 43	Brazil	40 47	United Arab Emirates[2]	40 37	Pakistan	40 40
Romania	41 41	Cyprus	41 38	Nigeria	41 –	Bulgaria	41 46
Qatar	42 42	Qatar	42 49	Algeria	42 38	Finland	42 39
Ukraine	43 45	Israel	43 45	Luxembourg	43 45	Morocco	43 42
Kuwait	44 44	Malaysia	44 46	Mexico	44 50	Malta	44 47
Cyprus	45 47	Kuwait	45 43	Romania	45 39	New Zealand	45 38
Morocco	46 –	Angola	46 44	New Zealand	46 46	Kazakhstan	46 41
Pakistan	47 46	New Zealand	47 48	Colombia	47 –	Taiwan	47 45
Slovakia	48 49	Hungary	48 41	Saudi Arabia	48 42	Brazil	48 49
Gibraltar	49 –	Iraq	49 –	Greece	49 47	Hungary	49 34
Malta	50 50	Gibraltar	50 –	Egypt	50 –	Israel	50 48

1 USA includes Puerto Rico
2 United Arab Emirates includes Abu Dhabi, Dubai, Sharjah, Ajman, Umm al Qaiwain, Ras al Khaimah and Fujairah

9.13 Trade in services
Trading partners ranked[1]

£ million

Exports								
	2008	2007		2008	2007		2008	2007
USA	36 173	32 964	Algeria	208	194	Belize	21	13
Germany	11 815	10 661	Peru	189	191	North Korea	21	8
Netherlands	9 731	8 417	Bulgaria	183	170	Mali	21	14
France	9 683	8 332	Chile	177	175	Chad	21	34
Ireland	8 449	7 436	Bangladesh	168	145	Macedonia	19	31
Switzerland	7 083	6 441	Malta	168	129	Democratic Republic Congo	18	8
Spain	5 522	5 114	Kenya	162	141	Guinea	18	11
Japan	4 991	4 573	Tunisia	150	79	Aruba	17	6
Italy	4 479	4 178	Argentina	144	127	Uzbekistan	17	6
The Channel Islands	4 049	2 816	Oman	135	99	Dominican Republic	16	12
Australia	4 016	3 105	Ghana	134	136	Moldova	16	7
Belgium	3 648	2 890	Trinidad & Tobago	127	68	Bolivia	15	13
Singapore	3 458	3 328	Mauritius	119	90	Belarus	14	13
Canada	2 851	2 559	Bahamas	114	136	Gambia	14	16
Saudi Arabia	2 633	2 815	Sri Lanka	114	125	Mauritania	14	12
Norway	2 478	2 546	Croatia	109	97	Swaziland	14	5
China	2 471	1 547	Vietnam	105	83	Bosnia & Herzegovina	13	8
Denmark	2 426	2 345	Barbados	101	57	Cuba	13	10
Sweden	2 316	2 100	Jordan	92	74	Costa Rica	12	6
Russia	2 187	2 208	Colombia	89	75	Saint Lucia	11	4
Cayman Islands	2 154	1 654	Fiji	87	66	Nepal	11	17
Hong Kong	2 121	1 640	Latvia	86	245	Togo	10	9
Luxembourg	2 077	1 537	Cameroon	84	65	Andorra	9	9
India	1 827	1 648	Slovenia	84	74	Burkina Faso	9	4
United Arab Emirates[2]	1 683	1 298	Morocco	77	73	Maldives	9	12
South Africa	1 580	1 454	Cote d'Ivoire	75	34	Rwanda	9	3
Nigeria	1 279	875	Netherlands Antilles	74	75	Turks & Caicos Islands	9	16
Greece	1 201	887	Gabon	70	41	Falkland Islands	8	8
Finland	1 139	1 186	Venezuela	70	62	Lesotho	8	6
British Virgin Islands	1 104	835	Equatorial Guinea	68	74	Armenia	7	3
South Korea	1 080	956	Liechtenstein	68	97	Benin	7	5
Poland	1 031	1 007	Lebanon	62	56	Guatemala	7	8
Kazakhstan	915	894	Tajikistan	62	31	Cambodia	7	11
Bermuda	864	785	Sudan	61	36	Mongolia	7	5
Portugal	724	647	Mozambique	60	60	Marshall Islands	6	5
Austria	718	613	Senegal	58	37	Paraguay	6	6
Taiwan	694	639	Syria	58	32	Honduras	5	4
Egypt	690	607	Congo	57	29	Kyrgyzstan	5	3
Turkey	648	748	Tanzania	57	33	Macao	5	6
Brazil	594	447	Afghanistan	56	43	Cape Verde	4	3
Cyprus	586	629	Georgia	55	16	Haiti	4	2
Qatar	579	397	Uganda	51	36	Laos	4	2
Israel	549	482	Yemen	48	51	Myanmar	4	4
Malaysia	535	453	Brunei	44	34	Niger	4	1
Kuwait	532	515	Estonia	43	109	San Marino	4	1
Angola	512	484	Sierra Leone	40	13	St Vincent & the Grenadines	4	9
New Zealand	456	433	Botswana	39	38	U.S. Virgin Islands	4	6
Hungary	455	548	Papua New Guinea	38	30	Eritrea	3	4
Iraq	433	273	Jamaica	34	27	Vanuatu	3	1
Gibraltar	426	259	Serbia & Montenegro	33	64	America Samoa	2	1
Czech Republic	415	521	Ecuador	32	47	Guam	2	1
Mexico	345	342	Seychelles	32	18	St Kitts & Nevis	2	1
Thailand	333	318	Zambia	32	36	Nicaragua	2	1
Pakistan	321	320	Ethiopia	31	35	El Salvador	2	2
Azerbaijan	300	287	Namibia	31	32	Tonga	2	1
Indonesia	297	252	Panama	30	27	Vatican City State	2	–
Slovakia	290	190	Guyana	27	22	Burundi	1	2
Romania	272	252	Malawi	26	28	Djibouti	1	1
Lithuania	270	121	Albania	25	11	Grenada	1	–
Iran	256	163	Liberia	25	11	Guinea-Bissau	1	1
Libya	244	197	Zimbabwe	25	33	Kiribati	1	2
Bahrain	243	165	Uruguay	24	14	Solomon Islands	1	1
Philippines	229	110	Antigua & Barbuda	23	8	St Helena	1	3
Iceland	225	183	Madagascar	23	16	Somalia	1	2
Ukraine	223	206	Suriname	23	13			
Isle of Man	216	272	Turkmenistan	22	13			

1 Any country not included in this table is estimated having Trade in Services of less than £500,000
2 United Arab Emirates includes Abu Dhabi, Dubai, Sharjah, Ajman, Umm al Qaiwain, Ras al Khaimah and Fujairah

9.13 Trade in services
Trading partners ranked[1]

continued £ million

Imports

	2008	2007		2008	2007		2008	2007
USA	19 703	18 387	Maldives	127	121	Botswana	16	13
Spain	10 707	10 014	Angola	123	154	Mali	16	4
Germany	10 093	8 235	Indonesia	123	112	Suriname	16	15
France	9 842	9 793	Azerbaijan	120	107	Netherlands Antilles	15	5
Italy	4 955	4 755	Slovakia	112	99	Dominica	15	5
Ireland	4 185	3 936	Ghana	109	108	Cote d'Ivoire	13	9
Netherlands	3 749	3 295	Sri Lanka	105	74	Eritrea	13	6
Japan	3 635	2 945	British Virgin Islands	100	116	Somalia	12	5
Belgium	2 624	2 274	Dominican Republic	97	74	Panama	11	10
Switzerland	2 582	2 793	Gibraltar	93	105	Uzbekistan	9	11
Greece	2 261	2 249	Lithuania	89	100	Guatemala	8	5
India	2 229	1 839	Algeria	88	145	Laos	8	3
Australia	2 051	2 019	Peru	86	71	Liechtenstein	8	19
Portugal	1 909	1 699	Iceland	85	91	Rwanda	8	4
Canada	1 497	1 381	Vietnam	84	38	Moldova	7	4
Turkey	1 470	1 165	Antigua & Barbuda	77	93	Armenia	6	4
Bermuda	1 438	1 229	Tanzania	72	93	Bosnia & Herzegovina	6	10
Singapore	1 347	899	Latvia	71	137	Belize	6	6
Sweden	1 344	1 204	Zambia	67	41	Cook islands	6	1
China	1 272	983	Slovenia	65	44	Georgia	6	3
Poland	1 261	1 170	Andorra	63	46	Sao Tome & Principe	6	1
United Arab Emirates[2]	1 242	1 020	Serbia & Montenegro	63	71	Chad	6	8
Cyprus	1 178	1 167	Bahrain	60	53	Uruguay	6	7
Norway	1 150	992	Costa Rica	60	44	Paraguay	5	8
Denmark	1 113	1 017	Estonia	60	132	Benin	4	4
Russia	1 102	912	Bahamas	58	39	Brunei	4	1
Hong Kong	1 050	1 213	Chile	52	68	Falkland Islands	4	2
The Channel Islands	1 040	1 142	Cayman Islands	51	56	Guinea	4	13
Austria	957	827	Oman	51	25	Equatorial Guinea	4	1
South Africa	899	948	Fiji	50	29	Guyana	4	10
Egypt	747	598	Jordan	49	19	Cambodia	4	10
Thailand	677	693	Saint Lucia	48	73	Togo	4	3
Luxembourg	599	469	Iran	45	44	Cape Verde	3	2
Barbados	570	466	Zimbabwe	45	36	Djibouti	3	1
Saudi Arabia	564	516	Ecuador	42	48	Honduras	3	7
Nigeria	484	211	Trinidad & Tobago	41	48	North Korea	3	1
Czech Republic	476	469	Grenada	39	24	Macedonia	3	4
Mexico	448	363	Afghanistan	38	25	Mauritania	3	3
South Korea	401	339	Venezuela	38	37	Burkina Faso	2	1
Pakistan	400	413	Ethiopia	37	36	Bhutan	2	1
Bulgaria	397	334	Namibia	37	10	Haiti	2	–
Finland	395	418	Isle of Man	36	67	Liberia	2	2
Morocco	389	383	Nepal	36	21	Myanmar	2	1
Malta	379	313	Seychelles	35	25	Macao	2	1
New Zealand	377	438	Colombia	33	37	Nicaragua	2	–
Kazakhstan	363	402	Yemen	32	19	Tajikistan	2	3
Taiwan	357	338	Gambia	31	19	Turkmenistan	2	–
Brazil	348	285	Malawi	30	8	Anguilla	1	6
Hungary	335	471	Papua New Guinea	30	16	Burundi	1	1
Israel	302	303	Sudan	30	34	Guinea-Bissau	1	1
Malaysia	241	231	Mozambique	29	20	Kyrgyzstan	1	–
Jamaica	240	161	Uganda	26	31	St Kitts & Nevis	1	1
Tunisia	235	180	Albania	24	23	Lesotho	1	2
Qatar	234	174	Turks & Caicos Islands	23	8	Mongolia	1	–
Ukraine	234	175	Senegal	22	14	Niger	1	1
Croatia	228	159	Syria	22	14	El Salvador	1	4
Iraq	224	107	Bolivia	21	6	Swaziland	1	1
Kuwait	213	150	Madagascar	21	10	St Vincent & the Grenadines	1	2
Romania	208	170	Belarus	20	23	U.S. Virgin Islands	1	3
Philippines	192	153	Lebanon	19	21			
Bangladesh	175	119	Democratic Republic Congo	18	13			
Cuba	158	142	Cameroon	18	10			
Kenya	142	201	Aruba	17	22			
Libya	137	85	Congo	17	15			
Mauritius	136	112	Gabon	17	11			
Argentina	128	92	Sierra Leone	17	12			

1 Any country not included in this table is estimated having Trade in Services of less than £500,000
2 United Arab Emirates includes Abu Dhabi, Dubai, Sharjah, Ajman, Umm al Qaiwain, Ras al Khaimah and Fujairah

9.14 World total and G7 countries trade in services[1]

| | US$ million | | | | | | | | | % | |
| | | | | | | | | | | The UK as a percentage of: | |
	World	US	Canada	Japan	France	Germany	Italy	UK[2]	G7 total	World	G7
Exports											
1996	1 315 397	236 890	29 243	67 712	83 529	85 408	65 660	96 605	665 047	7.3	14.5
1997	1 364 176	254 317	31 596	69 303	80 790	82 735	66 991	107 366	693 098	7.9	15.5
1998	1 392 477	260 806	33 836	62 412	84 958	84 507	67 549	114 711	708 779	8.2	16.2
1999	1 441 626	279 610	36 117	60 998	81 635	83 267	58 788	123 840	724 255	8.6	17.1
2000	1 517 320	295 965	40 230	69 238	80 489	82 237	56 556	124 151	748 866	8.2	16.6
2001	1 521 210	283 054	38 804	64 516	80 125	87 775	57 676	126 393	738 343	8.3	17.1
2002	1 638 868	288 789	40 481	65 712	86 160	102 217	60 439	141 262	785 060	8.6	18.0
2003	1 888 004	301 053	44 242	77 621	98 814	122 560	71 767	167 313	883 370	8.9	18.9
2004	2 283 424	349 576	50 286	97 611	114 629	144 673	84 524	206 873	1 048 172	9.1	19.7
2005	2 548 919	385 295	55 444	110 210	122 209	161 684	89 216	216 883	1 140 941	8.5	19.0
2006	2 866 094	430 159	59 330	117 298	126 287	185 574	98 983	247 402	1 265 033	8.6	19.6
2007	3 386 225	493 157	62 988	129 117	145 736	214 958	111 999	301 561	1 459 516	8.9	20.7
Imports											
1996	1 335 402	150 629	35 906	129 988	67 275	135 977	57 605	74 251	651 631	5.6	11.4
1997	1 371 654	166 478	38 013	123 454	64 164	129 647	59 227	79 849	660 832	5.8	12.1
1998	1 393 988	180 666	38 156	111 833	67 728	134 799	63 379	89 851	686 412	6.4	13.1
1999	1 437 356	199 204	40 573	115 158	63 158	137 656	57 707	98 656	712 112	6.9	13.9
2000	1 509 904	223 740	44 118	116 864	60 691	133 431	55 601	101 405	735 850	6.7	13.8
2001	1 530 735	221 764	43 843	108 249	62 372	138 462	57 753	101 625	734 068	6.6	13.8
2002	1 628 914	231 049	45 069	107 940	68 960	141 973	63 166	111 763	769 920	6.9	14.5
2003	1 860 429	250 328	52 454	111 528	82 898	169 161	74 332	130 351	871 052	7.0	15.0
2004	2 217 431	291 191	58 776	135 514	98 371	191 508	83 246	154 819	1 013 425	7.0	15.3
2005	2 453 108	313 511	65 434	134 256	105 692	203 708	90 081	170 040	1 082 722	6.9	15.7
2006	2 730 796	348 889	72 295	135 556	113 734	219 076	100 511	183 302	1 173 363	6.7	15.6
2007	3 217 555	378 114	80 837	150 367	130 749	254 233	121 450	211 867	1 327 617	6.6	16.0
Balances											
1996		86 261	–6 663	–62 276	16 254	–50 569	8 055	22 354	13 416		
1997		87 839	–6 417	–54 151	16 626	–46 912	7 764	27 517	32 266		
1998		80 140	–4 320	–49 421	17 230	–50 292	4 170	24 860	22 367		
1999		80 406	–4 456	–54 160	18 477	–54 389	1 081	25 184	12 143		
2000		72 225	–3 888	–47 626	19 798	–51 194	955	22 746	13 016		
2001		61 290	–5 039	–43 733	17 753	–50 687	–77	24 768	4 275		
2002		57 740	–4 588	–42 228	17 200	–39 756	–2 727	29 499	15 140		
2003		50 725	–8 212	–33 907	15 916	–46 601	–2 565	36 962	12 318		
2004		58 385	–8 490	–37 903	16 258	–46 835	1 278	52 054	34 747		
2005		71 784	–9 990	–24 046	16 517	–42 024	–865	46 843	58 219		
2006		81 270	–12 965	–18 258	12 553	–33 502	–1 528	64 100	91 670		
2007		115 043	–17 849	–21 250	14 987	–39 275	–9 451	89 694	131 899		

1 G7 country data is not yet available for 2008
2 The analysis of UK data is based on the all accounts totals shown in table 3.1

Sources: G7 and world data provided by IMF;
UK data provided by ONS

Geographical breakdown of the UK international investment position

Chapter 10

Chapter 10: Geographical breakdown of the UK international investment position

Summary

The latest available geographical breakdown of the UK's international investment position (IIP) is for the end of 2007. The geographical breakdown of IIP lags that of the current account as much of the data are sourced from annual inquiries which are not available until 12 months after the reference year.

Foreign direct investment geographical breakdown levels are derived from annual inquiries to outward and inward direct investors in the UK. Portfolio investment consists of equity and debt securities holdings, in the form of bonds and notes and money market instruments. Information on the geographical breakdown of UK holdings of portfolio investment assets are broadly based on the UK contribution to the IMF's Coordinated Portfolio Investment Survey (CPIS).

Geographical breakdowns of UK banks' deposits abroad and loans made abroad are derived from banking data supplied by the Bank of England. This information is also used to apportion securities dealers' deposits abroad. Country breakdowns of UK private sector (excluding banks and securities dealers) deposits with banks abroad are derived from the banking statistics of countries in the Bank for International Settlements (BIS) reporting area. Geographical breakdowns of foreign deposits with UK banks are derived from banking data, with foreign loans made to securities dealers apportioned in the same way. Country breakdowns of UK private sector (excluding banks and securities dealers) loans from abroad are derived from the banking statistics of countries in the BIS reporting area.

Geographical international investment position

At the end of 2007 the UK's net IIP was -£282.5 billion with reported assets totalling £6,384.6 billion and reported liabilities totalling £6,667.2 billion. These are respectively equal to 456 per cent and 477 per cent of GDP (GDP at current market prices, as published in the National Accounts Blue Book 2009). In 2007 the UK retained its net asset position with the Americas and with Australasia & Oceania but continued to have a net liability position with the EU27, Other Europe, Asia and Africa. The UK also had a net liability position with the United States of America (USA), though much reduced in 2007 compared to the previous year.

Geographical breakdown of assets

Of the assets held by UK residents at the end of 2007, 55 per cent were issued in Europe. In total 43 per cent were held in the EU27. France remained the most popular European destination for UK investors, at £515.1 billion. The Netherlands and Germany accounted for £450.6 billion and £425.8 billion of UK assets respectively at the end of 2007.

Investments in the Americas amounted to £1,994.1 billion, which represented 31 per cent of UK investment holdings

abroad. Most of these investments in the Americas were held in the USA, at £1,453.5 billion which was an increase on the previous year of £153.8 billion. UK residents held 23 per cent of their total investment in the USA, nearly three times the size for the next largest country, France.

An additional 10 per cent of UK assets were investments held in Asia. Japan, the UK's main investment partner in this region, represented 4.0 per cent of total UK assets, at £256.5 billion, down from 6.6 per cent of UK assets in 2004. Investments in Australasia, Africa and International Organisations accounted for only 2.7 per cent of total assets.

Geographical breakdown of liabilities

The distribution of liabilities by region largely mirrored that of assets at the end of 2007. Investments in the UK from Europe amounted to 57 per cent of total investments. The EU27 accounted for £2,783.0 billion, or 42 per cent of total investment.

Figure 10.1

International Investment Position

10 largest counterparts to assets of the UK, 2007

£ billion

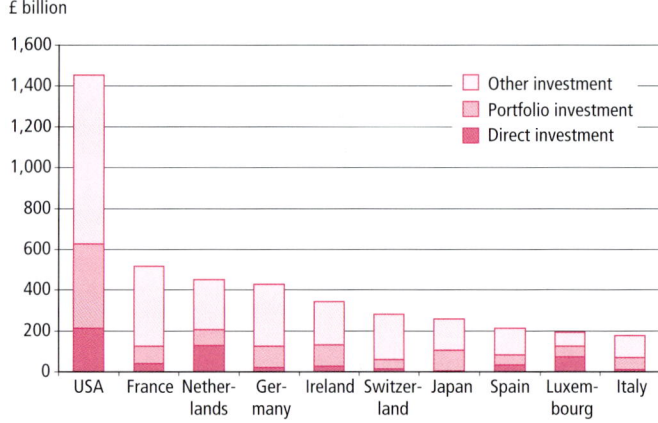

Figure 10.2

International Investment Position

10 largest counterparts to liabilities of the UK, 2007

£ billion

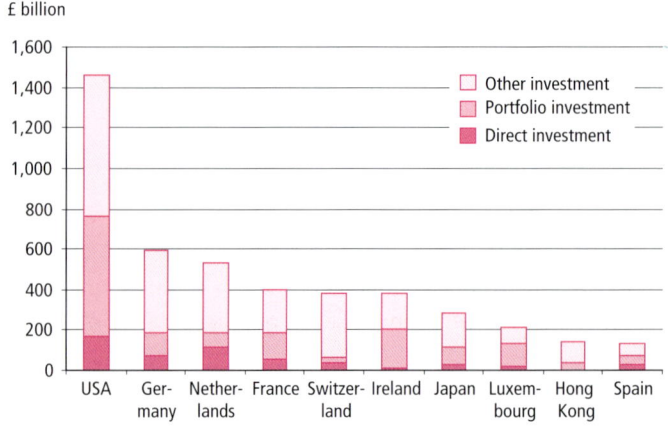

Investment in the UK from the Americas was 28 per cent of total UK liabilities at the end of 2007, while the USA itself accounted for 22 per cent of total investment into the UK. Investments in the UK from Asia totalled 12 per cent of UK liabilities. UK liabilities with Australasia & Oceania, Africa and International Organisations amounted to 2.9 per cent of total investments in the UK.

Geographical breakdown of direct investment

UK direct investment abroad contributed 14 per cent to the total stock of UK assets at the end of 2007, at £913.9 billion. Of these investments, 42 per cent were in holdings issued by countries in the EU27 and 23 per cent in the USA. The country in the EU accounting for the highest level of UK assets was the Netherlands, with total investments in that country amounting to £128.7 billion; this represents 34 per cent of UK direct investment in the EU. Holdings within the Netherlands grew strongly in 2007 but were still at a lower level than at the end of 2004, after which they fell sharply.

Direct investment in the UK equalled 9 per cent of the total level of UK liabilities in 2007. The USA accounted for 27 per cent of direct investment into the UK and the EU27 for a further 50 per cent. The country in the EU27 with the most significant direct investment into the UK was the Netherlands with total investments of £113.5 billion. This was followed by Germany at £70.3 billion and France at £54.1 billion worth of UK liabilities. Direct investment into the UK by the USA was higher than for any of these EU27 countries, totalling £167.6 billion.

Geographical breakdown of portfolio investment

UK portfolio investment assets at the end of 2007 stood at £1,693.8 billion, 27 per cent of total UK assets. The geographical breakdown of UK portfolio investment assets is compiled using the UK's contribution to the Coordinated Portfolio Investment Survey (CPIS). The largest issuer of holdings (in the UK's 2007 CPIS return to the International Monetary Fund) was the USA, contributing 25 per cent of total investments. Long term debt issues comprised 57 per cent of portfolio investment held in the USA. Banks, insurance and pension funds and trust funds were the UK sectors investing most heavily in the USA (46 per cent of investment was from banks and 39 per cent from insurance and pension funds). Residents of the EU27 were the issuers of 38 per cent of UK portfolio investment holdings at the end of 2007. Issues by Ireland were £105.0 billion, the largest share of which, 51 per cent, were held by banks. The Netherlands, Germany, and France were also significant EU countries for UK investors. The USA was the main location for short term debt assets, at £11.1 billion, of which £7.9 billion were invested by banks. A majority of Japanese-issued holdings were equity issues, at 71 per cent.

The concentration of investment in just four countries where each reached more than £100 billion (United States, at £415.2 billion, Ireland at £105.0 billion, Germany at £104.9 billion and Japan at £101.5 billion) represents 43 per cent of total portfolio investment assets. In 2007 there were 197 countries in which the UK invested less that £1 billion each; the sum of these investments accounted for only £14 billion, 0.8 per cent of total portfolio investment assets.

Portfolio investment liabilities are derived from the CPIS returns of other countries reporting assets held in the UK. The country holding most portfolio investments in the UK was the USA, at £589.4 billion. Ireland also reported high levels of investment in the UK, at £196.9 billion.

Geographical breakdown of other investment

The UK's other investment assets totalled £3,750.2 billion at the end of 2007 with £1,739.4 billion invested in EU27 countries; 22 per cent of this was in France, 17 per cent in Germany and 14 per cent in the Netherlands. The UK's assets in the USA amounted to £826.3 billion or 22 per cent of total other investment assets. At the end of 2007 a significant proportion of UK assets were also held in Japan, at £152.8 billion or 4.1 percent of the world total.

Other investment liabilities totalled £4,119.4 billion in 2007. The USA accounted for 17 per cent of total other investment liabilities, at £702.9 billion. A total of 69 per cent of German investment holdings in the UK were other investments, at £409.9 billion.

Time series: comparisons

Following a slight fall between 2001 and 2002, there was an increase in total UK IIP assets from £3,051.9 billion in 2002 to £6,384.6 billion in 2007. Investment in the EU27 increased from £1,395.9 billion in 2002 to £2,768.7 billion in 2007. Between 2001 and 2002 there was a fall in overall assets held but in some countries a build up of assets was apparent, notably Australia, Belgium, Canada, Japan and the Netherlands. In the broad geographical regions there was roughly a doubling of assets held between 2002 and 2007. The UK's assets in the EU27 grew by 98 per cent. Investments in Asia grew by 78 per cent, though assets in Japan, the Asian country with the highest liabilities to the UK, grew by only 21 per cent over the period. Investments in India and China have grown strongly from a low base. The USA remained the most important country for UK investment, growing from £625.9 billion in 2002 to £1,453.5 billion in 2007.

IIP liabilities also increased in each of the years from 2002 to 2007. There were increases in investments in the UK from the EU27, rising from £2,342.5 billion in 2006 to £2,783.0 billion in 2007. Between 2002 and 2007 there was growth of 128 per cent in UK liabilities to the EU27. Investment by the USA in the

Figure 10.3
International Investment Position
Total assets by region

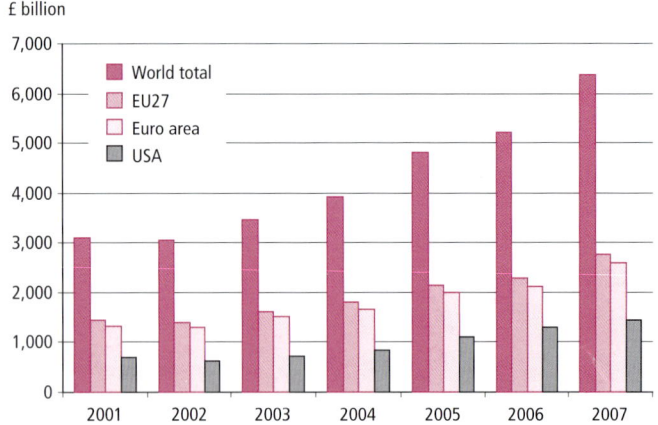

Figure 10.4
International Investment Position
Total liabilities by region

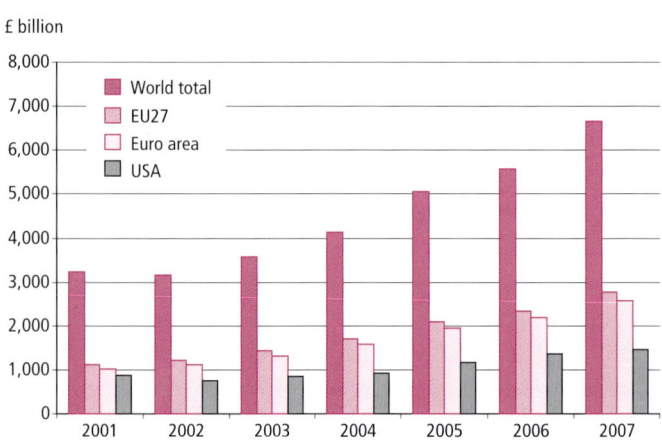

UK increased from £1,350.7 billion in 2006 to £1,459.9 billion in 2007.

Rates of return

Regional rates of return are calculated by dividing income earned and paid on investments by the total value of the investment. Taking the EU27 as an example, the UK earned £117.8 billion from its average investments of £2,523.1 billion in 2007, equivalent to an annual rate of return of 4.7 per cent. (The average investment in 2007 is calculated by taking the mean of the end-2006 and end-2007 levels.) In 2007 the UK earned a 5.0 per cent rate of return on its total external assets and paid out a 4.4 per cent rate of return on external liabilities. Usually the UK has earned a higher rate of return with its main partners and globally on its external assets than it pays out on its liabilities. However, in 2007 the USA earned a higher rate on its assets in the UK than it paid on its liabilities to the UK.

Regional rates of return

External assets (per cent)	2005	2006	2007	External liabilities (per cent)	2005	2006	2007
EU 27	3.6	4.1	4.7	EU 27	3.6	4.1	4.5
Total Europe	3.8	4.3	4.9	Total Europe	3.5	4.1	4.3
USA	4.6	4.9	4.8	USA	4.0	4.7	4.9
Total Asia	4.5	5.4	5.6	Total Asia	2.9	3.9	3.8
Rest of the World	4.6	4.3	4.3	Rest of the world	2.3	3.0	3.1
World total	4.3	4.7	5.0	World total	3.6	4.3	4.4

10.1 International Investment Position: by type of investment
Balance sheets valued at end of year
2007

£ billion

	Assets				Liabilities			
	Type of Investment				Type of Investment			
	Direct	Portfolio	Other	Total	Direct	Portfolio	Other	Total
Belgium	7.0	10.5	127.0	144.5	3.9	22.7	87.9	114.5
France	39.7	85.4	390.0	515.1	54.1	131.4	212.3	397.9
Germany	18.9	104.9	302.0	425.8	70.3	115.9	409.9	596.0
Ireland	25.8	105.0	210.5	341.3	8.0	196.9	175.9	380.9
Italy	10.5	58.3	108.4	177.2	4.6	30.4	53.6	88.6
Luxembourg	72.3	50.3	71.1	193.7	18.5	112.3	78.7	209.5
Netherlands	128.7	78.0	243.9	450.6	113.5	71.5	342.0	526.9
Spain	31.1	50.1	131.0	212.1	29.3	39.2	64.6	133.2
Total EU27	**383.3**	**646.0**	**1 739.4**	**2 768.7**	**314.6**	**874.5**	**1 593.9**	**2 783.0**
Norway	2.3	14.6	46.3	63.2	1.3	16.5	41.4	59.2
Switzerland	14.5	43.5	223.2	281.2	31.1	34.3	317.3	382.8
Total EFTA	**18.6**	**62.0**	**285.9**	**366.5**	**32.7**	**51.9**	**363.4**	**448.0**
Total Europe	**495.5**	**771.5**	**2 217.7**	**3 484.7**	**371.3**	**1 017.8**	**2 428.4**	**3 817.5**
Canada	46.9	9.5	69.8	126.2	20.5	36.2	23.9	80.7
USA	212.0	415.2	826.3	1 453.5	167.6	589.4	702.9	1 459.9
Total America	**324.6**	**546.5**	**1 123.1**	**1 994.1**	**203.9**	**661.2**	**1 021.6**	**1 886.7**
Hong Kong	25.4	21.6	26.0	73.0	–	38.5	101.9	140.4
Japan	2.2	101.5	152.8	256.5	25.2	92.3	161.1	278.6
Singapore	6.3	10.9	47.5	64.7	–	21.6	72.1	93.7
Total Asia	**61.6**	**249.3**	**334.7**	**645.7**	**42.7**	**170.0**	**558.4**	**771.2**
Australia	13.4	39.5	34.6	87.5	8.7	19.7	28.3	56.7
Total Australasia and Oceania	**14.1**	**41.8**	**37.5**	**93.5**	**9.1**	**20.8**	**30.1**	**60.0**
South Africa	9.1	5.1	10.6	24.8	0.9	17.8	17.1	35.8
Total Africa	**18.1**	**11.2**	**21.6**	**51.0**	**3.1**	**18.4**	**72.0**	**93.5**
International Organisations	–	11.1	15.6	26.7	–	29.3	8.9	38.2
World Total	**913.9**	**1 693.8**	**3 750.2**	**6 384.6**	**630.2**	**1 917.6**	**4 119.4**	**6 667.2**

10.2 Geographical breakdown of International Investment Position: UK assets
Balance sheets valued at end of year

£ million

		2001	2002	2003	2004	2005	2006	2007
Europe								
European Union (EU)								
Austria	HCZI	15 013	13 839	17 825	21 025	20 199	21 282	23 450
Belgium	A54T	57 216	59 068	72 219	91 158	126 491	113 572	144 470
Bulgaria	HCZU	1 102	364	436	610	937	1 200	1 028
Cyprus	A3OB	2 209	1 648	1 678	1 777	3 902	5 161	7 246
Czech Republic	HDFF	2 642	2 050	2 200	2 076	3 020	3 030	3 845
Denmark	HDRV	18 996	19 550	24 521	35 024	48 299	43 822	50 377
Estonia	HDSA	265	196	238	372	110	79	63
Finland	HDSJ	19 475	16 755	15 625	15 417	19 488	18 589	27 793
France	HDSL	224 478	213 594	233 014	273 314	335 540	439 138	515 113
Germany	HDQJ	276 726	267 203	297 359	326 962	342 911	360 297	425 815
Greece	HDSM	17 860	19 957	22 241	25 503	23 542	31 331	38 051
Hungary	HDXA	4 193	4 759	4 582	5 750	5 145	6 333	7 044
Ireland	HDZG	93 637	91 255	120 109	139 794	236 402	271 499	341 285
Italy	HEGT	132 842	127 829	148 566	147 907	157 722	154 004	177 198
Latvia	HFHZ	102	120	70	118	176	380	1 078
Lithuania	HFHY	156	166	117	152	957	65	152
Luxembourg	A5BW	111 247	105 816	147 451	168 171	194 423	144 459	193 684
Malta	A3OC	589	719	956	2 470	536	2 647	4 667
Netherlands	HFID	299 006	307 486	324 626	321 763	313 185	338 565	450 572
Poland	HFII	5 336	6 224	7 279	7 144	7 556	7 253	9 084
Portugal	HFIJ	19 872	20 653	25 843	22 904	27 197	26 110	27 761
Romania	HFIX	558	714	1 032	1 564	2 131	1 832	3 158
Slovak Republic	HFJI	436	592	817	386	657	552	1 094
Slovenia	HFJH	496	309	426	631	892	789	1 172
Spain	HDSC	59 757	55 974	85 285	112 645	182 542	192 318	212 144
Sweden	HFJA	50 748	38 078	45 071	51 883	69 078	71 442	83 942
European Central Bank	HBKQ	–	–	–	–	–	–	–
EU Institutions	HBKP	17 654	20 983	21 845	19 356	20 441	21 654	17 424
Total EU27	GB6F	1 432 611	1 395 901	1 621 361	1 795 876	2 143 479	2 277 403	2 768 710
European Free Trade Association (EFTA)								
Iceland	HDZZ	1 128	909	1 519	2 071	3 723	6 094	21 164
Liechtenstein	HFCE	841	819	960	520	652	846	927
Norway	HFIE	17 900	19 290	23 254	28 707	41 319	55 184	63 243
Switzerland	HCZZ	153 198	147 300	171 774	147 533	166 161	148 143	281 195
Total EFTA	HBKW	173 067	168 318	197 507	178 831	211 855	210 267	366 529
Other Europe								
Albania	HBLA	–	–8	1	20	25	27	79
Belarus	HCZX	1	1	1	1	–	29	119
Croatia	HDWZ	635	1 053	1 184	1 153	1 529	1 099	1 158
Russia	HFIY	7 619	8 395	12 058	16 511	39 725	34 396	54 786
Turkey	HFJK	7 004	8 126	6 576	8 423	15 789	19 377	25 323
Ukraine	HFJM	106	167	243	828	3 608	4 134	6 607
Serbia and Montenegro	HFJQ	49	51	37	45	250	272	693
Other	HFIP	83 795	96 939	109 993	129 645	170 058	220 064	260 690
Total Europe	HDRW	1 704 887	1 678 943	1 948 961	2 131 333	2 586 318	2 767 068	3 484 694
Americas								
Argentina	HCPD	5 199	3 108	3 292	3 571	6 774	5 266	6 232
Brazil	HCZW	11 780	9 219	8 810	9 606	12 323	16 048	22 559
Canada	HCZY	45 615	49 275	43 014	42 561	63 631	84 825	126 223
Chile	HDER	3 362	3 401	3 311	3 644	4 659	2 319	2 214
Colombia	HDEZ	2 113	2 656	2 943	2 553	2 815	2 207	2 605
Mexico	HFIB	10 165	7 790	7 961	9 495	14 725	12 187	11 863
United States of America	HFJN	699 158	625 858	716 946	832 034	1 109 879	1 299 727	1 453 486
Uruguay	HFJO	301	324	243	144	389	297	286
Venezuela	HFJP	1 807	1 733	1 077	1 606	3 906	1 572	951
Other Central American Countries	HFIR	106 271	119 271	146 435	192 622	276 452	302 336	361 463
Other	HFIV	912	1 427	1 741	3 342	4 419	4 282	6 264
Total Americas	HDRZ	886 683	824 062	935 773	1 101 178	1 499 972	1 731 066	1 994 146
Asia								
China	HDES	5 943	6 484	7 029	9 181	11 924	14 972	36 219
Hong Kong	HDSN	39 310	30 365	35 746	43 098	56 401	67 617	73 046
India	HDZX	5 541	4 993	6 979	8 681	13 592	16 206	42 667
Indonesia	HDZD	3 038	2 592	2 958	3 237	4 034	4 541	5 245
Iran	HDZY	1 115	1 591	2 496	3 419	4 717	3 294	2 692
Israel	HDZK	1 672	2 301	2 463	2 593	2 735	3 402	3 666
Japan	HEIC	198 151	212 085	212 204	259 585	267 189	235 543	256 527
Malaysia	HFIC	4 941	5 234	5 361	6 658	7 058	7 336	7 893
Pakistan	HFIH	1 228	847	944	1 145	1 399	1 712	2 083
Philippines	HFIG	2 221	2 492	3 316	2 496	3 657	3 532	4 067
Saudi Arabia	HFIZ	6 028	5 830	5 736	4 868	6 910	6 280	13 126
Singapore	HFJG	48 384	39 117	43 991	42 740	46 295	46 105	64 704
South Korea	HEJH	11 502	14 890	17 460	21 184	30 452	26 711	35 054
Taiwan	HFJL	7 460	5 189	11 476	20 531	25 474	20 406	20 742
Thailand	HFJJ	3 054	3 731	4 417	4 679	4 817	4 936	4 948
Residual Gulf Arabian Countries	HFIS	19 999	20 184	20 840	25 915	33 017	33 105	57 317
Other Near & Middle Eastern Countries	HDSG	1 122	1 092	616	1 496	1 602	2 883	3 564
Other	HFIT	5 771	3 834	3 890	3 819	5 766	8 371	12 122
Total Asia	HDSF	366 480	362 851	387 922	465 325	527 039	506 952	645 682
Australasia & Oceania								
Australia	HCZT	44 908	48 186	52 888	57 551	71 676	76 360	87 490
New Zealand	HFIF	5 136	5 971	5 773	6 891	5 305	5 663	5 553
Other	HFIU	368	407	320	304	311	274	430
Total Australasia & Oceania	HDSH	50 412	54 564	58 981	64 746	77 292	82 297	93 473
Africa								
Egypt	HDSB	2 254	1 917	1 520	2 004	3 504	5 536	6 623
Morocco	HFIA	574	323	473	535	651	595	496
South Africa	HFJR	11 357	16 598	18 770	22 850	28 913	22 827	24 802
Other North Africa	HFIW	601	1 428	1 020	1 073	872	1 219	1 623
Other	HFIQ	8 262	7 795	9 047	11 599	13 503	12 820	17 435
Total Africa	HDRY	23 048	28 061	30 830	38 061	47 443	42 997	50 979
International Organisations	HBKR	18 593	21 134	21 230	22 399	23 771	26 272	26 664
Unallocated	G972	26 182	56 794	56 961	65 103	19 747	32 690	62 310
Reserve Assets	LTEB	25 649	25 469	23 794	23 250	24 739	22 931	26 685
World total	HBQA	3 101 934	3 051 878	3 464 452	3 911 395	4 806 321	5 212 273	6 384 633

10.3 Geographical breakdown of International Investment Position: UK liabilities
Balance sheets valued at end of year

£ million

		2001	2002	2003	2004	2005	2006	2007
Europe								
European Union (EU)								
Austria	HFMW	17 268	17 581	18 452	21 578	22 604	26 419	29 650
Belgium	A56Z	53 143	62 333	71 151	88 358	98 801	94 517	114 494
Bulgaria	HFMY	522	513	507	648	1 086	1 443	1 589
Cyprus	A3SB	3 376	3 237	3 102	3 595	6 270	7 883	10 722
Czech Republic	HFNG	3 419	2 175	2 030	2 050	3 521	3 940	4 108
Denmark	HFNJ	21 138	20 075	28 699	36 277	38 632	39 678	58 403
Estonia	HFNO	125	310	232	345	385	396	442
Finland	HFOA	6 025	6 907	11 854	13 596	14 715	16 742	19 747
France	HFOB	162 393	185 427	197 228	243 830	344 672	337 532	397 850
Germany	HFNI	253 307	290 223	349 591	432 617	470 116	507 358	596 040
Greece	HFOD	13 981	17 847	18 814	24 113	33 403	36 237	44 672
Hungary	HFOG	741	1 259	929	1 345	1 799	1 328	1 892
Ireland	HFOI	110 211	133 012	162 583	203 176	269 356	306 731	380 865
Italy	HFOO	69 476	74 606	78 704	81 606	84 082	85 959	88 622
Latvia	HFOX	190	323	254	338	264	281	575
Lithuania	HFOW	104	180	133	293	216	347	474
Luxembourg	A5E4	82 117	83 907	116 495	128 419	146 268	179 913	209 536
Malta	A3SC	1 166	1 379	1 542	1 070	1 868	2 434	7 061
Netherlands	HFPD	200 410	196 011	218 789	253 629	356 637	442 952	526 893
Poland	HFPN	4 500	3 160	3 120	3 960	5 208	5 275	7 119
Portugal	HFPO	6 668	9 682	11 101	12 930	15 985	17 498	19 433
Romania	HFQB	533	422	615	771	1 041	1 395	961
Slovak Republic	HFQH	405	154	559	1 353	996	993	1 175
Slovenia	HFQG	1 008	938	764	255	451	355	599
Spain	HFNR	35 732	45 361	54 600	65 257	83 965	117 991	133 153
Sweden	HFQE	30 084	26 333	32 555	40 701	42 019	48 870	59 967
European Central Bank	HFMP	–	–	–	–	–	–	–
EU Institutions	HFMO	38 386	39 056	40 457	43 309	53 728	57 999	66 922
Total EU27	GB9A	1 116 428	1 222 411	1 424 860	1 705 419	2 098 088	2 342 466	2 782 964
European Free Trade Association (EFTA)								
Iceland	HFOM	488	294	826	1 462	3 219	4 861	3 070
Liechtenstein	HFOU	2 026	2 233	2 213	2 377	2 789	2 363	2 915
Norway	HFPG	16 574	20 341	27 246	28 452	50 061	62 361	59 226
Switzerland	HFNC	231 765	240 193	266 310	256 177	286 101	223 560	382 815
Total EFTA	HFMT	250 853	263 061	296 595	288 468	342 170	293 145	448 026
Other Europe								
Albania	HFMU	89	54	60	92	57	178	154
Belarus	HFNA	71	72	139	231	446	347	792
Croatia	HFOF	849	1 387	1 476	1 547	1 611	1 652	2 366
Russia	HFQC	9 567	13 967	17 348	23 893	55 181	64 233	71 725
Turkey	HFQJ	3 150	2 574	2 620	3 814	6 273	6 561	10 330
Ukraine	HFQL	213	1 262	1 496	2 712	7 464	7 653	9 611
Serbia and Montenegro	HFQP	218	469	360	462	292	982	696
Other	HFPT	212 398	222 075	225 150	268 637	330 909	383 555	490 840
Total Europe	HFNK	1 593 836	1 727 332	1 970 104	2 295 275	2 842 491	3 100 772	3 817 504
America								
Argentina	HFMV	475	256	232	253	375	395	1 824
Brazil	HFMZ	3 293	2 754	4 347	5 582	6 484	5 117	3 005
Canada	HFNB	41 486	35 548	43 058	50 600	59 434	74 484	80 661
Chile	HFND	985	797	1 083	1 211	1 170	2 218	3 694
Colombia	HFNF	1 344	589	818	780	856	1 501	1 970
Mexico	HFPB	5 802	2 645	2 839	2 971	3 676	2 585	7 316
United States of America	HFQM	875 866	746 839	858 407	934 299	1 163 167	1 350 749	1 459 929
Uruguay	HFQN	176	116	806	234	444	305	371
Venezuela	HFQO	1 056	1 040	1 130	1 127	1 400	2 368	3 238
Other Central American Countries	HFPV	119 863	107 560	156 136	197 590	267 348	255 862	320 210
Other	HFPZ	4 084	2 571	2 934	2 903	3 293	3 963	4 458
Total America	HFNN	1 054 430	900 715	1 071 790	1 197 550	1 507 647	1 699 547	1 886 676
Asia								
China	HFNE	8 287	9 407	7 234	10 437	12 406	14 105	24 686
Hong Kong	HFOE	84 118	71 722	80 077	86 840	97 292	100 578	140 393
India	HFOK	7 921	7 849	11 337	17 985	22 424	28 124	13 050
Indonesia	HFOH	3 127	2 847	2 729	2 286	2 312	1 785	2 259
Iran	HFOL	6 130	3 695	3 418	3 252	3 468	3 561	2 184
Israel	HFOJ	6 910	6 451	6 065	6 264	9 189	10 806	8 979
Japan	HFOP	225 644	206 255	178 025	213 901	214 771	224 998	278 596
Malaysia	HFPC	6 160	4 345	4 419	8 078	3 897	7 665	10 658
Pakistan	HFPM	2 254	3 497	3 790	2 720	2 645	3 229	3 986
Philippines	HFPJ	1 209	1 059	594	913	2 279	2 256	4 138
Saudi Arabia	HFQD	16 496	16 071	14 068	16 746	27 964	32 957	62 258
Singapore	HFQF	67 828	68 850	67 144	78 156	78 806	84 803	93 698
South Korea	HFOS	4 316	4 122	5 585	5 310	9 428	6 980	12 708
Taiwan	HFQK	4 217	3 073	7 221	10 423	10 475	7 113	14 682
Thailand	HFQI	4 135	1 348	3 521	3 089	4 985	5 173	8 328
Residual Gulf Arabian Countries	HFPW	39 603	32 233	27 239	33 937	39 341	49 513	70 823
Other Near & Middle Eastern Countries	HFNX	5 301	5 807	6 472	6 591	8 174	8 125	8 908
Other	HFPX	3 893	3 759	4 253	4 896	7 646	9 015	10 837
Total Asia	HFNT	497 549	452 390	433 191	511 824	557 502	600 786	771 171
Australasia & Oceania								
Australia	HFMX	26 538	26 904	32 469	44 814	43 774	44 684	56 681
New Zealand	HFPH	2 644	2 569	2 289	2 665	3 431	2 818	2 941
Other	HFPY	182	181	177	197	259	148	425
Total Australasia & Oceania	HFNZ	29 364	29 654	34 935	47 676	47 464	47 650	60 047
Africa								
Egypt	HFNQ	6 778	6 220	6 462	6 351	11 355	9 592	9 364
Morocco	HFOZ	897	754	831	869	1 625	2 282	1 732
South Africa	HFQQ	19 870	21 719	29 131	32 283	34 333	34 082	35 773
Other North Africa	HFQA	4 583	3 955	4 364	5 537	11 022	15 863	17 340
Other	HFPU	14 711	14 277	13 644	14 349	18 328	23 273	29 313
Total Africa	HFNM	46 839	46 925	54 432	59 389	76 663	85 092	93 522
International Organisations	HFMQ	16 461	14 867	17 150	20 373	27 146	30 986	38 233
World total	HBQB	3 238 479	3 171 883	3 581 602	4 132 087	5 058 913	5 564 833	6 667 153

10.4 Geographical breakdown of International Investment Position: Net
Balance sheets valued at end of year

£ million

		2001	2002	2003	2004	2005	2006	2007
Europe								
European Union (EU)								
Austria	IDBU	−2 255	−3 742	−627	−553	−2 405	−5 137	−6 200
Belgium	A58F	4 073	−3 265	1 068	2 800	27 690	19 055	29 976
Bulgaria	IDBW	580	−149	−71	−38	−149	−243	−561
Cyprus	A3V5	−1 167	−1 589	−1 424	−1 818	−2 368	−2 722	−3 476
Czech Republic	IDCE	−777	−125	170	26	−501	−910	−263
Denmark	IDCH	−2 142	−525	−4 178	−1 253	9 667	4 144	−8 026
Estonia	IDCM	140	−114	6	27	−275	−317	−379
Finland	IDCS	13 450	9 848	3 771	1 821	4 773	1 847	8 046
France	IDCT	62 085	28 167	35 786	29 484	−9 132	101 606	117 263
Germany	IDCG	23 419	−23 020	−52 232	−105 655	−127 205	−147 061	−170 225
Greece	IDCU	3 879	2 110	3 427	1 390	−9 861	−4 906	−6 621
Hungary	IDCX	3 452	3 500	3 653	4 405	3 346	5 005	5 152
Ireland	IDCZ	−16 574	−41 757	−42 544	−63 382	−32 954	−35 232	−39 580
Italy	IDDE	63 366	53 223	69 862	66 301	73 640	68 045	88 576
Latvia	IDDJ	−88	−203	−184	−220	−88	99	503
Lithuania	IDDI	52	−14	−16	−141	741	−282	−322
Luxembourg	A5FI	29 130	21 909	30 956	39 752	48 155	−35 454	−15 852
Malta	A3V6	−577	−660	−586	1 400	−1 332	213	−2 394
Netherlands	IDDN	98 596	111 475	105 837	68 134	−43 452	−104 387	−76 321
Poland	IDDS	836	3 064	4 159	3 184	2 348	1 978	1 965
Portugal	IDDT	13 204	10 971	14 742	9 974	11 212	8 612	8 328
Romania	IDEC	25	292	417	793	1 090	437	2 197
Slovak Republic	IDEI	31	438	258	−967	−339	−441	−81
Slovenia	IDEH	−512	−629	−338	376	441	434	573
Spain	IDCO	24 025	10 613	30 685	47 388	98 577	74 327	78 991
Sweden	IDEF	20 664	11 745	12 516	11 182	27 059	22 572	23 975
European Central Bank	IDBN	–	–	–	–	–	–	–
EU Institutions	IDBM	−20 732	−18 073	−18 612	−23 953	−33 287	−36 345	−49 498
Total EU27	GC25	316 183	173 490	196 501	90 457	45 391	−65 063	−14 254
European Free Trade Association (EFTA)								
Iceland	IDDD	640	615	693	609	504	1 233	18 094
Liechtenstein	IDDH	−1 185	−1 414	−1 253	−1 857	−2 137	−1 517	−1 988
Norway	IDDO	1 326	−1 051	−3 992	255	−8 742	−7 177	4 017
Switzerland	IDCA	−78 567	−92 893	−94 536	−108 644	−119 940	−75 417	−101 620
Total EFTA	IDBR	−77 786	−94 743	−99 088	−109 637	−130 315	−82 878	−81 497
Other Europe								
Albania	IDBS	−89	−62	−59	−72	−32	−151	−75
Belarus	IDBY	−70	−71	−138	−230	−446	−318	−673
Croatia	IDCW	−214	−334	−292	−394	−82	−553	−1 208
Russia	IDED	−1 948	−5 572	−5 290	−7 382	−15 456	−29 837	−16 939
Turkey	IDEK	3 854	5 552	3 956	4 609	9 516	12 816	14 993
Ukraine	IDEM	−107	−1 095	−1 253	−1 884	−3 856	−3 519	−3 004
Serbia and Montenegro	IDEQ	−169	−418	−323	−417	−42	−710	−3
Other	IDDU	−128 603	−125 136	−115 157	−138 992	−160 851	−163 491	−230 150
Total Europe	IDCI	111 051	−48 389	−21 143	−163 942	−256 173	−333 704	−332 810
America								
Argentina	IDBT	4 724	2 852	3 060	3 318	6 399	4 871	4 408
Brazil	IDBX	8 487	6 465	4 463	4 024	5 839	10 931	19 554
Canada	IDBZ	4 129	13 727	−44	−8 039	4 197	10 341	45 562
Chile	IDCB	2 377	2 604	2 228	2 433	3 489	101	−1 480
Colombia	IDCD	769	2 067	2 125	1 773	1 959	706	635
Mexico	IDDL	4 363	5 145	5 122	6 524	11 049	9 602	4 547
United States of America	IDEN	−176 708	−120 981	−141 461	−102 265	−53 288	−51 022	−6 443
Uruguay	IDEO	125	208	−563	−90	−55	−8	−85
Venezuela	IDEP	751	693	−53	479	2 506	−796	−2 287
Other Central American Countries	IDDW	−13 592	11 711	−9 701	−4 968	9 104	46 474	41 253
Other	IDEA	−3 172	−1 144	−1 193	439	1 126	319	1 806
Total America	IDCL	−167 747	−76 653	−136 017	−96 372	−7 675	31 519	107 470
Asia								
China	IDCC	−2 344	−2 923	−205	−1 256	−482	867	11 533
Hong Kong	IDCV	−44 808	−41 357	−44 331	−43 742	−40 891	−32 961	−67 347
India	IDDB	−2 380	−2 856	−4 358	−9 304	−8 832	−11 918	29 617
Indonesia	IDCY	−89	−255	229	951	1 722	2 756	2 986
Iran	IDDC	−5 015	−2 104	−922	167	1 249	−267	508
Israel	IDDA	−5 238	−4 150	−3 602	−3 671	−6 454	−7 404	−5 313
Japan	IDDF	−27 493	5 830	34 179	45 684	52 418	10 545	−22 069
Malaysia	IDDM	−1 219	889	942	−1 420	3 161	−329	−2 765
Pakistan	IDDR	−1 026	−2 650	−2 846	−1 575	−1 246	−1 517	−1 903
Philippines	IDDQ	1 012	1 433	2 722	1 583	1 378	1 276	−71
Saudi Arabia	IDEE	−10 468	−10 241	−8 332	−11 878	−21 054	−26 677	−49 132
Singapore	IDEG	−19 444	−29 733	−23 153	−35 416	−32 511	−38 698	−28 994
South Korea	IDDG	7 186	10 768	11 875	15 874	21 024	19 731	22 346
Taiwan	IDEL	3 243	2 116	4 255	10 108	14 999	13 293	6 060
Thailand	IDEJ	−1 081	2 383	896	1 590	−168	−237	−3 380
Residual Gulf Arabian Countries	IDDX	−19 604	−12 049	−6 399	−8 022	−6 324	−16 408	−13 506
Other Near & Middle Eastern Countries	IDCQ	−4 179	−4 715	−5 856	−5 095	−6 572	−5 242	−5 344
Other	IDDY	1 878	75	−363	−1 077	−1 880	−644	1 285
Total Asia	IDCP	−131 069	−89 539	−45 269	−46 499	−30 463	−93 834	−125 489
Australasia & Oceania								
Australia	IDBV	18 370	21 282	20 419	12 737	27 902	31 676	30 809
New Zealand	IDDP	2 492	3 402	3 484	4 226	1 874	2 845	2 612
Other	IDDZ	186	226	143	107	52	126	5
Total Australasia & Oceania	IDCR	21 048	24 910	24 046	17 070	29 828	34 647	33 426
Africa								
Egypt	IDCN	−4 524	−4 303	−4 942	−4 347	−7 851	−4 056	−2 741
Morocco	IDDK	−323	−431	−358	−334	−974	−1 687	−1 236
South Africa	IDER	−8 513	−5 121	−10 361	−9 433	−5 420	−11 255	−10 971
Other North Africa	IDEB	−3 982	−2 527	−3 344	−4 464	−10 150	−14 644	−15 717
Other	IDDV	−6 449	−6 482	−4 597	−2 750	−4 825	−10 453	−11 878
Total Africa	IDCK	−23 791	−18 864	−23 602	−21 328	−29 220	−42 095	−42 543
International Organisations	IDBO	2 132	6 267	4 080	2 026	−3 375	−4 714	−11 569
World total	IDBP	−136 545	−120 005	−117 150	−220 692	−252 592	−352 560	−282 520

Supplementary information

Part 4

Balance of payments and the relationship to national accounts

This section is intended to help users of the Pink Book gain a better understanding of how the data fit within the broader economic accounts framework. It can be read as a stand-alone, although it makes several references to Blue Book tables and so readers are advised to have access to these if possible.

Introduction

Conceptually, the balance of payments, including the international investment position, form part of the broader system of the UK national accounts. The national accounts provide a comprehensive and systematic set of statistics for the UK economy, with information on economic transactions, other changes in the levels of assets and liabilities, and the levels of assets and liabilities themselves. The UK national accounts have generally been compiled according to the *European System of Accounts (ESA95)*. Linkages between the UK balance of payments and national accounts are reinforced by the fact that the UK balance of payments are compiled at the same time as the national accounts, as a component of the sector accounts and using many common data sources.

The national accounts are a closed system in which both ends of every transaction involving a resident economic entity are recorded. A set of accounts is introduced to capture transactions that involve economic relationships with non-resident entities. These accounts are known as the 'rest of the world accounts' and are presented from the perspective of non-residents rather than residents. Consequently, entries in the balance of payments (which show transactions from the perspective of residents) are reversed in the presentation of the rest of the world accounts. The accounts for resident entities, which consist of the production, income and accumulation accounts, are described in more detail below.

Two important accounting differences occur when comparing the balance of payments and the national accounts. First, each transaction is recorded twice in the balance of payments (double entry) and four times in the national accounts (quadruple entry). This is because in the balance of payments the activity of only one transactor is recorded, that of the resident entity (with a non-resident entity), whereas in the national accounts the activity of both transactors is recorded (that is, the activity of either two residents or a resident and a non-resident). Second, in the balance of payments, transactions are shown from the perspective of the resident entity; whereas in the national accounts, transactions are shown from the perspective of the resident in the production, income and accumulation accounts, and from the perspective of the non-resident in the rest of the world account.

Relationship between national accounts and balance of payments concepts and classifications

Because the balance of payments, including the international investment position, forms an integral part of the national accounts, there is complete concordance between them in concept and classification, although the extent of cross-classifications may differ between the two systems.

The balance of payments and national accounts identify resident producers and consumers identically, and both invoke the same concepts of economic territory and centre of economic interest. Both use market prices as the primary concept of valuation of transactions and they adopt identical concepts of accrual accounting. The systems use identical conversion procedures to convert transactions which take place in foreign currency, to UK currency.

While for some purposes it would be convenient if classifications used in the rest of the world accounts and the balance of payments accounts were identical, differences between the two are justifiable because on occasion they serve different purposes. For example, in the balance of payments financial account, precedence is given to classification of transactions by type of investment (that is, direct, portfolio, reserve assets, other), whereas in the rest of the world financial account the instrument of investment is the primary classification. More important is the fact that concepts, definitions and classifications are consistent between the two systems.

The production, income and capital accounts of the national accounts

The national accounts tables reflect the basic aspects of economic life (production, income, consumption, accumulation and wealth). For many analysts, Gross Domestic Product (GDP) is the key economic aggregate as it measures the total value added for the UK economy in any period. GDP may be measured as:

- The total value of output less the cost of goods and services used in the production process (intermediate consumption). This is referred to as the *output (or production) approach*

- The value of income accruing from the production process to each of the factors of production (plus net taxes on production and imports). This is referred to as the *income approach*

- Total final expenditure on goods and services during the period, referred to as the *expenditure approach*

Conceptually these measures are equal, but because different and imperfect data sources are used to measure each approach the measures may differ in practice. This difference is reflected in the statistical discrepancy item. The national accounts are regularly benchmarked to balanced annual supply and use (input-output) tables. This ensures that, except for the latest year, the three measures of GDP are equal on an annual basis, though there will still be a statistical discrepancy between the quarterly estimates based on the three approaches.

Blue Book Table 1.2 presents the Gross Domestic Product Account for the whole economy, the derivation of GDP using the expenditure approach and the income approach. Table 1.7.1, the Production Account, shows the derivation of GDP using the production approach.

- The expenditure-based measure of GDP is derived as final consumption expenditure by government and households, plus investment in fixed capital formation and changes in inventories, plus exports minus imports of goods and services, plus (or minus) the statistical discrepancy. Exports and imports are the same as the balance of payments components, exports and imports of goods and services

- The income-based measure of GDP shows the components of factor income, namely compensation of employees, gross operating surplus and mixed incomes, plus taxes less subsidies on production and imports

- The production-based measure of GDP is shown as total gross output at purchasers' prices less intermediate consumption

For the purpose of discussion here, all values are in current prices.

Blue Book Table 1.7.3 presents the National Income and Use of Income Account, showing the derivation of gross national income, gross disposable income and use of gross disposable income. Gross national income is equivalent to GDP plus primary income receivable from non-residents, less primary income payable to non-residents. These primary income items are the same as the balance of payments income components which are used in the derivation of gross saving (gross disposable income less consumption) and net saving (gross saving less consumption of fixed capital). Table 1.7.3 illustrates how the various balance of payments income and current transfers components affect the nation's saving. To derive gross disposable income, net secondary income receivable from non-residents is added to gross national income; secondary income items are equivalent to the net current transfer components in the balance of payments. The segment of Table 1.7.3 dealing with use of gross disposable income shows the derivation of gross saving (gross disposable income less consumption) and net saving (gross saving less consumption of fixed capital).

Blue Book Table 1.7.7, the National Capital Account, shows the link between gross saving and net lending/ borrowing (to/from the rest of the world). The latter is derived as gross saving plus net capital transfers from non-residents less investment in fixed capital and inventories and the net acquisitions of non-produced, non-financial assets from non-residents. The items net capital transactions and net acquisitions of non-produced non-financial assets are both sourced from the balance of payments capital account. The capital account was introduced into the balance of payments to emphasise this clear relationship between the balance of payments and the national accounts.

The financial account and balance sheet of the national accounts

Net lending/borrowing is also the balance shown in *Blue Book* Table 1.7.8, the Financial Account. The financial account shows how the net lending/borrowing is financed through a combination of transactions in financial assets and liabilities. As Table 1.7.8 is a summary account for the economy, transactions between resident sectors are offset and eliminated. Therefore Table 1.7.8 is also equivalent to the balance of payments financial account. However, there are some important differences in classification emphasis between Table 1.7.8 and the balance of payments financial account. In Table 1.7.8 the emphasis is on instrument of investment (such as currency and deposits, securities, loans, and equity), while in the balance of payments financial account, the emphasis is on type of investment (direct investment, portfolio investment, and other investment). Both presentations give emphasis to the asset and liability classification.

It is worth noting that, if Table 1.7.8 were expanded to include the financial transactions taking place between the various resident sectors, it would show the full financial account for the economy (which is published monthly in *Financial Statistics* and quarterly in *UK Economic Accounts*).

Blue Book Table 1.7.9, the National Balance Sheet, shows the UK's non-financial assets (fixed assets, inventories, tangible and intangible non-produced assets such as land and copyright), financial assets, and liabilities and net worth at the end of the period. As Table 1.7.9 is a summary account for the economy, financial assets and liabilities only measure financial claims by residents on non-residents and liabilities by residents to non-residents. In other words, in this table the financial assets and liabilities components are the international investment position statement for the UK. Claims and liabilities between resident sectors have been offset and eliminated. Again, there are some important classification differences between Table 1.7.9 and the international investment position statement. In Table 1.7.9 the emphasis is on instrument of investment, while in the international investment position statement the emphasis is on type of investment. Both presentations give emphasis to the asset and liability classification.

Rest of the world accounts of the national accounts

There are five accounts for the rest of the world in the national accounts shown in the *Blue Book*. These are:

- Table 7.1.0, the External account of goods and services
- Table 7.1.2, the External account of primary incomes and current transfers
- Table 7.1.7, the External capital account
- Table 7.1.8, the External Financial Account
- Table 7.1.9, the External Balance Sheet Accounts

The External Financial Account is published quarterly in *UK Economic Accounts*. As mentioned earlier, these accounts are required to close the system of national accounts and, while essentially the same as the balance of payments accounts and international investment position statement, they are compiled from the perspective of the non-resident transactor. Table 7.1.2 is essentially the current account of the balance of payments, Table 7.1.7 the capital account, Table 7.1.8 the financial account, and Table 7.1.9 the international investment position. The reader should be able to readily identify the counterpart entries in all of these tables.

Transactions with the EU

Blue Book Table 12.1 shows UK official transactions with institutions of the EU from a UK national accounts perspective. It has been recreated in the *Pink Book* as Table 9.9 using balance of payments terminology.

The Pink Book: 2009 edition

Methodological notes

Trade in goods (Chapter 2)

Introduction

The IMF *Balance of Payments Manual,* 5th edition (BPM5) defines trade in goods as covering general merchandise, goods for processing, repairs on goods, goods procured in ports by carriers, and non-monetary gold.

General merchandise (with some exceptions) refers to moveable goods for which real or imputed changes of ownership occur between UK residents and the rest of the world.

Goods for processing: this covers goods that are exported or imported for processing on the basis of a contract and for a fee, where there is no change of ownership. There is a corresponding import or export (respectively) when the goods return to the originator. The inclusion of these transactions on a gross basis is an exception to the change of ownership principle. The value of the good before and after processing is recorded. This is included in total trade in goods but cannot be separately identified.

Repairs on goods: this covers repairs that involve work performed by residents on movable goods owned by non-residents (or vice versa). Examples of such goods are ships, aircraft and other transport equipment. The value recorded is the value of the repairs (fee paid or received) rather than the value of the goods before and after repair.

Goods procured in ports: this covers goods such as fuels, provisions, stores and supplies procured by UK resident carriers abroad or by non-resident carriers in the UK.

Non-monetary gold: this is defined as all gold not held as reserve assets (monetary gold) by the authorities. Non-monetary gold can be subdivided into gold held as a store of value and other (industrial) gold – for further information see the Glossary.

Coverage and other adjustments

The balance of payments statistics of trade in goods compiled by the Office for National Statistics (ONS) are derived principally from data published by HM Revenue & Customs (HMRC) on the physical goods exported from and imported to the UK. However, this information is on a different basis to that required for balance of payments statistics. In order to conform to the IMF definitions, ONS has to make various adjustments to include certain transactions which are not reported to HMRC and to exclude certain transactions which are reported to them but where there is no change of ownership. In addition, the value required for balance of payments purposes is the value of goods at the point of export (that is, the customs border of the exporting country) rather than the value of goods as they arrive in the UK. Therefore, the freight and insurance costs of transporting the goods to the UK needs to be deducted from the values recorded by HMRC. Table 2.4 summarises this transition onto a balance of payments basis for each of the last 11 years.

Overseas trade statistics compiled by HM Revenue & Customs (HMRC)

Statistics of the UK's overseas trade in goods have been collected for over 300 years by HMRC, formerly HM Customs and Excise (HMCE). Since 1993 these data comprise statistics of UK imports from and exports to countries outside the EU and statistics on trade with other EU member states collected via the Intrastat survey. Data are compiled from declarations made to HMRC by importers, exporters or their agents AND statistics of UK arrivals (imports) from and dispatches (exports) to other member states of the EU compiled from the Intrastat returns submitted by traders or their agents to HMRC.

Prior to 1993 statistics of UK imports from and exports to all countries in the world were compiled from declarations made to HMRC by importers, exporters or their agents.

Information on trade with EU countries

The Intrastat system has applied since 1993, with minor variations, in all EU member states. In the UK all VAT registered businesses are required to complete two additional boxes on their VAT returns, which are normally submitted quarterly. These show the total value of exports of goods to customers in other member states (dispatches) and the total value of imports of goods from suppliers in other member states (arrivals).

Traders whose annual value of arrivals or dispatches exceed given thresholds are required to provide an Intrastat declaration each month, showing full details of their arrivals and dispatches during the month. These thresholds are reviewed annually. For the calendar year 2009, the thresholds were £270,000, both for arrivals and for dispatches. These detailed Intrastat declarations cover approximately 97 per cent of the value of trade.

Link with VAT

The information on the VAT returns serves three purposes:

- to establish a register of traders and to determine which exceed the thresholds
- to provide a cross-check with the Intrastat declarations, and
- to provide an estimate of the total value of trade carried out by traders below the Intrastat thresholds

Traders not registered for VAT and private individuals who move goods within the EU have no obligations under the Intrastat system and their trade is therefore not included in the statistics. Examples of commodities where this trade can be significant are works of art and racehorses.

Below threshold trade

The total values of arrivals and dispatches by traders below the Intrastat thresholds are available from their VAT returns, although the coverage is slightly different. The figures are included in the month in which the VAT return is received by HMRC, although the VAT return itself may relate to a period of more than one month. Detailed information on below threshold trade is not available from the VAT data. However, it has been established that the pattern of that trade before the Intrastat system was introduced on 1 January 1993 was similar to that of traders just above the thresholds. Thus estimates enabling detailed allocations of below threshold trade can be made on this basis by HMRC.

Late response

Traders who have a legal responsibility to provide Intrastat declarations are required to do so by the end of the calendar month following the month to which the declaration relates. However, where traders have failed to provide returns to Intrastat by the due date, estimates of the total value of such trade are included. These are based on the trade reported by these traders in a previous period, and the growth rate since that period experienced by comparable traders who have provided returns for the current month.

Late declarations of trade with EU countries are subsequently incorporated into the month's figures to which they relate with a corresponding reassessment of the initial estimates for late response.

The methodology used to collect EU (Intrastat) data on natural gas and electricity was amended by the Commission of the European Communities (EC regulation no 1982/2004). As a result, from January 2005, HM Revenue & Customs (HMRC) has changed to collecting information relating to the trade in natural gas and electricity directly from the pipeline and grid operators. This has removed the need for individual companies to submit Intrastat (EU) import and export declarations for these goods. The new methodology records the physical flow of natural gas and electricity between the UK and the last country at the point the goods cross the border into the UK. Value data are estimated using the relevant market prices for gas and electricity.

Information on trade with non-EU countries

In general the figures for trade with non-EU countries show the trade as declared by

Methodological notes

The Pink Book: 2009 edition

importers and exporters or their agents and for which documentation has been received and processed by HMRC during the month.

Importers are usually required to present a Customs declaration before they can obtain Customs clearance and remove the goods. The great majority of imports are cleared immediately by a computerised system. Furthermore the import statistics include documents received by HMRC up to the third working day after the end of the month. Therefore the import figures correspond fairly closely to goods actually imported during the calendar month. Generally speaking about 90 per cent by value and 85 per cent by number of all entries relate to the calendar month with the bulk of the remainder relating to the immediately preceding month.

Under the procedures for the control of exports, the principle is the same – namely that goods cannot be cleared for export until a Customs declaration has been made. Traders can, if they wish, submit a simplified declaration so that the goods can be exported, which has to be followed within 14 days after date of shipment with a complete export declaration. Moreover the processing of these complete export documents begins three working days before the end of the calendar month (two working days for December). Thus the export statistics compiled for a month (which are based on the date of receipt of the complete export documents) do not correspond with goods actually shipped in the calendar month. Generally both in terms of the value and the number of documents, 70 per cent relates to the calendar month with the bulk of the remaining 30 per cent relating to the immediately preceding month.

HMRC's New Export System (NES), which replaced manual (paper) Customs declarations with electronic submissions, requires electronic messages from the trade once the goods have been exported in order to provide the departure date. The new system has led to greater efficiency; improving processing and thereby speeding up the flow of information. This means that, in terms of the value of trade, the proportion allocated to the correct month has increased from September 2003 onwards.

Basis of valuation

For statistical purposes the UK adopts the valuation bases recommended in the *International Merchandise Trade Statistics Concepts & Definitions* published by the United Nations.

The valuation of exports (dispatches) is on a free on board (f.o.b.) basis, that is, the cost of goods to the purchaser abroad, including:

- packaging
- inland and coastal transport in the UK
- dock dues
- loading charges
- all other costs such as profits, charges and expenses (for example, insurance) accruing up to the point where the goods are deposited on board the exporting vessel or aircraft or at the land boundary of Northern Ireland

The valuation of imports (arrivals) is on a cost, insurance and freight (c.i.f.) basis including:

- the cost of the goods
- charges for freight and insurance
- all other related expenses in moving the goods to the point of entry into the UK (but excluding any duty or tax chargeable in the UK)

When goods are re-imported after process or repair abroad, the value includes the cost of the process or repair as well as the value of the goods when exported.

Arrivals from and dispatches to EU countries

As part of the simplification procedure to reduce the burden on business, in the UK most traders are permitted to provide a valuation for trade in goods with EU countries based on the invoice value. Large traders in the calendar year 2009, those who have more than £16 million of trade in the year, are required to supply information on their delivery terms. Regular sample surveys to all traders are conducted by HMRC to establish conversion factors to adjust the invoice values to produce the valuation basis required for statistical purposes. Separate factors are imputed for a range of different delivery terms and for trade with each member state.

The value recorded for arrivals and dispatches includes any duties or levies that have been applied to goods originating in non-EU countries but which have since cleared EU Customs procedures in one EU country prior to moving onto other EU countries.

Imports from non-EU countries

The statistical value of imports of goods subject to duty is the same as the value for Customs purposes. This value is arrived at by the use of specific methods of valuation in the following order of preference:

- the transaction value of the imported goods (that is, the price paid or payable on the goods)
- the transaction value of identical goods
- the transaction value of similar goods
- the 'deductive method' – value derived from the selling price in the country of importation
- computed value based on the built-up cost of the imported goods

Imported goods are valued at the point where the goods are introduced into the Customs territory of the EU. This means that costs for delivery of the imported goods to that point have to be included in the Customs value.

For all other goods (that is, goods free or exempted from duty and goods subject to a specific duty) the statistical value is determined in relation to the point at which the goods enter the UK.

An amount expressed in foreign currency is converted to sterling by the importer using a system of 'period rates of exchange' published by HMRC. These rates are normally operative for a four weekly period unless there is a significant movement in the exchange rate.

Treatment of taxes

As described above, the value of all goods moving into and out of the UK is based on the transaction value recorded for Customs purposes or, in the case of trade in goods with EU countries, the invoice or contract value. In line with this principle, the values recorded exclude VAT. For trade in goods with non-EU countries, all other taxes such as duties and levies applied to goods after arrival in the UK are excluded. For trade in goods with EU countries, the value recorded for imports and exports includes any duties or levies that have been applied to goods originating in non-EU countries but which have since cleared Customs procedures prior to moving onto other EU countries. However excise duties are excluded from the value recorded for trade.

Balance of payments statistics for trade compiled by ONS

Table 2.4 summarises the transition from trade in goods statistics on an Overseas Trade Statistics basis (compiled and published by HMRC) to those on a Balance of Payments basis (compiled by ONS).

Valuation adjustments

Freight: the cost of freight services for the sea legs of dry cargo imports is estimated by applying freight rates (derived from the rates for a large sample of individual commodities imported from various countries) to tonnages of goods arriving by sea. For the land legs, estimates of freight rates per tonne-kilometre for different commodities and estimated distances are used. Estimates of rail freight through the Channel Tunnel are estimated from data provided by Le Shuttle and freight operators. The cost of freight on imports arriving by air is derived from information on the earnings of UK airlines on UK imports and the respective tonnages landed by UK and foreign airlines at UK airports. Pending investigations of an alternative methodology the cost of freight and insurance on oil and gas imports is projected from data formerly supplied by the Department of Trade and Industry.

Sources: tonnages from HMRC; information on freight rates from Chamber of Shipping, Civil Aviation Authority and road hauliers; information from Eurotunnel.

Insurance: the cost of insurance premiums on non-oil imports is estimated as a fixed percentage of the value of imports.

Source: ONS estimate.

Coverage adjustments

Second-hand ships: to include purchases and sales of second-hand ships which are excluded from the Overseas Trade Statistics.

Source: inquiries to UK ship owners conducted by the Department for Transport until late 2005. Estimates are now made by ONS where possible.

New ships delivered abroad: to include deliveries of new ships built abroad for UK owners while the vessel is still in a foreign port.

Source: inquiries to UK ship owners conducted by the Department for Transport until late 2005. Data now provided by HMRC are when the change of ownership/sale takes place.

North Sea installations: to include goods (including drilling rigs) directly exported from and imported to the UK production sites in the North Sea. This adjustment is also used when there is a redistribution of the resources of fields which lie in both UK and non-UK territorial waters (for example, the Frigg, Murchison and Statfjord). In these circumstances the contribution to (or reimbursement of) a proportion of the development costs has been treated as a purchase (or sale) of fixed assets at the date of the re-determination and appears as an adjustment to imports (exports) of goods.

Source: ONS inquiries to the petroleum and natural gas industry.

NAAFI: to exclude goods exported by the Navy, Army and Air Force Institute for the use of UK forces abroad since these are regarded as sales to UK residents.

Source: quarterly returns from NAAFI.

Goods not changing ownership: the Overseas Trade Statistics exclude temporary trade (that is, goods that are to be returned to the original country within two years and there is no change of ownership). However, goods may well have originally been recorded as 'genuine' trade but which are subsequently returned to the original country. Examples of these 'returned goods' are goods traded on a 'sale or return' basis, goods damaged in transit and returned for replacement or repair, and contractor's plant. The same amount is deducted from both imports and exports for the month in which the return movement is declared to Customs.

Source: HMRC (non-EU trade in goods identified by reference to Customs Procedure codes (CPCs) and by 'Nature of Transaction Code' on Intrastat submissions).

Gold: trade in gold (that is, gold bullion, gold coin, unwrought or semi-manufactured gold and scrap) is reported to HMRC but it is excluded from the statistics of total exports and imports published in the Overseas Trade Statistics. However, trade in ores and concentrates and finished manufactures of gold (for example, jewellery) are included in total exports and imports.

For balance of payments purposes, all trade in non-monetary gold should be included under trade in goods. Non-monetary gold is defined as all gold not held as reserve assets (monetary gold) by the authorities. Non-monetary gold can be subdivided into gold held as a store of value and other (industrial) gold. The UK currently makes adjustments to include industrial gold. In exports, the adjustment reflects the value added in refining gold and producing proof coins. In imports, the adjustment reflects the value of gold used in finished manufactures (such as jewellery and dentistry).

Within the transactions of the London Bullion Market, the UK cannot currently distinguish between monetary gold and non-monetary gold held as a store of value. Accordingly, the UK has obtained an exemption from adopting IMF recommendations, as specified in BPM5 and for the time being these transactions are included in the Financial Account.

The treatment of non-monetary gold is being reviewed as part of the worldwide process to revise the IMF *Balance of Payments Manual*. UK BoP will continue current practice until the treatments defined in the revised manual are implemented.

Source: ONS estimate.

Letter post: to include exports by letter post which are not included in the Overseas Trade Statistics.

Sources: books – ONS estimate based on historic information from publishers and booksellers; other items – ONS estimate based on historic sample inquiry made by the former Post Office.

Additions and alterations to ships: to include work carried out abroad on UK-owned ships and work carried out in UK yards on foreign-owned ships.

Sources: Inquiries to UK ship owners conducted by the Department for Transport, (imports) until late 2005, then HMRC data (exports).

Repairs to aircraft: to include the value of repairs carried out in the UK on foreign-owned aircraft.

Source: ONS estimate.

Goods procured in ports: to include fuels, provisions, stores and supplies purchased for commercial use in ships, aircraft and vehicles. (Estimates of goods dispatched are recorded by HMRC.)

Sources: Chamber of Shipping and Civil Aviation Authority for goods procured in foreign ports by UK transport companies (imports); UK oil companies, Civil Aviation Authority, BAA, municipal airports and port authorities for goods procured in UK ports by overseas transport companies (exports).

Smuggling of alcohol and tobacco: Customs provide volume figures for smuggled goods entering the UK based on published estimates of revenue loss and revenue evasion through smuggling. This information is supplemented by information on the average prices for alcohol and tobacco goods in France and Belgium from the published sources of the statistical and banking institutions in those countries in order to estimate the value of smuggled alcohol and tobacco entering the UK.

Sources: HMRC, INSEE and National Bank of Belgium.

Territorial coverage adjustment: for the purposes of the Overseas Trade Statistics, 'UK' is defined as Great Britain, Northern Ireland, the Isle of Man, the Channel Islands and the Continental Shelf (UK part). Therefore the Overseas Trade Statistics exclude trade between these different parts of the UK but include their trade with other countries.

For balance of payments purposes the Channel Islands and the Isle of Man are not considered part of the UK economic territory. Adjustments are made to exports to include UK exports to those islands and to exclude their exports to other countries; and to imports to include UK imports from those islands and to exclude their imports from other countries.

Source: ONS estimate.

Other adjustments

Diamonds: much of the world's trade in rough (uncut) diamonds is controlled from London by the Diamond Trading Company, part of De Beers. Prior to 2001, in order not to distort the trade statistics, all imports into and exports from the UK of uncut diamonds which remain in the ownership of foreign principles are excluded from the Overseas Trade Statistics by HMRC. In addition the value of diamonds imported into the UK can be reassessed after the diamonds have been cleared by Customs. Prior to 2001, this adjustment reflects these changes in valuation. From 2001 the procedure for recording movements of diamonds was changed so that all trade was included in the Overseas Trade Statistics by HMRC. From 2001, this adjustment removes movements of diamonds where no change of ownership has taken place.

Source: Diamond Trading Company.

Adjustments to imports for the impact of VAT Missing Trader Intra-Community (MTIC) fraud: VAT missing trader intra-community fraud is a systematic, criminal attack on the VAT system, which has been detected in many EU member states. In essence, fraudsters obtain VAT registration to acquire goods VAT-free from other member states. They then sell on the goods at VAT inclusive prices and disappear without paying over the VAT from their customers to the tax authorities. The fraud is often carried out very quickly, with the fraudsters disappearing by the time the tax authorities follow up the registration with their regular assurance activities.

Acquisition fraud is where the goods are imported from the EU into the UK by a trader who then goes missing without completing a VAT return or Intrastat declaration. The 'missing trader' therefore has a VAT-free supply of goods, as they make no payment of the VAT monies due on the goods. The trader sells the goods to a buyer in the UK and the goods are available on the home market for consumption.

Carousel fraud is similar to acquisition fraud in the early stages, but the goods are not sold for consumption on the home market. Rather, they are sold through a series of companies in the UK and then re-exported to another country. Goods may be imported and exported several times, hence the goods moving in a circular pattern or 'carousel'.

The VAT system (and therefore the Intrastat collection of trade statistics) picks up the exports of any 'carouselled' goods, but does not always pick up the associated import at the time the carouselled goods entered the UK. As a consequence, UK import statistics had been under reported.

Originally, most carousel chains only involved EU member states. From the beginning of 2004, there was an increase in carousel chains that involve non-EU countries, for example, Dubai and Switzerland. However, the MTIC trade adjustments are added to the EU import estimates derived from Intrastat returns as it is this part of the trading chain that is not recorded. Changes to the pattern of trading associated with MTIC fraud can therefore make it difficult to analyse trade by commodity group and by country. In particular, adjustments affect trade in capital goods and intermediate goods – these categories include mobile phones and computer components (now covered by the UK's reverse charge derogation).

HMRC estimates for the impact of MTIC on the trade statistics. The method used relies heavily on information uncovered during HMRC's operational activity and as such it cannot be detailed for risk of prejudicing current activity, including criminal investigations and prosecutions and more generally undermining HMRC's ability to tackle the fraud effectively. The method specifically excludes adjustments for the acquisition variant of the fraud which cannot be quantified at present. HMRC regularly reviews the methodology for producing the estimates of the impact on the trade statistics to take account of mutations in the fraud. Estimates may change as the analysis of the fraud continues. The UK is the first member state to make adjustments in their trade statistics for this type of fraud.

Source: HMRC estimate.

Adjustment for under-recording and for currency and other valuation errors: these adjustments compensate for the following types of error:

- failure on the part of traders or their agents to submit details of shipments
- incorrect valuations recorded
- declarations wrongly given in foreign currency instead of sterling

Regular reviews show the adjustments for non-EU trade remaining broadly constant over time. Those for EU trade have reduced since the early days of the Intrastat system. The adjustments, expressed as percentages of total trade excluding oil and erratics, are shown in Table 1.

Adjustments to estimates for late response: a review of the introduction of the Intrastat system carried out in 1994 identified a number of issues in the initial monthly estimates of trade with EU countries provided by HMRC. The following describes the adjustments made by ONS to cope with these difficulties.

The HMRC method of estimation for late response relies on linking the values of trade reported by traders in the current period with previous periods. Issues can arise when traders change their VAT registration (perhaps as a result of an internal reorganisation, mergers or sales) or when a trader starts submitting returns for the first time. If the trader then becomes a late responder there may be no history of previous trade upon which to base an estimate. The current HMRC adjustments make an allowance for this, but recent changes in the overall trader profile, with an increasing proportion of smaller traders, means the current methodology needs to be revised. In the meantime, ONS and HMRC have agreed that ONS makes an initial monthly adjustment of +£30 million to both exports and imports (reducing to zero over the following two months).

Furthermore, some traders may submit first declarations for a month that do not include all their trade in that month. Later declarations are then received for the rest of their trade. The pattern of receipt at HMRC of these partial returns is analysed to enable ONS to make initial adjustments to both exports and imports to anticipate these later declarations. These initial adjustments are progressively reduced in subsequent months as late declarations are processed.

Currently the profile of these adjustments is as shown in Table 2.

When Intrastat was introduced it was envisaged that the vast majority of declarations in respect of any particular month would be made within six months of the end of that month. As a consequence HMRC computer programs were designed to recalculate its initial estimates for late response for six months after those estimates first appear in the Overseas Trade Statistics. However the reality is that some declarations (around half a per cent) are still being received and processed after that six month period. These are being included as additions to the value of reported trade with no corresponding reduction in the value of monthly estimated trade (until the annual HMRC closedown of the trade year). ONS therefore, in order to eliminate this element of double counting on a monthly basis, makes a negative adjustment to the value of estimated trade equal to the value of these late amendments. Note that where the value of late amendments exceeds the value of estimated trade the level of estimated trade is set to zero.

Source: ONS estimate.

Price and volume indices

Any difference between time periods in the total value of trade reflects changes in prices as well as changes in the levels of the underlying economic activity (for example, the physical amounts of goods exported or imported). Separation of these changes greatly enhances the interpretation of the data and, for this reason, ONS compiles separate data measuring changes in price and changes in volume. These data are presented in index number form.

Classifications and definitions

The Overseas Trade Statistics (OTS), on which the trade data are based, have been compiled under the United Nations Standard International Trade Classification Revision 4 (SITC R4) from January 2007. However, the data have been converted back to SITC R3 for publication in order to help users to compare data over time. There are some discontinuities at detailed levels, particularly between capital and intermediate goods where some products are allocated from January 2007 to intermediate goods rather than capital goods as done previously. It is also possible that volume and price changes between 2006 and 2007 may be less reliable than usual.

References

Aggregate estimates of trade in goods, seasonally adjusted and on a balance of payments basis, are published monthly by ONS in a Statistical Bulletin (previously known as a First Release). More detailed figures are available from the Time Series Data Service and are also contained in the *Monthly Review of External Trade Statistics* (Business Monitor MM24). This is available, free of charge, in electronic format as a PDF on the Office for National Statistics website.

The latest *UK Trade Statistical Bulletin* can be found at: www.statistics.gov.uk/StatBase/Product.asp?vlnk=1119

The *Monthly Review of External Trade Statistics*, previously published as MM24, can be found at: www.statistics.gov.uk/StatBase/Product.asp?vlnk=613

An article entitled 'UK visible trade statistics – the Intrastat system' was published in *Economic Trends,* August 1994.

An article describing MTIC fraud and its effect on Balance of Payments Statistics and the UK National Accounts was published in *Economic Trends* No. 597, August 2003. A copy can be found at: www.statistics.gov.uk/cci/article.asp?id=402

A follow-up report was published on 17 February 2005 which summarised the work carried out since July 2003 to review the estimates of the impact on the trade figures; a copy can be found at www.statistics.gov.uk/cci/article.asp?id=1066

A fuller version of these methodological notes appears in *Statistics on Trade in Goods* (Government Statistical Service Methodological Series 36). It also describes the methodology employed to derive volume and price indices and is available on the Office for National Statistics website at: www.statistics.gov.uk/StatBase/Product.asp?vlnk=14943

Trade in services (Chapter 3)

Introduction

Trade in services covers the provision of services by UK residents to non-residents and vice versa. Trade in services are disaggregated into 11 broad categories of services, as follows:

Table 1

	Exports to:		Imports from:	
	EU	non-EU	EU	non-EU
Under-recording	+¼%	+1½%	+¼%	0
Currency errors	0	–½%	0	0
Other valuation errors	0	–¼%	0	0

Source: ONS estimates based on historic quality surveys conducted by HMRC

Methodological notes

- Transportation (Sea, Air and Other) – Passenger, freight and other
- Travel (Business and Personal)
- Communications services
- Construction services
- Insurance services
- Financial services
- Computer and information services
- Royalties and licence fees
- Other business services (Merchanting and other trade-related services; operational leasing services; miscellaneous business, professional and technical services)
- Personal, cultural and recreational services (Audio-visual and related services; other cultural and recreational services)
- Government services

Separate tables appear at chapter 3 of this publication for each of the above categories except construction services, which are shown in the trade in services summary Table 3.1.

Trade in services data has been compiled and presented on a product rather than an industry basis since the 1998 *Pink Book*, when the BPM5 changes were implemented. This change was facilitated by the introduction of the International Trade in Services (ITIS) survey in 1996. A full product-based dataset is available from this date. Account totals, and some additional product estimates have been constructed back to 1991 or 1992, based on the relationship between the new ITIS data and the previous industry-based data. For the transport, travel, royalties and government services accounts, there were only small changes from the industry-based data, and it was possible to construct longer time series.

Construction services (shown within Table 3.1)

Construction services covers work done on construction projects and installations by employees of an enterprise in locations outside the resident economic territory of the enterprise. The source of information is the International Trade in Services (ITIS) survey. For construction services, where a permanent base is established which is intended to operate for over a year, the enterprise becomes part of the host economy and its transactions are excluded from the trade in services account. Transactions where a permanent base is established are recorded under direct investment, within investment income.

Transportation services (Table 3.2)

The transportation account covers sea, air and other (that is, rail, land, and pipeline) transport. It includes the movement of passengers and freight, and other related transport services, including chartering of ships or aircraft with crew, cargo handling, storage and warehousing, towing, pilotage and navigation, maintenance and cleaning, and commission and agents' fees associated with passenger/freight transportation.

Freight and the valuation of UK trade in goods

The trade in goods estimates included in the balance of payments value *imports* as they arrive in the UK f.o.b. (free on board) at the frontiers of the exporting country. This is net of the *cost of freight* to the UK border and any loss and damage incurred in transit to the UK. For UK importers who purchase goods f.o.b. and arrange transport themselves, their payment for the goods at the exporting countries' frontiers comprises:

(i) the value included in the trade in goods estimates (which is net of subsequent loss and damage)

(ii) the value of loss and damage incurred in transit

In addition, such importers bear the costs of:

(iii) freight services outside the exporting countries

(iv) insurance services (the excess of insurance premiums paid for the journeys over claims made)

Where importers purchase goods c.i.f. (cost, insurance and freight) on arrival in the UK, items (ii) to (iv) are paid by the foreign exporters in the first instance. The c.i.f. prices are set accordingly, however, and the UK importers are regarded as bearing the costs of items (i) to (iv).

Therefore, irrespective of the payment basis, items (ii) to (iv) represent costs to UK importers additional to the trade in goods entries, item (i). Item (ii), the value of loss and damage, is part of the price paid to the foreign exporter and so always represents a debit entry in the balance of payments accounts. Items (iii) and (iv), freight and insurance services, also represent debit entries when provided by non-residents; where such services are provided by UK residents there is no balance of payments entry. The debit entries above relating to freight are included in imports of transportation services.

The estimates of trade in goods cover exports valued f.o.b. The valuation of exports at the UK frontier must, by definition, include any subsequent loss or damage en route to the importer. Therefore, unlike imports, there is no need to make an explicit adjustment for loss and damage to exports. However, foreign importers must additionally bear the costs of freight and insurance services for the journeys outside the UK and where such services are provided by UK residents this gives rise to credit entries in the services accounts.

The f.o.b. value for UK imports includes the cost of transport within the exporting country. Where this service is provided by a UK operator then the trade valuation of imports overstates the balance of payments effect and an offsetting credit entry is therefore included under 'Road transport'. Similarly, an offsetting debit entry is included for foreign operators' carriage of UK exports within the UK.

Sea transport

Exports by UK operators consist of freight services on UK exports (but not imports – see 'Freight and the valuation of UK trade in goods', above) and on cross-trades, the carriage of non-resident passengers and the provision to them of services, and the chartering of ships to non-residents. Exports also include port charges and other services purchased in the UK by non-resident operators. Conversely, imports comprise services purchased abroad by UK operators, their chartering of ships from non-residents, and the carriage by non-resident operators of UK imports (but not exports) and goods on UK coastal routes and UK passengers.

Statistics relating to UK operators are provided by the Chamber of Shipping (CoS), which conducts inquiries into its members' participation in foreign trade. Until 1995, inquiries covering all CoS members were made every four years, with sample surveys for intervening years. Since 1995, the CoS has surveyed all its members annually. The data from the Chamber of Shipping are uplifted to account for UK sea transport companies who are not members using estimates for the gross tonnage of the UK fleet for different types of ship.

Exports

Passenger revenue: the value of services provided to non-resident passengers comprises fares and passengers' expenditure on board. Since UK operators are not able to distinguish between fares received from UK residents and non-residents, fares collected abroad are assumed to represent fares received from non-residents (passenger revenue collected abroad from UK residents is thought to be small and is likely to be counter-balanced by that collected in the UK from foreign residents). An estimate of passengers' expenditure on board is added. It is assumed that the non-residents' proportion of this is the same as for fares.

Freight: earnings consist of freight services on UK exports and are based on data supplied to the Chamber of Shipping. Time charter receipts include receipts for charters with crew. Time

Table 2 £ million

	Exports	Imports
First published estimates	+600	+650
Second estimates	+250	+250
Third estimates	+120	+150
Fourth estimates	+50	+70
Fifth estimates	+10	+20
All subsequent estimates	0	0

Source: ONS (derived from HMRC estimates)

charters without crew are included within the operational leasing component of 'Other business services' (Table 3.9).

Disbursements: estimates of disbursements in the UK by foreign operators are formed from a variety of sources. UK income from port charges, towage, handling costs and other port-related services was collected in 1996 from a survey of port authorities and has been projected forward from this. Crews' expenditure is estimated from information on numbers of visiting seamen, supplied by the Home Office. Regular returns are received on light dues from Trinity House. Estimates of expenditure on ships stores and on bunkers are included within the trade in goods data. Time charter payments made to UK residents are included under 'Ships owned or chartered-in by UK residents'.

Imports

Passenger revenue: estimates of passenger fares paid to non-resident operators are derived mainly from the results of the International Passenger Survey which is described in the notes below on 'Travel'. A further allowance is made for on-board sales of goods and services. However, 'Travel' imports includes, but does not separately identify, passenger fares paid to non-resident operators for fly-cruises, together with other expenditure by UK passengers aboard non-resident shipping.

Freight: estimates of freight services on UK imports provided by non-resident operators are compiled as follows; the estimates of total freight services (provided by all operators) on the sea legs of UK imports of goods are taken as the starting point, as described in the methodological notes to Table 2.4. Estimates of the element provided by UK-operated ships, based on data from the Chamber of Shipping are then deducted to obtain the non-resident operators' element, which is then used in the transportation account. Charter payments cover payments for charters with crew.

Disbursements: disbursements abroad include payments for canal dues, the maintenance of shore establishments, port charges, agency fees, handling charges, crews' expenditure, pilotage and towage, light dues and other miscellaneous port expenditure abroad. Payments for bunkers, ships stores and other goods purchased are included within the trade in goods data.

Air transport

The exports of UK airlines comprise the carriage of non-resident passengers to, from or outside the UK; the carriage of UK exports of goods (but not imports – see 'Freight and the valuation of UK trade in goods', above); and cross-trades and the chartering of aircraft to non-residents. Exports also include airport charges and services purchased in the UK by foreign airlines. Purchases of fuel and other goods are included within trade in goods.

Imports include for example, expenditure abroad by UK airlines on airport charges, crews' expenses, and charter payments. They also include payments to foreign airlines for the carriage of UK imports of goods (but not exports) and of UK mail, and for the carriage of UK passengers on flights covered by tickets for journeys to or from the UK. The carriage of UK passengers on other non-resident flights is included under 'Travel'.

The transactions of UK airlines are derived from returns supplied by the airlines to the Civil Aviation Authority.

Exports

Passenger revenue: this relates to all tickets sold outside the UK and used on UK aircraft, together with receipts from carrying passengers' excess baggage. An exercise by British Airways plc demonstrated that the value of tickets sold abroad to UK residents is roughly counter-balanced by sales in the UK to non-residents.

Freight: this consists of freight services on UK exports and the carriage of non-resident airmails, and is based on data supplied to the Civil Aviation Authority.

Disbursements and other revenue: these comprise expenditure in the UK by non-resident airlines on landing fees, other airport charges, handling charges, crews' expenses, office rentals and expenses, salaries and wages of staff at UK offices, commissions to agents and advertising. The estimates are based on returns from the Civil Aviation Authority, BAA plc and municipal airports on their receipts from non-resident airlines for air traffic control, landing fees and other airport charges; and survey information collected from large non-resident airlines operating in the UK on their other UK expenses. Purchases of fuel and other goods are included within trade in goods.

Also included are receipts from the charter or hire of aircraft, and gross receipts of sums due from non-resident airlines under pooling arrangements and for services such as consultancy and engine overhaul.

Imports

Passenger: the information on fares paid by UK passengers to non-resident airlines is derived from the International Passenger Survey; see notes on 'Travel' below.

Freight: estimates of non-resident airlines' freight on UK imports are derived by subtracting from the estimates of total freight on imports of goods arriving by air (see the methodological notes to Table 2.4) the element provided by UK airlines, the residual being the freight services supplied by non-resident airlines. Other imports comprise payments to non-resident airlines for carrying UK airmails as reported by the Royal Mail Group to the Civil Aviation Authority.

Disbursements and other payments: disbursements abroad include airport landing fees, other airport charges, charter payments, crews' expenses, the operating costs of overseas offices, agents' commissions, advertising, settlements with non-resident airlines under pooling arrangements, and miscellaneous expenditure abroad. Purchases of fuel and other goods are included within trade in goods.

Other Transport

This covers the movement of passengers and freight, and other related transport services, by rail, road and pipeline.

Rail: this consists primarily of expenditure on fares and rail freight through the Channel Tunnel. Passenger revenue estimates are based on numbers of passengers through the tunnel and average fare information. Estimates of rail freight through the tunnel are based on data provided by Eurotunnel and freight operators.

As the tunnel operators are a joint UK/French enterprise, half of passenger and freight transactions are taken to accrue to the UK part of the business. All tickets sold in France are assumed to be sold to non-UK residents (likewise, all tickets sold in the UK are assumed sold to UK residents). Of these, 50 per cent are assumed to accrue to the UK as they represent exports of rail transport services.

Road: exports comprise the earnings of UK road hauliers for the carriage outside the UK of UK exports of goods and the carriage within the exporting countries of UK imports (although such earnings from lorries leaving the UK via the Northern Ireland land boundary are only included from 2002). Estimates of numbers of journeys to various countries are derived from the International Road Haulage Survey, and rates for each journey are estimated from trade and other sources.

Imports include payments to all non-resident land transport operators for the carriage of UK imports of goods between the frontiers of the exporting countries and the foreign sea ports. Estimates are made by subtracting from the estimate of total freight on imports for land legs (see the methodological notes to Table 2.4) an estimate of the element earned by UK operators (derived as for exports). Imports also include the earnings of non-resident road hauliers for carrying UK exports and imports within the UK, although estimates of the trade with the Republic of Ireland are only included from 1996. These are estimated from the statistics of ferry movements of foreign-registered lorries, average loads, and average lengths of haul within the UK and estimated freight rates. The disbursements abroad by UK road hauliers, and in the UK by non-resident road hauliers, are included within 'Travel'.

Pipeline: this covers the cost of transport of oil freight via undersea pipelines. Data are derived from a survey of North Sea oil and gas companies.

Travel (Table 3.3)

Travel covers goods and services provided to UK residents during trips of less than one year abroad (and provided to non-residents during similar trips in the UK). Transport to and from the UK is excluded and shown as passenger services under transportation (see above). Internal transport within the country being visited is included within travel.

A traveller is defined as an individual staying, for less than one year, in an economy of which he/she is not a resident. The exceptions are those military and diplomatic personnel, whose expenditure is recorded under government services. The one-year rule does not apply to students and medical patients, who remain residents of their country of origin, even if the length of stay in another economy is more than a year.

The estimates are based primarily on the International Passenger Survey (IPS), which is a frontier sample survey which collects information on the expenditure of non-resident visitors leaving the UK and of UK residents returning from abroad. For package tourists, estimates of the transport elements are deducted from the reported total package costs. Estimates of the expenditure of UK residents visiting the Republic of Ireland and of Irish residents visiting the UK have been covered by the survey since the second quarter of 1999. Prior to this, data were derived from statistics published by the Irish Central Statistics Office.

Business travel

Business travel is divided into expenditure by seasonal and border workers (individuals who work some or all of the time in economic territories that differ from their resident households) and other business travel. Estimates are based on the IPS.

Personal travel

Personal travel covers holidays, visits to friends and relatives, the expenditures of people visiting for education and health reasons and miscellaneous purposes. Visits for more than one purpose, where none is distinguished as the main purpose, are classified as other.

Education related travel exports cover the tuition fees and other expenditure of students who are funded from abroad and studying in the UK (imports cover the expenditure of UK students studying abroad). The figures also include the fees and other expenditure of pupils in UK private schools and students at other colleges and language schools. Income received direct from abroad by examining bodies and correspondence course colleges is included within personal, cultural and recreational services.

Fees and other expenditure paid by non-resident students for higher education are collected via a special IPS trailer which commenced in 1997.

Health related travel covers the cost of medical and other expenses of those travelling abroad for medical treatment. Estimates are based on information supplied to the IPS.

Communication services (Table 3.4)

Communication services covers two main categories of international transactions: telecommunications (telephone, telex, fax, email, satellite, cable and business network services) and postal and courier services. Information is obtained through the ONS International Trade in Services survey (ITIS) and direct from the Royal Mail Group.

Insurance services (Table 3.5)

Insurance services covers the provision of various types of insurance to non-residents by resident insurance enterprises and vice versa. Insurance services include freight insurance on goods being imported or exported, direct insurance (such as, life, accident, fire, marine, and aviation) and reinsurance. The amounts recorded in the accounts reflect the service charge earned on the provision of insurance services. This is equal to net premiums from abroad (premiums less claims), plus property income attributed to policy holders, less the change in the reserves for foreign business, less foreign expenses. The figures for UK insurance companies' and brokers' underwriting activities are derived from annual inquiries conducted by ONS. Lloyd's of London underwriting activity is based on data supplied by the Corporation of Lloyd's; they also include receipts for management services provided to overseas members of Lloyd's syndicates.

Life insurance and pension funds

Life insurance covers underwriting services associated with long-term policies. Data are collected in the ONS inquiry into insurance companies. Pension fund services include service charges relating to occupational and other pension schemes, but not compulsory social security services.

Freight

Treatment of freight insurance is consistent with the f.o.b. valuation of trade in goods (see 'Freight and the valuation of UK trade in goods', above). That is, non-resident importers pay for freight and insurance on journeys outside the UK. Where such services are provided by UK residents to foreign enterprises, this gives rise to a credit entry.

Other direct insurance

Other direct insurance covers accident and health insurance; marine, aviation and other transport insurance; fire and property insurance; pecuniary loss insurance; general liability insurance; and other (such as travel insurance and insurance related to loans and credit cards).

Reinsurance

Reinsurance represents subcontracting parts of risks, often to specialised operators, in return for a proportionate share of the premium income. Reinsurance may relate to packages which mix several types of risks. Exports of services are estimated as the balance of flows between resident reinsurers and non-resident insurers. Imports are estimated as the balance of flows between resident insurers and non-resident reinsurers.

Auxiliary insurance services

This covers insurance broking and agency services, insurance and pension consultancy services, evaluation and adjustment services, actuarial services, salvage administration services, regulatory and monitoring services on indemnities and recovery services. These are measured by net brokerage earnings on business written in foreign currencies, and sterling business known to relate to non-residents. The main source of information on auxiliary insurance services is the ITIS survey.

Financial services (Table 3.6)

Financial services cover financial intermediary and auxiliary services other than those of insurance companies and pension funds. They include services provided in connection with transactions in financial instruments, as well as other services related to financial activity, such as advisory, custody and asset management services. These services may be charged for explicitly, for example through fees and commissions or implicitly, for example in the price spread offered in market making and foreign currency transactions. From the 2008 edition of the *Pink Book*, financial services also include financial intermediation services indirectly measured (FISIM). FISIM represents the implicit charge for the services related to borrowing and lending that are provided by monetary financial institutions and paid for by the interest differential between borrowing and lending rather than by fees and commissions. FISIM is exported by UK monetary financial institutions and imported by UK insurance companies and pension funds, private non-financial corporations and households. Prior to the 2008 edition of the *Pink Book*, the data for FISIM imports and exports were implicitly included as part of earnings on other investment debits and credits within income.

Estimates of financial services are based on returns from the Bank of England (for banks), ITIS, ONS's security dealers survey and directly from other sources including the Baltic Exchange.

From the 2001 edition of the *Pink Book*, the service earnings of financial institutions are presented on a gross exports and imports basis. This treatment is consistent with the BPM5 edition of the accounts. Trade in services transactions covered by type of financial institution are detailed below:

Monetary financial institutions (banks and building societies)

This covers UK banking services giving rise to:

- commissions for credit and bill transactions such as advising, opening and confirming documentary credits, and collection of bills
- financial intermediation services indirectly measured (FISIM)
- spread earnings (net service earnings through spreads on market making) including those on transactions in foreign exchange, securities and derivatives
- fees and commissions on foreign exchange dealing
- commission on new issues of securities, investment management and securities transactions
- commission on derivatives transactions
- banking charges, income arising from lending activities, fees and commissions in respect of current account operations, overdraft facilities, executor and trustee services, guarantees, securities transactions and similar services

Estimates are based on inquiries carried out annually from 1986 to 1990 and for some earlier years. A quarterly survey was run in 1991. A new survey was introduced in 1992 to collect data on UK banks' current account transactions including services. A further new survey was introduced in 2004, which enabled the collection of spread earnings on foreign exchange, securities and derivatives transactions – the data prior to 2004 are estimated by the Bank of England largely on the basis of information on the volumes of transactions and movements in spreads. The survey is completed quarterly by a selected sample of banks and annually by a larger sample of the UK banking population. From 2008, the Bank of England additionally included a sample of UK building societies in the quarterly reporting population.

FISIM is calculated by assuming the existence of an interest rate that represents the pure costs of borrowing funds, known as the reference rate. When monetary financial institutions lend money, FISIM is the difference between the interest they actually charge on the loan and the amount that would be charged if this reference rate were used. When financial institutions accept deposits (or borrow money), FISIM is the difference between the amount of interest they actually pay on the deposit (or loan) and the amount that would be paid if the reference rate were used. Exports of FISIM from 1992 onwards have been estimated by the Bank of England based on survey information relating to UK banks' balance sheet data for loans and deposits with non-residents and their interest receipts and payments on loans and deposits with non-residents. The reference rate used in these calculations is the average of the implied rates of return for loans and deposits. The implied rates of return are calculated by dividing the annualised amounts of interest paid or received in a quarter by the balance sheet level. FISIM on loans is calculated by multiplying the balance sheet level for loans by the quarterly reference rate and subtracting the result from the actual interest receipts on loans. FISIM on deposits is calculated by subtracting the actual interest paid on deposits from the result of multiplying the balance sheet level for deposits by the quarterly reference rate. Separate reference rates and FISIM estimates are calculated for sterling and foreign currency loans and deposits. As the information on interest receipts and payments with non-residents is not available before 1992, exports of FISIM have been estimated by ONS using balance sheet levels and interest rates based on LIBOR and the spread between implied rates of return on loans and deposits in the period for which data is available.

Fund management companies

From 2001, information on investment management fees and fees generated from advisory and other related functions has been collected via the ITIS survey. Earlier estimates were derived from a survey of companies whose main activity is fund management. Earnings are net of any foreign expenses by the institutions concerned. They exclude earnings of insurance companies, which are covered by separate returns made to ONS (see above, under 'Insurance Services').

Securities Dealers

The earnings of securities dealers are derived from a survey run by ONS. From the 1998 edition of the *Pink Book*, security dealers' spread earnings (service earnings through market making activities) are included as part of securities dealers' overseas earnings. This treatment is consistent with the domestic accounts as described in the European System of Accounts (1995). Estimates of these spread earnings are based on information on acquisitions and realisations of various classes of securities derived from ONS inquiries, together with the bid and offer prices for certain international bonds.

Baltic Exchange

This covers the brokerage and other service earnings of members of the Exchange for chartering, sales and purchases of ships and aircraft and other associated activities. Estimates are based on a survey of Exchange members.

Other

This includes commissions and other earnings received from abroad by UK residents (other than banks and oil companies, whose earnings are included elsewhere) for dealings in physical goods and in futures and options contracts. From 1990 to 2004 ONS carried out an annual survey of dealers in physical commodities. This data is now collected via the ITIS survey. The foreign earnings of financial futures and options dealers are assumed to have moved in line with the corresponding total earnings of such dealers reported in statutory returns to supervisory bodies.

This component also includes those financial services not included elsewhere, including financial service transactions (exports and imports) picked up from the ITIS survey, service charges on purchases of IMF resources and estimates of imports of net spread earnings, which are based on the UK's share of world turnover data for cross-border foreign exchange and derivatives transactions and the UK's share of global imports of financial services.

Imports of FISIM are included under this section as well. Estimates are made for imports of FISIM by UK insurance companies and pension funds, non-financial corporations and households. These estimates are based on Bank for International Settlements (BIS) balance sheet data for UK private sector loans from and deposits with non-resident banks, described in more detail in the methodological notes for Tables 8.7 and 8.8. FISIM is calculated separately for each sector's loans and deposits by multiplying the sectorised balance sheet data from BIS by a fixed margin, which represents the difference between the reference rate and the interest rate paid or received on loans or deposits. The margins used are based on the margins observed in the calculation of exports.

Computer and information services (Table 3.7)

Computer and information services covers computer, news agency and other information provision related service transactions. Examples of these services include data processing; hardware consultancy; software implementation; maintenance and repair of computers and peripheral equipment; the provision of news, photographs and feature articles to the media; database development, storage and dissemination both through the internet and through magnetic, optical or printed media; and direct, non-bulk subscriptions to newspapers and periodicals. Information is obtained from the ITIS survey. Excluded from computer services are the provision of packaged non-customised software on magnetic media, which are included in trade in goods.

Royalties and licence fees (Table 3.8)

Royalties and licence fees covers the exchange of payments and receipts for the authorised use of intangible, non-produced, non-financial assets and proprietary rights (such as patents, copyrights, trademarks, industrial processes, and franchises) and with the use, through licensing agreements, of produced originals or prototypes (such as manuscripts and films).

The heading includes royalties, licences to use patents, trade marks, designs, copyrights; manufacturing rights and the use of technical 'know-how'; amounts payable or receivable in respect of mineral royalties; and royalties on printed matter, sound recordings and performing rights. Data are obtained through the ITIS survey. Film royalties from the ONS Films and TV inquiry are also included. Royalties incorporated in the contract prices of UK exports and imports of goods are recorded under 'Trade in Goods'. The outright sale of a copyright is treated as a sale of a non-produced, non-financial asset and is recorded within the Capital Account (Table 6.1).

Other business services (Table 3.9)

'Other business services' covers a range of services including merchanting and other trade-related services, operational leasing (rental) without operators and miscellaneous business, professional and technical services.

Merchanting and other trade related services

Merchanting is defined as the purchase of a good by a resident from a non-resident and the subsequent resale of the good to another non-resident, without the good entering the compiling economy. The difference between the purchase and sale price is recorded as the value of merchanting services provided. Other trade related services covers commissions on cross-border goods and service transactions paid to, for example, merchants, commodity brokers, commission agents and auction houses.

Estimates of the net profits of UK firms from third country trade in goods are derived from ONS surveys. From 1990 to 2004, ONS carried out a specific sample survey of export houses, but information from these institutions is now collected via the ITIS survey, which has always collected information from other institutions on merchanting and trade related services. This component also covers fees charged for ship classifications and other related services, including information supplied by Lloyd's Register of Shipping.

Operational leasing

Operational leasing covers leasing (other than financial leasing) and charters of ships, aircraft and other transportation equipment without crews. Operational leasing data are derived from the ITIS survey and from the Chamber of Shipping.

Miscellaneous business, professional and technical services

Miscellaneous business, professional and technical services include legal, accounting, management consulting, recruitment and training and public relations; advertising and market research and development; architectural, engineering and other technical services; agricultural, mining and on-site processing services associated with agricultural crops (protection against disease or insects), forestry, mining (analysis of ores); and other services such as placement of personnel, security and investigative services, translation, and photographic. This item includes data from a number of different data sources, the most important of which is the ITIS survey.

Estimates of the earnings of solicitors are based on surveys held in respect of 1980 and annually since 1986 by the Law Society (in which amounts forwarded to barristers are included). From the 2000 edition of the *Pink Book*, earnings of solicitors are collected as part of the ITIS survey. Other legal services also include estimates of the overseas earnings of UK barristers as supplied by the Commercial Bar Association.

Estimates of banks' and securities dealers' non-financial service transactions appear in the other business services account.

Personal, cultural and recreational services (Table 3.10)

Personal, cultural and recreational services are divided into audio-visual and related services and other. The first category covers services and associated fees relating to the production of motion pictures (on film or video tape), radio and television programmes (live or on tape), and musical recordings. It includes rentals; and fees received by actors, directors and producers. The second category covers all other personal, cultural and recreational services including those associated with museums, libraries, archives, and provision of correspondence courses by teachers or doctors. Income received direct from abroad by examining bodies and correspondence course colleges is also included. Most of the information is obtained from the ITIS survey but there is a separate ONS inquiry for the film and television industry.

Government services (Table 3.11)

Government services include all transactions by embassies, consulates, military units and defence agencies with residents of staff or military personnel in the economies in which they are located. Other services included are transactions by other official entities such as aid missions and services, government tourist information and promotion offices, and the provision of joint military arrangements and peacekeeping forces (for example, United Nations). Information comes directly from government departments (including the Ministry of Defence and the Foreign and Commonwealth Office), foreign embassies and United States Air Force bases in the UK.

Exports

Expenditure by foreign embassies/consulates in the UK: this comprises the cost of operating and maintaining Commonwealth High Commission offices, foreign embassies and consulates in the UK, including the personal expenditure of diplomatic staff, but excluding the salaries of locally engaged staff, which are included within income; and similar expenditure by the UK offices of non-territorial organisations. In 1993 ONS conducted an inquiry to all high commission offices, embassies, consulates and international organisations in the UK. This figure has been updated for subsequent years using information obtained from several key high commissions and embassies and information on the number of diplomats in the UK.

Military units and agencies: this includes expenditure by the United States Air Force (USAF) in the UK (excluding the pay of locally engaged staff which is included within compensation of employees), together with receipts for services provided by UK military units in the UK and elsewhere to non-residents, such as military training schemes, which is sourced from the Defence Analytical Services Agency (DASA).

European Union institutions exports: these are services of the UK Government in collecting the UK contributions to the EU Budget, and services provided at the site of the EU's Joint European Torus project in Oxfordshire.

Other: this comprises goods and services which the government provides to non-residents under its economic aid programmes (these are offset under 'Bilateral aid' transfer debits) and miscellaneous goods and services supplied by the UK Government to foreign countries, including the reimbursement from other member states of the EU for treatment given by the National Health Service to their nationals.

Imports

Expenditure abroad by UK embassies and consulates: goods and services provided by local residents to UK embassies, high commission offices, consulates and the British Council account for most of this heading. It also includes the goods and services provided by local residents to UK diplomatic and other non-military personnel stationed abroad, excluding the salaries of locally engaged staff. The source for this information is the Foreign and Commonwealth Office.

Expenditure abroad by UK military units and agencies: this includes expenditure on food, equipment, fuel and services purchased locally. These items are recorded partly on a net basis – that is, after deducting receipts arising locally. The source for this information is DASA.

Other: this includes goods and services provided by local residents to the UK Government, excluding military and diplomatic expenditure. It covers expenditure abroad of the British Council and the reimbursement to other member states of the EU for medical treatment given to UK nationals.

References

United Kingdom Trade in Services, UKA1

UKA1 has been discontinued as a separate publication. All of the tables that were in Section A of UKA1 are now included in the *Pink Book*. New tables that were formerly in UKA1 but not in the *Pink Book* have been added to chapter 9. The tables that were formerly in Sections B and C of UKA1 are now in a web-only publication which focuses on the results of the ITIS survey.

Old editions of UKA1 can be found at the following web address: www.statistics.gov.uk/StatBase/Product.asp?vlnk=3343

The publication containing the ITIS survey results can be found at the following web address:

www.statistics.gov.uk/StatBase/Product.asp?vlnk=14407

Sea transport

An annual analysis describing the international activities of the UK shipping industry is published by the Department for Transport, in *Transport Statistics Great Britain* (The Stationery Office).

Transport Statistics Great Britain, 2008 edition can be found at: www.dft.gov.uk/pgr/statistics/datatablespublications/tsgb/

Air transport

Information relating to passenger expenditure is published by the Civil Aviation Authority in *CAA Monthly and Annual Statistics*.

CAA statistics are available at: www.caa.co.uk/default.aspx?catid=80&pagetype=90

Travel

Details are published regularly in National Statistics monthly Statistical Bulletins (previously First Releases) and quarterly Business Monitors (MQ6), both titled *Overseas Travel and Tourism*, and in the annual publication *Travel Trends*.

Overseas Travel and Tourism Statistical Bulletins can be found at: www.statistics.gov.uk/StatBase/Product.asp?vlnk=8168

MQ6 can be found at: www.statistics.gov.uk/StatBase/Product.asp?vlnk=1905

Travel Trends can be found at: www.statistics.gov.uk/Statbase/Product.asp?vlnk=1391

Income (Chapter 4)

The income account covers compensation of employees and investment income. For compensation of employees, estimates for total credits, debits and the balance appear at Table 4.1 but no detailed breakdown of the account is available. Investment income is broken down into five main categories: direct investment, portfolio investment, financial derivatives, other investment, and reserve assets.

Compensation of employees (Table 4.1)

Compensation of employees comprises wages, salaries, and other benefits paid by employers, in cash or in kind, to individuals who work in economies other than those in which they are residents. Employees, in this context, include seasonal or other short term workers (who stay for less than one year) and workers who cross international borders to get to their regular place of work. Compensation of employees also includes pay received by local (host country) staff of embassies, international organisations, consulates and military bases, as such entities are considered non-resident of the host economy.

Personal expenditure made by non-resident seasonal and border workers in the economies in which they are employed is recorded under travel within trade in services. Wages and salaries are recorded gross, with taxes paid recorded under current transfers.

Credits

There are three components:

- Wages, salaries and other benefits earned by UK seasonal and border workers, together with employers' contributions. These are estimated using data from the International Passenger Survey on the number of UK resident seasonal and border workers working abroad and average earnings data
- Wages and salaries earned by UK employees in US military bases in the UK. Information has been supplied to ONS by US military bases
- Wages and salaries earned by UK employees of foreign embassies in the UK. In 1993, ONS conducted an inquiry to all high commission offices, embassies, consulates and international organisations in the UK, asking for information on expenditure – including that on locally employed staff. This figure has been updated for subsequent years using information from a small sample of key embassies

Debits

There are two components:

- Wages, salaries and other benefits earned by non-resident workers employed in the UK for less than one year. These are estimated using data from the International Passenger Survey on the number of foreign resident seasonal and border workers working in the UK and average earnings data
- Wages, salaries and other benefits earned by foreign workers working in UK embassies and military bases abroad. Information on pay of locally engaged staff in UK embassies and military bases abroad is obtained from HM Treasury's Combined Online Information System (COINS), the Foreign and Commonwealth Office (FCO) and the Ministry of Defence (MOD)

International investment (Chapters 4, 7 and 8)

International investment comprises investment between resident and non-resident economies. Five functional categories of investment are distinguished in the international investment accounts:

- Direct investment
- Portfolio investment
- Financial derivatives
- Other investment
- Reserve assets

The international investment accounts measure investment income (chapter 4), transactions in financial assets and liabilities (chapter 7) and the international investment position (chapter 8).

Investment income (Chapter 4)

The investment income account covers earnings (for example, profits, dividends and interest payments and receipts) arising from foreign investment in financial assets and liabilities. Credits are the earnings of UK residents from their investments abroad and other foreign assets. Debits are the earnings of foreign residents from their investments and funds held in the UK and other UK liabilities. The flow of investment is recorded separately from the earnings in the Financial Account, although reinvested earnings of companies with foreign affiliates are a component of both. The total value of UK assets and liabilities held at any time is also recorded separately under the international investment position. The presentation of these three sections is almost identical, although there are small differences in coverage in some cases, mainly because complete information is not available for all items.

Earnings on the credit side of the account cover such items as interest on UK residents' deposits with banks abroad, profits earned by UK companies from their foreign affiliates, and dividends and interest received by UK investors on their portfolio investments in foreign companies' securities. Similarly, debits cover earnings by foreign investors on deposits held with UK banks, profits of foreign companies from their investments in their affiliates in the UK, and dividends and interest paid to foreign investors on their holdings of UK bonds and shares, including British government stocks.

Earnings on assets and liabilities are defined to include all profits earned and interest and dividends paid to UK residents from non-residents or to non-residents by UK residents. They are, where possible, measured net of income or corporation taxes payable without penalty during the recording period by the enterprise to the economy in which that enterprise operates and, in the case of profits, after allowing for depreciation. Dividends are recorded when they are paid (on a cash basis), whereas interest is recorded on an accruals basis.

Profits and dividends include the (credit) earnings from foreign affiliates of UK registered companies and the (debit) earnings of profits and dividends by UK-based affiliates of foreign-based companies. Conceptually, stock appreciation and other holding gains and losses should be excluded from the income flows entered in the balance of payments accounts because they represent only valuation changes. However, data on these are included in banking sector statistics provided by the Bank of England. Profits retained abroad by foreign affiliates or retained in the UK by affiliates of foreign companies are included in the flows of earnings and offset in the financial account. All interest flows between UK residents and non-residents are in principle included.

Interest on loans extended by and deposits with UK banks is now presented net of FISIM (Financial Intermediation Services Indirectly Measured). Likewise, UK non-bank loans from and deposits with banks abroad are also presented net of FISIM. FISIM is an estimate of the value of the services provided by financial intermediaries, such as banks, for which no explicit charges are made; instead these services are paid for as part of the margin between rates applied to savers and borrowers. The supposition is that savers would receive a higher interest rate and borrowers pay a lower interest rate if all financial services had explicit charges. FISIM received by UK banks is now recorded as an export of financial services while FISIM paid by UK non-banks is now recorded as an import of financial services. Information on the estimation of FISIM is included in the methodological notes for 'Trade in services'.

Financial account (Chapter 7)

The financial account covers transactions which result in a change of ownership of financial assets and liabilities between UK residents and non-residents. The financial account is broken down into five main categories: direct investment, portfolio investment, financial derivatives, other investment, and reserve assets.

In the balance of payments accounts, the term 'investment' has a wide coverage. It refers not only to the creation of physical assets but also, for example, to the purchase (or sale) of paper assets, such as shares, bonds and other securities. Investment also covers the financing of trade movements and other financial transactions between related companies in the UK and abroad. These 'other financial transactions' consist mainly of borrowing and lending by banks, both transactions by UK banks with non-residents and transactions of banks abroad with UK residents. Such borrowing and lending may be associated with UK trade in goods. For example, a non-resident may borrow from a UK bank to pay a UK exporter; alternatively he may use money already on deposit with the bank. Such borrowing or use of deposits will be included in the appropriate item in the financial account offsetting the entry under trade in goods.

Banking transactions may also arise from the financing of other financial transactions. For example, a UK company may borrow from a foreign bank in order to finance investment ('direct investment') in one of its subsidiary companies abroad. In this case, both the bank borrowing and the investment would be recorded in this section of the accounts and the two entries would offset each other; the investment would increase UK assets abroad while the borrowing would increase UK liabilities to foreign residents.

The total value of assets and liabilities held at

the end of each year is recorded separately under the international investment position (see chapter 8) and the income earned from them is recorded under investment income within the income account (see chapter 4). The presentations of these sections are almost identical although there are small differences in coverage in some cases, mainly because full information is not available for all items. The financial account tables appearing at chapter 7 show net debits (UK assets) above net credits (UK liabilities), in order to allow easier read across with the investment income and international investment position tables which appear at chapters 4 and 8.

International investment position (Chapter 8)

The international investment position brings together the available estimates of the levels of identified UK external assets (foreign assets owned by UK residents) and identified UK external liabilities (UK assets owned by foreign residents) at the end of each calendar year.

The presentation of the international investment position is almost identical to the presentation of investment income, within the income account (see chapter 4) and the financial account (see chapter 7) although there are small differences in coverage in some cases, mainly because full information is not available for all items.

Changes in balance sheet levels will reflect not only transactions in the corresponding assets and liabilities but also changes in valuation and certain other changes. Changes in valuation will occur in the following circumstances:

- where assets and liabilities are denominated in foreign currencies, their equivalent sterling value may change because of changes in foreign exchange rates
- where assets and liabilities are regularly bought and sold (for example, British government stocks, UK and foreign company securities), the current market value may be different from the value at which they were acquired
- where the holders of assets and liabilities change their values in preparing their accounts to reflect what is thought to represent the current position (for example, bad debts may be written off and direct investment assets may be written up or down in the books of the investing company)

In addition to changes in the valuation of identical underlying assets and liabilities, changes in recorded levels of external assets and liabilities will also reflect some changes in coverage which introduce discontinuities in the series.

Assessment of the international investment position

Because of the very varied data sources used to derive the estimates for the international investment position, there are some inconsistencies between the different figures in the tables, resulting particularly from different methods of valuation. Wherever possible, figures are at market values. However, for significant items such as direct investment, the figures are at own funds of book value and are subject to all the limitations of data taken from accounting balance sheets as a reflection of current market values. To the extent that the conventional valuation basis for direct investment is own funds at book value or, in the case of banks, often historical cost values, an up-to-date valuation closer to market values is likely to be higher.

In addition, some assets and liabilities are measured very imperfectly (for example, for a number of items, levels of assets and liabilities are not directly reported but derived from cumulating recent identified transactions and allowing for estimated valuation changes). The balance between the estimates of identified external assets and liabilities has always been an imperfect measure of the UK's debtor/creditor position with the rest of the world.

To the extent that net errors and omissions reflect unrecorded or misrecorded financial transactions, the external balance sheet will tend to fail to capture the corresponding levels of assets and liabilities, although much will depend on the categories of assets and liabilities concerned:

- where both levels and transactions are reported (for example, portfolio investment by most financial intermediaries), there may be similar deficiencies to estimates of both levels and transactions, although levels may tend to be more accurate to the extent they are derived from annual accounting data
- where only levels are reported and transactions are derived from changes in levels, allowing as far as possible for valuation changes, (for example, non-portfolio transactions of UK and foreign banks), there may be errors in the estimates of transactions (for example, in allowing for valuation changes) with no corresponding error in levels
- where only transactions are reported and levels are calculated by cumulating transactions and allowing for valuation changes (for example, inward portfolio investment in UK company bonds), errors in recording transactions will lead to corresponding errors in levels. Thus if part of the net errors and omissions represents such missing portfolio investment inflows, the identified net assets figures will be overstated

Allocation of Special Drawing Rights

These are issued to the UK by the IMF but are not regarded by them as a liability of the UK and do not form part of total external liabilities in this table.

Direct investment

Introduction

A direct investment relationship exists if the investor has an equity holding in an enterprise, resident in another country, of 10 per cent or more of the ordinary shares or voting stock. The direct investment relationship extends to branches, subsidiaries and other businesses where the enterprise has significant shareholding. Equity investment in which the investor does not have an effective voice in the management of the enterprise (that is, the investor has less than 10 per cent of the voting shares) is regarded as portfolio investment. The estimates of direct investment include the investor's share of the reinvested earnings of the subsidiary or associated company, the net acquisition of equity capital, changes in inter-company accounts and changes in branch/head office indebtedness. Further details are given in the Glossary.

Income (Tables 4.3 and 4.4)

Direct investment earnings include interest on loan capital, profits from branches or other unincorporated enterprises abroad and the direct investor's share of the profits of subsidiary and associate companies. It includes the direct investor's portion of reinvested earnings, which is also treated as a new investment flow out of the parent's country into the affiliate's and appears in the financial account (Table 7.3) as an offsetting entry to the earnings one. Estimates of profits are made after providing for depreciation, the companies' own estimates of depreciation being used. Although depreciation is estimated at replacement cost in the national accounts, there is little doubt that the estimates in the balance of payments are, in the main, measured at historic cost (different treatments of depreciation result in different entries in the current and financial accounts, but the sum of the two entries will always be the same).

International reporting standards recommend that direct investment enterprises report their profits on a 'current operating performance' basis and not include any realised or unrealised holding gains/losses, exceptional items, write-downs or write-offs. This is generally the case with the exception of the profits of monetary financial institutions, which report to the Bank of England on an 'all inclusive basis' and include realised and unrealised holding gains/losses, write-downs or write-offs.

Refunds of tax made retrospectively under double-taxation agreements are included in the period when they were made rather than the earlier periods in which they could be deemed to have accrued. Dividend receipts and payments include subsidiaries payments of withholding tax.

Estimates for reinvested earnings are not collected separately but are derived by deducting dividends paid from total subsidiaries' profits.

Financial account (Tables 7.3 and 7.4)

The components of the direct investment financial account comprise equity capital, reinvested earnings and other capital associated with inter-company debt transactions. Inter-company transactions between affiliated monetary financial institutions and between affiliated other financial institutions (for example, securities dealers) are limited to those associated with permanent debt. The usual inter-company deposits and other claims and liabilities associated with these financial institutions are reported under other investment.

Methodological notes

The Pink Book: 2009 edition

International investment position (Tables 8.3 and 8.4)

The estimate of the international investment position relates to total net asset values attributable to investing companies, that is, book values of fixed assets less accumulated depreciation provisions plus current assets less current liabilities. The book values of direct investments are likely to be less than the values at written down replacement cost and less than the market values. There are no official estimates of the market value of UK direct investment assets and liabilities. However, research by Cliff Pratten (Department of Applied Economics, University of Cambridge) indicated that, on certain assumptions, the market value of UK direct investments abroad at end-1989 might be about double their book value, while the market value of foreign direct investment in the UK might be just under double their book values at the same point of time. However there are considerable uncertainties in making such estimates.

The comparison between transactions in the balance of payments account and changes in total assets and liabilities is not affected by allowances for depreciation of fixed assets as charged to the profit and loss account; such allowances are deducted before arriving at the earnings included in the current account, and the provision for depreciation is regarded as maintaining the total book value of the existing assets. Similarly, the comparison is unaffected by the treatment of reinvested earnings from direct investments, since these appear both in the current account as earnings and in the financial account as a flow of capital adding to the stock of assets. However, the values are affected by the treatment applied in their consolidated accounts by UK companies to value newly acquired foreign companies. Under both merger and acquisition accounting the increase in the net book value can be less than the net investment to complete the acquisition. The difference represents goodwill and the other costs associated with the transaction that are written off directly against reserves.

Direct investment abroad by UK residents

Monetary financial institutions (banks): information on the direct investment by UK registered banks in their foreign branches, subsidiaries and associates is collected quarterly by the Bank of England from a selection of banks that have a direct investment enterprise abroad. Income data are supplemented by additional information from certain banks that only report to the Bank of England on an annual basis. Direct investment balance sheet data are collected annually from a panel of banks selected by the Bank of England.

Insurance companies and other financial intermediaries: an annual inquiry forms the basis for estimates of direct investment by UK insurance companies and other financial intermediaries; these results are supplemented by a quarterly survey. Investment in foreign property by financial companies is also included here. They are estimated from the levels of such assets held by financial companies and information on their total income from abroad.

In line with international standards, the investment of other financial intermediaries includes those of all holding companies.

Private non-financial and public corporations: information on direct investment by all private and public non-financial corporations is estimated from the results of ONS's annual direct investment inquiry. This inquiry covers a sample of UK companies that either have foreign affiliates or are affiliated to a foreign parent. Returns are imputed for companies that are not approached in the inquiry but which are known to have direct investment links. The estimates for the latest year are based on a quarterly inquiry with a smaller population sample. Results of the annual inquiry are available about twelve months after the end of the year and are published in a National Statistics First Release (which will in future be renamed a Statistical Bulletin) and in Business Monitor MA4.

Copies of the FDI First Release can be found at: www.statistics.gov.uk/StatBase/Product.asp?vlnk=728

Copies of the FDI Business Monitor can be found at: www.statistics.gov.uk/StatBase/Product.asp?vlnk=9614

Households: this comprises household sector investment in property abroad. Investment in property includes the ownership of 'second homes' located outside the UK. Estimates of property ownership are based on information from the Department for Communities and Local Government (DCLG)'s Survey of English Housing (SEH). The SEH collects information from English households on the number of properties owned outside the UK. These estimates have been grossed to include all UK households. Average dwelling prices are applied as well as an estimate of property rental. For more information on the latest methodology see the *Economic Trends* article: www.statistics.gov.uk/CCI/article.asp?ID=1176

Direct investment in the UK by foreign residents

Estimates for direct investment in the UK are based on the same inquiries to banks, financial institutions and private non-financial corporations as direct investment abroad. For direct investment in UK banks, the Bank of England surveys a sample of UK branches and subsidiaries of foreign-owned banks.

Households: limited information on property transactions was originally based on information obtained from the then Inland Revenue and on ONS estimates. From 2003, the Inland Revenue ceased to collect data, and from this point the data should be regarded as being of lower quality. ONS estimates are based on publicly reported property transactions.

Portfolio investment

Introduction

Portfolio investment comprises investment in either equity or debt securities that are not considered to have led to the acquisition of a foreign affiliate (that is, less than 10 per cent ownership) and so are classified as portfolio rather than direct investment. Portfolio investment is sub-divided into investment in equity or debt securities; debt securities are further sub-divided into investment in bonds and notes (long-term) and investment in money market instruments (short-term).

Income (Tables 4.5 and 4.6)

Earnings on equity securities consist of dividends received by investors on their holdings of shares of registered companies. Earnings on debt securities consists of interest received on investment in bonds and notes (government and municipal loan stock, and bonds and notes of private and public corporations) and money market instruments (for example commercial paper, certificates of deposit, and Treasury bills). Dividends are recorded on a paid basis and interest is recorded on an accrued basis.

Financial account (Tables 7.5 and 7.6)

Financial accounts transactions in equity securities comprise the acquisitions or disposals in the ordinary shares of registered companies. Transactions in bonds and notes consist of the acquisition and disposal of government and municipal loan stock, and bonds and notes of registered companies. Transactions in money investment comprise the acquisition and disposal of government short-term paper (such as Treasury bills, certificates of deposits, and commercial paper).

International investment position (Tables 8.5 and 8.6)

As with investment income and the financial account, the international investment position is divided into investment in equity and debt securities with debt securities further subdivided into investment in bonds and notes and investment in money market instruments. Investment in both equity and debt securities are recorded at market value.

Portfolio investment abroad by UK residents

Monetary financial institutions (MFIs) (banks and building societies): estimates are derived from statutory inquiries conducted by the Bank of England. Prior to 2006, portfolio transactions by UK MFIs were based on reported transactions. From 2006 onwards, estimates of net transactions in both equity and debt securities by UK MFIs are derived from changes in reported balance sheets adjusted for both price and exchange rate effects. UK banks' earnings on portfolio investment abroad are collected on a quarterly basis by the Bank of England.

Insurance companies, pension funds and securities dealers: estimates are largely derived from quarterly ONS inquiries. These quarterly inquiries are supplemented by a more comprehensive annual inquiry.

Other financial intermediaries and private non-financial corporations: estimates are derived from survey-based asset levels to which rates of return on comparable assets shown by financial institutions are applied.

Households: estimates of investment by the household sector largely consist of investment by members of Lloyd's of London which are supplied annually by Lloyd's. They include portfolio investment income on funds which are held abroad to support business underwritten in those countries. Also included are estimates of investment in foreign equity securities acquired by UK households in exchange for their holdings of UK equities following an acquisition by a foreign direct investor. Typically, such acquisitions are funded by the issuance of shares by the investing company, rather than a cash payment. Significant levels of household ownership are most likely to exist when the UK company is a demutualised building society or privatised public utility.

Portfolio investment in the UK by foreign residents

As with portfolio investment abroad, portfolio investment in the UK is subdivided into investment in equity securities and debt securities with investment in debt securities further subdivided into investment in bonds and notes and investment in money market instruments.

Equity securities

Prior to 2007, the main sources for estimates of new investment in UK equity securities were a range of statistical inquiries conducted by ONS. Data were then adjusted to take account of total levels of foreign investment in shares as indicated by the results of ONS's biennial Share Ownership Survey. The Share Ownership Survey identifies the beneficial owner of listed UK equity securities held by both UK and foreign residents. Adjustments are made to exclude holdings of a direct investment nature and to establish the beneficial ownership of nominee and third party shareholdings. From 2007, new investment in UK equity securities by non-residents is derived by residual. Non-resident investment in UK equity securities is obtained by assuming that any net transactions in UK equity securities not attributable to the domestic sectors of the UK (using all available data sources) are attributable to foreign residents.

Estimates of foreign earnings from UK equity securities consist of dividends paid to foreign holders of UK company ordinary shares. These estimates are calculated from Stock Exchange data on dividend payments, which are applied pro-rata to levels of non-resident holdings of UK shares derived from ONS's Share Ownership Surveys.

The latest Share Ownership Report, covering end-2006, was published by ONS in July 2007. Copies of the Share Ownership Report can be found at: www.statistics.gov.uk/StatBase/Product.asp?vlnk=930

No precise sector breakdown is available and an assumption is made by ONS that non-resident holdings by sector of issuer are proportional to the overall equity liabilities of each sector.

Debt securities – bonds and notes

Non-resident investment in bonds and notes are comprised of those issued by HM Government and those issued by other sectors such as monetary financial institutions and private non-financial corporations.

Monetary financial institutions: estimates for non-resident investment in bonds and notes issued by UK banks and building societies stem from statistical surveys carried out by the Bank of England and ONS estimates. Information collected by the Bank of England for identified non-resident investment is supplemented by ONS estimates. ONS estimates allocate any residual investment to non-residents (for example, any securities not identified as being held by a specific sector are assumed to be held by non-residents). Earnings on bonds and notes issued by UK banks are reported by those banks to the Bank of England.

General government: investment in government bonds and notes comprises investment in British government securities (gilts) and other foreign currency bonds. Investment in British government securities by foreign central banks, international organisations and private foreign residents are measured from banking statistics and other Bank of England sources including the Central Gilts Office. Foreign earnings on British government stocks (gilts) are estimated from information on the levels outstanding and appropriate rates of interest. These earnings are calculated gross of UK income tax. Most gilts are issued by the UK Government at a discount to the redemption value. This is recorded as interest accruing over the lifetime of the gilt. Non-resident investment UK foreign currency bonds and notes issued by central government relates to bonds issued by HM Government (the latest of which is the $3 billion 5-year eurobond issued in 2003). Information on the total issue of these foreign currency bonds is supplied by the Bank of England. Holdings by non-residents are once again derived as the residual of total securities in issue less those held by domestic sectors. Earnings are estimated on a pro-rata basis, proportional to the levels of investment.

Other sectors (other financial institutions and private non-financial corporations): foreign investment in bonds and notes issued by other sectors is primarily estimated on the residual basis where investment by non-residents is assumed to be the difference between total other sector bonds and notes in issues less those acquired or owned by UK residents. Information on total bonds and notes in issue and acquisition by UK residents is derived from the Bank of England and London Stock Exchange records of UK company bond issues, accumulated financial transactions, ONS surveys, and price and exchange rate movements. Earnings are estimated on a pro-rata basis, proportional to the levels of investment.

Debt securities – money market instruments

Non-resident investment in UK money market instruments consist of foreign investment in UK treasury bills, certificates of deposit and commercial paper.

Monetary financial institutions: estimates for non-resident investment in money market instruments issued by UK banks and building societies stem from statistical surveys carried out by the Bank of England and ONS. Information collected by the Bank of England for identified non-resident investment is supplemented by ONS estimates. ONS estimates allocate any residual investment to non-residents (for example, any securities not identified as being held by a specific sector are assumed to be held by non-residents). Earnings on bonds and notes issued by UK banks are reported by those banks to the Bank of England.

General government: non-resident investment in government money market instruments comprises investment in UK treasury bills. Estimates for custody holdings held with UK banks are supplied by the Bank of England, and ONS allocates a fixed proportion of the residual (total issue less known acquisitions) to non-residents. Earnings are estimated from information on the levels outstanding and appropriate rates of interest.

Other sectors (other financial institutions and private non-financial corporations): foreign investment in money market instruments issued by other sectors is primarily estimated on the residual basis where investment by non-residents is assumed to be the difference between total other sector money market instruments in issues less those acquired or owned by UK residents. Information on total money market instruments in issue and acquisition by UK residents is derived from the Bank of England and London Stock Exchange records of UK company money market instruments issues, accumulated financial transactions, ONS surveys and price and exchange rate movements. Earnings are estimated on a pro-rata basis, proportional to the levels of investment.

Financial derivatives

Financial derivatives are defined as financial instruments that are linked to the price performance of an underlying asset and which involve the trading of financial risk. Examples of the underlying asset might include a financial instrument, commodity, bilateral foreign exchange rate, movement in stock index, or interest rate. Financial derivatives include options (on, for example, currencies, interest rates, commodities, and indices), traded financial futures, warrants, currency and interest rate swaps, forward rates agreements (FRAs), and certain credit derivatives. The rationale for separate recording of derivatives contracts in the financial account is to keep the distinction between them and other transactions (for example, securities) to which they may be linked for hedging purposes. An article examining the use of derivatives in the UK accounts was published in the May 2005 edition of *Economic Trends*. It can be found at: www.statistics.gov.uk/cci/article.asp?ID=1139

Financial account (Table 7.1)

Derivatives are valued at current market prices. Estimates for financial derivatives are currently unavailable except for net transactions by UK banks. Prior to 2005, the banks' transaction only covered net settlement receipts/payments on interest rate swaps and forward rate agreements. From 2005 onwards, the coverage is for all UK bank derivative transactions, data for which are supplied by the Bank of England.

Balance sheets (Table FD)

Data on UK banks' gross asset and liability positions in derivatives are collected quarterly by the Bank of England; no data are available prior to 1998. Data on securities dealers'

Methodological notes

assets and liabilities are collected by ONS; similarly there are no data available prior to 1998.

Data published in Table FD (in chapter 8) form supplementary information as estimates for financial derivatives have yet to be fully implemented in either the UK international investment position or in the UK's national accounts balance sheets. Work is continuing to validate and improve the estimates and obtain more information on the types of derivatives traded, and the underlying transactions.

Other investment

Introduction

Other investment abroad is subdivided into trade credit, loans, currency and deposits and other assets/liabilities.

Trade credit consists of claims and liabilities arising from the direct extension of credit by suppliers and buyers for goods and services transactions and advance payments for work to be undertaken or currently in progress. Lending activity to facilitate trade, including those loans underwritten by the Export Credit Guarantee Department (ECGD), are treated as loans and not trade credit within the accounts. Trade credit between related firms (that is, credit received or extended between a UK business and a foreign affiliate or parent company) is treated as an investment in the affiliate or parent company, and is therefore recorded under direct investment.

Loans comprise financial assets created by the direct lending of funds by a creditor (lender) to a debtor (borrower). This includes loans to finance trade, other loans and advances, financial leases and repurchase agreements.

Currency consists of notes and coins that are in circulation and commonly used to make payments. UK resident holdings of foreign currency are deemed a UK asset while non-resident holdings of sterling are a UK liability. Deposits comprise both transferable (accessible on demand without penalty or restriction) and other deposits.

Other assets and liabilities comprise any other items that are not trade credit, loans or deposits. The most notable other asset comprises the UK's subscriptions to international organisations while the most notable other liabilities are non-residents' prepayments of premiums and reserves against outstanding insurance claims.

Income (Tables 4.7 and 4.8)

Income predominantly comprises the interest accruing on trade credit, loans or deposits. Interest is presented net of FISIM, which is recorded within exports and imports of financial services. 'Other income payments' includes an estimate of imputed income to foreign households from UK insurance companies' technical reserves and is recorded in the balance of payments because households are regarded as owning the net equity of pension funds and life assurance reserves; that is, the funds set aside for the purpose of satisfying the claims and benefits foreseen. The estimates are derived from data collected on ONS statistical inquiries.

Financial account (Tables 7.7 and 7.8)

The financial account records the drawing/repayment of loans, the addition to or withdrawals from deposits, subscriptions to international organisations, debt forgiveness, adjustments for accrued interest and prepayments of premiums and reserves against outstanding insurance claims.

International investment position (Tables 8.7 and 8.8)

The international investment position presents total trade credit, loans and deposits outstanding at end period. It also records total capital subscribed to the international organisations and levels of prepayments of premiums and reserves against outstanding insurance claims.

Other investment abroad by UK residents

Trade credit

At present only a minimal amount of data is recorded within trade credit. Some data previously recorded in this area have been reclassified as bank lending and are now within the loans data in other investment abroad. Other data are no longer suitable for inclusion and have been removed from the accounts, generally back to 1999.

Loans

These are subdivided into earnings on long-term loans and earnings on short-term loans; short-term loans are those which are repaid in full within one year.

Monetary financial institutions: MFI long-term loans comprise UK bank loans under the Export Credit Guarantee Department's guarantee. MFI short-term loans comprise sterling and foreign currency loans extended by UK banks and building societies. Information on loans extended by UK banks and from 2008, UK building societies, is collected by the Bank of England using a range of statistical inquiries. Prior to 2008, information on building society loans was supplied to the Bank of England by the Financial Services Authority. It is not possible to separate out UK banks' earnings on lending abroad from their earnings on deposits abroad. Estimates for earnings on such loans are therefore included indistinguishably within earnings on deposits (see below).

General government: government loans are all long-term and comprise inter-government loans. Estimates are sourced from information supplied by the Department for International Development.

Public corporations: public corporation loans are all long-term and are sourced from the Export Credit Guarantee Department and the Commonwealth Development Corporation.

Currency and deposits

Currency

Estimates for transactions in foreign notes and coin by the UK private sector other than monetary financial institutions are based on tourists' expenditure.

Deposits

Estimates comprise both transferable (accessible on demand without penalty or restriction) and other deposits held abroad.

Monetary financial institutions: MFI deposits comprise UK banks' and building societies' sterling and foreign currency deposits held with deposit taking institutions abroad. Information on deposits held abroad by UK banks and from 2008, UK building societies, is collected by the Bank of England using a range of statistical inquiries. Prior to 2008, information on building society deposits was supplied to the Bank of England by the Financial Services Authority. It is not possible to separate out UK banks' earnings on lending abroad from their earnings on deposits abroad. Estimates for earnings on such loans are therefore included indistinguishably within earnings on deposits.

Securities dealers: deposits held abroad by UK securities dealers are derived from quarterly ONS inquiries. Financial transactions and interest accrued are reported directly by the institutions while end-period positions are estimated by ONS.

Other UK residents: estimates of other UK private sector deposits with banks abroad are derived from the banking statistics of countries in the Bank for International Settlements (BIS) reporting area (as defined in the Glossary). End-period positions are reported to the Bank of England, who in turn estimate net transactions. These data are then supplied to ONS. ONS then deducts deposits held abroad by UK securities dealers to avoid potential double counting. Interest on these deposits is then estimated by ONS using average quarterly levels and appropriate interest rates. Due to the limitations in the coverage of the BIS data, statistical adjustments have been applied to the financial flows data since 1994 to improve the overall coherence of the sector financial accounts. In order to maintain consistency between financial flows and balance sheet levels, corresponding coherence adjustments have been applied to the international investment position. Transactions in non-monetary gold are included here and comprise net transactions in gold which are held as financial assets by listed institutions in the London Bullion Market (LBM). These estimates are currently derived from banking statistics collected by the Bank of England. The treatment of non-monetary gold is being reviewed as part of the worldwide process to revise the IMF *Balance of Payments Manual*. The main proposal is that the concept of non-monetary gold would be replaced by two categories – allocated gold (a commodity) and unallocated gold (a financial instrument). UK balance of payments will continue current practice until the treatments defined in the revised manual are implemented.

Other assets

Comprise any other items that are not trade credit, loans or deposits.

Central government: this includes central government subscriptions to international organisations and covers capital subscriptions to international lending bodies other than the IMF, that is, regional development banks, the International Finance Corporation and the International Fund for Agricultural Development. Some transactions are in the form of non-interest-bearing promissory notes and are included in the accounts as the subscriptions fall due, irrespective of the time of encashment of the notes. The information is obtained from official records.

Monetary financial institutions and public corporations: estimates reflect UK banks' and the Export Credit Guarantee Department's (ECGD) debt forgiveness and offset the corresponding entry in the capital account. Information on debt forgiveness comes from the Bank of England and the ECGD.

Other sectors: these short-term assets largely relate to assets of UK insurance companies and pension funds and other financial intermediaries other than those classified under portfolio investment, estimates for which are obtained from ONS statistical inquiries.

Other investment in the UK by non-residents

Trade credit

At present only a minimal amount of data are recorded within trade credit. Some data previously recorded in this area have been reclassified as bank lending (see above), and are now within the loans data in other investment abroad. Other data are no longer suitable for inclusion and have been removed from the accounts, generally back to 1999.

Loans

These are subdivided into earnings on long-term loans and earnings on short-term loans; short-term loans are those which are repaid in full within one year.

General government and public corporations: general government loans are all long-term and comprise loans received by both central government and local authorities. Central government long-term loans such as Lend-Lease and the Lines of Credit were reported by HM Treasury. The final payment on these loans was made in 2005. Also included are the loans received under the Very Short-term Financing Facility (VSTFF) taken out during 1992 and repaid in 1993. Public corporations' borrowing directly from foreign residents under the exchange cover scheme is included. Repayments under the scheme by former public corporations that have since been privatised are included under repayments from central government, to whom their foreign debt was transferred following privatisation; such debt is known as novated debt. In recent years only local authorities have engaged in long-term borrowing from abroad; estimates are obtained from the Department for Communities and Local Government (DCLG).

Securities dealers: estimates for securities dealers' short-term loans from abroad are estimated from information collected through ONS inquiries. Since 1995 statistical adjustments have been applied to the data for securities dealers' short-term loans in order to improve the overall coherence of the sector financial accounts.

Other sectors: estimates of borrowing by other sectors are based on data reported to the Bank for International Settlements (BIS), and are generally confined to borrowing from commercial banks based within the BIS reporting area (see Glossary). End-period positions are reported to the Bank of England, who in turn estimate net transactions. These data are then supplied to ONS. ONS then deducts UK securities dealers' loans from banks abroad to avoid potential double counting. Interest on these loans is then estimated by ONS using average quarterly levels and appropriate interest rates. Due to the limitations in the coverage of the BIS data, statistical adjustments have been applied to the financial flows data since 1994 to improve the overall coherence of the sector financial accounts. In order to maintain consistency between financial flows and balance sheet levels, corresponding coherence adjustments have been applied to the international investment position. Additional information on borrowing from the European Investment Bank (EIB) is supplied directly to ONS on a quarterly basis by the EIB.

Currency and deposits

Currency

Estimates of transactions in sterling notes and coin by private foreign residents (other than monetary financial institutions) are based on ONS statistics of tourists' expenditure. While sterling bank notes are issued by the Bank of England, which is classified to monetary financial institutions, coins are issued by the Royal Mint, which is classified to the central government sector. In the absence of any separate data for notes and coin, it is assumed that notes make up 90 per cent of total notes and coin.

Deposits

Foreign deposits with UK monetary financial institutions are subdivided into deposits with banks and deposits with building societies. Also included are deposit liabilities of central government.

Central government: deposit liabilities of UK central government include short-term inter-government loans and transactions with non-residents under minor government accounts in the form of changes in balances not attributable elsewhere in the accounts. Since 1973 this has consisted entirely of balances held by the Paymaster General on the European Union (EU) account.

Monetary financial institutions: it is not possible to separate out foreign deposits with UK banks from foreign loans to UK banks. The estimates for foreign loans to UK banks are therefore included indistinguishably within deposits. Within deposits with UK monetary financial institutions, estimates for sterling deposits are derived from banking statistics and include both current and deposit accounts. Foreign currency deposits comprise all external borrowing denominated in foreign currencies by UK banks (sometimes described as euro currency transactions). They consist of changes in deposits with, and other lending to, UK banks from abroad. These transactions may be a reflection of (that is, the counterpart to) a variety of other foreign or domestic transactions by UK banks. These other transactions could be: foreign currency lending to UK residents (which are not balance of payments transactions); net purchases of foreign securities by the banks (which are included in direct or portfolio investment abroad as appropriate); any switching of banks' liabilities between foreign currencies (including gold) and sterling; or any change in the amount of foreign currency capital raised by banks. Estimates for foreign currency deposits with UK monetary financial institutions have been calculated from the end-quarter balance sheets as reported by all UK banks and building societies to the Bank of England. Adjustments are made to the reported changes in balance sheets to exclude revaluations resulting from changes in exchange rates. UK banks' income payments also include income payments associated with repurchase agreements and stock lending activities.

Other liabilities

These comprise any other items that are not trade credit, loans or deposits.

Central government: these short-term liabilities largely consist of non-interest-bearing notes, estimates for which are obtained from the Bank of England. Non-interest-bearing notes are issued by HM Government and are held by international organisations.

Other sectors: long-term liabilities consist of net equity of foreign households in life assurance reserves and in pension funds and prepayments of premiums and reserves against outstanding claims which are recorded in the balance of payments because households are regarded as owning the net equity of pension funds and life assurance reserves; that is, the funds set aside for the purpose of satisfying the claims and benefits foreseen. The estimates are derived from data collected on ONS statistical inquiries. Short-term liabilities largely consist of additions to insurance companies' technical reserves, estimates for which are derived from ONS statistical inquiries.

Reserve assets

Introduction

Reserve assets comprise gold, convertible foreign currencies, IMF Special Drawing Rights (SDRs) and the UK's reserve position in the IMF. Currencies may be held in the form of financial instruments. From July 1979 convertible currencies also include European Currency Units acquired when 20 per cent of the gold and dollar holdings in the reserve assets were deposited on a swap basis with the European Monetary Co-operation Fund, the swap arrangement being renewed quarterly. As from January 1994 the swap was with the European Monetary Institute and as from January 1998 was with the European Central Bank. The swap arrangement was terminated in December 1998. All information on the reserve assets is recorded within the Exchange Equalisation Account by the Bank of England.

Income (Table 4.1)

Interest received on the official foreign exchange reserves and on the UK's holdings of Special Drawing Rights with the IMF and other remuneration received from the IMF (related to its holdings of sterling), is recorded within the Exchange Equalisation Account by the Bank of England.

Financial account (Table 7.9)

This item consists of the sterling equivalent, at current rates of exchange, of drawings on, and additions to the gold, convertible currencies and Special Drawing Rights (SDRs) held in the Exchange Equalisation Account; and of changes in the UK reserve position in the IMF.

International investment position (Table 8.9)

Until 1999 securities were valued at historic cost and translated to sterling. Gold was valued at the ruling official price of 35 SDRs per fine ounce until end-1977 and at end-year market rates from end-1978 to end-1999. Since 2000, all reserve assets are valued at end-period market prices and exchange rates. SDRs and convertible currencies are valued throughout at closing middle market rates of exchange.

External debt (Table 8.10)

Gross external debt is defined as the outstanding amount of those actual current, and not contingent, liabilities that require payment(s) of principal and/or interest by the debtor at some point(s) in the future and that are owed to non-residents by residents of an economy.

UK External Debt data are compiled according to the IMF's *External Debt Statistics: Guide for Compilers and Users* (www.imf.org/external/pubs/ft/eds/Eng/Guide/index.htm#Guide). The data are consistent with those contained in the UK's international investment position (IIP) statement.

End-period stocks of external liabilities are classified according to institutional sector (General government, monetary authorities, Banks and Other sectors), type of instrument, and original maturity of instrument. Direct investment liabilities are separately identified.

Current transfers (Chapter 5)

Introduction

Transfers represent the provision (or receipt) of an economic value by one party without directly receiving (or providing) a counterpart item of economic value. In plain terms a transaction representing 'something for nothing' or without a *quid pro quo*. Transfers can be in the form of money, or of goods or services provided without the expectation of payment. Transfers are broken down into current or capital transfers. Capital transfers relate to the transfer of ownership of a fixed asset, or the forgiveness of a liability by a creditor, when no counterpart is received in return. Current transfers are all other types of transfer. Current transfers are subdivided into those made or received by general government and by other sectors. The UK's contributions to and receipts from the European Union budget are recorded on a gross basis.

General government current transfers

General government transfers include receipts, contributions and subscriptions from or to European Union (EU) institutions and other international bodies, bilateral aid and military grants. Information mainly comes from government departments (HM Treasury, Foreign & Commonwealth Office and Department for International Development).

Credits

These mainly comprise receipts of the UK general government from EU institutions, taxes on income, and social contributions paid by non-resident workers.

Current taxes on income and wealth: these are the receipts of the UK Government from taxes on the incomes of non-resident seasonal and border workers working in the UK (the incomes themselves are recorded as compensation of employees) and withholding taxes paid abroad by UK direct investment corporations. The former are estimated on the basis of the compensation of employees information derived from the International Passenger Survey and the latter from ONS inquiries into foreign direct investment.

Social contributions: these represent social contributions paid to the UK National Insurance Fund by non-residents.

EU institutions: these receipts comprise the VAT Abatement and other smaller, miscellaneous EU receipts. From the 1998 edition of the *Pink Book*, the VAT Abatement is treated as a credit entry to the UK balance of payments, rather than netted off VAT-based contributions.

Debits

These comprise payments by the UK general government to international organisations and other non-residents.

Social security benefits: these mainly consist of National Insurance Fund retirement and war pensions paid to foreign residents.

European Union institutions: these payments are mainly the central government part of the UK contribution to the EU budget. For more detailed information, please see the methodological notes to Table 9.9.

Other international organisations: this includes contributions to the military budget of NATO, contributions to the European Regional Development Fund and agencies of the United Nations to provide economic assistance to developing countries, and subscriptions to cover the administrative expenses of various other international bodies.

Bilateral aid: this covers technical co-operation and non-project grants (project grants are included within capital transfers as they fund capital projects). Technical co-operation covers the provision of technical 'know-how' to developing and transitional countries either as qualified manpower or as facilities for the training of nationals of these countries. It is wholly funded by the UK Government and is included as a credit in 'Trade in services'. Non-project grants are cash grants to developing countries for use in financing imports and budgetary support, together with the value of goods and services provided by the UK Government as food aid or disaster relief.

Military grants: these consist of cash grants for military purposes and the value of goods and services of a military nature provided without charge to foreign countries and international organisations by the UK Government.

Other sectors' transfers

Other sectors' transfers cover current taxes paid, receipts and payments to EU institutions, net non-life insurance premiums and claims, and other payments and receipts of households, including remittances.

Credits

Private social contributions: this consists of the actual social contributions paid by non-residents to UK private pension schemes, plus the related imputed contribution supplement, less the related service charge. Data are sourced from ONS surveys to pension funds.

Receipts from EU institutions: comprise those paid out of the EU's Agricultural Guarantee Fund and Social Fund. They are treated as non-government transfers within the national accounts and balance of payments, as the UK Government acts only as an agent for the ultimate beneficiary of the transfer.

Net non-life insurance premiums: comprise the actual premiums received by UK insurance companies from non-residents plus the related imputed premium supplement, less the related insurance service charge. The sources for these data are ONS surveys of insurance corporations, which collect premiums by type of insurance product, and Lloyd's of London.

Net non-life insurance claims: these are based on information supplied to the International Trade in Services survey on insurance claims received from non-resident insurance companies.

Other receipts of households: consists of two main components:

- Remittances, which are current transfers in cash or in kind sent by households resident in foreign economies to households resident in the UK. These estimates are statistical projections mainly based on bilateral information on partner countries' remittance flows to the UK, where these are published or have been made available to ONS, or on the basis of entries in the IMF *Balance of Payments Statistics Yearbook*, with fixed percentages of the total workers' remittances for certain countries assumed to go to the UK

- UK charities transfer receipts from abroad. These are based on information from a 1995 survey to charities

Debits

Current taxes on income: these are taxes on the incomes of UK seasonal and border workers (recorded as compensation of employees) working abroad and withholding taxes paid abroad by UK direct investment corporations. The former are estimated on the basis of the compensation of employees information derived from the International Passenger Survey and the latter from ONS inquiries into foreign direct investment.

Private social benefits: comprise private pensions paid abroad, plus the change in net equity in pension fund reserves of non-residents. The data source is the ONS survey of pension funds.

Payments to EU institutions: these comprise agricultural and sugar levies, customs duties and VAT-based contributions. The data source is HM Treasury.

Net non-life insurance premiums: this covers premiums paid by UK companies to non-resident insurance companies collected via the International Trade in Services survey.

Net non-life insurance claims: this covers settlement of claims by UK insurance companies to non-resident claimants, which are regarded as a transfer debit. The total of claims equals the total of net premiums (service charges having been deducted), as the essential function of non-life insurance is to redistribute resources. The sources for these data are ONS surveys of insurance corporations, and Lloyd's of London.

Other payments of households: these include two main components:

- Remittances, which are current transfers in cash or in kind sent by UK households to households resident in foreign economies. In many cases these are sent by long-term migrant workers in the UK to friends or relatives still resident in their country of origin. Data were obtained from exchange control records until 1979. Estimates since 1979 are statistical projections mainly based on the exchange control data and also some bilateral information on partner countries' remittance flows to the UK. The projections also take account of information on the value of gifts of money and goods sent abroad by parcel post
- UK charities' transfers abroad. These are based on information from a 1995 survey to charities

Capital account (Chapter 6)

The capital account comprises two components: capital transfers and the acquisition/disposal of non-produced, non-financial assets.

Capital transfers

Capital transfers are those involving transfers of ownership of fixed assets, transfers of funds associated with the acquisition or disposal of fixed assets, and cancellation of liabilities by creditors without any counterparts being received in return. As with current transfers, they can be subdivided into general government transfers and other sectors transfers. The main sources of information are government departments (Department for International Development and HM Treasury) and the Bank of England. Compensation payments from the EU related to the destruction of animals to combat BSE and foot and mouth disease are also included here.

General government capital transfers

These consist of debt forgiveness and project grants (there are no receipts in recent years).

Debits

Debt forgiveness is defined as the voluntary cancellation of debt between a creditor, in this case the UK Government, and a debtor in another country. Data are supplied by the Department for International Development. Project grants are cash grants to developing countries for the establishment of production and infrastructure facilities. Such transfers are distinguished from current transfers as they are conditional on the acquisition of fixed assets. Data are supplied by the Department for International Development.

Other sectors capital transfers

These include migrants' transfers, debt forgiveness and capital transfers from European Union institutions.

Credits

Migrants' transfers: these are recorded as being equal to the net worth of the migrants, as they arrive in the UK. Estimates are based on information on number of migrants and average assets being transferred as collected on the International Passenger Survey.

Transfers from EU institutions: Regional Development Fund and Agricultural Fund for Regional Development receipts from the EU are assumed to be capital rather than current transfers as they relate to infrastructure projects. Data are supplied by HM Treasury. Other capital transfers include agricultural compensation scheme payments relating to the destruction of animals to combat BSE and Foot and Mouth Disease.

Debits

Migrants' transfers: these represent the net worth of emigrants as they leave the UK. Estimates are based on information on the number of migrants and average assets being transferred as supplied to the International Passenger Survey.

Debt forgiveness: this consists of non-government debt forgiveness by monetary financial institutions and public corporations. Data on monetary financial institutions is supplied by the Bank of England and data on public corporations is supplied by the Export Credit Guarantee Department.

Sales/purchases of non-produced, non-financial assets

This heading covers intangibles such as patents, copyrights, franchises, leases and other transferable contracts, and goodwill; and transactions involving tangible assets that may be used or needed for the production of goods and services but have not themselves been produced, such as land and sub-soil assets. The use of such assets is recorded under trade in services as royalties and license fees; only the outright purchase or sale of such assets is recorded in the capital account.

The International Trade in Services (ITIS) survey has collected information on the sale and purchase of copyrights, patents and transferable contracts from 1996. Such transactions are indistinguishable from other areas of the current account for years before 1996.

Geographical breakdown on the current account and international investment position (Chapters 9 and 10)

Introduction

The geographical data is broadly consistent with level 2 of Eurostat's Vade Mecum (66 individual countries, nine geographical regions and five continents). Data for the European Union (EU) relate to the membership following the enlargement of 1 January 2007. EU Institutions are included in the EU aggregate and are excluded from the International Organisations total. Separate data for Belgium and Luxembourg are not available for periods before 1999. Data for China exclude Hong Kong, which is shown as an individual item.

Reliability of estimates

The UK's balance of payments accounts are primarily compiled on a global basis. Not all of the data sources used in preparing the accounts attempt to distinguish transactions on a full country basis, although the majority do. Where individual country information is not reported, estimates are made by using the geographical detail for a related category; for example, the geographical breakdown of financial assets and liabilities is used to allocate some components of investment income.

In addition to the imputation of geographical detail for some categories where the data are incomplete, there remains a margin of uncertainty regarding the accuracy of reported data by country. The finer the level of geographical detail sought, the greater the likelihood of misallocation. Enterprises are encouraged to make their best estimates when asked to report geographical data but, as country allocation may not be a crucial aspect of the information from which details are extracted, a significant degree of estimation may occur.

Given these conceptual and practical limitations, these estimates should be seen as a broad indication of the economic relationships between the UK and the rest of the world economies. They will be more reliable and meaningful in terms of broad geographical areas and major partner countries than for smaller partners. Estimates for recent years are currently more reliable than those for earlier years since some data sources do not extend back over the whole published period.

Approach for country allocation

The following notes summarise the main criteria of country allocation adopted for the various categories of the current account. In general the figures are not likely to be consistent with those recorded by countries which allocate regional balance of payments estimates on a cash settlements basis. An analysis of UK asymmetries with its EU and US partners was published in the March 2005 edition of *Economic Trends*, which can be found at: www.statistics.gov.uk/cci/article.asp?ID=1056

Trade in goods

Exports of goods are allocated to the country of destination; imports of goods are allocated according to the country of consignment. However, export figures from a country (A) to another country (B) may over-estimate the value of goods actually consumed in that country (B) if the importer forwards the goods on to another country (C). There are several reasons for this: 'the Rotterdam/Antwerp effect' (exports are properly attributed to the country where the port of discharge is located, following international convention, but are then re-exported to the country of final destination); other transit trade

Methodological notes

(goods passing straight through the country); and triangular trade (where goods are sold from member state A to B and on to C, but the goods move directly from A to C). 'The Rotterdam/Antwerp effect' is a particular issue with the UK because of exports routed through Rotterdam in the Netherlands and Antwerp in Belgium. No information is available on the value of UK exports that are subsequently shipped on to other countries, although investigations are taking place. The principal data source for trade in goods is HMRC (see the methodological notes on 'Trade in goods (Chapter 2)' for more details).

Trade in services

The geographical breakdown of exports and imports of services are largely based on the existing sources of information for the global estimates, although there is some use of proxy information for some components. The change from an industry to a product-based presentation with the introduction of the fifth edition of the IMF *Balance of Payments Manual* in 1998, and the consequent change to data collection, means that data from 1996 onwards are largely based on reported geographical breakdowns of the new products. Earlier geographical estimates are based on the industry-based geographical breakdowns in the fourth edition of the IMF *Balance of Payments Manual*, adjusted to take the changes to the trade in services classification into account.

Sea transport: estimates relating to ships owned or chartered by UK operators are taken from inquiries carried out by the Chamber of Shipping.

Geographical breakdowns of freight services on exports and cross trades are allocated using the ports at which the goods are unloaded. For non-resident operators' freight on UK imports, the nationality of the exporting country is used as a proxy to allocate the freight payments. The resulting proportions are used to calculate the shares of non-resident operators' disbursements in the UK. Disbursements abroad by UK operators are supplied annually by the Chamber of Shipping.

Passenger revenue export estimates are derived from information supplied annually by the Chamber of Shipping. Passenger revenue import estimates are based on assumptions about the likely markets for cruises and on other information relating to the movements of UK shipping.

Air transport: passenger revenue exports are based on information supplied to ONS by the Civil Aviation Authority, which gives the required country analysis of fares paid. Other transactions with foreign airlines are allocated by nationality of airline. Receipts by UK airlines from foreign passengers are allocated to the countries in which tickets are purchased. Freight services on UK imports earned by foreign airlines are allocated to the countries of consignment of the imports.

Other transport: rail passenger exports are based on assumptions of the likely nationality of channel tunnel users. Rail imports are allocated entirely to France. Estimates for road freight exports and imports are based on information supplied by the Road Haulage Association. This information includes details of vehicle load and country of destination or country of origin. Pipeline transport is based on those countries that are assumed to import / export North Sea oil and gas.

Travel: a detailed geographical split of travel expenditure, both exports and imports, are obtained from the International Passenger Survey. Allocation of expenditure of overseas visitors to the UK is by country of residence. UK residents' expenditures abroad are allocated to the country in which most time was spent or, if this cannot be determined, the furthest country visited. As a result, expenditure in countries with appreciable numbers of transit tourists may be understated.

Other services: data for communication, construction, computer and information, royalties, other business and personal services are largely based on information supplied to the ITIS survey, supplemented with information from Royal Mail, ONS's Film and Television inquiries and Lloyd's registry for shipping.

Insurance services: estimates are based on detailed geographical data provided by Lloyd's of London, as well as the ITIS survey for insurance imports provided to non-insurance institutions. The geographical split of trade in goods' imports is used as a proxy for freight insurance imports. Geographical splits for other insurance services are based on fixed weights.

Financial services: regular geographical information on gross flows is obtained from the Bank of England for banking services (including FISIM), and from the ITIS survey for financial service exports and imports from non-financial institutions. The geographical breakdown of non-bank financial corporation service exports are imputed using banking geographical data as a proxy.

Government services: for the major components, detailed geographical information on the location of those receiving or making payments is available from returns provided by the Ministry of Defence, Department for Work and Pensions, and the Foreign and Commonwealth Office. The United States Air Force has also provided data on expenditure of US Forces in the UK. Expenditure by foreign embassies and consulates in the UK is based on information supplied by some overseas embassies and statistical institutions, supplemented by information on numbers of accredited diplomats by country.

Income

Compensation of employees: estimates of the geographical breakdown of seasonal and border workers' earnings are based on information supplied to the International Passenger Survey. Figures for the earnings of locally engaged staff are based on information supplied by government departments.

Investment income and international investment position

Direct investment income: figures are based on the quarterly and annual foreign investment inquiries and include reinvested profits. Geographical information is based on the country of registration of the immediate foreign parent company and the location of the foreign affiliate, except for banks where the information relates to the country of residence of the ultimate owner (for inward investment) or the country of residence in which the direct investment enterprise is located.

Portfolio investment income: credits are the earnings accruing to UK residents from their investment in equities and debt securities, in the form of bonds and notes and money market instruments, issued by foreign institutions. Global estimates are derived from surveys of UK end-investors (banks, securities dealers, unit and investment trusts, insurance companies, pension funds and some non-financial companies).

Deriving a geographical breakdown of portfolio investment income flows has been one of the most problematic areas of balance of payments compilation. Portfolio investment income is particularly difficult to allocate correctly to the actual country owning or issuing the security, as the transactions are often made through financial intermediaries in a third country. However, with the launch and subsequent expansion of the IMF's Coordinated Portfolio Investment Survey (CPIS), an important new data source has become available. Participants in the CPIS collect a geographical breakdown of their portfolio investment assets, which are co-ordinated and disseminated by the IMF.

Data on the geographical breakdown of portfolio investment credits are derived from the UK's contribution to the CPIS exercise from 2001. For banks, Bank of England information on the geographical breakdown of levels is applied to the estimates of global earnings obtained by surveys of UK banks. Similarly for non-banks, a geographical breakdown of portfolio investment income is derived from the geographical breakdown of portfolio investment assets.

Information on the geographical breakdown of UK portfolio investment debits (dividends and interest payments made to overseas residents by issuers of UK securities), are based on other countries' participation in the CPIS exercise. The IMF acts as a central clearing house for the compilation of aggregate data from countries that have participated in the CPIS and disseminate the information to balance of payments compilers. These data can provide us with information on participating countries' holdings of UK-issued equity and debt securities. For earlier years, surveys of share ownership are used to allocate portfolio holdings of UK equity securities and associated dividends by country of holder. For interest on holdings of debt securities, data derived from the CPIS exercises from 2001 onwards have been used to estimate the geographical breakdown.

Other investment income: gross interest flows between UK banks and the rest of the world are estimated by the Bank of England by allocating global interest receipts and payments in proportion to the corresponding levels of assets and liabilities of UK banks. Interest flows for UK non-bank deposits with, and borrowing from, banks in the BIS reporting area are allocated in proportion to the levels supplied by the BIS. The interest on reserve assets is estimated from official records. Figures for UK banks are used as proxies to estimate a country breakdown for the remaining components of earnings on other investment.

Adjustments applied to the global earnings on other investment to exclude the Channel Islands and the Isle of Man have been used to estimate other investment income between the UK and the offshore islands. These data are included within 'Other Europe'.

Current transfers

There are very few data sources for current transfers that allocate transactions on a country basis – these are outlined below. The geographical allocation of withholding taxes is based on the geographical allocation of inward and outward direct investment as published in Business Monitor MA4. The geographical allocation of insurance premiums is based on information supplied by Lloyd's of London. Data on EU transfers are provided by HM Treasury, and the geographical allocation of social security and aid payments are supplied by the Department for Work and Pensions and the Department for International Development, respectively. Other geographical breakdowns are based on proxy data and global transfer estimates.

UK official transactions with institutions of the EU (Table 9.9)

This table presents all the official transactions between the UK Government and the Institutions of the European Union. The series are the same as those shown in Table 12.1 of the *Blue Book* but the presentation here reflects Balance of Payments rather than National Accounts classification of transactions.

Some of the transfers are classified to Other sectors (rather than central government) as they are paid by or to non-government sectors; however they are still classified as official transactions because the money is collected from or paid to non-government sectors by the UK Government on behalf of the EU. The source for much of the data is HM Treasury (HMT), who are responsible for the UK's official transactions with the EU. These data represent the cash movements in and out of government bank accounts for Transactions with the EU. Any divergences from this source – to accord with the reporting conventions required for Balance of Payments and National Accounts – are detailed below. The data sourced from HMT are also available in chapter 3 of the HMT White Paper on EU Finances found at the following web address: www.hm-treasury.gov.uk/int_eu_statefraud.htm

Credits

Exports of services

This series represents the part of the import levies collected by the UK Government on behalf of the EU that the UK Government retains to cover the costs of collection. The percentage retained was 10 per cent up until 2000 and has been 25 per cent from 2001 onwards. It is treated as an export of a government service.

The exports of services to EU Institutions series in Table 9.3 differs from this one in that the series includes services provided to EU Institutions by UK private companies.

Other sectors current transfers

These largely comprise receipts from the Agricultural Guarantee Fund and the European Social Fund. The receipts from the Agricultural Guarantee Fund are classified as subsidies and are recorded on an accruals basis based on the subsidies paid to farmers by the Rural Payments Agency.

Central government current transfers

These mainly comprise the Fontainebleau Abatement but also include a small number of miscellaneous payments to EU institutions and research councils. Since 1984, the UK's third own resources (VAT-based) contribution to the EU budget has been abated in recognition of the relatively low level of its receipts, compared with its contributions to the Community Budget. Broadly, the UK receives a VAT abatement of its gross contributions equal to two-thirds of the difference between its unabated contribution and its receipts. This is deducted a year in arrears. Since the 1998 edition of the *Pink Book*, this abatement has been treated as a credit entry to the UK balance of payments rather than simply being netted off VAT-based contributions.

Other sectors capital transfers

In most years these consist entirely of receipts from the Agricultural Fund for Regional Development and the European Regional Development Fund. Other capital transfers from EU institutions are payments to farmers under agricultural compensation schemes related to the destruction of animals during the BSE and Foot and Mouth disease outbreaks.

Debits

Other sectors current transfers

These comprise the UK's traditional own resource and third own resource contributions to the EU. The former are customs duties paid on a range of products imported from non-member states, and levies charged on the production of sugar to recover part of the costs of subsidising the export of surplus EU sugar on to the world market. EU third own resources are VAT-based contributions which represent a notional extra 1 per cent on the VAT base, but are capped at 0.5 per cent of Gross National Income (GNI), hence the adjustment to VAT contributions. Payments of both traditional and third own resource contributions are classified as taxes paid direct to the EU. Estimates are sourced from HMRC and are converted to an accruals basis using agreed methodologies.

Central government current transfers

This mainly consists of the UK Government's fourth own resource contribution. This is calculated as a fixed percentage of UK GNI, increased or rebated according to whether within the EU budget as a whole, expenditure exceeds or falls short of revenue. There are also a small number of miscellaneous payments to EU institutions under this heading.

Trade in Goods and Services additional tables (Tables 9.10, 9.11, 9.12, 9.13 and 9.14)

Tables 9.10 and 9.11 show imports of services from and exports of services to selected partner countries broken down by the 11 broad categories of services for the latest two years. The details of the methods of country allocation are outlined in the trade in services section above. To avoid disclosing data on individual companies, the tables have been arranged to remove these disclosive items. This is done wherever possible by suppressing the item so that non-disclosing headings are preserved.

Table 9.12 shows the top-50 trading partners for imports and exports of goods and services for the last two years for which data are available. Again the details of the methods of country allocation are outlined above in the goods and services sections.

Table 9.13 shows estimates of the UK's exports and imports of services with all partner countries for the latest two years. Countries not listed in the tables are assumed to have total transactions in services with the UK of less than £0.5 million. The details of the methods of country allocation are outlined in the section on trade in services above. The data sources which have full country breakdowns of transactions in services are the ITIS survey and the IPS, which between them account for around 70 per cent of the source data for total trade in services. Data from these sources have been used as proxies to estimate the very detailed country breakdowns where these are not available for other data sources.

Table 9.14 shows the UK's data for trade in services compared with world totals and those for G7 countries. The data for these are sourced from the IMF. This data is not available for the latest year as it will not have been published yet. No world balance is included as this should in theory be zero, but in practise because of asymmetries it tends to have either positive or negative values.

Further information on UK balance of payments

The following articles of interest relate to UK balance of payments statistics:

Revisions Analysis to Quarterly Current Account Balance of Payments Data

An analysis of revisions made to balance of payments quarterly current account data between 1998 Q4 and 2003 Q3, an update of the previous article published in the August 2005 issue of *Economic Trends*.

Author: Mala Mistry

This article focuses on revisions to current account credits and debits and how these influence revision to the current account balance. The article also explores the chronological evolution of revisions, revisions to current account components and provides explanation for more prominent revisions occurring over the period analysed.

www.statistics.gov.uk/cci/article.asp?ID=1800

CPIS 2004 Data – Preliminary Results

Analysis of the UK's preliminary CPIS results 2004 including total portfolio investment assets by type of investment.

Author: Ellie Turner

This paper analyses preliminary UK results for the Coordinated Portfolio Investment Survey (CPIS) 2004. Data was delivered to the International Monetary Fund (IMF) on 1 November 2005 and was published on their website in January 2006.

www.statistics.gov.uk/CCI/article.asp?ID=1303

Analysis of past revisions to UK Trade statistics

The past revisions performance for UK Trade statistics explained.

Author: David Ruffles

This article presents an analysis of the past revisions performance for UK Trade statistics, looks at the statistically significant mean or average revisions seen in the figures for total trade, identifies the main causes of these revisions, and describes what is being done to improve the first published estimates.

www.statistics.gov.uk/cci/article.asp?ID=1063

Current Account Asymmetries with the European Union, Annual Report 2004

A report on current account asymmetries for 2004.

Author: Libby Cox

Current account asymmetries occur when one country's data does not correspond to the same data for the same transaction reported by its partner countries. This report analyses asymmetries between the UK current account and the rest of the European Union. Additional data is presented regarding asymmetries between the UK and the US.

www.statistics.gov.uk/cci/article.asp?ID=1056

Report on impact of MTIC on UK Trade statistics

Report on further research into the impact of Missing Trader Fraud on UK Trade Statistics, Balance of Payments and National Accounts.

Authors: David Ruffles, Tricia Williams (HM Revenue & Customs)

This article was a follow-up to the article published in the August 2003 edition of *Economic Trends* which is available on the ONS website. It summarises the work carried out since July 2003 to review the estimates of the impact of Missing Trader Intra-Community (MTIC) VAT Fraud on UK Trade Statistics, Balance of Payments and National Accounts, and to investigate potential methods of estimating acquisition fraud.

www.statistics.gov.uk/cci/article.asp?ID=1066

Methodological improvements to UK foreign property investment statistics

New methodology to measure ownership of foreign property by UK households and estimates the value of property owned at end 2003 to be £23 billion.

Author: Deborah Nicole Aspden

This article presents new methodology to measure ownership of foreign property by UK households. It is based on the Office of the Deputy Prime Minister's (ODPM) Survey of English Housing (SEH). The new methodology estimates the value of foreign property ownership in 2003/04 to be just above £23 billion – more than double the estimate for 1999/2000. Investment is highest in Europe, with Spain and France being the preferred locations for investment.

www.statistics.gov.uk/cci/article.asp?ID=1176

Financial Derivatives in the UK Sector Balance Sheets and Financial Accounts

Although the availability and quality of data on financial derivatives has improved, a number of methodology and coverage issues remain outstanding.

Author: Graham Semken

This article re-assesses the area of derivatives statistics following expanded data availability. It examines a number of issues, both conceptual and practical, which will need to be resolved before the collective data on derivatives can be integrated into the UK accounts.

www.statistics.gov.uk/cci/article.asp?ID=1139

Other articles

Older articles which may be of interest, published in *Economic Trends*, include:

- 'Overseas trade in services: publication of monthly estimates', September 1997
- 'Geographical breakdown of exports and imports of UK trade in services by component', January 1998
- 'Geographical breakdown of income in the balance of payments', November 1999

www.statistics.gov.uk/cci/article.asp?id=44

- 'Geographical breakdown of income in the balance of payments: further improvements to the methodology for portfolio investment income', December 2000

www.statistics.gov.uk/cci/article.asp?id=61

- 'IMF Co-ordinated Portfolio Investment Survey', May 2003

www.statistics.gov.uk/cci/article.asp?ID=345

- 'Geographical breakdown of the UK International Investment Position', June 2004

www.statistics.gov.uk/cci/article.asp?ID=907

Glossary

Acceptances
See 'Bills and acceptances'.

Accrued interest
A method of recording transactions to relate them to the period when the exchange of ownership of the goods, services or financial asset applies. For example, value added tax accrues when the expenditure to which it relates takes place, but HM Revenue & Customs (HMRC) receive the cash some time later. The difference between accruals and cash results in the creation of an asset and liability in the financial accounts, shown as amounts receivable or payable.

Advance and progress payments
Payments made for goods in advance of completion and delivery of the goods.

Affiliates
Branches, subsidiaries or associate companies.

Allocation of SDRs
See 'Special Drawing Rights'.

Arbitrage
Buying in a market in one centre and selling in a similar market in another centre, in order to exploit a temporary misalignment of prices at little or no risk.

Assets
This term commonly refers to financial assets that are claims on non-residents, from whose point of view the same item is a liability to a UK resident. Among reserve assets, however, gold and SDRs have a value which exists independently of any corresponding liabilities. Real assets such as merchandise, although they may be entered in company accounts as assets, are seldom described as assets in balance of payments analysis.

Associated companies
Companies in which the investing company has a substantial equity interest (usually this means that it holds between 10 per cent and 50 per cent of the equity share capital) and is in a position to exercise a significant influence on the company. (See 'Subsidiary'.)

Balancing item
See 'Net errors and omissions'.

Bank of England – Issue Department
This part of the Bank of England deals with the issue of bank notes on behalf of central government. It was formerly classified to central government though it is now part of the central bank/monetary authorities sector. Its activities include, inter alia, market purchases of commercial bills from UK banks.

Bank for International Settlements (BIS)
An international institution based in Basle, Switzerland, established in 1930. Its main functions today are to promote international monetary co-operation; to observe the work of the IMF, Finance Ministers and Central Bank Governors of the Group of Ten countries; and to provide monetary research. The most recent BIS data used within the UK balance of payments accounts covers non-bank borrowing from banks in the following countries: Australia, Austria, the Bahamas, Bahrain, Belgium/Luxembourg, Bermuda, Brazil, Canada, Cayman Islands, Chile, Denmark, Finland, France, Germany, Greece, Guernsey, Hong Kong SAR, India, Ireland, Isle of Man, Italy, Japan, Jersey, Mexico, Netherlands, Netherlands Antilles, Norway, Panama, Portugal, Singapore, Spain, South Korea, Sweden, Switzerland, Taiwan, Turkey and United States of America. The data used for balance of payments purposes are locational banking statistics on a residence basis.

Banking statistics
A term used in this publication to denote an integrated set of returns, covering all UK banks, and collected by the Bank of England. The returns were first introduced in late 1974 and during 1975. Since then, various reviews of the requirements of data from banks have been conducted and forms amended, introduced or dropped as necessary. The data collected covers all listed banks up to the end of 1981 and the revised group of institutions classified as UK banks from 1982 onwards. It collects on a regular basis extensive information relating to the levels of, and changes in, assets and liabilities. Revised banking returns were introduced from the end of 1997 to reflect the requirements of the IMF *Balance of Payments Manual* 5th edition and to remove the Channel Islands and the Isle of Man from the definition of the economic territory of the UK.

Banks (UK)
Banks are defined as all financial institutions recognised by the Bank of England as UK banks. For statistical purposes, this includes:

- institutions which have a permission under Part 4 of the Financial Services and Markets Act 2000 (FSMA) to accept deposits, other than (i) credit unions, (ii) firms which have a permission to accept deposits only in the course of carrying out contracts of insurance in accordance with that permission, (iii) friendly societies, and (iv) building societies

- European Economic Area credit institutions with a permission under Schedule 3 to FSMA to accept deposits through a UK branch

- the Banking and Issue Departments of the Bank of England (the latter from April 1998)

Prior to December 2001, banks were defined as all financial institutions recognised by the Bank of England as UK banks for statistical purposes, including the UK offices of institutions authorised under the Banking Act 1987, the Banking and Issue Departments of the Bank of England (the latter from April 1988), and deposit-taking UK branches of 'European Authorised Institutions'. This includes UK branches of foreign banks, but not the offices abroad of these or of any British owned banks.

An updated list of banks appears regularly in the Bank of England's *Monetary and Financial Statistics* publication (available at: www.bankofengland.co.uk/statistics/ms/index.htm). The most recent list can also be found on the Financial Services Authority website at: www.fsa.gov.uk/Pages/Library/Other_publications/Banks/index.shtml

Bills and acceptances
A bill is an unconditional order in writing addressed by the drawer to the drawee to pay to the drawer a fixed sum on a specified date. A UK resident may draw a bill in sterling on a foreign resident representing credit extended by the UK resident to the foreign resident. If the UK resident sells the bill to a UK bank, generally at a price less than the nominal value of the bill, the bank is said to discount the bill, and the claim on the foreign resident is transferred to the UK bank.

A bill is known as an acceptance when the drawee accepts the bill. A UK bank may accept a bill on behalf of a foreign resident in which case the UK resident draws the bill on the UK bank and not on the foreign resident. The accepting bank has a claim on the foreign resident and expects to be paid by him before the bill matures.

Bond
A financial instrument that usually pays interest to the holder. Bonds are issued by governments as well as companies and other institutions, for example, local authorities. Most bonds have a fixed date on which the borrower will repay the holder. Bonds are attractive to investors since they can be bought and sold easily in a secondary market. Special forms of bonds include deep discount bonds, equity warrant bonds, Eurobonds, and zero coupon bonds.

BPM5
The *Balance of Payments Manual,* 5th Edition, published in 1993 by the IMF.

Branch
An unincorporated enterprise, wholly or jointly owned by a direct investor.

British government stocks
Securities issued or guaranteed by the UK government, also known as gilts.

Building societies

Building societies are mutual institutions specialising in accepting deposits from members of the public and in long-term lending to members of the public, mainly to finance the purchase of dwellings; such lending being secured on dwellings. Their operations are governed by special legislation which places restrictions on their recourse to other sources of funding and other avenues of investment.

Capital account

The capital account consists of capital transfers (see 'Transfers') and acquisition/disposal of non-produced, non-financial assets (see separate entry in glossary).

Capital transfers

See 'Transfers'.

Certificate of deposit

A short-term interest-paying instrument issued by deposit-taking institutions in return for money deposited for a fixed period. Interest is earned at a given rate. The instrument can be used as security for a loan if the depositor requires money before the repayment date.

c.i.f. (cost, insurance and freight)

The basis of valuation of imports for Customs purposes, it includes the cost of insurance premiums and freight services. These need to be deducted to obtain the *free on board* valuation consistent with the valuation of exports which is used in the economic accounts.

Collective investment institution (CII)

Incorporated (investment companies or investment trusts) and unincorporated undertakings (mutual funds or unit trusts) that invest the funds, collected from investors by means of issuing shares/units (other than equity), in financial assets (mainly marketable securities and bank deposits) and real estate. (See also 'Trusts'.)

Commercial paper

This is an unsecured promissory note for a specific amount and maturing on a specific date. The commercial paper market allows companies to issue short-term debt direct to financial institutions who then market this paper to investors or use it for their own investment purposes.

Commodity gold

See 'Gold'.

Commonwealth Development Corporation

A public corporation which finances development projects abroad.

Compensation of employees

Total remuneration payable to employees in cash or in kind, and includes the value of social contributions payable by the employer.

Coordinated Portfolio Investment Survey (CPIS)

A survey coordinated and disseminated by the IMF. Participants in the CPIS collect a geographical breakdown of their portfolio investment assets.

Counterpart items

Certain items in the balance of payments exist only as counterpart items, introduced to balance the inclusion of other items that do not fall naturally into the double-entry system. The allocation of SDRs is an example of an artificial counterpart item introduced into the balance of payments to offset the corresponding increase in SDR holdings within official reserves (as SDRs are no one sector's liabilities). (For SDRs see 'Special Drawing Rights'.)

Cross-trades

The provision of transportation services by resident operators between two foreign economies.

Currency swaps

A *currency swap*, also known as a *cross-currency interest-rate swap* contract, consists of an exchange of cash flows related to interest payments and, at the end of the contract, an exchange of principal amounts in specified currencies at a specified exchange rate.

Current account

The account of transactions in respect of trade in goods and services, income and current transfers.

Current balance

The balance of current account transactions.

Current transfers

See 'Transfers'.

Debt forgiveness

The voluntary cancellation of all or part of a debt within a contractual arrangement between a creditor in one country and a debtor in another country.

Debt securities

Debt securities cover bonds, debentures, notes etc., and money market instruments. These are split into long and short (up to one year) term, based on original maturity.

Derivatives

See 'Financial derivatives'.

Direct investment

Net investment by UK/foreign companies in their foreign/UK branches, subsidiaries or associated companies. A direct investment in a company means that the investor has a significant influence on the operations of the company, defined as having an equity interest in an enterprise resident in another country of 10 per cent or more of the ordinary shares or voting stock. (See 'Branch indebtedness', 'Subsidiary' and 'Associated companies'.) Investment covers not only acquisition of fixed assets, stock building and stock appreciation, but also all other financial transactions, such as: additions to or payments of working capital; other loans and trade credit; and acquisitions of securities. Estimates of investment flows allow for depreciation in any undistributed profits. Funds raised by the subsidiary or associate company in the economy in which it operates are excluded as they are locally raised and not sourced from the parent company.

Disbursements

Operating expenses, for example, by operators of ships or aircraft.

Dividend

A payment made to company shareholders from current or previously retained profits. Dividends are recorded when they become payable.

Equity

Equity is ownership or potential ownership of a company. Equities differ from other financial instruments in that they confer ownership of something more than a financial claim. Shareholders are owners of the company whereas bond holders are outside creditors.

Equity securities

Equity securities are shares issued by companies to shareholders. Purchases of equity securities in which the purchaser does not have any significant degree of control over the company (that is, less than 10 per cent of the equity capital) fall within portfolio investment; otherwise it falls within direct investment. Equity securities include mutual fund shares.

Euro area

The euro area encompasses those member states of the European Union in which the euro has been adopted as the single currency and in which a single monetary policy is conducted under the responsibility of the decision-making bodies of the European Central Bank. In 2008 the euro area comprised Austria, Belgium, Cyprus, Finland, France, Germany, Greece, Ireland, Italy, Luxembourg, Malta, the Netherlands, Portugal, Slovenia and Spain.

Eurocurrency market

All borrowing and lending by banks in currencies other than that of the country in which the banks are situated.

Euro/European Currency Unit (ECU)

The ECU was officially introduced in 1979 in connection with the start of the European Monetary System (EMS). In the EMS, the ECU served as the basis for determining exchange rate parities and as a reserve asset and means of settlement. It was a composite currency which contained specified amounts of the currencies of the member states of the European Union. The currencies making up the ECU were weighted according to their economic importance and use in short-term finance. As from September 1989 the weightings of the ECU were revised to include both the Spanish peseta and Portuguese escudo. The ECU was converted into the euro at the start of European Monetary Union on 1 January 1999, with Greece joining on 1 January 2001. From 1 January 2003, the euro became the currency of the member states of the European Monetary Union.

European Central Bank (ECB)

The Monetary Authority for the euro currency, based in Frankfurt. The ECB, together with the national central banks of the member states, manages monetary policy and the banking system across the European Monetary Union area.

European Investment Bank (EIB)

This was set up to assist economic development within the European Union. Its members are the member states of the EU.

European Monetary System (EMS)

The EMS was established in March 1979. Its most important element was the mechanism known as the ERM (Exchange Rate Mechanism) whereby the exchange rates between the currencies of the participating member states were kept within set ranges. The UK joined the ERM on 8 October 1990. On 16 September 1992 the UK's membership of the ERM and the EMS was suspended. The EMS was superseded by the single currency when 11 of the participating member states joined European Monetary Union on 1 January 1999, with Greece joining on 1 January 2001.

Eurosystem

The Eurosystem comprises the European Central Bank (ECB) and the national central banks of the member states which have adopted the euro in Stage Three of Economic and Monetary Union (EMU). In 2008 there were 15 national central banks in the Eurosystem. The Eurosystem is governed by the Governing Council and the Executive Board of the ECB and has assumed the task of conducting the single monetary policy for the euro area since 1 January 1999. Its primary objective is to maintain price stability.

Exchange control

A legal control imposed by governments on the ability of persons, businesses and others to hold, receive and transfer foreign currency. The extent of the Exchange Control Act of 1947 was considerably reduced in June and July 1979 and the Act was repealed in 1987.

Exchange cover scheme (ECS)

A scheme first introduced in 1969 whereby UK public bodies raise foreign currency from abroad, either directly or through UK banks, and generally surrender it to the EEA (see below) in exchange for sterling for use to finance expenditure in the UK. HM Treasury sells the borrower foreign currency to service and repay the loan at the exchange rate that applied when the loan was taken out. The transactions relate to net borrowing by British Nuclear Fuels plc and repayment by HM Government following the privatisation of other former public corporations (see 'Novations').

Exchange Equalisation Account (EEA)

The government account with the Bank of England in which transactions in reserve assets are recorded. These transactions are classified to the central government sector. It is the means by which the government, through the Bank of England, influences exchange rates.

Export credit

Credit extended abroad by UK institutions, primarily in connection with UK exports but also including some credit in respect of third-country trade.

Export Credit Guarantee Department (ECGD)

A non-ministerial government department, classified to the public corporations sector, the main function of which is to provide insurance cover for export credit transactions.

External debt

A measure of balance sheet liabilities owing to non-residents. Liabilities relating to trade credit, debt securities, and loans and deposits (including inter-company liabilities within direct investment) are included; equity liabilities are excluded.

Financial account

The financial account records transactions in external assets and liabilities of the UK, for example, the acquisitions and disposals of foreign shares by UK residents. The financial account consists of direct investment, portfolio investment, other investment, financial derivatives and reserve assets.

Financial auxiliaries

Auxiliary financial activities are ones closely related to financial intermediation but which are not financial intermediation themselves, such as the repackaging of funds, insurance broking and fund management. Financial auxiliaries therefore include insurance brokers and fund managers.

Financial corporations

All bodies recognised as independent legal entities whose principal activity is financial intermediation and/or the production of auxiliary financial services. However, the UK currently treats financial auxiliaries as non-financial corporations.

Financial derivatives

Any financial instrument the price of which is based upon the value of an underlying asset (typically another financial asset). Financial derivatives include options (on, for example, currencies, interest rates, commodities, and indices), traded financial futures, warrants, and currency and interest swaps. Under *BPM5*, transactions in derivatives are treated as separate transactions, rather than being included as integral parts of underlying transactions to which they may be linked as hedges. Only estimates for settlement receipts/payments on UK banks' interest rate swaps and forward rate agreements are currently included.

Financial gold

See 'Gold'.

Financial leasing

See 'Leasing'.

Financial surplus or deficit (FSD)

The former term for Net lending(+)/Net borrowing(-), the balance of all current and capital account transactions for an institutional sector or the economy as a whole.

FISIM

FISIM is an acronym for Financial Intermediation Services Indirectly Measured. It represents the implicit charge for the service provided by monetary financial institutions paid for by the interest differential between borrowing and lending rather than through fees and commissions.

f.o.b. (free on board)

An f.o.b. price excludes the cost of insurance and freight from the country of consignment but includes all charges up to the point where the goods are deposited on board the exporting/importing vessel or aircraft. Trade in goods exports are valued on an f.o.b. basis in the balance of payments accounts.

Foreign

In this publication 'foreign' denotes residence outside the UK rather than nationality. In some contexts 'external', 'abroad' or 'non-resident' are used with the same meaning. (See 'Residency'.)

Forwards

In a *forward contract,* the counterparties agree to exchange, on a specified date, a specified quantity of an underlying item (real or financial) at an agreed-upon contract price (the strike price). If a future exchange of currencies is carried out in a forward contract, the counterparties exchange, in accordance with prearranged terms, cash flows based on the reference prices of the underlying items. Forward rate agreements and forward foreign exchange contracts are common types of forward contracts.

Futures

Futures are forward contracts traded on organised exchanges. They give the holder the right to purchase a commodity or a financial asset at a future date.

Gilts

Bonds issued or guaranteed by the UK Government. Also known as gilt-edged securities or British government securities.

Gold

In the accounts, a distinction is drawn between gold held as a financial asset (financial gold) and gold held like any other commodity (commodity gold). Transactions in commodity gold are recorded in the trade in goods account and include foreign trade in finished manufactures together with net domestic and foreign transactions in gold moving into or out of finished manufactured form (that is, for jewellery, dentistry, electronic goods, medals and proof – but not bullion – coins).

All other transactions in gold (that is, those involving semi-manufactures such as rods and wire or bullion, bullion coins or banking-type assets and liabilities denominated in gold, including reserve assets) are treated as financial gold transactions and included in the financial account. The distinction between commodity and financial gold differs from that drawn by the

IMF, in its *Balance of Payments Manual* (5th edition, 1993), between non-monetary and monetary gold. The UK has obtained an exemption from adopting the *BPM5* recommendations on treatment of gold in order to avoid distortion of its trade in goods account by the substantial transactions of the London Bullion Market.

The treatment of non-monetary gold is being reviewed as part of the worldwide process to revise the IMF *Balance of Payments Manual*. The main proposal is that the concept of non-monetary gold would be replaced by two categories – allocated gold (a commodity) and unallocated gold (a financial instrument). UK balance of payments will continue current practice until the treatments defined in the revised manual are implemented.

Gross

The separate identification of both credit/debit, export/import for any particular transaction.

Hedging

Hedging is accomplished by the temporary purchase or sale of futures/swaps contracts to offset the position or anticipated position in the cash markets. This may benefit banks, financial institutions, pension funds and corporate treasuries who hold interest rate, exchange rate or stock price sensitive assets or liabilities.

Holding companies

A holding company is a company that usually confines its activities to owning stock in and supervising management of other companies. A holding company usually owns a controlling interest in the companies whose stock it holds. Holding companies exist for legal, commercial and tax reasons. In line with international standards, holding companies are classified as other financial intermediaries.

Households

Individuals or small groups of individuals as consumers and in some cases as entrepreneurs producing goods and market services.

Import credit

Credit extended to UK institutions by non-residents, primarily in connection with UK imports.

Income

The income account forms part of the current account and consists of compensation of employees and investment income, both of which have separate entries in this glossary.

Inter-company accounts

Accounts recording transactions between parent and subsidiary or associated companies, and balances owed by one to the other.

Interest rate swaps

An obligation between two parties to exchange interest-related payments in the same currency from fixed rate into floating rate, or vice versa, or from one type of floating rate to another. A swap can be used to reshape the coupon payments of either new or existing debt. The only movement of funds is a net transfer of interest payments between the two parties. The interest payments are calculated on an agreed principal amount, which is not exchanged. The settlement receipts/payments on UK banks' interest rate swaps appear in the financial account under financial derivatives.

International investment position (IIP)

The international investment position records end of period balance sheet levels of UK external assets and liabilities. The IIP consists of direct investment, portfolio investment, other investment and reserve assets. Financial derivatives are not currently included in the IIP, but presented separately in Table FD.

International Monetary Fund (IMF)

A Fund set up as a result of the Bretton Woods Conference of 1944 and which began operations in 1947. It includes most of the major countries of the world. The Fund was set up to supervise the fixed exchange rate system agreed at Bretton Woods and to make available to its members a pool of foreign exchange resources to assist them when they have balance of payments difficulties. Further definitions relating to the IMF are given in the IMF section in the 1981 and earlier editions of this publication. (See also 'Special Drawing Rights'.)

Intervention Board for Agricultural Produce (IBAP)

The UK government agency which used to operate the support arrangements of the EU Common Agricultural Policy within the UK. It has now been replaced by the Rural Payments Agency (RPA).

Investment

In a balance of payments context this is categorised as either direct, portfolio or other investment. See appropriate headings for definitions.

Investment income

All investment income accruing to UK residents from non-residents or payable abroad by UK residents after allowing for depreciation. The balance on credits and debits equals 'net property income from abroad' as shown in the national accounts.

Investment trust

See 'Trusts'.

Leasing

In the balance of payments accounts all financial leases and some long-term operating leases (for example, for aircraft) are regarded as loans to finance the purchase of goods. The lessor thus makes a loan to the lessee who subsequently repays this with interest. The lessee is regarded as the purchaser of the goods.

Liabilities

In balance of payments terminology, liabilities are the financial claims of non-residents on the UK.

LIBOR

London Interbank Offered Rate. The rate of interest at which banks borrow funds from other banks, in marketable size, in the London Interbank market.

Local authorities

Elected councils responsible for the administration of certain services in particular areas within the UK.

Merchanting

Merchanting is defined as the purchase of a good by a resident from a non-resident and the subsequent resale of the good to another non-resident, without the good entering the compiling economy. The difference between the purchase and sale price is recorded as the value of merchanting services provided.

Monetary authorities

Institutions (usually central banks) which control the centralised monetary reserves and the supply of currency in accordance with government policies, and which act as their governments' bankers and agents. In the UK this is equivalent to the Bank of England and part of the Treasury (the Exchange Equalisation Account). Data is not separately available in the UK accounts for monetary authorities.

Monetary financial institutions

Banks and building societies.

Monetary gold

See 'Gold'.

Money market

The market in which short-term loans are made and short-term securities traded. 'Short term' usually applies to periods up to one year but can be longer in some instances.

Money market instruments

Money market instruments, within portfolio investment, generally give the holder the unconditional right to receive a stated, fixed sum of money on a specified date. These are short-term instruments usually traded at a discount; the discount being dependent upon the interest rate and the time remaining to maturity. Included are such instruments as acceptances, treasury bills, commercial paper and certificates of deposit.

MTIC

VAT missing trader intra-community fraud. A systematic, criminal attack on the VAT system, which has been detected in many EU member states. In essence, fraudsters obtain VAT registration to acquire goods VAT free from other member states. They then sell on the goods at VAT inclusive prices and disappear without paying over the VAT paid by their customers to the tax authorities.

Navy, Army and Air Force Institute (NAAFI)

A body which provides goods and services for use by the UK armed forces abroad.

Net

In this presentation of the balance of payments accounts, the term 'net' is generally applied only to transactions in financial assets or liabilities. Purchases of assets are recorded net of sales; similarly with liabilities. In the current and capital accounts, where the operations of UK and foreign residents are taken together in particular transactions areas, the term 'balance' is used.

Net errors and omissions

The item included to bring the sum of all balance of payments entries to zero. Also known as the balancing item.

Non-monetary gold

See 'Gold'.

Non-produced, non-financial assets

Non-produced, non-financial assets, within the capital account, include land purchased or sold by a foreign embassy, patents, copyrights, trade marks, franchises and leases and other transferable contracts, but not finance leasing. Only the purchase and sale of such assets are proper to the capital account; earnings from them are recorded under trade in services.

Novations

This term defines the reassignment of debt (for balance of payments, usually foreign debt) of public corporations to central government following the privatisation of the public corporation. This does not normally change the overall balance of payments situation as the debt is still regarded as a UK liability.

NPISH

Non-profit institutions serving households.

Official reserves

See 'Reserve assets'.

Offshores

The economic territory of a country consists of the geographic territory administered by a government; within this territory, persons, goods, and capital circulate freely. In the context of the UK, the offshore islands of the Channel Islands and the Isle of Man are subject to their own fiscal authorities and have their own tax systems, there are impediments to taking up residency, and they are not part of the EU. They are therefore not recognised as part of the economic territory of the UK for balance of payments purposes and are classified as non-resident in the UK.

Operating leasing

Operational leasing (rental) covers resident/non-resident leasing (other than financial leasing), charter of ships, aircraft and transportation equipment without crew. Leasing of ships, aircraft and transportation equipment with crew are included in the transportation account.

Ordinary share

The most common type of share in the ownership of a corporation. Holders of ordinary shares receive dividends. (See also 'Equity'.)

Other financial intermediaries (OFIs)

A diverse group of units constituting all financial corporations other than depository corporations, insurance corporations, pension funds, and financial auxiliaries. They generally raise funds by accepting long-term or specialised types of deposits and by issuing securities and equity. These intermediaries often specialise in lending to particular types of borrowers and in using specialised financial arrangements such as financial leasing, securitised lending, and financial derivative operations.

Other investment

Investment other than direct and portfolio investment. Includes trade credit, loans, currency and deposits and other assets and liabilities.

Parent

In a balance of payments context this means a company with direct investments in other countries.

Pension funds

The institutions that administer pension schemes. Pension schemes are significant investors in securities. Self-administered funds are classified in the financial accounts as pension funds. Those managed by insurance companies are treated as long-term business of insurance companies. They are part of S.125, the Insurance corporations and pension funds sub-sector.

Portfolio investment

Investment in equity and debt securities issued by foreign registered companies, other than that classed as direct investment, and in equity and debt securities issued by foreign governments. A portfolio investment, unlike a direct investment, does not entitle the investor to any significant influence over the operations of the company or institution, and represents less than 10 per cent of the equity capital.

Preference share

This type of share guarantees its holder a prior claim on dividends. The dividend paid to preference shareholders is normally more than that paid to holders of ordinary shares. Preference shares may give the holder a right to a share in the ownership of the company (participating preference shares). However in the UK they usually do not, and are therefore classified as bonds.

Private sector

Private non-financial corporations, financial corporations other than the Bank of England (and Girobank when it was publicly owned), households and the NPISH sector.

Promissory note

A security which entitles the bearer to receive cash. These may be issued by companies or other institutions. (See 'Commercial paper'.)

Public corporations

These are public trading bodies which usually have a substantial degree of financial independence from the public authority which created them. A body is normally treated as a trading body when more than half its income is financed by fees. A public corporation is publicly controlled to the extent that the public authorities appoint a majority of the board of management or when public authorities can exert significant control over general corporate policy through other means. Since the 1980s many public corporations, such as British Telecom, have been privatised and reclassified within the accounts as private non-financial corporations.

Public sector

Central government, local authorities and public corporations.

Refinanced export credit

Identified long-term credit extended for UK exports initially by banks and refinanced with the ECGD, the Trustee Savings Banks and the Central Trustee Savings Bank.

Reinvested earnings

The direct investor's share of earnings not distributed as dividends (by subsidiaries) or branch profits. As this income remains with the foreign subsidiary or branch (it is reinvested by the parent) an amount will appear in the financial account equal to (and with opposite sign) the corresponding entry within direct investment income.

Related companies

Branches, subsidiaries, associates or parents.

Remittances

Current transfers in cash or in kind sent by households resident in one economy to households resident in another economy. Closely related to *BPM5* concept workers remittances which are current transfers sent by migrants who are employed in new economies and are considered to be residents of their new economy to their home economy.

Repo

This is short for 'sale and repurchase agreement'. One party agrees to sell bonds or other financial instruments to other parties under a formal legal agreement to repurchase them at some point in the future – usually up to six months – at a fixed price. Repo transactions are treated as borrowing/lending within other investment, rather than as transactions in the underlying securities.

Reserve assets

Short-term assets which can be very quickly converted into cash. They comprise the UK's official holdings of gold, convertible currencies, Special Drawing Rights, and changes in the UK reserve position in the IMF. Also included between July 1979 and December 1998 are European Currency Units acquired from swaps with the European Cooperation Fund, EMI and the ECB. Reserve assets were referred to as 'official reserves' in editions of the *Pink Book* prior to 1998.

Reserve position in the Fund

The UK's position in the IMF's General Resources Account. This position is the sum of the UK's reserve tranche purchases, and any indebtedness to the Fund (under a loan agreement) that is readily payable to the UK.

Residency

UK residents are those with a centre of economic interest within the UK of at least one year's duration – nationality does not play a part in determining residency status. There are a number of exceptions to the standard residency classification: regardless of length of stay, UK personnel of UK embassies and military bases abroad are deemed to be residents of the UK (conversely foreign personnel of other nations' embassies and military bases in the UK are classed as non-residents), as are students studying abroad or patients being treated abroad who are normally resident in the UK. (See also 'Offshores'.)

Royalties

These form part of trade in services. They represent payments for services by, or to, UK residents in respect of the right to use processes and other information, for example, licences to use patents, trade marks, designs, or copyrights. Sales and purchases of patents are included within the capital account.

Rural Payments Agency (RPA)

The UK government agency which operates the support arrangements of the EU Common Agricultural Policy within the UK. This replaced the Intervention Board for Agricultural Produce (IBAP).

Securities dealers

Securities and futures dealers are those institutions whose main activity is dealing in securities and futures either on their own account or on behalf of customers and clients. This activity also includes stock exchange money brokers, inter-dealer brokers and dealing in commodities for investment purposes. They should not be confused with monetary financial institutions (banks and building societies) that are licensed as able to take deposits.

Security

Security against loans involves the depositing of a document or asset which is retained by the bank as a charge for an advance. This form of security may include stocks and share certificates, debentures, and insurance policies.

Smuggling

Smuggling is the importation of goods acquired duty free or duty paid in another country for re-sale in the UK without payment of UK duty and (where appropriate) VAT. (See also 'MTIC'.)

Special Drawing Rights (SDRs)

These are reserve assets created and distributed by decision of the members of the IMF. Participants accept an obligation to provide convertible currency, when designated by the IMF to do so, to another participant, in exchange for SDRs equivalent to three times their own allocation. Only countries with a sufficiently strong balance of payments are so designated by the IMF. SDRs may also be used in certain direct payments between participants in the scheme and for payments of various kinds to the IMF.

Spread earnings

Net spread earnings are the part of market making activities that represent payment for the performance of a service. The value of the spread earning for each transaction is calculated as the margin earned between the transaction price and the mid-market price at the time of the transaction. This represents the 'added value' gained from market making activities. Spread earnings can be made on, for example, foreign exchange, securities and derivatives transactions.

Stock lending

Lending of securities by long-term holders or custodians such as banks, pension funds or insurance companies when securities are in short supply.

Subsidiary

A registered company in which another registered company has ownership of the majority of the voting share capital, that is, greater than 50 per cent.

Subsidies

Current unrequited payments made by general government or the EU to enterprises. Those made on the basis of a quantity or value of goods or services are classified as 'subsidies on products'. Other subsidies based on levels of productive activity (for example, numbers employed) are designated 'Other subsidies on production'.

Swaps

See 'Interest rate swaps' and 'Currency swaps'.

Trade credit

See 'Export credit' and 'Import credit'.

Trade in goods

Trade in goods covers general merchandise, goods for processing, repairs on goods, goods procured in ports by carriers and commodity gold (see 'Gold'). General merchandise is defined for balance of payments purposes as covering, with a few exceptions, all movable goods for which actual or imputed changes of ownership occur between residents and non-residents.

Trade in services

Provision of services between UK residents and non-residents, and transactions in goods which are not freighted out of the country in which the transactions take place, for example purchases for local use by foreign forces in the UK and by UK forces abroad, and purchases by tourists. Transactions in goods which are freighted into/out of the UK are included under trade in goods.

Transfers

Transfers are payments or receipts where there is no corresponding exchange of an actual good or service. These transfers are split between current transfers, which form part of the current account, and capital transfers which form part of the capital account. Most transfer payments are general government transfers; that is, receipts from and payments to institutions of the EU.

Travel

The travel account gives the earnings from, and expenditure on, international tourism and business and other travel, but excludes transport between the UK and other countries (included within the transportation account). An international traveller is defined as a resident of one country who visits another country and stays there for a period of less than 12 months. This definition excludes travellers who visit another country to take up pre-arranged employment or education there, military and diplomatic personnel, merchant seamen and airline crews on duty.

Treasury bills

Short-term securities or promissory notes that are issued by government in return for funding from the money market. In the UK every week, the Bank of England invites tenders for sterling Treasury bills from the financial institutions operating in the market. ECU/euro-denominated bills were issued by tender each month but this programme has now wound down; the last bill was redeemed in September 1999. Treasury bills are an important form of short-term borrowing for the government, generally being issued for periods of three or six months.

Trusts (unit and investment)

Unit trusts are institutions through which investors pool their funds to invest in a diversified portfolio of securities. Individual investors purchase units in the fund representing an ownership interest in the large pool of underlying assets, that is, they have an equity stake. The selection of assets is made by professional fund managers. Unit trusts therefore give individual investors the opportunity to invest in a diversified and professionally-managed portfolio of securities without the need for detailed knowledge of the individual companies issuing the stocks and bonds. Unit trust units are issued and bought back on demand by the managers of the trust, the value of the unit reflecting the value of the underlying pool of securities.

Investment trusts are institutions that invest capital in a wide range of other companies' shares. Investment trusts issue shares (which are listed on the stock market) to raise this capital. The price of shares is driven by the usual market forces.

Unit trusts are 'open-ended funds' which means the fund gets bigger as more people invest and gets smaller as people withdraw their money. Investment trusts are 'close-ended funds' because there are a set number of shares and this number does not change regardless of the number of investors. (See also 'Collective investment institutions'.)

Very short term financing facility (VSTFF)

This is a facility available within the EMS where a central bank makes short-term credit facilities in its own currency available to another central bank.

The Pink Book: 2009 edition

Index

Bold indicates name of chapter. **Figures** indicate table numbers. **P** indicates page number. **G** indicates the item appears in the Glossary.

A

Accrued interest,	G
Acquisition/disposal of Non-produced, non-financial assets,	p195
Administrative and diplomatic expenditure,	3.11
Advertising,	3.9
Air transport,	p184, 3.2
Arbitrage,	G
Assets,	G
summary of UK external assets,	1.3, 8.1
Associated companies,	G

B

Balance of Payments,	p1
Balancing item,	G
– see "Net Errors and Omissions"	
Baltic Exchange,	p186, 3.6
Bank of England,	G
Bills and acceptances,	G
Bonds,	G
– see also "Debt securities"	
Bonds and notes:	
earnings,	4.5
transactions in,	7.5
stock outstanding,	8.5
Borrowing – see "Loans"	
Branch,	p10
British government foreign currency bonds and notes:	
earnings,	4.5
transactions in,	7.5
stock outstanding,	8.5
British government stocks,	G
earnings,	4.5
transactions in,	7.5
stock outstanding,	8.5
Building societies,	G

C

Capital account,	G, p14, p195, 6.1
Capital transfers,	G, p14, p195, 6.1
Cargo – dry and wet,	3.2
Certificates of Deposit,	G
earnings,	4.5
transactions in,	7.5
stock outstanding,	8.5
Chartering of ships,	3.2
c.i.f.,	G
Commercial paper,	G
earnings,	4.5
transactions in,	7.5
stock outstanding,	8.5
Commonwealth Development Corporation,	G
earnings,	4.7
transactions in,	7.7
stock outstanding,	8.7
Communication services,	p185, 3.4
Companies' securities,	G
– see "Debt securities" and "Equity securities"	
Compensation of employees,	G, p12, p188, 4.1
Consultancy firms,	3.9
Counterpart items,	G
Coverage adjustments – trade in goods,	2.4
Currency and deposits,	4.7, 7.7, 8.7
Current account,	G, 1.2, 9.1, 9.2, 9.8
Current balance,	G, 1.1, 1.2
Current transfers,	G, p14, p194, 5.1, 9.7

D

Debt forgiveness,	G, p195, 6.1
Debt securities,	G
earnings,	4.5
transactions in,	7.5
stock outstanding,	8.5
Deposits abroad	
– see "Currency and deposits"	
Deposits, earnings on,	4.7
Derivatives,	G
– see "Financial derivatives"	
Direct investment,	G
earnings,	4.3, 4.4
transactions,	7.3, 7.4
stock of investment,	8.3, 8.4
Disbursements,	G, 3.2
Double entry accounting principle,	p5

E

Equity,	G
Equity capital,	G
– see "Direct investment" earnings,	4.3
transactions,	7.3
stock of investment,	8.3
Equity securities,	G
earnings,	4.5
transactions,	7.5
stock of investment,	8.5
Euro/European Currency Unit,	G
European Union,	p187, p194, p197, 3.11, 5.1, 6.1, 9.1–9.9
European Monetary System,	G
Exchange control,	G
Exchange cover scheme,	G
Exchange Equalisation Account,	G
Export credit,	G
Exports	
goods; commodity analysis,	2.1
services; summary,	3.1
External borrowing and lending	
– see "Loans"	
External debt,	G, 8.10

F

Films and television,	p186, 3.8
Financial account,	G, p14, p188, 7.1–7.9
Financial derivatives,	G, p15, p188, p191, FD
Financial leases,	p10
Financial leasing	
– see "Leasing by specialist finance leasing companies"	
Financial services,	p185, 3.6
Financial gold,	G
FISIM	G, p10, p185, p186, p188, p192, 3.6
f.o.b.,	G
Foreign – definition of,	G
Foreign military forces expenditure,	3.11
Freight and insurance - trade in goods,	2.4
Freight on cross-trades,	3.2
Freight on UK trade,	3.2
Fund management companies,	p186

G

Goods and services,	G
– see "Trade in goods" and "Trade in services"	
Goods for processing,	p10
Gross recording,	G, p11

I

Import credit,	G
Imports	
goods; commodity analysis,	2.1
services; summary,	3.1
Income,	G, p12, p187, 4.1–4.8, 9.6

Index

Instruments of investment, p16
Insurance services, p185, 3.5
Inter-company accounts, G, 7.3, 8.3
Inter-government loans
– see "Loans"
International investment position, G, p2, p189, 8.1–8.9, 10.1–10.4
International Development Association, 7.7, 8.7
International Monetary Fund (IMF), G
Intervention Board for Agricultural Produce, G
Investment, G
– see "Direct investment", "Portfolio investment" and "Other investment"
Investment income, G, p188, 4.1–4.8

L

Land transport, 3.2
Leasing by specialist finance leasing companies, G
  earnings, 4.7
  transactions, 7.7
  stock of investment, 8.7
Liabilities, G
License fees
– see "Royalties and license fees"
Local authorities, G
  earnings, 4.2
  transactions, 7.2
  stock of investment, 8.2
Loans
  earnings, 4.7
  transactions, 7.7
  stock of investment, 8.7

M

Management and economic consultants, 3.9
Migrants transfers, p9, p195, 6.1
Military expenditure and receipts, 3.11
Miscellaneous financial institutions, G
Monetary authorities, G
Monetary financial institutions, G
  earnings, 4.2
  transactions, 7.2
  stock of investment, 8.2
Money market brokers, 3.6
Money market instruments, G
  earnings, 4.5
  transactions, 7.5
  stock of investment, 8.5
MTIC fraud G, p32, p124, p181

N

Navy, Army and Air Force Institute – "NAAFI", G
Net, G
Net errors and omissions, G, p6, 1.1
Non-produced, non-financial assets, G
North Sea oil and natural gas companies, 3.9
Notes and coin
– see "Currency and deposits"

O

Oil – exports and imports, p33, 2.1–2.3
Other business services, p186, 3.9
Other investment, G, p15, p192
  earnings, 4.7, 4.8
  transactions, 7.7, 7.8
  stock of investment, 8.7, 8.8
Overseas Trade Statistics
- see "Trade in goods"

P

Portfolio investment, G, p15, p190
  earnings, 4.5, 4.6
  transactions, 7.5, 7.6
  stock of investment, 8.5, 8.6
Private sector, G
Public corporations, G
  earnings, 4.2
  transactions, 7.2
  stock of investment, 8.2
Public sector, G

R

Refinanced export credit, G
Reimbursement by EU for NHS treatment, p187
Reinvested earnings, p9, p189, 4.3, 7.3
Reserve assets, G, p15, p193
  earnings, 4.1
  transactions, 7.9
  stock of investment, 8.9
Reserve position in the Fund, G, 7.9, 8.9
Residency, G
Revaluation of assets and liabilities, p11
Revisions, p17, p23, 1.1R
Royalties and license fees, G, p186, 3.8

S

Sea transport, p183, 3.2
Sectorisation, p17
Securities dealers, 3.6, 7.5, 8.5

Shares
– see "Equity securities"
Sign convention, p6
Solicitors and barristers, 3.9
Special Drawing Rights, G
  in reserve assets, 7.9, 8.9
Subscriptions to international organisations, 7.7, 8.7
Subsidiary, G

T

Telecommunications and postal services
– see "Communication services"
Territorial coverage, p3
Timing of transactions, p8
Trade credit, p192, p193
  earnings, 4.7
  transactions, 7.7
  stock of investment, 8.7
Trade in goods, G, p12, p179, 2.1-2.4, 9.4
Trade in services, G, p12, p182, 3.1-3.11, 9.5, 9.10-9.13
Trade in ships – trade in goods, 2.4
Transactions with EU institutions, p197, 9.9
Transfers, G
– see "Current transfers" and "Capital transfers", p14
Travel, G, 3.3
Treasury bills, G
  earnings, 4.5
  transactions, 7.5
  stock of investment, 8.5

U

United Kingdom, p3
UK banks, G
– see "Monetary Financial Institutions"
UK companies' securities, G
– see "Debt Securities" and "Equity Securities"
Unremitted profits
– see "Reinvested earnings"

V

Valuation, p7
Very short term financing facility, G